Melbourne · Oakland · London · Paris

Chris Baty

Chicago

The Top Five

1 Lincoln Park Zoo
The city's free zoo has a fantastic new African exhibit (p75)
2 Sears Tower
Sky-high views from Chicago's tallest tower (p65)
3 Wrigley Field
The perfect ballpark (p77)
4 Navy Pier
A playground for Chicago kids and young-at-heart adults (p68)
5 Field Museum of Natural History
Where dinosaurs still roam the earth (p91)

Contents

Published by Lonely Planet Publications Pty Ltd
ABN 36 005 607 983

Australia Head Office, Locked Bag 1, Footscray,
Victoria 3011, ☎ 03 8379 8000, fax 03 8379 8111,
talk2us@lonelyplanet.com.au

USA 150 Linden St, Oakland, CA 94607,
☎ 510 893 8555, toll free 800 275 8555,
fax 510 893 8572, info@lonelyplanet.com

UK 72–82 Rosebery Ave, Clerkenwell, London,
EC1R 4RW, ☎ 020 7841 9000, fax 020 7841 9001,
go@lonelyplanet.co.uk

France 1 rue du Dahomey, 75011 Paris,
☎ 01 55 25 33 00, fax 01 55 25 33 01,
bip@lonelyplanet.fr, www.lonelyplanet.fr

© Lonely Planet 2004
Photographs © Ray Laskowitz and as listed (p255), 2004

Printed through The Bookmaker International Ltd
Printed in China

The Author

CHRIS BATY

A Midwesterner by birth and Chicagoan by grace of the University of Chicago's lax admissions policies, Chris Baty has long had a love affair with the Windy City. Chris' infatuation with the place began in 1995 when he visited Chicago in April expecting some sun and fun, only to have his car buried under 3ft of snow.

Impressed by the moxie of a city that refused to be constrained by conventional notions of springtime, Chris immediately vowed to move to Chicago. When he was admitted to graduate school at the U of C in 1996, Chris sold his battered futon and relocated to Hyde Park, eager to begin his new life. The unforgettable experiences that followed – eating hash browns at 3am at the Golden Apple, watching a nervous Jeff Tweedy play his first solo show at Lounge Ax, riding out to Gary, Indiana, in the middle of the night for no good reason – were some of the most memorable in his life. Now living in California, Chris spends most of his time listening to Chicago bands and skimming the *Reader* online for sublets when he should be working. Chris is ready to move back to Chicago as soon as Mayor Daley agrees to cover the city in a large, weather-resistant dome.

PHOTOGRAPHER
Ray Laskowitz

For photographer Ray Laskowitz, photographing Chicago was a break from the heat and humidity of his hometown of New Orleans. Although he had passed through Chicago on many occasions, he really had never spent much time there. He was delighted to find a wealth of cultural diversity, very friendly people and great food. He has been photographing all manner of subjects for 27 years, and lists making travel images among his favorite work. This is his fifth book for Lonely Planet, having previously photographed Los Angeles, Las Vegas, New Orleans and San Francisco.

Introducing Chicago

The trumpeter's cheeks look like they're about to explode. You're in an overheated, matchbox-sized nightclub on the city's South Side, watching an unknown horn player rewrite the rules of jazz in sweat and noise. The tune is familiar, but the treatment is revelatory. Explosive. The crowd screams their approval, and you scream right along with them. The night is young, your face is flushed and you have a sneaking suspicion that you may have to reschedule tomorrow's 8am pancake breakfast.

Welcome to Chicago, a city that has a way of confounding visitors' best-laid plans. Though it ranks third behind Los Angeles and New York size-wise, the Windy City is a vast and vibrant metropolis – a place where running shoes and a good train map are a must if you even hope to make a dent in the city's copious and unique attractions.

Unique? You bet. This is the city that invented both Twinkies and house music, after all. The Chicago spirit is one of unlikely improvisations and delicious discoveries. You can taste the restless adventuring in its weird, pan-everything restaurants, see it in the myriad of groundbreaking, rib-tickling theater companies and feel it in the Blue Line train that roars along ancient tracks, depositing today's crop of computer programmers and next-wave filmmakers among the towering forests of 19th-century skyscrapers.

And there's something else unique about Chicago: people are downright *friendly* to tourists here. It's kind of creepy for those accustomed to big-city brusqueness. If you ever find yourself lost along Lake Michigan, or disoriented in Daley Plaza, you can count on Midwestern hospitality

Lowdown

Population 2.9 million
Time zone Central (GMT -6 hours)
Nicknames Second City, Windy City, Chi-town (pronounced Shy town), City of Big Shoulders
Downtown hotel room $150
Chicago-style hot dog $2.50
Cup of coffee $1.25
El fare $1.50 (transfer $0.30)
Essential drink Old Style beer ($2)
No-no Unflattering comparisons to New York

to help get you out of the jam. Just pantomime distress and a Good Samaritan will be along shortly. (Note: this kindliness does not apply to Chicago's bloodthirsty population of taxicab drivers, who help maintain the city's urban credibility by honking and yelling at anything that moves.)

The quintessential Midwesternness of the natives – cheerful, hard-working and a little conservative – acts as a steadying anchor for the city's more adventuresome impulses. For all its eagerness to embrace the new, Chicago is still a place where steak wins out over soy, and where a half-pound of crème-filled donuts is considered a legitimate breakfast.

There is something, though, that Chicago's artsy, reckless yin and no-nonsense yang both agree on: drinking. True to its long-established reputation as a bootlegger's paradise, Chicago is a place that knows how throw a party. The best times to come to Chicago are when the myriad of city-sponsored music and food festivals transform the lakefront Grant Park into a boogeying, carousing mass of humanity. June, with its Gospel and Blues Festivals, is especially prime, as are September and October. Summers are deadly hot and miserably humid, and winters… Sheesh. Bring a parka and plan on spending *a lot* of time getting to know the area's museums and drinking establishments (not such a bad fate, really).

The other best time to come to Chicago is between conventions. During the larger trade shows, power-suited attendees will snap up most of the city's available rooms. Even if you're lucky enough to find a room, you'll end up paying twice or three times what you should. If your arrival date happens to coincide with a major convention, plan on reserving far, far in advance. With violent crime on the decline, Chicago's streets may be friendly, but it's best not to try and sleep on them.

CHRIS' TOP CHICAGO DAY

Wake up in Ukrainian Village with a cup of locally roasted Intelligentsia coffee. Head down Division St to Flo for a breakfast burrito and more coffee before taking the Blue Line El two stops to Wicker Park. After trolling through the used-CD bins at Reckless, walk up to Quimby's and grab the latest copy of the *Reader*, flipping through the music listings on the cab ride to Wrigley Field for an afternoon Cubs game. By the seventh inning, the Cubs are down by five runs. Slip out, taking the Red Line down to the Art Institute for a stroll through photography exhibits. Grab two hot dogs from a vendor's cart for dinner, and eat them with relish in Burnham Park, watching the boats bob in the lake and the lights flicker on along Navy Pier. Then it's another quick cab ride to the Hideout for a frosty glass of Old Style and some live country music.

Essential Chicago

- **Art Institute** (p62) – miraculous finds in every room
- **John Hancock Center Signature Lounge** (p137) – at dusk, you'll cry into your beer it's so beautiful up here
- **Wicker Park/Bucktown** (p82) – quirky shopping + live music = love
- **Navy Pier Ferris Wheel** (p68) – exhilarating and way scarier than it should be
- **Chicago Mercantile Exchange** (p63) – a heady mix of capitalism and modern dance

City Life

City Life

CHICAGO TODAY

Whether or not you make it out to Second City for some comedy while you're in Chicago, you're going to see acts of tremendous improv. Much of the dynamism on the streets of Chicago today comes from the city's bullheaded determination to invent its own cultural trends and lifestyle niches, regardless of the winds blowing in from New York or California.

That energetic, maverick spirit is most visible in the city's creative realms. Between the Pilsen artists creating canvases from the innards of taxidermized animals to the Andersonville thespians whose stock-in-trade is staging 30 hilarious plays in 60 minutes, Chicago is a city that marches to the beat of its own drummer. A desperately overworked drummer who waits tables in the Ukrainian Village during the day and plays in five different indie rock bands at night.

All the actors, artists, and musicians have made Chicago such an attractive place to live, in fact, that they've inadvertently created a monster. After years of losing residents to the surrounding suburbs, Chicago actually posted a population increase in the 2000 census, part of which was due to thirtysomethings moving back to the city for an urban experience (and a shorter commute). With violent crime rates down and luxury lofts and condos going up, the funky, sketchy 'emerging neighborhoods' that the artsy types once called home are gentrifying at a bewildering pace.

Neighborhoods like Wicker Park and Ukrainian Village – places where prostitutes and drug dealers ruled just 10 years ago – have become havens for yuppies looking for great real-estate values. The dramatic change from affordable working-class neighborhood to spa-filled, boutique-land has forced out many of the residents that gave those areas their unique character in the first place. Gentrification, coupled with the continued razing of the city's disastrous experiments in public housing, has made Chicago's marginal neighborhoods tense battlegrounds in the future of housing in the city.

Thankfully, the city's restaurateurs have stepped in to comfort the masses. After a brief spike in adventuresome, high-concept fusion dining in the early 2000s, current menus across the city emphasize the basics. From Lake View to Logan Square, chefs are wooing patrons with reassuring portions of mashed potatoes and meatloaf. Tater Tots have even made a comeback in some chichi places. Sound dull? It can be. Which is why the city's array of Chinese, Thai, Vietnamese, Indian and Mexican restaurants have never been more essential (or more popular – you can wait an hour or more on weekends for a plate of curry on Devon Ave).

Chicago skyline

Chicago's other great unifier is sport. Regardless of their age, ethnicity, or annual income, Chicagoans can come together in the city's stadiums and sports bars and share the experience of watching their home team get trounced. Despite the constant losses of Chicago teams, locals keep the faith, buying tickets and reading the sports pages to stay up to date on the latest failures.

It's not the most realistic behavior for the fans, perhaps, but it's perfectly in keeping with a city fanatically dedicated to doing things its own way.

CITY CALENDAR

Chicago stages an exhausting array of festivals, concerts and events. The moment the thermometer registers a single degree above freezing, you can count on some group lugging out a stage and speakers to Grant Park to celebrate the good news. We've listed some of the major events here, but a complete listing would likely provoke hernias in anyone who tried to pick it up: between March and September alone, Chicago throws over 200 free day- or weekend-long shindigs. And that's not counting the events that last all summer, like the **Grant Park Music Festival** (www.grantparkmusicfestival.com), which presents top-notch free pop and classical concerts in the park most Wednesdays, Fridays and Saturdays.

Like the Grant Park Music Festival, the big events of the summer – Blues Fest, the Jazz Fest and Taste of Chicago – all go down in Grant Park, and many of the major parades take place along S Columbus Dr nearby. But even if you can't make it down to Grant Park during festival time, you're still likely to get caught up in some local celebration. Check the Mayor's Office of Special Events website (www.ci.chi.il.us/specialevents) for details on all the fun.

A word on holidays: public holidays in Chicago will likely affect business hours and transit schedules. And while holidays have little impact on shopping, eating and entertainment opportunities, things like banks, post offices and government offices will be shuttered for the day. Plan your important mail runs and bank deposits around the holidays listed below to ensure you don't get shut out in the cold (or the heat, as the case may be).

JANUARY & FEBRUARY

Ah, January. The city wakes to another year with a lampshade on its head and fuzzy memories of the night before. These are the months with the most snowfall in Chicago, the coldest temperatures – average 24°F (-4°C) – and the fewest festivals. Sigh. New Year's Day is celebrated on January 1. Martin Luther King Jr Day is celebrated on the third Monday of January. President's Day falls on the third Monday of February.

CHINATOWN'S CHINESE NEW YEAR
☎ 312-225-6198
A massive celebration with millions of little firecrackers, a parade and more takes place in Chinatown. Exact date varies according to the ancient Chinese calendar.

BLACK HISTORY MONTH
☎ 877-244-2246
Events and exhibits all around the city celebrate African-American history in February.

CHICAGO AUTO SHOW
☎ 312-225-6198
Detroit, Tokyo and Bavaria all introduce their latest and finest vehicles to all the excited gear-heads in a huge show mid-February at McCormick Place.

MARCH

Is that the sun making a long-awaited reappearance? It is! Hope reappears on the horizon, as the daily high moves up to 45°F (7°C) and Chicagoans can feel their toes and noses for the first time in weeks. Easter Sunday brings out tentative forays to backyards for egg-hunts.

CHICAGO FLOWER AND GARDEN SHOW
☎ 312-222-5086; www.chicagoflower.com
It may be sleeting outside, but this mid-March garden event on Navy Pier puts a little spring into everyone's step.

ST PATRICK'S DAY PARADE

☎ 312-942-9188; www.chicagostpatsparade.com

This city institution starts with dyeing the Chicago River green near the N Michigan Ave bridge, then continues with a parade along S Columbus Dr by the Buckingham Fountain.

POLISH CONSTITUTION DAY PARADE

☎ 773-282-6700

Chicago's Polish community comes out to party at this annual parade on S Columbus Dr.

HELLENIC HERITAGE GREEK PARADE

☎ 773-994-2222; Halsted St, from Randolph St to Van Buren St

The streets of Greektown come alive in this celebration and parade, held the last Sunday of the month.

APRIL

The windiest month in the Windy City. The temperatures are rising, and can break 60°F (16°C) during the day, but freak snowstorms still threaten all those cute little blooms and buds appearing throughout the city.

SPRING FLOWER SHOW

☎ 312-746-5100; www.garfield-conservatory.org

Zillions of blooms are at their best at the Garfield Park Conservatory and Lincoln Park Conservatory just north of the zoo.

EARTH DAY

☎ 773-755-5111; www.naturemuseum.org

The Peggy Notebaert Nature Museum sponsors an annual Earth Day event with lots of activities and exhibits, and even a little eco-themed comedy. Held on the fourth Saturday of the month.

MAY

The average temperatures are hovering around 70°F (21°C), and Chicagoans are starting to mow their lawns in earnest. Memorial Day falls on the last Monday.

CINCO DE MAYO FESTIVAL AND PARADE

☎ 773-843-9738

This annual bash celebrating the Mexican army routing the French in 1862 draws more than 350,000 people to Pilsen with food, music, rides and games.

ART CHICAGO

☎ 312-587-3300; www.artchicago.com

This massive mid-month festival on Navy Pier is a Very Big Deal in Chicago's art world. Over 3000 artists are featured, and city-wide events are held at museums and galleries. Also features the Stray Show, a separate event for up-and-coming artists.

GREAT CHICAGO PLACES AND SPACES FESTIVAL

☎ 312-744-3370

This architectural festival includes boat, bike and walking tours of some of Chicago's treasures.

JUNE

Highs are over 80°F (27°C), lows down to 50°F (10°C). Grant Park is packed most weekends with festival-goers glad to be outdoors. Summer– and the festival season – has arrived. This is a great time to be here.

CHICAGO TRIBUNE PRINTERS ROW BOOK FAIR

☎ 312-222-3986; www.printersrowbookfair.org

This event features thousands of rare and not-so-rare books on sale, plus author readings, at the beginning of the month on the 500-700 blocks of S Dearborn St.

CHICAGO BLUES FESTIVAL

☎ 312-744-3370

This highly regarded three-day festival features more than 70 performers on six stages in Grant Park on the first weekend of the month.

CHICAGO GOSPEL FESTIVAL

☎ 312-744-3370

Hear soulful gospel music on the second weekend of the month in Grant Park.

ANDERSONVILLE MIDSOMMARFEST

☎ 773-664-4682; www.andersonville.org

The Swedes go nuts at this Andersonville event, featuring plenty of Swedish dances, songs and Maypole activities. Held mid-month.

CHICAGO COUNTRY MUSIC FESTIVAL

☎ 312-744-3370

A hoedown takes over Grant Park on the third weekend of the month, with music spanning the gamut from slick new artists to old-school favorites like Loretta Lynn.

GAY AND LESBIAN PRIDE PARADE
☎ 773-348-8243
Held the last Sunday in June along Halsted St, the Pride Parade is packed with colorful floats and revelers.

TASTE OF CHICAGO FESTIVAL
☎ 312-744-3370
This enormous festival closes Grant Park for the 10 days leading up to Independence Day on July 4. More than 60 local eateries serve some of the greasiest food you've ever tried to rub off your fingers. Live music features on several stages.

JULY
The weather takes a turn for the hot and humid, with average highs around 85°F (29°C). Block parties take over the streets and flip-flops become the official city shoe. Independence Day is celebrated on July 4.

FOURTH OF JULY FIREWORKS
Though it really happens the day before Independence Day, on July 3, the city pulls out all the stops for this concert, which features a long fireworks show bursting out over Lake Michigan and Tchaikovsky's '1812 Overture,' played with gusto by the Grant Park Symphony Orchestra. For the best view, try the embankment east of Randolph St and Lake Shore Dr.

CHICAGO FOLK AND ROOTS FESTIVAL
☎ 773-728-6000; www.oldtownschool.org
Mid-month, one of Chicago's coolest organizations throws this two-day party that features everything from alt-country to Zimbabwean vocalists.

CHICAGO OUTDOOR FILM FESTIVAL
☎ 312-744-3370
Running from mid-July to the end of August, this Grant Park festival is like a drive-in but without all the obnoxious cars. Screened on Tuesdays at sundown, the films are all classics, and are preceded by Chicago shorts.

TALL SHIPS CHICAGO
☎ 312-744-3370
The 30 or so wind-powered ships that show up for this celebration at month's-end travel through the St Lawrence Seaway on their way to Navy Pier. Ship-boarding encouraged.

VENETIAN NIGHT
☎ 312-744-3370
Late in the month, yacht owners decorate their boats with lights and parade them at night in Monroe Harbor to the adulation of the rabble. Fireworks follow.

AUGUST
The bad news: you're most likely to get rained on in August. The good news: it's so hot, you probably won't care. Temperatures range from 72°F (22°C) to 84°F (29°C), and the beaches are crowded.

BUD BILLIKEN PARADE
☎ 877-244-2246
Held on the second Saturday of the month, this huge parade features drill teams, dancers and floats; it runs along Martin Luther King Dr, from 39th St to 51st St and features a picnic in Washington Park afterwards.

NORTH HALSTED MARKET DAYS
☎ 773-883-0500
The costumes and booths get wild at this gay neighborhood street festival, held in mid-August.

CHICAGO AIR AND WATER SHOW
☎ 312-744-3370
The latest military hardware flies past the lakefront from Diversey Pkwy south to Oak St Beach. Acrobatic planes and teams perform both afternoons on the third weekend in August. North Ave Beach is the best place for viewing.

VIVA! CHICAGO LATIN MUSIC FESTIVAL
☎ 312-744-3370
This festival, held the third weekend in August in Grant Park, features *cumbias*, merengue, salsa, and ranchero music delivered by some of the biggest names in the industry.

CHICAGO JAZZ FEST
☎ 312-744-3370
Usually held at the very end of August in Grant Park, the 25-year-old Chicago Jazz Fest features national and international acts.

SEPTEMBER
Fall colors begin to strut their stuff towards the end of the month, and the mild weather

makes this an excellent time for a visit. Labor Day is on the first Monday.

AROUND THE COYOTE ARTS FESTIVAL
☎ 773-342-6777; www.aroundthecoyote.org
A great introduction to the alternative world of the Wicker Park/Bucktown arts community, this series of gallery open houses and performances features hundreds of local artists in and around the Flat Iron Building at 1579 N Milwaukee Ave.

MEXICAN INDEPENDENCE DAY PARADE
☎ 773-328-8538
You'll see lots of cute kids dressed to the nines at this colorful and loud event, held in early September along Columbus Dr.

CELTIC FEST CHICAGO
☎ 312-744-3370
Bagpipers, storytellers and Celtic culture abound at this mid-month festival.

BERGHOFF OKTOBERFEST
☎ 312-427-3170
The Berghoff restaurant's Oktoberfest holds true to the traditional German dates in mid-September. Huge crowds cram Adams St in front of the Berghoff during the week.

GERMAN-AMERICAN FESTIVAL
This much more enjoyable Oktoberfest happens on the third weekend of the month in the heart of the old German neighborhood at Lincoln Square, 4700 N Lincoln Ave.

WORLD MUSIC FESTIVAL
☎ 312-742-1938
Musicians and bands from around the world come to Chicago late in the month to perform and take classes with the masters.

AUTUMN GARDEN SHOW
☎ 312-746-5100; www.garfield-conservatory.org
Beginning in late September the Garfield Park Conservatory shows off its autumn finery in a wonderful display.

DAY OF THE DEAD CELEBRATIONS
☎ 312-738-1503
The Mexican Fine Arts Center Museum in Pilsen puts on exciting Day of the Dead events over two months, running from late September to mid-December.

Day of the Dead art, Mexican Fine Arts Center Museum (p89)

OCTOBER

Temperatures have dropped substantially from the previous month – lows around 42°F (6°C) and highs 63°F (17°C). Halloween is one of the mayor's favorite holidays and the city pulls out all the stops for it. Columbus Day is on the second Monday.

CHICAGO BOOK FESTIVAL
☎ 312-747-4999
The Chicago Public Library organizes this month's worth of readings, lectures and book events, held throughout the city.

CHICAGO INTERNATIONAL FILM FESTIVAL
☎ 312-425-9400; www.chicagofilmfestival.org
Early in the month, scores of films compete during this weeklong event.

LASALLE BANK CHICAGO MARATHON
☎ 312-904-9800; www.chicagomarathon.com
Runners from all over the world compete on the 26-mile course, cheered on by a million spectators.

CHICAGOWEEN
☎ 312-744-3370
From mid-October through Halloween, the city transforms Daley Plaza into Pumpkin Plaza and sets up a Haunted Village for the kids.

NOVEMBER

The first wee snowflakes have begun to fall over the city. The thermometer registers a cold 40°F (4°C). Late in the month, Michigan Ave takes on a cheery glow. Veteran's Day is celebrated on the 11th and Thanksgiving falls on the fourth Thursday.

MAGNIFICENT MILE LIGHTS FESTIVAL
☎ 312-642-3570

The lighting of all 600,000 lights on the trees lining the streets takes place mid-month, after which the little fellas twinkle sweetly on Michigan Ave north of the river through January.

TREE LIGHTING CEREMONY
☎ 312-744-3370

The mayor flips the switch to light up Chicago's Christmas tree in Daley Plaza on Thanksgiving Day.

CHICAGO'S THANKSGIVING PARADE
☎ 312-781-5681

The annual turkey day parade runs along State St from Congress St to Randolph St.

DECEMBER

Everyone loves Chicago's museums, and this a perfect opportunity to get to know some of them (not to mention the underground walkways connecting some parts of the Loop). Lows around 20°F (-6°C). Christmas falls on the 25th.

KWANZAA
☎ 312-744-2400

The increasingly popular African American holiday celebration adds new events and locations each year.

NEW YEAR'S EVE FIREWORKS AT BUCKINGHAM FOUNTAIN
☎ 312-744-3370

Ring in the New Year with fireworks at Chicago's famous fountain.

Top Five Quirky Chicago Events

- **Mayor Daley's Hall of Fame 16in Softball Tournament** Grant Park. The World Series for a uniquely Chicago brand of softball. The ball's bigger, the games are shorter and no one wears mitts (ouch).
- **Buskerfest** North Loop. The world's best street performers come to Chicago to compete for pocket change.
- **Carol to the Animals** Lincoln Park Zoo. Hordes of people sing Christmas tunes to perplexed zoo critters.
- **72-Hour Feature Project** Around Chicago. The Chicago Film Office is one of the sponsors of this annual contest, in which participants shoot, edit and show a feature-length film or video in three days. Sleep is not included.
- **Smelt Season** Chicago beaches. When the tiny fish swarming into Chicago harbors to spawn are met by amateur anglers, nets and deep-fat fryers.

CULTURE

The cultures of some big cities – Berlin, say, or New York – can be tough nuts to crack. Visits to these hectic, polished places are invariably exciting, but can also be frustrating for those looking to move beyond the tourist/customer role and dive into the social fabric of the city. No matter how many times you go back to the same store or eat at the same restaurant, it seems, the cities' cultures remain tucked politely out of view.

Not so with Chicago, a city that wears its passions, beliefs and lifestyles on its sleeve. You'll find that almost everywhere you go in the Windy City – bars, stadiums, museums, El stops – you'll have a chance to get to know real Chicagoans and gain insight on what makes them tick. What follows is an overview of Chicago culture, a bare-bones guide to help launch your own explorations of this open and friendly city.

IDENTITY

When actor (and *Friends* star) David Schwimmer's Lookingglass Theatre Company opened its sparkling, renovated digs in Water Tower Water Works building in 2003, its choice for an inaugural play seemed odd – an adaptation of Studs Terkel's nonfiction book *Race: How Blacks and Whites Think and Feel about the American Obsession.* However unusual, the play was perfect for Chicago, where a decidedly heterogeneous population grapples with racial understanding and misunderstanding on a daily basis.

White Flight

From the late 1950s through the '70s, Chicago's ethnic neighborhoods in the southern, western and southwestern areas of the city underwent rapid change. Whole neighborhoods that had been filled with Irish, Lithuanian and other immigrant residents became populated entirely by Black residents in a matter of months.

The causes were both simple and complex. White residents, raised with racist assumptions about the dangers of having Blacks as neighbors, engaged in panic selling at the first appearance of an African American on the block. 'For Sale' signs sprouted like weeds throughout the neighborhoods. People who had worked two or more jobs to afford their dream home sold at below-market prices and fled with their families to the suburbs.

The Blacks who could afford to do so fled the slums and snapped up the homes but soon found they had a new set of problems: insurance companies and mortgage lenders engaged in 'redlining,' the practice of refusing to write policies and grant loans in areas that had 'gone Black.' The new homeowners were often forced to purchase mortgages and insurance from unscrupulous businesses – many of them owned by African Americans – that charged far more than market rates. Soon some families were forced to default on their loans, and their once-tidy homes became derelict, blighting otherwise healthy blocks.

Discrimination also took the form of 'housing covenants,' unwritten agreements in the real estate industry whereby houses in certain neighborhoods were not sold to people deemed 'unsuitable.'

Government agencies attempted to alleviate these problems by outlawing 'For Sale' signs, punishing firms that engaged in redlining, and requiring banks to open branches in African American communities and to grant mortgages under the same conditions that applied to White communities. These new policies slowed the destabilizing turnover of neighborhoods, and in the few places where true integration has occurred, neighboring black and white homeowners find that they share many of the same concerns: good schools, low crime rates, affordable taxes, timely trash removal, instant eradication of snow and a melancholy wish for the return of Michael Jordan and Mike Ditka.

The 2000 census tells the story pretty clearly. Chicago's 'diversity index' – a percentage likelihood that two randomly chosen people in an area will be of different races – is 74%, a full 25% higher than the US as a whole. Blacks actually outnumber Whites in Chicago, with Latinos running a close third.

Despite the high diversity, integrated neighborhoods are rare in Chicago, with Blacks tending to live on the city's south and west sides, Latinos showing a strong presence in Pilsen and many areas on the North Side, and Asians in Chinatown and along Argyle St in Uptown. Whites tend to make up the bulk of the population in areas visited by tourists (which is why visitors who don't venture off of the beaten path will get a mistakenly monochromatic – and much less interesting – view of the city).

The paucity of mixed-race neighborhoods has its roots in Chicago history, including the 'White Flight' of the 1950s, '60s, and '70s, where whites on the city's South, West, and Southwest Sides engaged in panic selling at the first sight of black families moving onto the block (see boxed text opposite).

Whatever its many causes, segregation is a fact of life in Chicago. Locals tend to socialize with others of their race and class and live in areas where most of their neighbors look and talk like they do. This makes visiting Chicago's distinct neighborhoods sometimes feel a little like globetrotting – it's not uncommon to find stretches of the city where stores advertise their specials only in Polish, or where understanding the difference between *damas* and *caballeros* is essential in avoiding some serious bathroom embarrassment. (Hint: the *damas* door is for women.)

Segregation among Chicago Whites falls along ideological and political lines, with artists and alternative types living and socializing in out-of-the-way neighborhoods like Logan Square and Humboldt Park, carefully avoiding wealthier neighborhoods like Lincoln Park, where post-collegiate, career-oriented conservatives tend to roam.

However much Chicago sometimes feels like a series of homogenous enclaves, though, there are plenty of places where the lines between groups are blurred. Music – especially dance clubs – has helped bring young Chicagoans together, giving them a chance to forget about skin color and class, and address the *real* problem of the day: how to get the phone number of the hottie by the bar.

Religion-wise, Catholicism is running strong in the Windy City. Chicago has the largest Catholic archdiocese in the country, and ongoing immigration from Catholic countries like Mexico and Poland ensures that those pews will stay full for decades to come. In Black neighborhoods, Baptist churches are the mainstay, and Chicago has a sizable Jewish population as well. As with most major cities in the US, though, church attendance in the under-40 set is declining, and faith often takes a back seat to issues of friendship, recreation, and family.

For younger folks, hashing out what it means to be a Chicagoan requires its own sort of devotional intensity. Chicagoans have a zealous faith in their city, but also nurse a deep-seated insecurity that comes from being regularly discounted by coastal tastemakers. Chicago's 'Second City' nickname once proudly proclaimed the town's powerhouse size and status in the country – from 1890 to 1990, only New York could give the headstrong city a run for its money. When Los Angeles supplanted Chicago in 1990, it confirmed the worst fears of Chicago's backers – that Chicago had become a flyover city on the way to America's *real* urban hot spots. That drop from number two to number three, however insignificant it seems to outsiders, threw the civic identity of the city into a muddle, sparking an ongoing debate on what, exactly, it means to be a Chicagoan.

It's a question that the area's scholars and philosophers have taken to heart. One of Chicago's best-known writers, Studs Terkel, has made a celebrated career out of collecting vivid oral histories that often feature Chicago voices puzzling out issues of personal and national identity. Terkel's humanistic torch has been carried on by the radio program *This American Life*, broadcast from Chicago's WBEZ on Navy Pier. Hosted by Ira Glass, the program draws heavily on the lives and stories of ordinary Chicagoans to help illuminate the truths and fictions of an uncertain age.

Even lofty academics here love to roll up their sleeves and wrangle with issues of Chicago identity. University of Chicago – best known for ivory-tower philosophizing and its phone book's worth of Nobel Prize winners in economics – regularly uses its massive brain trust to help understand what makes locals tick. To wit: the popular U of C professor Richard Epstein recently wrote a high-level economics paper about 'Dibs in the Snow,' a quirky Chicago tradition of squatters' rights for winter parking spaces. Another U of C prof published a groundbreaking ethnography called *Slim's Table* on the Black regulars at a Hyde Park cafeteria.

All of the civic and academic navel-gazing has yet to produce an acceptable answer explaining what it means to be a Chicagoan in the 21st century. And in some ways, Chicago's insecurity about its identity has itself become a vital part of its self-conception. It's an ongoing issue that will come up in a myriad of guises when you talk to locals about their city. Here's hoping they'll never figure it out; watching the debate unfold is one of the great joys of a visit to this ever-changing city.

LIFESTYLE

The pace of life in Chicago has two speeds: driving and not. When behind the wheel – which they are frequently – Chicagoans move at a velocity that would make jet pilots nervous. Pause for a fraction of a second too long at a stop sign or slow down at a yellow light, and you can be sure you'll hear about it from the car behind you. The vibe on the streets is bossy, loud, and more than a little chaotic. Witness the famed 'Chicago Left' – as soon as the light turns red, rows of cars ten deep gleefully fling themselves into the intersection, blocking oncoming cars to a chorus of honks as the left turners slowly push their way through the clogged crossing.

This ire-raising Chicago Left is indicative of the city's go-go pace in the mornings. Once Chicagoans have made it safely to work, they move at a less breakneck speed. That's not to say people loaf – jobs and working are taken seriously here, and questions about occupation are usually one of the first bits of information strangers will exchange when getting to know one another. Accountant or auto mechanic, the workers in Chicago tend to clock in early and eat lunch on the go. Unlike New Yorkers, Chicagoans head home at sane hours: the Loop empties around 5:30pm on weeknights, as commuters pile into outbound trains and hit the traffic-clogged highways for the commute home.

Home – be it an apartment, condo or Astor St mansion – is a sanctuary for Chicagoans. Even in more modest neighborhoods, lawns are kept tidy and weed-free, and fixing up the house on weekends is a time-honored creative outlet for older Chicago males. The typical pied-à-terre for twenty- and thirty-somethings, though, is an apartment.

The flats in Chicago tend to be large and long, and often shared by a friend or two. Backyards and back porches are common, and in warm weather these outside areas serve as staging grounds for regular barbecues and impromptu get-togethers. A gas grill and a collection of mismatched lawn chairs are must-have accoutrements for young Chicagoans.

For those without the space to entertain, the city's copious neighborhood parks serve as a much-loved space for cookouts and picnics. In spring and summer, Chicago's parks are overrun with parents keeping one eye on the cooking hamburgers and another on their gleefully screaming offspring.

At the fall of night (or the onset of winter), though, Chicago hits the bars. Free of California's niggling health concerns and New York's antismoking laws, Chicago is a bar-based bacchanal. The anything-goes phi-

South Loop lofts

losophy, coupled with late bar hours on weekends and easy availability of cabs and public transportation make Chicago a place where having a beer or two is often just a warm-up for a long evening of merriment.

The city's bars are also the choice hunting grounds for Chicago singles. Online dating, while growing in popularity, still carries a stigma that a drunken hookup in a Wrigleyville sports bar apparently does not. Make no mistake, the majority of Chicago watering holes are friendly but not *that* friendly, and table-hopping and number-exchanges aren't an integral part of most pubs' scenes. But if you are looking to get to know Chicago on a more, ahem, intimate level, you'll find a plethora of establishments to suit your needs.

Chicagoans also make plenty of time for diversions that don't involve beer coasters. With so many musicians in Chicago, almost everyone knows someone in a band, and getting out to see the friend's group is a common Saturday activity. Heading out to a serious play is a beloved pastime for older Chicagoans; the younger audiences spend their money at the raucous improv and comedy houses like Second City and ImprovOlympic.

FOOD

Though the city's foodies would kill us for saying so, the Weber Grill restaurant at the corner of State and Grand says a lot about Chicago's food scene. Only the Windy City could make an unequivocal success out of a theme restaurant based on backyard cookouts.

Chicagoans simply love meat. And not in that fussy 'nouvelle cuisine' way, where a sliver of steak tartar lists artfully against a single asparagus tip. In the Chicago restaurant world, you'd better serve heaping portions with plentiful sides or you're not going to last long. You can see the city's populist tastes writ large on *Check, Please!*, the local TV show on Channel 11 that allows everyday citizens to play restaurant critic and bring down the hammer on Chicago eateries whose serving sizes are found lacking.

It's fitting then, that Chicago's best-known culinary contributions are ones that will never show up on a Weight Watchers plan. If you really want to sample the culinary delight of the city, seek out a Chicago hot dog (see the boxed text p136). Or try some ribs, another Chicago speciality. Ribs have their roots in African American culture on the South Side. The preferred variation, slabs of pork baby-back ribs, get the long, slow treatment in an oven, usually with lots of smoke. The sauce is sweet, tangy and copious. Another popular variation is rib tips, the cheap bits of pork chopped away near the ribs. These meaty pieces can be a real mess to eat but are usually excellent.

Chicago-style pizza is absolutely nothing like any pizza that was ever tossed in Italy; lofting one of these deep-dish leviathans in the air could actually hurt someone. To prepare their mammoth pies, pizza chefs line a special pan – not unlike a frying pan without a handle – with dough and then pile on the toppings. These must include a red sauce, chopped plum tomatoes and a mountain of shredded American-style mozzarella cheese. Optional extras include Italian-style herb sausage (actually almost mandatory), onions, mushrooms, green bell peppers, pepperoni, black olives and more. Although Pizzeria Uno (p135) likes to claim that it invented Chicago-style pizza in the 1940s, some of its rivals also vie for credit.

You'll find a good representation of regional American cuisine throughout the city, but it's in purely ethnic cuisine where Chicago excels. The waves of immigrants who populated the city have created restaurants devoted to scores of cultures. Italian remains the most common variety by far, with pasta joints in every corner of the city. The breadth of cuisine served in these places ranges from northern Italian to Sicilian, as well as plenty of local interpretations. Chicago's improvised 'Italian' dishes include garlicky chicken Vesuvio (sautéed chicken with potatoes and peas) and Italian beef sandwiches.

Mexican food and flavors also shine in Chicago. Gringo kitchens like Topolobampo (p133) and Flo (p149) play with Mexican spices and staples, and real-deal *taquerias* stay open all night throughout the city, giving carousing Chicagoans a place to go after the bars close. And in the bars themselves, the tamale has become as common as Pabst Blue Ribbon, thanks to enterprising Mexican heroes who lug cooler-loads of homemade pork and chicken delights though the smoky pubs after midnight.

Don't get us wrong, Chicagoans do not subsist entirely on barbecue, five-pound pizzas and Mexican fast food. The fine-dining scene here is world class, spurred on by the millions of business travelers who come here and are every night in need of a setting that will impress a client or colleague. The chefs of Chicago regularly pull in James Beard awards for culinary excellence, and some of the country's most innovative dishes can be found on Chicago menus.

Regardless of whether Chicagoans are doing it in a Kentucky Fried Chicken or Charlie Trotter's (p137), dining out is a key setting for socializing. The 'dinner and a movie' outing is still very much alive in the city, and weekend brunch is similarly beloved. For twenty- and thirtysomethings especially, a late breakfast outing to the nearest upscale diner is an ideal way to start a Saturday (not to mention an efficient way to get the scoop on any scandal from the bar hopping the night before).

FASHION

Chicago is a casual town. The apex of fashion for most men is a pair of khakis and a Gap button-down shirt. Women's dress is similarly low-key, valuing comfort over high fashion. In the scorching summer, much of the population looks like they're heading off for a life-guard shift at the local pool – flip-flops, shorts, and T-shirts are acceptable attire most everywhere in the city. (Though arctic-cold air-conditioning in shops and movie theaters can sometimes make tank tops a regrettable choice.)

In winter, fashion disappears entirely beneath layers of Thinsulate, Gore-Tex and North Face merchandise. Even when summer is a distant memory, though, a surprising number of Chicago residents have the bronzed look of someone who commutes in from the Bahamas, courtesy of discreet visits to Chicago's hundred-plus tanning salons.

These tanned and fashion-forward locals are often horrified by the lack of attention their peers pay to appearance. Happily for the fashionistas, things are slowly changing. A quick tour of Wicker Park boutiques turns up a wealth of hip, international labels mixed in with high-concept, high-priced outfits from local designers. These sleek little stores have virtually eliminated the lag between Milan runways and Chicago shop displays, allowing Chicagoans to spend $200 on a belt just like they do in New York.

Chicago even boasts its own underground fashion scene. Hipsters proudly sport the latest creations from local button-maker Busy Beaver, and attend ramshackle, box-wine fashion shows where works by XNX Designs and fashion artist Cat Chow debut before making their way to Ukrainian Village resale shops.

If you plan on hitting the clubs while you're in town, tight black clothing is the rule for both men and women. Some clubs don't allow blue jeans, tennis shoes or baseball caps; if you only brought Levi's and Adidas and still want to go dancing, do yourself a favor and call ahead to make sure there won't be a problem.

SPORT

Chicago doesn't exactly have a recent reputation for domination in the sporting arena. While its teams aren't laughingstocks of their leagues, they haven't been the subject of ticker-tape parades along State St either.

Despite it all, almost every Chicagoan will declare a firm allegiance to at least one of the city's teams, and going to a game is a great way to bond with Windy City natives. For details on venues and getting to games, see Watching Sports (p184).

Baseball

Winning is not a tradition in Chicago baseball. The Cubs, one of Chicago's two baseball teams, last hoisted the World Series trophy four generations ago. Despite adding a popular new manager, Dusty Baker, in 2003, and making it to the play-offs that year, the team has an impressive knack for falling apart when things start to go their way.

With little to celebrate on the field, fans have instead celebrated the field itself. Known as 'the friendly confines,' Wrigley Field dates from 1914. Although often changed through the years, it retains its historic charm and remains the smallest and most intimate field in Major League Baseball. Popular new stadiums in other cities, such as Baltimore and Denver, have borrowed heavily from its charm.

Few experiences in Chicago can equal an afternoon at Wrigley: the clatter of the El, the closeness of the seats, the spectators on the rooftops, the derisive return of the opposing team's home-run balls, the often-friendly folks around you and, yes, the green leaves of the ivy glistening in the sun. Whether it's riding the El to the Addison stop, grabbing a pre-game beer on the patio at Bernie's or going a little nuts in the bleachers, each Cubs fan has his or her own rituals that make a day at Wrigley not a spectator sport but an almost religious experience.

Chicago's other baseball team, the White Sox, play in less charming surroundings. Comiskey Park (officially known by its corporate sponsors – and precious few others – as US Cellular Field) was one of the last large, antiseptic stadiums to be built before trends began favoring smaller designs like Wrigley. The team itself labors under one of the least popular owners in baseball, Jerry Reinsdorf (who also owns the Bulls), a perplexing man who makes no effort to win any popularity contests. His legendary cheapness means that he regularly trades away popular players who might ask for a raise.

As is the case with many ballparks, the best reason to go to Comiskey is the fans. They love the team despite the stadium and

Hot Conversation Topics

So you're in a bar in Wrigleyville and you want to strike up a conversation with the native sitting next to you. Here are some opening salvos that are guaranteed to get Chicagoans talking.

- The new Soldier Field is exactly the creative jolt Chicago architecture needed.
- Yuppies moving to the South Side will be the saviors of the neighborhood.
- The blues is a dead musical form; the city needs to find another cash cow.
- Bringing Scottie Pippen back to the Bulls was the worst $10 million the team ever spent.
- As soon as it gets a Starbucks, Pilsen is going to be the new Bucktown.
- The Cabrini-Green housing projects should be renovated, not destroyed.
- The sooner Chicago bans smoking in bars, the safer everyone will be.
- The Cubs are loved because Chicago can relate to a team that never comes in first.

owner, and they direct many creatively profane slogans toward the latter. And the food isn't bad either – the tasty burritos for sale on the mall-like concourse are only part of a long list of good and greasy choices. Finally, there's the fireworks – if the Sox hit a home run at night, plumes of color shoot into the air.

Basketball

Chicago is in a similar slump on the basketball court. The Bulls, once the stuff of legend, haven't posed much of a threat since the 1997–98 season, when Michael Jordan was still with the team. Since then the Bulls have stunk. The controversial owner Jerry Reinsdorf allowed Jordan, coach Phil Jackson, Scottie Pippen and other key parts of the Bulls juggernaut to leave after that championship year. In 2003, though, the Bulls made two announcements that may portend a brighter future – former player (and Bulls broadcaster) John Paxson was taking over as general manager, and legendary Scottie Pippen was leaving the Portland Trailblazers and coming back to Chicago. The latter, especially, caused a happy uproar in the city's sports bars. The Bulls play on the West Side in the huge United Center.

Football

As for football, once upon a time the Chicago Bears were one of the most revered franchises in the National Football League. Owner and coach George Halas epitomized the team's no-nonsense, take-no-prisoners approach. The tradition continued with players such as Walter Payton, Dick Butkus and Mike Singletary and coach Mike Ditka. In 1986 the Bears won the Super Bowl with a splendid collection of misfits and characters, such as Jim McMahon and William 'the Refrigerator' Perry, who enthralled and charmed the entire city. Over 15 years of mediocrity have taxed all but the most loyal fan's allegiance. Tickets, once a hot commodity, now sell for just a little cold cash. But Chicagoans still cling to that 1985–86 season, as Ditka maintains his hold over the Chicago psyche.

And as if they needed more infamy attached to their reputation, the Bears unveiled the $580 million renovation of their home, Soldier Field, in 2003 to almost unanimous derision. The long-awaited enlargement of the stadium looks a little like a DUI UFO has crashed into the original classical building.

Hockey

The Stanley Cup last came to Chicago in 1961, but Chicago's hockey team, the Blackhawks, wins enough games every year to keep their rabid fans frothing at the mouth.

The fans' fervor is a show in itself, though it never quite reaches the bloodletting antics of the players on the ice. Games against the Detroit Red Wings and the New York Rangers call for extra amounts of screaming, and the crowd always seems to come with bottomless reserves of lung power. The action starts with the traditional singing of the national anthem, which here becomes a crowd performance of raw emotion.

Soccer

Thanks to support from Chicago's Latino and European communities, Chicago's soccer team, the Fire, has been attracting a growing fan base. The team has made the Major League Soccer playoffs a few times in recent years and won the championship in 1998.

Until they settle on a location for a new stadium, the Fire play at Soldier Field.

MEDIA
Newspapers

Chicago is a newspaper town, one of the few cities in the country to support two competing dailies, the *Chicago Tribune* and the *Sun-Times*. The *Tribune* (www.chicagotribune.com), the higher-brow of the two papers, excels at arts and culture coverage; its writers tend to be articulate experts in their field. For entertainment and dining information, check out the *Tribune*'s www.metromix.com.

The *Sun-Times* (www.sun-times.com) is a tabloid, and, true to its format, tends to favor sensationalized stories that play up sex, violence and scandal. Recently it has drawn criticism for its palpable lean to the far right under the ownership of conservative Conrad Black. Among other well-known writers, the *Sun-Times* is home to America's most famous movie reviewer, Roger Ebert.

Both newspapers produce digest versions for twentysomething readers. The *Tribune* hatched their *Red Eye* first. Sensing a good thing in the making, the Sun-Times raced to release their own youth-oriented paper, the *Red Streak*. Both papers look almost identical, and though they're popular, no one in Chicago can tell you which company puts out which paper.

God's gift to Chicago, though, is the *Chicago Reader* (www.chireader.com). This mammoth four-section tabloid lists virtually everything going on in town, from theater to live music to offbeat films to performance art. Navigating your way through the behemoth, which brims with cool comics and popular advice columns, can take up the better part of a very pleasurable morning. Peter Margasak's long-running 'Post No Bills' column will help you dive into the local music scene.

Other arts papers include the *New City* (www.newcitychicago.com), a slim weekly that is a little edgier than the *Reader*, and the monthly *UR*, which offers extensive coverage of DJ and club culture in Chicago. The *Chicago Free Press* (www.chicagofreepress.com) is the city's main gay and lesbian weekly, with local, national and entertainment news.

Magazines

The monthly magazine *Chicago* (www.chicagomag.com) features excellent articles and culture coverage. But for visitors, the magazine's greatest value lies in its massive restaurant listings. The hundreds of expert reviews are up to date and indexed by food type, location, cost and more. It's worth picking up to find the latest and greatest places in Chicago's vibrant dining scene.

Moguls and would-be moguls consult *Crain's Chicago Business* (www.chicagobusiness.com), a business tabloid that regularly scoops the dailies despite being a weekly.

Chicago also has a wealth of locally produced indie magazines. *Venus Magazine*, (www.venuszine.com) a hip and entertaining read, covers up-and-coming women in music. *Roctober* (www.roctober.com) features an array of articles on old and new music, along with a healthy dose of weird comics. Beautifully designed *Stop Smiling* keeps an eye on Chicago's indie rock world. The *Baffler* (www.thebaffler.com) has been dishing out informed cultural criticism for nearly a decade. *Found Magazine* (www.foundmagazine.com), put out by *This American Life* contributor Davy Rothbart, is an always-amusing collection of found photos, letters, to-do lists and other heartbreaking ephemera. You can pick up all of Chicago's offbeat publications at Quimby's (p212).

Radio

The radio spectrum screeches with a cacophony of local stations. National radio personalities who work in Chicago include Paul Harvey, the amazingly stalwart conservative fossil on WGN, and Jim Nayder, host of WBEZ's *The Annoying Music Show*, which plays such duds as Leonard Nimoy crooning 'Proud Mary' and the Brady Bunch demolishing 'American Pie.'

During some parts of the day, WGN (720 AM) broadcasts from its street-level studio in the Tribune Tower overlooking N Michigan Ave. You can press your nose up against the glass and make stupid faces at hosts such as the duo of Kathy O'Malley and Judy Markey, two irreverent delights.

WBEZ (91.5 FM), the National Public Radio affiliate, is well funded and popular. It's the home station for the hit NPR show *This American Life*. Located on Navy Pier, WBEZ (☎ 312-832-9150) produces radio dramas and dramatic readings. Some of these recordings are taped before a live audience: call for details.

WBBM (780 AM) blares news headlines all day long, with traffic reports every 10 minutes. Newcomers to the US will want to listen to talk radio on WLS (890 AM) for a few minutes to hear a succession of the kind of paranoid blabbermouths who give the nation a bad rep.

You'll find the most interesting music on WXRT (93.1 FM), a rock station that aggressively avoids falling into any canned format trap. Other notables in Chicago are WHPK (88.5 FM), the eclectic University of Chicago station, and Q101 (101.1 FM), a modern rock station that features hyper-popular morning DJ Mancow.

TV

Chicago's local network affiliates are little different from their counterparts in other large cities. WLS (channel 7, the ABC affiliate) is generally the ratings leader for newscasts, covering the latest murders and mayhem from the streets. WMAQ (channel 5, the NBC affiliate) is a ratings loser after years of being adrift. WFLD (channel 32, the Fox affiliate) features the usual Fox neon effects, but also has the well-respected Walter Jacobsen, who has been around for decades. Other stations in town each have their own niches. WGN (channel 9) is owned by the Tribune Company. Its meteorologist, Tom Skilling, will tell you more than you could ever want to know about the weather, but that's good if you're traveling. The station also shows all the games played by fellow Tribune-empire denizens, the Cubs, and carries Bulls games as well. WTTW (channel 11) is a good public broadcasting station. *Chicago Tonight*, at 7pm weekdays, takes an in-depth look at one of the day's news stories.

LANGUAGE

As elsewhere in the US, English is the major language spoken here. In the heart of some ethnic enclaves you'll hear Spanish, Polish, Korean or Russian, but almost all business is conducted in English. Midwestern accents tend to be a bit flat with just a touch of nasal twang, but compared to other parts of the US, most of the English you'll hear is pretty standard – the middle of the country has always produced a large share of plain-spoken TV announcers.

In your wanderings, you may also encounter 'Black English,' a variation of English that's spoken by many African Americans. Generally reserved for casual encounters with friends, its lexicon and cadences can be cryptic to nonnative English speakers.

ECONOMY & COSTS

First the good news: it's possible to eat and drink very well in Chicago and not spend an arm and a leg. And thanks to the occasional (though increasingly rare) free days at local museums, coupled with the discounts offered in the invaluable 'Chicago Guidebook of Special Values' coupon book available in the Visitor Information Center in the Cultural Center (p62), the chances are good you can get in without paying full price at some attractions.

Now the bad news: your motel room is going to cost you. The rack rates on hotel rooms here are outrageous. This is partially because of the 14.9% hotel tax levied by the city, which Chicago depends on to maintain its parks and public buildings. But the city is only partially to blame for the price tags on hotel and motel rooms. Business travelers are the other culprit. Because of the huge number of conventioneers in Chicago at any given moment, hotel rooms are almost always at a premium. And unlike leisure travelers, the business travelers 1) have to come here whether they want to or not, and 2) get reimbursed for their lodging costs.

The high demand and looser purse strings of the conventioneers have put the city's hotels and motels in a position where they charge whatever the market will bear for rooms. And with the city getting such a substantial cut of the revenues, there's little incentive for anyone to bring the prices down.

With visitors being such a heady income stream for the city – around $15 billion in expenditures each year – you'd think they'd try to give us a break. The brutal nature of supply and demand, however, make that unlikely. Given the facts, there are two things you can do to save money on lodgings in Chicago. First, shop around as much as possible on the Internet before committing to anything – sometimes the room price listed on a discount travel website can be almost $100 lower than the price quoted by the reservation agent at the hotel. Second, start wooing those long-lost family members you have in Chicago. Aunt Bertha's fold-out couch is probably sounding better all the time.

How Much?

El ticket from O'Hare to Loop $1.50
Near North hotel, one night $150
Art Institute admission $10
Small bag of Garrett's caramel popcorn $2
One hour of meter parking $1
Taxi ride from Loop to Navy Pier $7
Blues club cover charge $15
Martini at the Green Mill $6
Cup of coffee $1.50
Taco in Pilsen $1.25

GOVERNMENT & POLITICS

Chicago's official motto is 'City in a Garden,' but the late *Tribune* columnist Mike Royko had more than one supporter when he suggested changing it officially to 'Where's mine?' The entire system of Chicago city politics is based on one hand washing the other, with Mayor Daley overseeing a city council of 50 aldermen, each elected every four years.

Maintaining so many politicians and their related offices and staffs is expensive, but proposals to shrink the city council always run aground for the simple reason that the voters like things as they are. Certainly, this amount of bureaucracy is ripe for abuse and corruption (more on that later), but for the average Chicagoan it works well. You got a pothole in front of your house? Somebody stole your trash can? The neighbor's leaving banana peels all over your stoop? Mundane as they are, these are the kinds of matters that directly affect people's lives, and they can be taken care of with a call to the alderman.

With the districts so small in size, the politicians and their staffs can't afford to anger any voters, because angry voters start voting for somebody else. Because of this, the aldermen (the term refers to both men and women) are constantly trying to put themselves in a position to do someone a favor. During your visit to Chicago, you'll likely see traces of this mercenary friendliness on billboards and bus shelter ads – aldermen rent them out to help spread their phone numbers and offers of help to their constituents.

Politics are a popular spectator sport in Chicago, in part because of the ongoing scandals associated with the aldermen and other elected officials. In a late 1990s scandal referred to as 'Operation Silver Shovel,' six alderman were indicted for refusing no bribe, no matter how small. In 2000 former city treasurer Miriam Santos pleaded guilty to campaign extortion while she still had her job. She served time in the federal slammer, although her conviction was later overturned. (She was eventually resentenced for a lesser crime.) Things are getting better though – when former alderman Virgil Jones dropped out the race in 2003, he left only one(!) convicted felon running for an alderman position.

Above Mayor Daley and the pack of aldermen is Illinois governor Rod Blagojevich (pronounced Blah GOY oh vich), a Democrat who replaced incumbent George Ryan in 2003. Blagojevich (referred to in Chicago as 'Blago') immediately made some enemies in the Windy City by rejecting a proposal to allow city-sponsored gambling.

Blagojevich's early work in the governor's office has been overshadowed by the final act of his predecessor. With three days left in his term, Ryan shocked death penalty advocates and foes alike when he announced he was commuting the sentences for all 156 inmates on the state's death row. Ryan, a Republican, had stopped all executions in Illinois three years earlier after it was discovered that 13 inmates awaiting execution had been wrongly convicted. 'Because the Illinois death penalty system is arbitrary and capricious and therefore immoral, I no longer shall tinker with the machinery of death,' he said upon announcing his decision. The inmates were given life sentences without the possibility of parole.

White Blight

Any Chicago politician can tell you that snow is a substance sent by God to ruin political careers, and because of that, the powers that be view each and every delicate little flake as an invader to be eradicated, whatever the cost.

At the first sign of flurries, official Chicago mounts a counterattack that rivals the Normandy invasion in its fury and single-minded sense of purpose. After all, everybody in city government remembers what happened to Mayor Michael Bilandic, who was sunning himself in Florida in January 1979, when the city was smothered by one of the worst blizzards of the century. Never mind that experts say the volume of snow precluded any response that would have saved the city from being buried for weeks. Images of the tanned Bilandic tut-tutting about the white stuff while people suffered heart attacks digging out their cars stuck with voters when they went to the polls two months later and sent a message that rocked Chicago's political machine.

Since then every mayor has gone to battle at the fall of the first flake. If you're in Chicago for a snowfall, you'll be treated to quite a show. First, more than 400 salt trucks with plows hit the streets with flashing yellow lights. Next come hundreds of garbage trucks hurriedly fitted with plows, followed by bulldozers, graders, dump trucks and other heavy equipment. Snow-parking rules go into effect, and any mope who leaves his or her car parked on an arterial street will find it towed.

At 10pm, watch the local newscasts. Each will have breathless reporters live at the command center of the Department of Streets and Sanitation, a milieu much like NASA's mission control, with reports of snow incursions immediately dispatched.

Tiny snowdrift forming at Clark and Diversey? Send in a platoon of plows! Patches of ice on the Randolph Bridge? Get a battalion of salt trucks over there! Homeless man refusing to leave box on Lower Wacker Dr? Send in a squad of cops to arrest him and toss him into a toasty cell. (Less stubborn sorts can avail themselves of the scores of 'warming centers' the city opens around the city.)

Outsiders might consider this response overkill, but Chicagoans take pride in this display of can-do attitude. No matter that the thousands of tons of salt dumped every year dissolve concrete, bridges, cars, trees, boots and everything else – nobody complains. In 1992 a deep cold snap hit the Midwest and several cities ran out of salt. 'What's the situation locally?' reporters asked. While cars skated on other cities' streets, everyone was delighted to learn that Chicago still had enough salt for several years, because each year the city buys at least three times what it needs. You can see some of these huge bluish-white mountains on vacant land around town.

Of course, anybody who has been to places such as Washington, DC, Atlanta or Dallas, where just a few flakes can cause pandemonium, might appreciate Chicago's war on the stuff. And they might enjoy the show as well.

ENVIRONMENT

Ah, pity the Chicago River. The ugly step-sibling to majestic Lake Michigan, the river has been rerouted, polluted and ignored for most of the city's history. Despite the fact that it essentially saved Chicago's population from gruesome death by waterborne disease, the poor thing has gotten all the respect of a garbage disposal.

Happily, that's changing. After monitoring and remediation efforts, the levels of toxic chemicals in the river have declined. The city has also started putting in a series of public river walkways, and mandating developers working along the riverfront to do the same. You won't see Chicagoans inner-tubing down it any time soon, but the river is clearly making a comeback after a century of misuse.

Also thriving are the city's populations of wild animals. Coyote and deer both live in the large parks on the outskirts of the city, and sometimes have been known to wander into the Loop. Raccoons are also plentiful here, and if you drive through suburban neighborhoods like Oak Park at night, your car headlights are likely to catch them as they bound across the road.

No animal species does better in Chicago, though, than rats. Walk through any Chicago alley, and you'll see the 'Target: Rats' sign that explains when the most recent dose of poison was laid out for the wee beasties. A pet peeve of Mayor Daley's, the rats have met a formidable foe in the city's Streets and Sanitation department. One brigade of agents actually patrols the alleys of infested neighborhoods, attacking the rodents with golf clubs. 'We work as a team,' one employee cheerfully reported to the *Sun-Times*, 'One will whack, while the other one will get the final kill.'

Visitors to Chicago in the summer will witness an infestation of a more beautiful sort. Lightning bugs – a flying beetle with a phosphorescent abdomen – are prevalent in Chicago in July and August. A park full of their twinkling lights is one of the most beautiful things you'll see in the Windy City.

Arts

Arts

Be they actors, painters or musicians, the Windy City holds a magnetic appeal to creative types. The housing is affordable, the community of like-minded right-brained folk is welcoming and, most importantly, the audiences in Chicago are happy to take chances on diamonds in the rough. Art – the good, the bad and the just plain puzzling – is everywhere in Chicago these days.

While you're here, you'll see that creative risk-taking is paying big dividends on stages, and in stores and galleries throughout the city. Whether its a band like Wilco, a theater company like Steppenwolf, or even a TV show like *Oprah*, Windy City arts-lovers have long been treated to front-row seats on tomorrow's trendsetting stars and cultural movements.

The gallery scene that was once contained in the River North area has jumped its banks and spilled into the West Loop. And those who can't get wall space in galleries happily take it to the streets. Art students and graffiti artists undertake midnight 'improvements' of bus shelters and building facades with political posters, colorful stickers, and that much-maligned Chicago invention, spray paint.

River North art gallery (p69)

The musical offerings in the city are also broad. Tourists flock to the city's blues clubs, but most young locals don't know Muddy Waters from Mozart. The long lines are for visiting hip-hop impresarios like Chicago expatriate Common or Billy Corgan's post–Smashing Pumpkins incarnation, Zwan. Jazz is vital as well. Local legends like innovative free jazz saxophonist Ken Vandermark and singer Kurt Elling play weekly gigs at local clubs. For Chicago DJs, the weekend starts on Thursday, and local record shops help keep things grooving by stocking exceptional amounts of delicious old soul, funk, and techno on vinyl.

Of all the hot entertainment options in the city, though, it is theater that has probably brought the city its most recent notoriety. Theater is its own universe here, with household names like John Malkovich serving time as actors and founding members of local companies. Big theater companies such as the Goodman and Steppenwolf routinely stage premieres by world-famous playwrights, and Chicago's cadre of underground, itinerant companies put on productions wherever they can rent space – offices, church basements, backyards...you name it.

Being here is a great opportunity to immerse yourself in the unpretentious scene that has been the launching pad for some of the biggest names in American arts and entertainment. So grab a *Reader* and buy some tickets already. A world of art awaits.

THEATER & IMPROV

If anyone was surprised that *Time* magazine named the Goodman Theater as the Best Regional Theater in the US in 2003, they sure as hell weren't from Chicago. Acting has long been high art in this town, and Chicagoans are well aware of the treasures they have in local theater companies.

Moviegoers familiar with the scenery-chewing performances of John Malkovich and Gary Sinise already know the tenets of the Chicago style of acting, for which the two Steppenwolf Theater principals receive much credit: a fiery intensity marked by loud, physical acting. Beginning in the 1970s, the tough, machine-gun-fire bursts of dialogue in David Mamet's taut dramas only added to Chicago theater's reputation for hard-edged, raw emotion.

The Chicago theater scene today is much more than a bunch of guys having dramatic conversations about life and death. As in the past, the focus is on works by local playwrights, but these days, those works are as likely to be realized through the nimble puppetry of the Redmoon Theater Company or the funny, self-help sing-alongs of local musical theater performer Tony Rogers.

And then there's the whole other Chicago universe of improv. Improvisational acting – which forces troupes to create sketches on the fly and change plots and characters according to audience members' whims – came into its own in the 1950s at the University of Chicago. It's since become a part of life here, and the improv scenes at ImprovOlympic and Second City have launched the careers of such comedians as Bill Murray, Tina Fey, Rachel Dratch and Stephanie Weir. The genre's openness to newcomers – ImprovOlympic will put anyone on stage who signs up for their classes – has made the Chicago improv scene a beacon to office cut-ups everywhere, stoking the dream that they may someday follow dozens of other Chicagoans to Hollywood or, at the very least, *Saturday Night Live*.

Things only got brighter in the Chicago theater scene in 2000, with the rehabs and openings in the Loop's 'theater district.' This combination of several new and renovated theaters that includes the gorgeous Cadillac Palace Theater, the Chicago Theater and the Ford Center/Oriental Theater has brought vibrant nightlife to downtown for the first time in 40 years.

MUSIC

Chicago is serious about music. This is a city where mediocre railway buskers are shamed off the platform by a man who plays acoustic guitar and violin *simultaneously* (go see him at the Washington St station), or an R&B ensemble who choreograph intricate dance steps to go along with their karaoke-machine backed numbers. It's also the only city in the country where fans have actually sued a rock band (Creed) for putting on a halfhearted show.

Thanks to the availability of rehearsal spaces, and a plethora of live music and DJ venues throughout the city, Chicago continues to maintain its reputation as a Midwestern mecca for dance, rock, jazz and blues music. Smaller scenes for gospel, hip-hop and world music also thrive here. Classical music fans and opera lovers can get a nightly dose of culture in a host of beautiful, venerable concert halls throughout the city.

ROCK

Yes, Peter Cetera's soft-rock band Chicago got their start here. But don't hold that against the city. Chicago has also produced hundreds of innovative rock pioneers, and rock and pop music hold a special allure for the hearts of the city's citizens.

There was even a moment, back in 1994, when national trend-spotters crowned Chicago the 'next Seattle,' thanks to the success of groups like the Smashing Pumpkins and Liz Phair. The famously unpretentious city didn't handle the glare of the media spotlight very well. Before long, vociferous critics and music scenesters were spilling blood on the letters pages of the local weeklies, tearing each other apart as they argued which, if any, of the almost-famous musical acts in the city deserved attention from outsiders.

Thankfully that moment passed quickly (as did many of the era's next-big-thing bands like Veruca Salt and Urge Overkill). Today's rock scene is adventuresome but unpretentious, and divided into a multitude of overlapping, cross-pollinating camps.

The western-shirt-wearing, alt-country scene hovers around venues like Schubas (p177) and bands like the Waco Brothers and chanteuse Neko Case. Indie rock fans can be found drinking $1 Huber Bock beers at the Empty Bottle (p176) or catching bigger local acts like

Tortoise or the Alkaline Trio at the Abbey (p176) or the Metro (p177). All-ages punk and emo shows take place at the Fireside Bowl (p176), a dilapidated (but operational) bowling alley where the bands play behind the ball-return.

DANCE MUSIC

If Chicago had only thought to trademark the term 'house music' when it was invented here in the early '80s, the city's coffers would be forever recession-proof. The genre takes its name from a long-defunct club on the West Side called the Warehouse, where the legendary DJ Frankie Knuckles spliced and diced disco anthems – extending intros, repeating phrases, and adding beats and bits from other songs.

Since then, house music has mutated into a dozen subgenres, from trance to garage to glitchy broken-beat. (In the late '80s, it even spawned another Chicago institution, industrial music – see boxed text p30). Whatever the style, house music is still the staple of dance clubs throughout the city.

The club scene in Chicago is coming back down to earth after a brief period of wealth-fueled snootiness in the economic boom of the early 2000s. This has been both good and bad for dance fanatics in Chicago. With their smaller budgets, local clubs can't always attract the megastar DJs from New York and Europe. Instead, parties now have a more underground feel; the VIP rooms and big egos that are the hallmark of scenes in Miami or New York don't play much of a role here. Best of all, Chicago patrons rarely endure long lines or discriminatory bouncers who use the velvet rope to inflate their own sense of self-importance.

Mixed crowds of gay and straight dancers are fairly common in the city, with venues like Berlin (p180) being a prime example of a crossover club that everyone loves. While you're in town, keep an eye on the event listings for a set from Jesse de la Pena, who many hail as Chicago's best DJ. Chicago also boasts a larger number of women DJs – some names to look for include Margaret Noble and Brenda D.

BLUES

The blues is an institution here, as witnessed by the half-million people who pack Grant Park every June for the Blues Festival. Missed the festival? Don't worry, you can see live players every night of the week. Old-time-blues fanatics hungry for the raw, epiphanic feel of the music tend to avoid the North Side clubs (many of which feature gift shops as prominently as they do musicians) and head to the few remaining low-key Black establishments on the South Side, such as Rosa's (p179) or Lee's Unleaded Blues (p179). Most of that is pure snobbery – these days, you're just as likely to hear high-quality blues in Wicker Park as you are in an 'authentic' joint in the South.

Wherever you go, though, it's good to know a little history of the blues in Chicago. Early on, blues in the city closely resembled the variety played in the bayous of Mississippi and Louisiana. But the demands of noisy clubs and the pressures of urban life soon resulted in a more aggressive, amplified sound that is the basis of Chicago blues. Muddy Waters arrived on the scene in 1943 and is widely regarded as the most important blues musician to work in Chicago. His influence runs deep, extending to early rock

Top Five Chicago CDs

- *Resurrection*, Common (Relativity) Recorded back when he still lived in Chicago, Common's debut is a jazzy, lyric-packed underground hip-hop favorite.
- *Superfly*, Curtis Mayfield (Rhino) A funky and soulful masterwork that transcends the kitschy movie it was written to accompany.
- *Exile in Guyville*, Liz Phair (Matador) This brilliant, plainspoken record has become a cornerstone of '90s indie rock.
- *Insurgent Country Vol 1: For A Life of Sin*, Various Artists (Bloodshot) This 1993 snapshot of Chicago's nascent alt-country scene features tracks by Freakwater, Robbie Fulks, Jon Langford and others.
- *His Best: 1947 to 1955*, Muddy Waters (Chess) Blues classics from Waters' sessions at Chess Records on the Near South Side.

groups such as the Rolling Stones and the Paul Butterfield Blues Band. His sideman in later years was Buddy Guy, whose electric-guitar work shaped musicians such as Eric Clapton, Stevie Ray Vaughan and Jimi Hendrix. Guy continues to operate the club bearing his name in the South Loop (p178). Other important blues greats have included Willie Dixon, Sunnyland Slim and Koko Taylor, who also owns a club bearing her name (p178).

JAZZ

Many of the great names in jazz – Louis Armstrong, Jelly Roll Morton, Benny Goodman, Bix Beiderbecke and Nat King Cole – lived and worked in Chicago. And the Windy City is still a thriving home for the music, with clubs hosting everything from smooth vocal jazz to far-out, skronky caterwauling. The latter, of which there is plenty in Chicago, owes a big debt to the legacy of the Association for the Advancement of Creative Musicians (more commonly known as the AACM), a Chicago-based organization formed in the 1960s determined to push the envelope of jazz. The Art Ensemble of Chicago, the

Music on the streets of Pilsen

biggest name to come out of the scene, doesn't play much around town anymore. But their kitchen-sink instrumentation and creative rhythmic playfulness lives on in local improvisers like Ken Vandermark, who packs the Empty Bottle (p176) when he plays there every Tuesday night. Other local free jazz names to watch out for are tenor saxophonist legend Von Freeman, who plays the New Apartment Lounge (p179) on Tuesday nights, and Fred Anderson, who holds court at the club he owns, the Velvet Lounge (p179).

HIP-HOP, SOUL AND GOSPEL

Hip-hop is everywhere and nowhere in Chicago. Mainstream national artists like 50 Cent and Jay-Z boom from cars all around the city, and Chicago has one of the country's long-running rap radio shows in JP Chill's *Rap*, which airs Friday night on WHPK (88.5FM). But Chicago has yet to produce a rap star as well known as hometown R&B smash R Kelly. Talented hip-hop MCs – like one-time Chicagoan Common – tend to move to New York or Los Angeles as soon as they achieve any sort of notoriety.

Gospel has its roots in blues and jazz, and the music emanates from churches all over the South Side every Sunday. Huge choruses clap their hands, chant, shout, wail and create music that both inspires and speaks for the huge congregations of the primarily Baptist churches. Much of the credit for creating the gospel sound, at once mournful and joyous, goes to Thomas A Dorsey, music director at the Pilgrim Baptist Church in Bronzeville, who died in 1993 at age 93. Mahalia Jackson is just one of the great Chicago gospel singers who have launched careers in South Side churches.

Closely related to gospel is soul, a genre that primarily emerged from Detroit's Motown sound, though Chicago also made contributions. Chicagoan Curtis Mayfield wrote, produced and performed through the 1960s and '70s. His musical additions to a series of the so-called blaxploitation films of the early 1970s are largely credited with the low-budget films' success. Check out his pulsing beat in the 1972 hit *Superfly*.

Five Chicago Record Labels That Changed the World

From Chess Records in the '40s and '50s to Thrill Jockey Records today, Chicago labels have long been the trailblazing leaders in new music. Five labels deserve special credit in making Chicago such a musical hotbed over the past five decades.

Bloodshot (www.bloodshotrecords.com) What do you get when you combine punk rock with old-school country? Ask Bloodshot, which has been Chicago's bastion of brawling twang and barbed-wire heartache for over 10 years now. Bloodshot has put out some of the best records in the left-of-center American genre called No Depression, alt-country or (the label's preferred moniker) insurgent country. Known for releasing CDs by sensitive singer-songwriter types like Neko Case and Ryan Adams, Bloodshot also showcases the swinging, old-timey side of country music with records by roster artists like the Pine Valley Cosmonauts and Wayne Hancock.

Chess Records When the blues left The Delta and took the train for the city, its home in Chicago was Chess Records. Run by two brothers, Leonard and Phil Chess, the label helped launch the careers of Muddy Waters, Howlin' Wolf and legendary harmonica player Little Walter. Chess engineered their records to match the tone of their artists, creating an aggressive, redlining blues sound that remains synonymous with Chicago. The label also served as a catalyst for what would eventually become rock and roll, recording early sessions by Chuck Berry and Bo Diddley.

Delmark Records (www.delmark.com) The oldest independent jazz and blues label in the country, Delmark Records' has inspired countless other small start-ups around the world determined to promote the pioneers and mavericks of the two genres. Delmark was founded in 1953 by a 21-year-old music fan named Bob Koester, who, before his leap into the music recording business, had been selling out-of-print blues and jazz records from his dorm room. Over its 50-year life, the label has released blues works by artists like Junior Wells, Otis Rush, Little Walter and Sunnyland Slim, and jazz records by Art Ensemble Of Chicago, Sun Ra and Dinah Washington. Additionally, Koester runs the Jazz Record Mart (p94), a jazz and blues shopping heaven in Near North.

Thrill Jockey (www.thrilljockey.com) When indie rock discovered the nuanced sounds and textures of jazz in the mid-1990s, Thrill Jockey was there to document the 'eureka!' moment. Started by New York transplant Bettina Richards, the independent label has been the celebrated home of local bands like Tortoise and The Sea and Cake. The label isn't limited to the 'post-rock' bands that made it famous, however, with their signings ranging from local countryish acts like Freakwater and Califone to abstract European electronica artists like Mouse on Mars. Thanks to its consistently solid output and stratospherically high cachet, Thrill Jockey has opened the minds of tens of thousands of indie music fans worldwide to new genres and styles.

Wax Trax! It's hard to say what would have happened to industrial music in the '80s without the tireless work of local label (and record store) Wax Trax! Along with bringing the raw, electronic mayhem of European artists like KMFDM and Front 242 to the US, Wax Trax! put out seminal works by fledgling domestic acts such as Ministry, Meat Beat Manifesto and My Life With the Thrill Kill Kult. Though the label is now defunct, you can hear highlights in the extensive, 3-CD box set *Black Box: Wax Trax! Records, The First 13 Years*.

VISUAL ARTS

Chicago's young, dynamic contemporary arts scene blooms all around Chicago. Some of this, oddly enough, has to do with dorms, or a lack thereof. Big-name art schools like the Art Institute and Columbia College are primarily commuter schools, and the lack of a concentrated campus with housing means that the students live and work everywhere from the Gold Coast to Humboldt Park.

The spread of art throughout the city is also due in part to Chicago's fractured gallery scene. Up-and-coming, risk-taking galleries and a small but growing number of heavy hitters are located in the meatpacking district of the West Loop. The more established galleries that can afford the higher rents are located in River North. And Chicago's 'stray galleries' – an apt term used to describe new, less commercial galleries in off-the-beaten-path locations tend to be found in Pilsen and Wicker Park.

The cooperation and communication between the three camps can be spotty at best, and it mirrors a certain Chicago split between ragged, warts-and-all avant-garde art, and more traditional object-based or representational pieces that patrons will want to hang in their living rooms.

That high art/low art divide that critics and gallery owners are so conscious of is often gleefully crossed by the artists themselves. Comic artists like Chris Ware (see boxed text p211) take the art form to an almost architectural level of perfection, painter Kerry James Marshall's recent work plays with the idea of comics and super-heroes, and photographer Rashid Johnson gives nods to both 19th-century photographic techniques and hip-hop.

All of this juxtaposition of old and new is a far cry from the Chicago art scene of 100 years ago, which was largely designed to show the world that Chicago was a city 'that got taste.' The industrialists funded works that evoked imperial Europe in their grand scale. Meanwhile, the same industrialists bought up the latest art Europe had to offer. During this period, society matron Bertha Palmer and others gathered much of the Art Institute's wondrous collection of impressionist paintings.

During the 1920s Chicago art veered towards modernism and realism, led by the likes of Rudolph Weisenborn and Wassily Kandinsky. The gritty realm of the city proved a perfect inspiration for these new forms of art, with their hard-edged portrayals of urban life. Archibald Motley Jr captured the essence of life on the South Side.

Styles fragmented with the emergence of surrealism and abstract expressionism in the mid-20th century. Chicago artists who experimented with the new, unconventional techniques included Karl Wirsum and James Falconer.

Much to local sculptors' delight, in 1978 Chicago began to require that developers include financial provisions for public art in their projects, specifically 1% of the total cost. True to the city's art ubiquity, you can see the results throughout the Loop, in parks and along the city's traffic medians.

Top Five Art Museums

- **Art Institute of Chicago** (p62) From medieval armor to Mondrian abstracts, this giant has it all.
- **Museum of Contemporary Art** (p72) Chicago's home for brilliant, cutting-edge works.
- **Museum of Contemporary Photography** (p92) A record of our modern age.
- **Smith Museum of Stained Glass Windows** (p69) This find on Navy Pier is more hallway than museum, but the works are inarguably amazing.
- **Mexican Fine Arts Center Museum** (p89) Ambitious, innovative museum celebrates Mexican and Mexican-American artists.

Top Five Public Art Experiences

- Helping tourists photograph themselves in front of the beautiful **Buckingham Fountain** (Map pp282–3).
- Imagining Alexander Calder riding into the Loop with a circus in tow (true story!) for the dedication of his **Flamingo** (p114) sculpture.
- Watching kids climb around Jean Dubuffet's great **Monument with Standing Beast** (p115).
- Playing 'Hot or Not?' with the huge sculpted heads of the city's mercantile forefathers at the 'Hall of Fame' in **Merchandise Mart** (Map pp280–1).
- Learning Chicago riverfront history at the **Riverwalk Gateway** (Map pp282–3) on the way to Navy Pier.

CINEMA & TV

From shopping-channel infomercials filmed in quiet suburban studios to exploding tanks on the streets of downtown, Chicago serves as a frequent backdrop for TV shows and movies. Film, especially, has a special place in Chicago's heart from the days when the city was the Hollywood of the Midwest during the second decade of the 20th century. (For more on this see the Essanay Studios p79).

Part of the city's love of movies is simply the narcissistic joy of getting to see their streets, homes and restaurants projected onto the silver screen. Over the past hundred years, almost every landmark in the city has had some screen time. In recent years, *Barbershop* (and *Barbershop II*), *My Big Fat Greek Wedding* and *The Road to Perdition* all had scenes filmed in Chicago. But the bond between Chicago and the movies goes beyond ego-fulfillment. From the lovingly restored old movie houses like the Music Box (p173), to the beer-soaked,

Top 10 Chicago Films

- *North by Northwest,* Alfred Hitchcock (1959) The middle part of this Hitchcock classic contains scenes filmed on location at the Omni Ambassador East, on N Michigan Ave and at Midway Airport.
- *Blues Brothers,* John Landis (1980) In the best-known Chicago movie, Second City alums John Belushi and Dan Aykroyd tear up the city, including City Hall.
- *Ferris Bueller's Day Off,* John Hughes (1986) A cinematic ode to Chicago, from the director who set almost all of his movies, from *Breakfast Club* to *Home Alone,* in and around the Windy City. This one revolves around a rich North Shore teen discovering the joys of Chicago.
- *Native Son,* Jerrold Freedman (1986) Based on the 1940 novel of the same name by Richard Wright, this movie plays out the disturbing repercussions of a young white woman's accidental murder by Bigger Thomas, a poor young black man. Much of this tense drama was shot in Hyde Park and the South Side.
- *The Untouchables,* Brian DePalma (1987) Kevin Costner saves Chicago from Al Capone in this crime thriller. The infamous baby-carriage scene was filmed in Union Station, and the exploding grocery store stood at Clark and Roscoe.
- *The Fugitive,* Andrew Davis (1993) Harrison Ford stars as the falsely accused main character in this action film, which boasts great scenes in City Hall and the Chicago Hilton and Towers and on the El.
- *Hoop Dreams,* Steve James (1994) This stirring documentary follows the high school basketball careers of two African American teenagers from the South Side. The filmmakers interview the young men and their families, coaches, teachers and friends over several years, showing how the dream of playing college and pro ball – and escaping the ghetto – influences their life choices.
- *High Fidelity,* Stephen Frears (2000) This Chicago version of Nick Hornby's classic paean to music nerds stars Chicagoan John Cusack as a man uncommitted about commitment. The record store set for the film was located at Milwaukee and Honore in Wicker Park.
- *The Road to Perdition,* Sam Mendes (2002) Tom Hanks and Paul Newman star in this story of a hit man on the run in Depression-era Chicago.
- *I Am Trying to Break Your Heart,* Sam Jones (2002) First-time director Jones follows Chicago musical celebrities Wilco through the record company jiltings and inter-band tensions that arise after the recording of their classic *Yankee Foxtrot Hotel.*

yelling-at-the-screen-is-okay Brew & View (p173) at the Vic, Chicago embraces movies as a part of everyday life. It's no coincidence that Roger Ebert, the nation's most famous film critic, lives and writes here.

This hardy love for the moving image, though, hasn't kept Chicago out of a bind with moviemakers. Hamstrung by the Illinois state legislature, Chicago isn't able to match Canada's offers of tax credits to filmmakers who shoot in their cities. As a result of this, Hollywood movies have begun bypassing the Windy City and doing the bulk of filming – even for movies set in Chicago – in Toronto. In 2003 a new Illinois Film Office director stepped in, determined to get legislation passed to remedy the situation. With Illinois $5 billion in debt, though, the Film Office is a long way from a happy ending.

Chicago television is in similar straits. The Oprah and Jerry Springer talk shows are shot here. If you reserve tickets in advance, you can sit in the audience and watch episodes being taped. Afterward, you may get to meet the hosts and their guests.

The charismatic ratings leader of syndicated talk shows, Oprah Winfrey is also a local celebrity. From her own production facility in the West Loop – Harpo Studios (wondering about the name? Spell it backward) – she tapes her wildly popular show, which features celebrities, the occasional serious news investigation and discussions of issues as diverse as racial prejudice and whom to invite to your third wedding.

For tickets, call ☎ 312-591-9222 at least a month in advance. Warning: the ticket line is infamous for being constantly busy. Advice from people who have gotten through is to keep trying. Harpo Studios is at 1050 W Washington Blvd.

If Oprah is the class act of daytime TV, Jerry Springer is at the opposite end of the spectrum. Joining the audience here can be a raucous or sickening experience, as Springer disingenuously admits that his guests are vile but that he's really trying to communicate valid moral messages. Yeah, right. At the end of each episode Springer delivers a pious sermon that's a laugh in itself. During ratings periods he heroically books neo-Nazis whom he then throws out of the studio for being Nazis. For tickets, call ☎ 312-321-5365. The Jerry Springer show is taped at the NBC Tower (454 N Columbus Dr, east of Michigan Ave).

But apart from the daytime TV juggernaut, only a handful of prime-time shows – *ER* the most notable among them – ever set foot in Chicago.

This doesn't mean that Chicago actors and actresses don't have their mugs appearing on screens big and small across America. *Friends* star David Schwimmer lives here (and directs the Lookingglass Theatre), as do Joan and John Cusack. John Mahoney, who plays Frasier's father on *Frasier*, is an Oak Park resident. Comedian Bernie Mac (of Fox's *The Bernie Mac Show*) is a longtime Chicago fixture, as is Cedric 'The Entertainer' (who played a coach on *The Steve Harvey Show*).

LITERATURE

Though it has produced a number of award-winning works and offers a myriad of bookstores, Chicago is not a fiction powerhouse. Young authors from the Chicago area – Dave Eggers among them – tend to leave the area to make their name in New York or California. That said, there are plenty of great works by Chicagoans, many of which play up the gritty, noir urban side of the city.

Top Five Bookstores

- Old Town's **Barbara's Books** (p197), a Chicago institution for new books and author readings.
- Evanston's **Bookman's Alley** (p233), a cross between a garage sale and a royal library.
- Wicker Park's **Myopic Books** (p212), boasting a vast collection of contemporary and offbeat used fiction.
- Hyde Park's **Powell's** (p213), one of five great bookstores in the neighborhood.
- Wicker Park's **Quimby's** (p212), home of zines and indie media.

Chic-A-Go-Go *by Kathleen Munnelly*

A rat puppet with a skateboard, wearing blue jeans and Converse sneakers, sits on a platform beside a peppy young woman in a miniskirt and go-go boots. A singer in a homemade superhero costume makes odd trilling noises as a band mimes playing behind her. In front, an ethnically diverse audience ranging from leaping two-year olds to thirtysomethings in thrift-store finery doing the pony mug for the camera.

Wondering what exactly is going on here? You've just stumbled across *Chic-A-Go-Go*, the coolest public access television show in Chicago. A dance program for kids of all ages, *Chic-A-Go-Go* is one-third *American Bandstand*, one-third *Romper Room* and one-third CBGBs. Not even John Waters could concoct such a delightful display of eccentricity that also manages to be joyous and inclusive.

Dancers groove to a wide range of sounds from punk to classic soul, hip-hop to country, and everything in between. An astounding variety of 'live' performers (they're actually lip-synching to their own recordings) play the show, from septuagenarian blues men to blistering punk bands to performance art groups that defy any explanation. The divine mayhem is all presided over by the hosts, Ratso the Rat and Miss Mia.

While many of the performers are local unknowns, you may just have heard of some of the other acts that have showed up to play for the *Chic-A-Go-Go* gang: Shonen Knife, Pansy Division, The Cramps, Sleater-Kinney, The Specials, The Donnas, Fugazi – the list goes on.

Chic-A-Go-Go was founded in 1996 by married hipsters Jake Austen and Jacqueline Stewart. The couple also publish an underground music magazine called *Roctober*, and got the idea for the show when writing an article about *Kiddie A-Go-Go*, a 1960s children's dance program.

Anyone and everyone are welcome at *Chic-A-Go-Go*. Toddlers twist alongside adults wearing alien costumes, grandmas boogie down the line with pierced bike messengers, and everyone plays John Wayne during the 'fantasy sequence,' dancing in front of a screen showing westerns to the tune of 'I Wanna Be a Cowboy.'

Chic-A-Go-Go airs on Tuesdays at 8:30pm and Wednesdays at 3:30pm. If this sounds like too much fun to miss out on and you want to be a part of it, just show up for a taping and dance your heart out. For a show schedule and taping location, check out their website at www.roctober.com /chicagogo, where you can also see photos of some of the regular dancers.

Top 10 Chicago Books

- *Sister Carrie,* Theodore Dreiser (1900) In a lot of ways, it is the perfect Chicago book: the mean streets of the city rob our heroine of her virtue, but in the best 'Where's mine?' tradition, she turns this seeming setback into profitable gain.
- *The Jungle,* Upton Sinclair (1906) Riveting story about the exploited workers in Chicago's South Side meatpacking plants still holds up well today.
- *Chicago Poems,* Carl Sandburg (1916) This collection includes the oft-cited 1916 poem 'Chicago,' which captured the grand spirit of the city: 'Hog Butcher for the World, / Tool Maker, Stacker of Wheat, / Player with Railroads and the Nation's Freight Handler; /...City of the Big Shoulders.'
- *The Adventures of Augie March,* Saul Bellow (1953) The odyssey of a dirt-poor Chicago boy growing up during the Depression, written by the Nobel Prize winning Chicago author.
- *Annie Allen,* Gwendolyn Brooks, (1949) Chicago's one-time poet laureate won the Pulitzer Prize for this collection.
- *The Man With the Golden Arm,* Nelson Algren (1950) The National Book Award Winning-novel by one of Chicago's quintessential modern realists is set in a Wicker Park very different from today's playland.
- *Studs Lonigan Trilogy,* James T Farrell (1932–1935) This series conveys the aspirations of Irish American immigrants and the nightmarish realities of their lives.
- *The House on Mango Street,* Sandra Cisneros (1983) A series of interconnected vignettes about growing up Mexican-American in a Chicago barrio.
- *Paco's Story,* Larry Heinemann (1986) This work by a former CTA bus driver focuses on his experiences as a grunt in Vietnam. It won the National Book Award for Fiction.
- *Windy City Blues,* Sara Paretsky (1996) A series of short stories featuring Paretsky's beloved creation, Detective VI Warshawski. These detective novels at first seem like nothing more than escapist genre fiction, but within the gritty narratives about a woman private investigator, Paretsky weaves her own deep commitment to social justice.
- *Personal Injuries,* Scott Turow (1999) Arguably the best of Turow's taut legal thrillers. Fun fact: Turow still works as a Loop lawyer and writes his books during his commute on the Metra train.
- *The Coast of Chicago,* Stuart Dybek (1990) A collection of short stories from Dybek, who adds an impressive twist on the down-and-out stories of Nelson Algren.
- *Nowhere Man,* Aleksandar Hemon (2002) This Bosnian-born author has been hailed as the new Nabokov. His first novel follows a Bosnian in exile in Chicago in the 1990s.

Poetry, on the other hand, got very interesting in Chicago. In 2002 pharmaceutical heiress (and longtime amateur poet) Ruth Lilly changed the entire landscape of poetry in the country when she bequeathed $100 million to Chicago's Modern Poetry Association, publisher of the humble *Poetry* magazine. The gift stunned everyone in the writing world, including the tiny staff at the MPA. It remains to be seen how the organization will spend the windfall, but you can believe that the city's poets are already counting the dough.

Architecture

Architecture

Architecture is a contact sport in Chicago. Need proof? Look at the hullabaloo surrounding the recently remodeled Soldier Field. The long-overdue modernization brought more seats, better sight lines, and (not unimportantly) more bathrooms to the lakefront stadium. It also brought a two-year vitriolic public pillorying of the architects, the city, the football franchise and anyone else who appeared to be in any way related to the project. Blair Kamin, the Pulitzer Prize–winning architecture critic for the *Tribune* called the stadium a 'nightmare' in a widely read series of articles. One local group launched a lawsuit. And barstool pundits throughout the city's taverns fantasized about what they'd do if only they could get the developers responsible alone in a dark alley.

The city's response to the public outcry says a lot about the gloves-off spirit of architecture in Chicago. 'We feel really good about this design,' Lee Bey, the deputy chief of staff for planning and design in the mayor's office told the *New York Times*. 'Even if it infuriates, it puts its foot down. We have to get away from this idea of architecture that's polite.'

Politeness has rarely been an issue in Windy City construction. Ever since William Le Baron Jenney built the first 'skyscaper' at the corner of LaSalle and Adams Sts in 1885, the city's streets have been shaded by an endless succession of unabashedly ambitious marvels and monstrosities. More so than any other American city save New York, Chicago has always been a place where architects take chances, pushing the envelope on design, height and materials. And the public, far from being passive recipients of the developers' largesse, see each new addition to the skyline as a wonderful gift or a personal insult. With such a long history of architectural innovation, Chicagoans have a lot to be both thankful for and mad about.

THE CHICAGO FIRE AND THE YOUNG TURKS

Though the 1871 Chicago fire seemed to be an unmitigated disaster at the time, it actually set the stage for a dramatic architectural renaissance in the city. Attracted by the blank canvas of an empty downtown, architects from around the world flocked to the city for commissions. Most were young – the average age was under 30 – and had something to prove. They found a city happy to give them the scorched Loop as a stage, and in a short time they had invented the modern skyscraper, with its steel frame, high-speed elevators and impossibly high (for the time anyway) rooftops. These young architects also defined a new form of architecture that came to be called the 'Chicago School.' Tossed aside were the classical forms of Greece and Rome that architects everywhere else in the world continued to employ. The Chicago School stressed economy, simplicity and function.

These mavericks closely adhered to Chicago School architect Louis Sullivan's mandate that 'form follows function.' Though the basic tenet held true – the buildings did draw their facades from the underlying logic of the regular steel bracing beneath – that didn't result in a lack of adornment. The architects used a powerful language of simple geometric shapes, primarily strong vertical lines crossed by horizontal bands. Relief from the sharp lines came in the form of bay windows, curved corners, sweeping entrances and other details, which gave the buildings a pragmatic glory that reflected the city around them.

Twenty years after the fire, the works of architects like Sullivan and Daniel Burnham had reshaped the formerly rubble-filled Loop area. The city's recovery was highlighted in the 1893 World's Columbian Exposition, where Burnham's host of classical-influenced buildings on the city's south side heralded the transition from the Chicago School into one that drew inspiration from European re-imaginings of antiquity.

The beginning of the 20th century also marked the ascent of the Prairie School movement, headed by former Sullivan protégé Frank Lloyd Wright. In contrast to the grand edifices, Wright and his followers built on a more modest scale, stressing ground-hugging, low-slung structures where the horizontal was the most important axis.

WHAT TO SEE

Named after the pigeons that used to nest here, the **Rookery** (Map pp282–3; 209 S LaSalle St) was built from 1885 to 1888 and remains one of Chicago's most beloved buildings. The original design by Burnham and Root, with its load-bearing walls of granite and brick, surrounds a spectacular atrium space that was remodeled in 1907 by Frank Lloyd Wright. A lavish restoration in 1992 has returned the building to its peak grandeur. Another Burnham and Root classic from the same era is the **Reliance Building** (Map pp282–3; 32 N State St). With its 16 stories of shimmering glass framed by brilliant white terra-cotta details, it's like a breath of fresh air. Its lightweight internal metal frame – much of which was erected in only 15 days – supports a glass facade that gives the building a feeling of lightness, a style that didn't become universal until after WWII. Narrowly avoiding demolition – a common fate for Chicago's architectural gems in a town where preservation often takes a back seat to commercial interests – the Reliance underwent an exterior restoration in 1995 and reopened as the chic Hotel Burnham (p217) in 1999.

The **Auditorium Building** (Map pp282–3; 430 S Michigan Ave) to the southeast, dates from 1889. It was designed by Louis Sullivan with Dankmar Adler, and stands as one of the city's greatest structures. Behind its granite and limestone facade hides a magnificent 4300-seat theater with some of the best acoustics and sight lines in the city. Originally a hotel and office space, the building is now largely occupied by Roosevelt University. The 10th-floor library used to be an ornate restaurant. The arcade on Congress Pkwy was created when the sidewalk was sacrificed for the widening of the road in the 1950s.

Daniel Burnham had a hand in the **Marshall Field & Co** building (p191). Covering an entire block, Marshall Field's was built in five stages by Burnham and others between 1892 and 1914. The southeastern corner (at Washington St and Wabash Ave) went up during the earliest stage and features massive load-bearing walls. On the State St side, the soaring ground-floor retail spaces are topped by Tiffany skylights. The whole store underwent a costly reconstruction in 1992, when a central escalator atrium was added.

Built in 1893, the **Art Institute of Chicago** (p62) is very much in keeping with the buildings erected in Chicago for the World's Columbian Exposition the same year. The Beaux Arts beauty was designed by Shepley, Rutan and Coolidge, and has been expanded several times. Across the train tracks is the large Columbus Dr wing, designed by Skidmore, Owings and Merrill and added in 1977. The large Rice Building, designed by Hammond, Beeby and Babka, came along in 1988. The bronze lions fronting the main entrance have been beloved mascots since 1894. Also dating back to the year of the Exposition, the **Marquette Building** (Map pp282–3;

Who to Know – Young Turks

Daniel Burnham Designer of 'The Chicago Plan' which stressed an open lakefront and an easy-to-follow street grid, Burnham played a principal role in the development of the Chicago School of architecture and oversaw the Beaux Arts buildings of the 1893 World's Columbian Exposition.

John Wellborn Root Burnham's partner, Root designed the Monadnock Building (1891) and the Rookery (1888), among many other Chicago School classics, before his untimely death at age 41.

Louis Sullivan A master of ornamentation, Sullivan brought his skills to bear on the entrance to Carson Pirie Scott & Co (1903) and on the now-destroyed Chicago Stock Exchange; you can see preserved bits of the latter at the Art Institute. Sullivan usually created his work in partnership with engineer Dankmar Adler.

William Holabird & Martin Roche These partners took the Chicago School to commercial success, applying its tenets to more than 80 buildings in the Loop. Notable survivors include the Pontiac Building (1891) and the Marquette Building (1894).

Frank Lloyd Wright A visionary, Wright pioneered the revolutionary Prairie School style of architecture, which derived its form from its surroundings. Buildings were low, heavily emphasizing the horizontal lines of the Midwestern landscape. In contrast to the simple lines of the architecture, Wright added myriad precise details, which you'll notice on closer inspection of his buildings. For more about Wright, see the Oak Park section (p234) and Robie House (p109).

Five Ugly Buildings

Along with world-class architectural triumphs, Chicago has some world-class duds. The following buildings may mess up the landscape, but at least they make their neighbors look good.

Illinois Center (South of the Chicago River, west of N Michigan Ave) Not just one ugly building but a vast collection of them, this mixed-use development of offices, stores, apartments and hotels includes triple-decker roads and other atrocities that spoil the view from the river.

Apparel Mart (350 N Orleans St, just west of the Merchandise Mart) Check out the grime-streaked, windowless south side. This was commissioned by the same folks – the Kennedy clan of political fame – who own the regal Merchandise Mart next door.

Presidential Towers (555, 575, 605 and 625 W Madison Street) These four sinister towers would make an excellent headquarters for an international evil corporate empire. They were allowed to be built under the condition that they would include units of affordable housing. Do they? Nope. Doh.

Asbury Plaza (750 N Dearborn St) This structure breaks with high-rise apartment tradition by providing more walls than windows – the high-rise for people afraid of heights. It's a putrid green color, too.

University of Illinois Campus (601 S Morgan St) As the university demolishes them, there are ever-fewer of Walter Netsch's atrocious buildings on the UIC campus south of Greektown. Those that do remain, however, are almost lovably hideous.

140 S Dearborn St) is the work of Holabird and Roche. The architects made natural light and ventilation vital considerations, because of the skimpy light bulbs and nonexistent mechanical ventilation of the time. The same firm took on the building's 1980 renovation. Tiffany and others created the sculptured panels above the entrance and in the lobby, which recall the exploits of French explorer and missionary Jacques Marquette.

Considered the Loop Lourdes for architecture buffs on a pilgrimage, the **Monadnock Building** (Map pp282–3; 53 W Jackson Blvd) consists of two structures, both dating from the early 1890s. The two parts represent a crucial juncture in American skyscraper development. The original portion of the building consists of traditional, load-bearing walls that are 6ft wide at the base. Working with brick, architects Burnham and Root fashioned a free-flowing facade that becomes almost sensuous around the bottoms of the window bays. Constructed only two years later, the addition lacks the heavy walls and benefits from the latest advance in construction at the time – a then-revolutionary metal frame.

The main structure of the yellowish terra-cotta–clad **Fisher Building** (Map pp282–3; 343 S Dearborn St) was completed in 1896; the simpler northern addition was added in 1907. Inspired by the name of the developer, Lucius G Fisher, architect Daniel Burnham gave the exterior a playful menagerie of fish, crabs, shells and other sea creatures. There's nothing fishy about the **Chicago Cultural Center** (p62), which was born in 1897 as the Chicago Public library. After the 1871 fire, the British sent over more than 8000 books to establish a free library for the people of Chicago. Many were autographed by the donors, such as Thomas Carlyle, Lord Tennyson and Benjamin Disraeli. The Chicago Public Library was established on the basis of that donation, and this building was created by Shepley, Rutan & Coolidge to house the collection. In 1977 the building was renovated for use as a cultural center. Today the books have found a home in the Harold Washington Library Center (p41), but the magnificent public spaces remain.

Architect Daniel Burnham kept his offices in the sparkling white terra-cotta **Santa Fe Center** (Map pp282–3; 224 S Michigan Ave) which he designed in 1904. The unusual top-floor porthole windows make the structure stand out even more from its neighbors. Enter the lobby and look upward at the vast light well Burnham placed in the center. He gave this same feature to the Rookery. Dating from the same year, the 15-story 1904 **Chicago Building** (Map pp282–3; 7 W Madison St) is typical of many designed by the firm Holabird and Roche during the late 19th and early 20th centuries. The windows fronting State St show classic Chicago style: two narrow sash windows on either side of a larger fixed pane. After a modest career as home to miscellaneous small businesses, the building reopened in 1997 as a dorm for the School of the Art Institute – another innovative use of older Loop office buildings. The preserved cornice is unusual, since most older buildings have had theirs removed for maintenance reasons.

Constructed two years after the Chicago Building, **Carson Pirie Scott & Co** (p191) was originally criticized as being too ornamental to serve as a retail building. You be the judge, as you admire Louis Sullivan's superb metalwork around the main entrance at State and Madison Sts. Though Sullivan insisted that 'form follows function,' it's hard to see his theory at work in this lavishly flowing cast iron. Amid the flowing botanical and geometric forms, look for Sullivan's initials, LHS. The rest of the building is clad simply in white terra-cotta.

The **Wrigley Building** (Map pp280–1; 400 N Michigan Ave) was designed with Hollywood flair by architects Graham, Anderson, Probst and White. The group cast the white terra-cotta in six shades, which get increasingly brighter toward the top, ensuring that the building pops out of the sky whether it's high noon or midnight. Lights from neighboring buildings and across the river provide the nocturnal glow. The 'main building' actually occupies almost half the space of the much-larger northern addition. Both were designed and built between 1919 and 1924. Across the street, you'll find the **Tribune Tower** (p69). The self-proclaimed 'world's greatest newspaper' was never one to let modesty get in the way of bombast. When the *Tribune* announced an architectural competition in 1922 for a new headquarters, it asked for nothing less than 'the most beautiful office building in the world.' The chosen entry, by Howells and Hood, won out over 264 submissions. It borrowed elements of Gothic cathedrals such as flying buttresses and applied them to a skyscraper. Look up at the top of the building, where the purely decorative buttresses surround a small tower. As on cathedrals, carved figures frame the building's three-story entrance, although here they come from Aesop's fables rather than from the Scriptures. Completed in 1925, the tower gained its less-interesting addition to the north in 1934. Look for historic rocks embedded in the walls at its base.

The **Chicago Board of Trade** (see boxed text p63) is one of Chicago's few remaining art deco creations. The original 1930 Holabird and Root tower, fronting LaSalle St, is a classic 45-story skyscraper topped with a statue of Ceres, the Roman goddess of agriculture. To the rear, a 1980 addition by Helmut Jahn nicely complements the original. Inside, the earlier building features a sumptuous lobby; the addition contains a 12th-floor atrium with a classic mural of Ceres that once adorned the original's main trading floor. 1930 also saw the construction of the impressive **Merchandise Mart** (p194), designed by Graham, Anderson, Probst and White as a wholesale store for Marshall Field & Co. The famous Kennedy family purchased it in 1945 and converted it into commercial space. The Merchandise Mart's 4.1 million sq feet are encased in a massive limestone exterior.

LUDWIG MIES VAN DER ROHE AND THE NEW SKYSCRAPERS

Chicago again became the center of the architectural world after WWII. Led by Ludwig Mies van der Rohe, the new 'International Style' was the pared-down embodiment of Louis Sullivan's mandate. The very structure of buildings – the steel frame – was no longer the inspiration for a building's look, it *was* the look. The oft-copied steel-and-glass towers, similar to the Federal Center (Dearborn and Adams Sts), were built in every country around the world but often without Mies' careful eye for details. And the interior of Mies's bare-bones structures are as functional as their exteriors, featuring walls that can be moved according to the whims of the occupants.

From 1950 through 1980, the Chicago architectural partnership of Skidmore, Owings and Merrill became the IBM of their day. No corporate manager was ever fired for hiring SOM and their bands of Mies disciples to design a building. They built the John Hancock Center in 1970, and then topped that with the Sears Tower three years later. During the go-go era of the 1980s, commercial space in the Loop almost doubled, and high-rise offices spread to the Near North. Many of these buildings were influenced by postmodernism, the movement that emphasized eclectic designs drawn from older styles and other art forms. Postmodernism's playful mix of eras and materials made local architects like Helmut Jahn famous in some circles and infamous in others.

WHAT TO SEE

Mies' twin modernist landmarks, the **860-880 N Lake Shore Dr Apartments** (p70), changed the architectural world when they went up in 1951. Also by Mies, the **Chicago Federal Center** (Map pp282–3; Dearborn St btwn Jackson Blvd & Adams St) bears the same austere look. In 1964 the 30-story Dirksen Building became the first structure to be completed; it holds the federal courts. The 42-story Kluczynski Building came along in 1974; it's home to various federal agencies. The post office, finished the same year, completes the troika; Mies designed it to be as tall as the lobbies in its two neighbors. *Flamingo*, a bright red sculpture by Alexander Calder, provides a counterpoint to Mies' ebony palette.

Dominated by its twin 'corncob' towers, the 1962 mixed-use complex of **Marina City** (Map pp280–1; north bank of the river btwn Dearborn & State Sts) designed by Bertrand Goldberg has become an iconic part of the Chicago skyline, showing up most recently on the cover of the Wilco CD *Yankee Hotel Foxtrot*. The condos that top the spiraling parking garages are quite popular and especially picturesque at Christmastime, when the owners decorate the scalloped balconies with a profusion of lights.

The **Richard J Daley Center** (Map pp282–3; Dearborn St btwn Washington & Randolph Sts) is a classic Chicago Miesian building. The 31-story Daley Center was called the Chicago Civic Center when it was completed by CF Murphy Associates in 1965. The building is clad in Cor-Ten steel, a type developed to avoid the need for paint – a layer of oxidation forms on the steel's surface, which protects it and gives the metal its distinctive bronze color. Inside, the scores of county courtrooms have ceilings two floors high. Outside, the plaza hosts regular performances and protests; it also holds what Chicagoans refer to simply as 'the Picasso,' an untitled sculpture by the great 20th-century artist.

John Hancock Center (p71)

Built four years after the Daley Center, the **Bank One Building** (Map pp282–3; Dearborn St btwn Monroe & Madison Sts) boasts a gracefully curving shape. The 60-story tower, designed by Perkins and Will and finished in 1969, gives this large bank a distinctive profile on the skyline. The multilevel plaza on Monroe St is popular at lunch. Marc Chagall's mosaic *The Four Seasons* recently gained an architecturally sensitive weather cover. In stark, rectangular juxtaposition to the Bank One Building, the **IBM Building** (Map pp280–1; 330 N Wabash Ave) was built in 1971. Many consider the tower to be the signature office building by Mies van der Rohe; it was his last American commission. Here Mies' basic black palette gives way to an almost radical combination of rich browns. The building and its breezy plaza are fastidiously maintained by its persnickety owner.

Perhaps the most recognizable Chicago high-rise, the 100-story, 1127ft **John Hancock Center** (p71) combines, from bottom to top, shopping, parking, offices, condos, tourist attractions and broadcast transmitters. The first major collaboration of the Skidmore, Owings and Merrill architect Bruce Graham and engineer Fazlur Khan, this 1970 building muscles its way into the sky atop a series of cross-braces. If you look at the exterior, you can see where the shorter residential floors begin at the 44th floor. Three years after the John Hancock Center came the **Aon Center** (Map pp282–3; 200 E Randolph St), originally called the Standard Oil building. Chicago's second tallest building in overall height was originally clad in marble from the same quarry Michelangelo used – at the firm insistence of Standard Oil's then-chairman, John Swearingen, and his wife, Bonnie. To save money, the marble was cut more thinly than ever before, despite warnings from experts that, structurally, the marble would be too weak to withstand the very harsh Chicago climate. Within 15 years the precious marble began falling off the building's 1136-foot facade. The 43,000 panels covering the entire exterior had to be replaced with light-colored granite at a cost equal to the original construction.

The only building in Chicago that can look down on the Aon Center, the 110-story **Sears Tower** (p65) is one of the world's tallest. Completed in 1973, it owes its existence to the talents of Skidmore, Owings and Merrill architect Bruce Graham and structural engineer Fazlur Khan. It consists of nine structural square 'tubes' that rise from the building's base, two stopping at the 50th floor, two more ending at the 66th floor, three more calling it quits at 90 stories and two stretching to the full height.

The most popular Loop tower to emerge from the 1980s building boom is **333 W Wacker** (Map pp282–3). Completed in 1983, this curving green structure is the work of architect William E Pedersen, who did a masterful job of utilizing the odd triangular site on the curve in the river. Water and sky play across the mirrored glass in an ever-changing kaleidoscope of shapes and colors. The bulbous **James R Thompon Center** (Map pp282–3; 100 W Randoph St) – completed as the State of Illinois Center in 1986 – features a shape reminiscent of its namesake governor, who commissioned it. Controversial from the start, the oddly shaped structure aroused ire with its all-glass design. Architect Helmut Jahn thought the structure should be a metaphor for open government and left off doors, ceilings and walls from interior offices. As a result he produced a vast greenhouse with overheated bureaucrats, who held up thermometers showing temperatures of 110°F and higher for the gleeful media. When the imperious Jahn took a tour of what he had wrought, he was confronted by a secretary who complained about her heat stroke. Jahn suggested she get a new job. Vastly improved air-conditioning has lowered temperatures, and everybody loves the soaring atrium lobby.

Named after the man dubbed 'the people's mayor,' the **Harold Washington Library Center** (Map pp282–3; 400 S State St) building serves as 'the people's library.' Appropriately enough, the democratic process played a big role in its design. The city invited several architectural firms to submit designs, which were displayed in the Chicago Cultural Center for several months in 1989. Thousands of citizens inspected the competing proposals and voted for their choice. Robustly traditional, with details derived from many classic Chicago designs, this 1991 Hammond, Beeby and Babka building was the winner. Note the whimsical copper details on the roof, including studious-looking owls.

CHICAGO ARCHITECTURE TODAY

The real estate crash at the end of the '80s stalled new construction in Chicago, and the '90s were somewhat of a timid decade for the architecture scene here, with little in the way of innovation or artistic breakthroughs taking place. Much of the building from the late '90s to the early '00s focused on bringing homes (in the forms of towering condo projects) to the Near North, South Loop and Near South Side areas. The results haven't been so pretty. Cutting corners on ornamentation and design, prominent local developers and architects

Who to Know – New Skyscrapers

Bertrand Goldberg He used concrete to create fluid structures such as Marina City (1959–67) and River City (1986).

Bruce Graham A leading partner at Skidmore, Owings and Merrill, Graham designed massive structures such as the John Hancock Center (1969) and the Sears Tower (1974), which continued Chicago's burly and aggressive style of architecture.

Helmut Jahn This controversial architect reversed the Sullivan tenet and designed buildings in which function follows form. His early work, such as the modernist Xerox Centre (1980), is overshadowed by his later showy works, such as the notorious James R Thompson Center (1985) and the masterful United Airlines Terminal One at O'Hare (1988). His latest Chicago creation is the Illinois Institute of Technology (IIT) dorm (p98).

Ludwig Mies van der Rohe The legendary architect brought his Bauhaus School ideas to Chicago when he fled the Nazis and Germany in the 1930s. His early '50s buildings set the style for three decades of international architecture.

like Jim Loewenberg have created ugly concrete high-rises where parking lots dominate the first floors, followed above by basic, Eastern-bloc-styled dwellings. Any architecture tour of Chicago should take in a couple of these new structures, such as the one at 1 W Superior St in Near North and 222 N Columbus Ave in the Loop.

Buildings like these inspired Mayor Daley in 2003 to write a front-page article in the *Sun-Times* taking local architects and developers to task for failing to employ more eye-pleasing, innovative designs. The article, entitled 'No More Ugly Buildings,' did little to stop the bottom-line-focused builders of condos and townhouses. It did, however, resonate with a new breed of up-and-coming Chicago architect – names like Jeannie Gang, Brad Lynch and Doug Garofalo, who have already begun adding their distinctive, modern visions to the city's architectural legacy.

And the mayor's malaise was also no doubt eased by the 2003 opening of Helmut Jahn's impressive new dorm and Dutch architect Rem Koolhaas' vibrant new student center, both at the Illinois Institute of Technology (p98). Both designs drew accolades from the press and public, putting Chicago back on the international architectural map.

Chicago Home Cheat Sheet

As you explore Chicago's neighborhoods, you will see several types of housing repeated over and over. The following styles are listed roughly in their order of historical appearance in Chicago.

Cottages & Frame Houses Chicago's great contribution to residential construction was the two-by-four. Until the system of knocking houses together from precut boards and mass-produced nails was developed in the city in 1833, building a house was a long and costly process of sawing timber and stacking rocks. Thousands of cottages and frame houses burned like matchsticks in the 1871 fire, but many more were built later in areas of the city where they weren't outlawed by the city's fire code. Look for them in Wicker Park, Old Town and Pilsen (see the Wicker Park walking tour p117).

Queen Anne Houses Also called Victorian houses, these proliferated in the late 19th century and featured a wealth of detail and ornaments, which the masses could afford thanks to assembly-line production techniques developed in lumber factories southwest of the Loop. The houses can be found throughout the north and northwest sides of the city.

Graystones Two and three stories tall, these dignified residences met the city's tough fire code and became popular refuges from 1890 to 1920. The expensive limestone was used only in front; the rest of the structures were made out of ordinary brick. Some were built as single-family homes, others as apartments. Graystones dot the city – the Wrigleyville neighborhood contains a huge concentration of them.

Apartment Buildings These come in all shapes and sizes, from three-story multi-unit affairs built in the late 1800s to the airy courtyard buildings of the 1920s to some really awful concrete high-rises that appeared after WWII. In the early 20th century Chicago's population density rose so much that by 1920 two-thirds of the city's residents lived in apartments.

Three-Flats Joined by their less ambitious cousins, the two-flats, these buildings filled many of the city's neighborhoods from the 1910s through today. Set on the usual narrow Chicago lot, the buildings feature apartments with light front rooms and airy back kitchens with wooden porches (many of which are now enclosed to increase living space). Dark bedrooms open off a long hall that runs the length of the apartment. Since the 1970s thousands of these buildings have been renovated throughout the North Side for a new generation of apartment dwellers and condo buyers.

Storefronts with Apartments Throughout the 20th century storeowners and developers have placed living spaces above small retail shops. Examples of this practice can be found along any of Chicago's retail streets, especially in the neighborhoods. To see a contemporary equivalent of this practice, look up at the condos high above the Michigan Ave vertical malls, such as Water Tower Place and 900 N Michigan.

Bungalows Built by the tens of thousands along Chicago's outlying streets from the 1920s through the 1950s, bungalows filled the subdivisions of their day. Aimed squarely at factory workers, these homes commonly cost only $1000 down, plus easy payments on builder-financed $5000 mortgages; the affordable prices brought single-family homeownership to a generation. Stolid and compact on lots 25ft wide, the homes introduced the booming middle class to features their parents had considered luxuries: central halls, which gave privacy to bedrooms; ceramic-tiled bathrooms, which had hot and cold water; and kitchens with built-in cabinets and counters. Provisions were made for gas ranges, refrigerators and ever-growing collections of electrical appliances. Architectural details inspired by Frank Lloyd Wright's Prairie School brought character to the 'bungalow belts' that soon circled the city. These sturdy homes – most are still standing – have proven endlessly adaptable through the years. Today a bungalow in good shape easily costs $200,000 or much more.

History

History *by Chris Baty and Ryan Ver Berkmoes*

THE RECENT PAST

KING RICHARD THE SECOND'S REIGN CONTINUES

If you thought summer blockbuster sequels were repetitive, they've got nothing on Chicago history, especially when it comes to politicians. The recent era of Chicago history dawned in 2003, when Chicago handed Mayor Richard M Daley his fifth mayoral election in yet another landslide victory. Five terms for any mayor would be impressive, but Richard M Daley is not any mayor. He's the son of Richard J Daley, who ruled Chicago for almost *six* terms from 1955 to 1976.

What is it with Daleys and Chicago, you ask? Ah, that's a good question. And one we'll get to in a second. But first, back to that 2003 election. The four people in Chicago who voted against Daley may have been deeply disappointed, but the rest of the city was rejoicing, having seen little reason to risk breaking in a new mayor when so much was at stake. September 11 was still fresh in everyone's minds, and Daley had led the city competently through the unsettling aftermath of the terrorist attack. An ambitious, Daley-helmed restructuring of the Chicago public school system that began back in 1989 was finally showing results, as children who had been kindergartners when Daley took over were now showing improvements on their standardized test scores. And the aesthetic dictates of the mayor – tulips, planters and parks – had the city looking better than it had in decades. Even African Americans, who had long been alienated by Daley's father, turned out in support of the incumbent mayor.

Daley leveraged the turn-out in the polls to further consolidate his political power in the city. Nowhere was this more apparent than the infamous Meigs Field incident of March, 2003. Meigs was the tiny commuter airport on the edge of the Museum Campus downtown, a tantalizingly valuable piece of real estate that the mayor had repeatedly argued should be made into a park.

When he ran into opposition from the airport's users – CEOs and other corporate types, mostly – he dropped the plan. Or appeared to, anyway. Then, at 11:30pm on March 30, he shocked the city by sending bulldozers to Meigs under the cover of darkness. The bulldozers made quick work of the airport's runway, as news helicopters flew overhead, capturing images of the affair. The next day, the Mayor defended the closure of the airport as a long-overdue move needed to protect the city's skyscrapers from a Meigs-launched terrorist attack. Editorials in both papers bristled at the autocratic action, and the airport's users talked about taking legal action to force the reopening of the airstrip. But legally, the mayor appeared to be within his rights, and the fallout over the incident soon passed.

LIFE IN THE MID-'00s

The scandal was helped off the newspaper editorial pages that year by the ongoing reactions to two city disasters. In the first, 21 clubgoers at a South Side nightclub were crushed to death when a bouncer's chemical spray set off a stampede for the exit. In the other, a porch collapsed during a Lincoln Park party, killing 12 people. In such a bar- and porch-centric city, the one-two punch was hard to take. Clubs such as Phyllis's Musical Inn in Ukrainian Village began preceding concerts with flight-attendant-style reports on the nearest emergency exits, prompting nervous laughter from bar patrons.

1779
Chicago's first settler, Jean Baptiste Pointe du Sable, establishes a trading post on the north bank of the Chicago River

That sort of anxious laughter resounded throughout the city in 2003. The newly elected Illinois governor, Rod Blagojevich, faced a nearly $5 billion budget deficit, the largest in the state's history. Schools throughout the state were hit, especially the University of Illinois, Chicago, which was forced to return $89 million of their 2003 budget to the state. The flatlining of the economy also put a question mark next to the vast number of luxury lofts and town houses going up in the South Loop and Near South Side. The buildings had been blueprinted back in 2000, when money flowed through the city like the Chicago River. If, on completion, the buildings prove to be a flop, their failure could send an ice-cold ripple through the city's still-hot real estate market.

To all the possibility of gloom and doom, Chicago's famously resilient residents just shrug. What can you do, really, besides put one foot in front of the other? Scottie Pippen is back with the Bulls, employment rates are up and violent crime is down. And the tulips are just coming into bloom. So Chicagoans walk into the future with the same tenacious stride that has carried the city through almost two centuries of boom and bust, fortunes and fires. Tomorrow, after all, is just another day in the city that works.

FROM THE BEGINNING
OUT OF THE SWAMP

No one is sure when Native Americans first lived in the Chicago region, but evidence can be traced back to about 10,000 years ago. By the late 1600s, many tribes made their home in the region, the dominant one being the Potawatomi.

In 1673 Indians directed French explorer Louis Jolliet and missionary Jacques Marquette to Lake Michigan via the Chicago River. The two, who had been exploring the Mississippi River, learned that the Indians of the region called the area around the mouth of the river '*Checaugou*,' after the wild garlic (some say onions) growing there.

Various explorers and traders traveled through the area over the next 100 years. In 1779 Quebec trader Jean Baptiste Pointe du Sable established a fur-trading store on the north bank of the river. Of mixed African and Caribbean descent, Pointe du Sable was the area's first non–Native American settler and was possibly the first settler period, given that the Indians dismissed this part of the riverbank as a feverish swamp.

After the Revolutionary War, the United States increasingly focused its attention on the immense western frontier. Because of Chicago's position on Lake Michigan, the government wanted a permanent presence in the area and in 1803 built Fort Dearborn on the south bank of the river, on marshy ground under what is today's Michigan Ave Bridge.

Nine years later, the Potawatomi Indians, in cahoots with the British (their allies in the War of 1812), slaughtered 52 settlers fleeing the fort. During this war such massacres had been a strategy employed throughout the frontier: the British bought the allegiance of various Indian tribes through trade and other deals, and the Indians paid them back by being hostile to American settlers. The settlers killed in Chicago had simply waited too long to flee the rising tension and thus found themselves caught.

After the war ended, bygones were quickly forgotten, as the Americans, French, British and Indians turned their energies to profiting from the fur trade. In 1816 Fort Dearborn was rebuilt. Two years later Illinois became a state, although much of its small population lived in the south near the Mississippi River.

During the 1820s, Chicago developed as a small town with a population of fewer than 200, most of whom made their living from trade. Records show that the total taxable value of Chicago's land was $8000.

Indian relations took a dramatic turn for the worse in 1832, when Chief Black Hawk of the Sauk Indians led a band of Sauk, Fox and Kickapoo from what is now Iowa to reclaim

1803	1833
Fort Dearborn built on the South Bank of the Chicago River	Chicago incorporated as a town

land swiped by settlers in western Illinois. The US reacted strongly, sending in hundreds of troops who traveled through Chicago, fueling its nascent economy. The army routed the Indians, and the US government requisitioned the rest of the Indian lands throughout Illinois, including those of the Potawatomi in Chicago. The Indians were forced to sign treaties by which they relinquished their land at a fraction of its worth, and all were moved west, ending any significant Native American presence in the city or region.

Chicago was incorporated as a town in 1833, with a population of 340. Within three years land speculation had rocked the local real estate market; lots that had sold for $33 in 1829 went for $100,000. The boom was fueled by the start of construction on the Illinois & Michigan Canal, a state project to create an inland waterway linking the Great Lakes to the Illinois River and thus to the Mississippi River and New Orleans.

The swarms of laborers drawn by the canal construction swelled the population to more than 4100 by 1837, when Chicago incorporated as a city. But the bullish city boosters quickly turned bearish that same year, after a national economic depression brought the unstable real estate market crashing down. On paper, Illinois was bankrupt; canal construction stopped for four years.

By 1847 the economy had recovered and the canal was being pushed forward at full pace. More than 20,000 people lived in what had become the region's dominant city. The rich Illinois soil supported thousands of farmers, and industrialist Cyrus Hall McCormick moved his reaper factory to the city to serve them. He would soon control one of the Midwest's major fortunes.

In 1848 the canal opened, and shipping began flowing through the Chicago River from the Caribbean to New York via the Great Lakes and the St Lawrence Seaway. It had a marked economic effect on the city. One of its great financial institutions, the Chicago Board of Trade, opened to handle the sale of grain by Illinois farmers, who had greatly improved access to Eastern markets thanks to the canal.

Railroad construction absorbed workers freed from canal construction. By 1850 a line had been completed to serve grain farmers between Chicago and Galena, in western Illinois. A year later, the city gave the Illinois Central Railroad land for its tracks south of the city. It was the first land-grant railroad and was joined by many others, whose tracks eventually would radiate out from Chicago. The city quickly became the hub of America's freight and passenger trains, a status it would hold for the next hundred years.

RAPID GROWTH

In the 1850s Chicago grew quickly. State St south of the river became the commercial center, as banks and other institutions flourished with the growing economy. The city's first steel mill opened in 1857, the forerunner of the city's economic and industrial diversification. By the end of the decade, Chicago supported at least seven daily newspapers. Immigrants poured in, drawn by jobs at the railroads that served the expanding agricultural trade. Twenty million bushels of produce were shipped through the city that year. The population topped 100,000.

By then Chicago was no longer a frontier town. Its central position in the US made it a favorite meeting spot, a legacy that continues to this day. In 1860 the Republican Party held its national political convention in Chicago and selected Abraham Lincoln, a lawyer from Springfield, Illinois, as its presidential candidate.

Like other northern cities, Chicago profited from the Civil War, which boosted business in its burgeoning steel and toolmaking industries and provided plenty of freight for the railroads and canal. In 1865, the year the war ended, an event took place that would profoundly affect the city for the next hundred years: the Union Stockyards opened on the South Side, unifying disparate meat operations scattered about the city. Chicago's rail network and the development of the iced refrigerator car meant that meat could be shipped

1837	1865
Chicago incorporated as a city (pop: 4170)	Union Stockyards open, bacon plentiful

east to New York, spurring the industry's consolidation.

The stockyards become the major supplier of meat to the entire nation. But besides bringing great wealth to a few and jobs to many, the yards were also a source of many problems, including water pollution (see the boxed text, p98).

The stockyard effluvia polluted not only the Chicago River but also Lake Michigan. Flowing into the lake, the fouled waters spoiled the city's source of fresh water and caused cholera and other epidemics that killed thousands. In 1869 the Water Tower and Pumping Station began bringing water into the city through a two-mile tunnel that had been built into Lake Michigan in an attempt to draw drinking water unpolluted by the Chicago River. But this solution proved resoundingly inadequate, and outbreaks of illness continued.

Two years later, the Illinois & Michigan Canal was deepened so that the Chicago River would reverse its course and start flowing south, away from the city. Sending waste and sewage down the reversed river provided

Water Tower (p73)

relief for Chicago residents and helped ease lake pollution, but it was not a welcome change for those living near what had become the city's drainpipe. A resident of Morris, about 60 miles downstream from Chicago, wrote, 'What right has Chicago to pour its filth down into what was before a sweet and clean river, pollute its waters, and materially reduce the value of property on both sides of the river and canal, and bring sickness and death to the citizens?'

The river still occasionally flowed into the lake after heavy rains; it wasn't permanently reversed until 1900, when the huge Chicago Sanitary & Ship Canal opened.

THE CHICAGO FIRE

On October 8, 1871, the Chicago fire started just southwest of downtown. Although the cause is now debated (see the boxed text, p48), the results were devastating. The fire burned for three days, killing 300 people, destroying 18,000 buildings and leaving 90,000 people homeless. 'By morning 100,000 people will be without food and shelter. Can you help us?' was the message sent east by Mayor Roswell B Mason as Chicago and City Hall literally burned down around him.

The dry conditions set the stage for a runaway conflagration, as a hot wind carried flaming embers to unburned areas, which quickly caught fire. The primitive, horse-drawn firefighting equipment did little to keep up with the spreading blaze. Almost every structure was destroyed or gutted in the area bounded by the river on the west, what's now Roosevelt Rd to the south and Fullerton Ave to the north.

Mayor Mason earned kudos for his skillful handling of Chicago's recovery. His best move was to prevent the aldermen on the city council from getting their hands on the millions of dollars in relief funds that Easterners had donated after the mayor's fireside plea, thus ensuring that the money actually reached the rabble living in the rubble.

1871	1885
Chicago Fire destroys city, re-brands cows as dangerous pyromaniacs	The world's first steel-frame 'skyscraper,' the Home Insurance Building, built in Chicago. It is 10 stories (138ft) tall

Don't Look at Me – It Was the Cow

For more than 125 years, legend has had it that a cow owned by a certain Mrs O'Leary kicked over a lantern, which ignited some hay, which ignited some lumber, which ignited the whole town. The image of the hapless heifer has endured despite official skepticism from the start. Now that story may have been milked for the last time.

Richard Bales, a lawyer and amateur historian, has spent years examining the case from every angle. His conclusion is that the cow was a victim of circumstances. It seems that Mrs O'Leary's barn was shared by a neighboring family. Each day Daniel 'Peg Leg' Sullivan dropped by to feed his mom's cow. Bales' evidence, gathered from thousands of pages of post-inferno investigations, indicates that Peg Leg accidentally started the fire himself and then tried to blame it on the bovine. After all, if you had just burned down what was then the fourth-largest city in the US, who would you blame?

The Chicago City Council has accepted Bales' version of the story; in 1997 the cream of Chicago politics passed a resolution officially absolving the O'Leary family of blame. Of course, for proponents of the cow story, this revision is udder nonsense.

CHICAGO REBORN

Despite the human tragedy, the fire's effect on Chicago was much the same as that of a forest fire; within a few years there was rapid new growth, a wealth of new life. The best architects in the world poured in to snare the thousands of rebuilding contracts, giving Chicago an architectural legacy of innovation that endures today. Rebuilding efforts added to the city's economy, which had been scarcely slowed by the conflagration, and by 10 years after the fire, the population of Chicago had tripled.

The later decades of the 19th century saw Chicago on a boom-and-bust economic cycle. While in general the economy grew, it often fell prey to short-lived recessions. During one of these in 1873, thousands of men thrown out of work marched on City Hall, demanding food. The police, who were always on call for governmental and economic interests, beat the protesters, who had dispersed after they were promised free bread. It was the beginning of a history of clashes between labor and police that would stretch over the next 50 years.

In 1876 strikes began in the railroad yards as workers demanded an eight-hour workday. Traffic was paralyzed, and the unrest spread to the McCormick Reaper Works, which was then Chicago's largest factory. The police and federal troops broke up the strikes, killing 18 civilians and injuring hundreds more.

By then, May 1 had become the official day of protest for Chicago labor groups. On that day in 1886, 60,000 workers in the city went on strike, demanding an eight-hour workday. As was usual, police attacked the strikers at locations throughout the city. Three days later, self-described 'anarchists' staged a protest in Haymarket Square where a bomb exploded, killing seven police officers. The government reacted strongly to what became known as 'the Haymarket Riot.' Eight anarchists were convicted of 'general conspiracy to murder' and four were hanged, although only two had been present at the incident and the actual bomber was never identified.

While the city's workers agitated for better working conditions, other progressive social movements were also at play in Chicago. Immigrants were pouring into the city at a rate of 10,000 a week, and they lived in squalid conditions, enjoying few if any government services. In 1889 two young women from middle-class families, Jane Addams and Ellen Gates Starr, founded Hull House on the city's West Side. The two women opened soup kitchens, set up schools for immigrant children, established English classes for adults and offered other services, such as medical care, to ease the immigrants' hardships.

Meanwhile, the city went on a big annexation campaign, nabbing the independent townships of Lake View, Hyde Park and others to gain their tax revenues. Civic leaders hoped that Chicago's increased population would give it prominence on the world stage.

1886	1892
Haymarket Riot	First elevated train begins operation

In 1892 society legend Bertha Palmer followed the lead of other Chicago elite by touring Paris. A prescient art collector, she nabbed a score of Monets, Renoirs and other impressionist works before they had achieved universal acclaim. Her collection would later form the core of the Art Institute.

The 1893 World's Columbian Exposition marked Chicago's showy debut on the international stage. Centered on a grand complex of specially built structures on the lakeshore south of Hyde Park, the exposition became known as 'the White City' for its magnificent white-painted buildings, which were brilliantly lit by electric searchlights. Designed by architectural luminaries such as Daniel Burnham, Louis Sullivan and Frederick Law Olmsted, the fairgrounds were meant to show how parks, streets and buildings could be designed in a harmonious manner that would enrich the chaotic urban environment.

Open only five months, the exposition attracted 27 million visitors, many of whom rode the newly built El to and from the Loop. The spectacular buildings surrounded ponds plied by Venetian gondolas. The entire assemblage made a huge impact not just in Chicago but around the world, as the fair's architects were deluged with huge commissions to redesign cities. The buildings themselves, despite their grandeur, were short lived, having been built out of a rough equivalent of plaster of Paris that barely lasted through the fair. The only survivor was the Fine Arts Building, which was really rebuilt from scratch to become the Museum of Science and Industry.

The El: on the rails since 1892

Chicago's labor troubles reached another critical point in 1894, when a recession caused the Pullman Palace Car Company to cut wages. Worker unrest spread from the huge South Side factory complex, which built railroad cars, to the railroads themselves, and more than 50,000 workers walked off their jobs, paralyzing interstate commerce. Federal troops were called in to Chicago and gradually broke the strike through a series of battles that left scores of workers injured.

At the turn of the century, Chicago's population had reached 1.7 million, and the city had become a far bigger place than anyone could have imagined just seven decades before. Despite this growth, though, Chicago still had its wild and woolly elements, many of which could be found in the notorious Levee District, a one-stop Sodom and Gomorrah south of the Loop run not by gangsters but by the top cops and politicians in the city.

Meanwhile, Chicago's industries continued to prosper at the expense of the environment and worker health. In 1906 Upton Sinclair's fictional account of the stockyards, *The Jungle*, was published. Although Sinclair hoped it would arouse sympathy for exploited workers living in squalid conditions, it ignited public fury with its lurid portrayal of conditions in the factories where the public's food was prepared.

Though working conditions were bad, they didn't stop the continual flow of immigrants to Chicago. People from Midwestern farms and impoverished nations in Europe continued to pour in, followed, in the early 20th century, by poor Blacks from the South.

1893	1900
World's Columbian Exposition opens. Cracker Jack, zipper invented	Chicago reverses flow of Chicago River, forever ingratiating itself with downstate neighbors

Why You Can't Get Lost in Chicago

As you make your way through Chicago's orderly system of streets and numbers, radiating from State and Madison Sts, you can thank the persistence and zeal of a frustrated bill collector for your ease of navigation. Scouring the city in search of deadbeats, Edward P Brennan got fed up trying to decide which of the city's 10 Oak Sts or 13 Washington Sts or eight 42nds might contain the address he was looking for. And those were just a few of his problems. Some streets changed their names every few blocks, and house numbers followed no set pattern.

In 1901 Brennan proposed a new system based on a regular grid and numbering system. Exhibiting a timeless skepticism of the Chicago City Council's ability to discern the wisdom of the plan, Brennan said of his proposal, 'It may be another job for the undertaker, as its fate is likely to be early death and burial.'

To his surprise, however, the plan was adopted and implemented beginning in 1909. During the next 30 years, Brennan attended more than 600 council meetings to see his plan to maturity, and after researching historical figures in the city's short past he renamed 300 duplicated streets. The only memorial to this toil – for which he refused payment – is a short street named Brennan Ave in Beverly at 2300 East, from 9600 South to 9772 South.

THE GREAT MIGRATION

In 1910 eight out of 10 Blacks still lived in the southern states of the old Confederacy. Over the next decade a variety of factors combined to change that, as more than two million African Americans moved north in what came to be known as the Great Migration.

Chicago played a pivotal role in this massive shift of population, both as an impetus and as a destination. Articles in the Black-owned and nationally circulated *Chicago Defender* proclaimed the city a worker's paradise and a place free from the horrors of Southern racism. Ads from Chicago employers promised jobs to anyone willing to work.

These lures, coupled with glitzy images of thriving neighborhoods like Bronzeville, inspired thousands to take the bait. Chicago's Black population zoomed from 44,103 in 1910 to 109,458 in 1920 and continued growing. The migrants, often poorly educated sharecroppers with big dreams, found a reality not as rosy as promised. Chicago did not welcome blacks with open arms. In 1919 White gangs from Bridgeport led days of rioting that killed dozens. Employers were ready with the promised jobs, but many hoped to rid their factories of White unionized workers by replacing them with blacks, which further exacerbated racial tensions. Blacks also found that they were promoted and advanced only so far before reaching an unofficial ceiling. Blacks were also restricted to living in South Side ghettos by openly prejudicial real estate practices that kept them from buying or renting homes elsewhere in the city.

CHICAGO GOES DRY (SORT OF)

Efforts to make the United States 'dry' had never found favor in Chicago; the city's vast numbers of German and Irish immigrants were not about to forsake their favored libations. During the first two decades of the 20th century, the political party that could portray itself as the 'wettest' would win the local elections. Thus, the nationwide enactment in 1920 of Prohibition, the federal constitutional amendment making alcohol consumption illegal, was destined to meet resistance in Chicago, where voters had gone six to one against the law in an advisory referendum. However, few could have predicted how the efforts to flout Prohibition would forever mark Chicago's image worldwide (see the boxed text, p80).

An important year for the city, 1933 saw Prohibition repealed and a thirsty populace return openly to the local bars in droves. Another world's fair, this time called the Century of Progress, opened on the lakefront south of Grant Park and promised a bright future filled with modern conveniences, despite the ongoing grimness of the Great Depression. And

1908	1920
Chicago Cubs win the World Series, 'Let's do this again soon,' says team	Chicagoans raise glasses of beer, whisky to celebrate onset of Prohibition

in 1933 Ed Kelly became mayor. With the help of party boss Pat Nash, he strengthened the Democratic Party in the city, creating the legendary 'machine' that would control local politics for the next 50 years. Politicians doled out thousands of city jobs to people who worked hard to make sure their patrons were reelected. The same was true for city vendors and contractors, whose continued prosperity was tied to their donations and other efforts to preserve the status quo.

ENTER THE DALEY

The zenith of the machine's power began with the election of Richard J Daley in 1955. Initially thought to be a mere party functionary, Daley was reelected mayor five times before dying in office in 1976. With an uncanny understanding of machine politics and how to use it to squelch dissent, he dominated the city in a way no mayor had before or has since. His word was law, and a docile city council routinely approved all his actions, lest a dissenter find his or her ward deprived of vital city services.

But Daley and those in the entrenched political structure were oblivious – both by intent and accident – to many of the changes and challenges that Chicago faced in the 1950s and later. After suffering through the Depression, the city experienced sudden affluence during WWII. Factories ran at full tilt, and once again people flocked to Chicago for jobs during the war years. In 1950 the population peaked at 3.6 million. But the postwar economic boom also made it possible for many Chicagoans to realize the dream of buying their own homes. Farms and wetlands surrounding the city were quickly turned into suburbs that attracted scores of middle-class people fleeing the crowded city.

The tax base diminished and racial tensions grew. Blacks moved from the ghettos on the South Side to other areas of the city, while Whites, succumbing to racism fueled by fears of crime, grew terrified at the prospect of ethnically integrated neighborhoods.

A 1957 *Life* magazine report that called Chicago's cops the most corrupt in the nation didn't make Chicagoans feel more secure. Although Daley and the machine howled with indignation over the article, further exposés by the press revealed that some cops and politicians were in cahoots with various crime rings. None of this was news to the average Chicagoan.

Chicago's voting practices were also highly suspect, never more so than in 1960, when John F Kennedy ran for president of the US against Richard Nixon, then vice president. The night of the election, the results were so close nationwide that the outcome hinged on the vote in Illinois.

Mayor Daley called up Kennedy and assured him, 'With a little bit of luck and the help of a few close friends, you're going to carry Illinois.' Kennedy did win Illinois, by 10,000 votes, which gave him the presidency. For many, that was the perfect embodiment of electoral politics in Chicago, a city where the slogan has long been 'Vote early and vote often' and voters have been known to rise from the grave and cast ballots.

Top Five Chicago History Reads

- *City of the Century: The Epic of Chicago and the Making of America*, Professor Donald Miller (1997) This book looks at the key players in Chicago's explosive growth, and analyzes the Windy City as a model for the change wrought by urban development throughout America.

- *Chicago Days: 150 Defining Moments in the Life of a Great City*, Stevenson Swanson, editor (1997) Put together by the Chicago *Tribune*, this book transcends the saccharine promise of its title to provide intimate snapshots of life throughout Chicago's history.

- *Lost Chicago*, David Lowe (2000) A readable account of all the marvels that have been torn down will have you shaking a fist at Chicago's urban planners.

- *The Devil in the White City: Murder, Magic, and Madness at the Fair that Changed America*, Erik Larson (2003) A riveting book that focuses on the 1893 world's fair and a gruesome killer who prayed on its attendees.

- *Working*, Studs Terkel (1974) This classic from 1974 features interviews with Chicago traffic cops, shoe shiners, bureaucrats and housewives, all of them discussing the everyday intricacies of their jobs.

1929	1933
St Valentine's Day massacre	Chicagoans raise glasses of beer, whisky to celebrate repeal of Prohibition

In 1964 the civil rights movement came to Chicago. Martin Luther King Jr spoke at rallies, demanding better conditions for Blacks and an end to segregation. He led marches through all-White neighborhoods where some racist residents attacked the marchers with rocks and bottles. In one march, King was hit in the head by a brick, foreshadowing events for which Daley and the machine would be ill prepared.

The year 1968 proved an explosive one for Chicago. When King was assassinated in Memphis, Tennessee, the West Side exploded in riots and went up in smoke. Whole stretches of the city were laid to waste, and Daley and the many Black politicians in the machine were helpless to stop the violence. Worse yet, the city's hosting of the Democratic National Convention in August degenerated into a fiasco of such proportions that its legacy dogged Chicago for decades (see the boxed text, p55).

Meanwhile, the city's economic structure was changing. In 1971 financial pressures caused the last of the Chicago stockyards to close, marking the end of one of the city's most infamous enterprises. Elsewhere in the city, factories and steel mills shut down as companies moved to the suburbs or the southern US, where taxes and wages were lower. A decade of economic upheaval saw much of Chicago's industrial base erode. Many companies simply went out of business during the recession of the late 1970s. Chicago and much of the Midwest earned the moniker 'Rust Belt,' which described the area's shrunken economies and their rusting factories. The human costs in the city were high; thousands of blue-collar workers lost their high-paying union jobs with virtually no hope of finding replacement work.

But two events happened in the 1970s that were harbingers of the city's more promising future. The world's tallest building (at the time), the Sears Tower, opened in the Loop in 1974, beginning a development trend that would spur the creation of thousands of high-paying jobs in finance, law and other white-collar areas. And in 1975 the Water Tower Place shopping mall brought new life to N Michigan Ave. It proved a surprising lure for suburbanites, despite the presence of the very same stores in their own malls. Developers began to realize that the urban environment was an attraction in itself.

Daley's death from a heart attack in 1976 began a process of political upheaval and reform that continued through the 1980s. Chicago's normally docile voters were enraged in 1978, when the city council cheerfully voted itself a 60% pay hike at the height of a recession amid record unemployment. Then, in January 1979, 4ft of snow hit Chicago. Daley's 'city that works' didn't, and voters gave Mayor Michael Bilandic a permanent Florida vacation (see boxed text p14), electing outsider Jane Byrne.

The colorful Byrne opened up Chicago to filmmakers, allowing the producers of *The Blues Brothers* to demolish part of Daley Center. She appointed her husband, a gregarious old journalist, as her press secretary, and he soon was answering questions at press conferences with amusing lines like 'The mayor told me in bed this morning...' As a symbolic overture to her minority constituents, Byrne moved into Cabrini-Green, the deeply troubled Near North housing project, but she also showed deep insensitivity to Blacks on several issues, stoking deep-seated anger.

THE PEOPLE'S MAYOR

In the fall of 1982, a who's who of Black Chicago gathered in activist Lu Palmer's basement on the South Side. The mood was tense. Newspaper columnist Vernon Jarrett was so angry he was ready to punch Harold Washington. So were a lot of other people who had spent months working their butts off to build the incredible movement that was ready to propel Chicago's first African American mayor – and a reformist to boot – into office. His election would present an obvious change in terms of race, but it was a far

1942	1960
First nuclear chain reaction occurs on a University of Chicago squash court	McCormick Place opens, immediately hailed as 'the mistake by the lake'

Water Tower Place shopping mall (p196)

bigger challenge to the entrenched interests that had dominated city politics for decades. And now the candidate was dithering about whether he wanted to make the huge commitment to run.

Then-congressman Washington was making it clear that he didn't want to be the sacrificial lamb to a reelection juggernaut by Mayor Jane Byrne. But months earlier, in another meeting in Palmer's basement, he had told Jarrett and the rest that he would consider running if they registered 50,000 new voters. They registered 150,000. The movement to elect Washington was bigger than anybody could have hoped.

Eventually, an irate Washington stormed out of the meeting at midnight, but he couldn't stop the phenomenon he'd tacitly allowed to take root. He did run, and he won the Democratic primary when Byrne and Richard M Daley split the White vote. He then went on to win the general election.

Washington's first term was best described by the *Wall Street Journal*, which called Chicago 'Beirut on the Lake.' The entrenched political machine reacted to him with all the hostility you'd expect from people who saw their cozy system under full attack. Much of the political and social chaos that marked city politics from 1983 to 1987 had ugly racial overtones, but at the heart of the conflict was the old guard refusing to cede any power or patronage to the reform-minded mayor. In retrospect, the chaos benefited the city, because it opened up the political process.

The irony is that when Washington died seven months after he was reelected in 1987, he and his allies were just beginning to enjoy the same spoils of the machine they had once battled. Washington had amassed a solid majority of allies on the city council and was poised to begin pushing his own ambitious programs.

A lasting legacy of the Washington years has been the political success of the African American politicians who followed him. Democrat Carol Moseley-Braun's election to the US

1968	1972
Chicago cops go nuts at Democratic National Convention	Chicagoan Curtis Mayfield releases *Superfly* soundtrack

senate in 1992 can be credited in part to Washington's political trailblazing. And John Stroger, the first Black president of the Cook County Board of Commissioners, was elected in 1994.

Overall, the 1980s meant good times for the city. The mid-decade economic boom in the US was especially strong in Chicago. Many young urban professionals – the oft-reviled 'yuppies' – found jobs in the fast-growing service and professional sectors and helped spark extensive real estate development that left large portions of the aging North Side renovated and beautified. As these yuppies aged and started families, many of them stayed in the city rather than following their parents to the suburbs. As a result, gentrification keeps on going and going and going, for two decades and counting. As values in some neighborhoods soar, adjoining areas begin to benefit; the comparatively low prices attract new residents and investors. Development has now spread to portions of the city west and south of the Loop.

A NEW DALEY DAWNS

In 1989 Chicago elected Richard M Daley, the son of Richard J Daley, to finish out the remaining two years of Harold Washington's term as mayor. Like his father, Daley owned an uncanny instinct for city politics. Unlike his father, though, he showed much political savvy in uniting disparate political forces. He shrewdly kept African Americans within his political power structure, thus forestalling the kind of movement that propelled Washington to the mayor's office.

After Daley's election the city enjoyed two years of cooperation between City Hall and then-governor Jim Thompson, who lived in and loved Chicago. Until then, the squabbles in city government had prevented the city from working effectively with the state. These newly friendly relations meant that state legislators freed up hundreds of millions of public dollars for the city's use, instead of letting the funds languish in state coffers (as they did throughout the '80s). Among the projects that bore fruit were an O'Hare airport expansion, the construction of a new South Building and hotel at McCormick Place, and the complete reconstruction of Navy Pier, which turned the pier into a meeting site and tourist attraction.

Daley moved to solidify his control of the city in a way his father would have applauded but in a much more enlightened manner. Old semi-independent bureaucracies such as the Park District and Department of Education were restructured under Daley protégés. And the new mayor entertained the city as well. To the delight of residents and commentators, Daley proved himself prone to amusing verbal blabber, such as this classic, his explanation for why city health inspectors had closed down so many local restaurants: 'Whadda ya want? A rat in yer sandwich or a mouse in yer salad?'

Despite falling to third largest US city, population-wise, in the 1990 census, the '90s were a good decade for Chicago. In 1991 the Chicago Bulls won the first of six national basketball championships. The 1994 World Cup soccer opening ceremony focused international attention on the city. And in 1996 a 28-year-old demon was exorcised when the Democratic National Convention returned to Chicago. City officials spent millions of dollars spiffing up the town, and thousands of cops underwent sensitivity training on how to deal with protests. The convention went off like a dream and left Chicagoans with a distinct sense that they were on a roll.

In 1999 Mayor Daley won his fourth mayoral election when he handily beat popular Black congressman Bobby Rush in the primary election. It was an auspicious win that set Daley firmly in control as Chicago headed into Y2K. It was Y2K01, however, that proved to be the more unsettling year for the city. On September 11, the terrorist attacks on Washington DC and New York City cast Chicago's skyline in a much different light. Long a symbol of the city's strength, the tall buildings suddenly became Chicago's Achilles' heel.

1974	1986
Sears Tower completed	*Ferris Bueller's Day Off* spikes teens' interests in French impressionist masters

When Cops Riot

With the war in Vietnam rapidly escalating and general unrest spreading through the US, the 1968 Democratic National Convention became a focal point for protest groups of all stripes. Even though then-president Lyndon Johnson announced he was washing his hands of the mess and not running for reelection, the mass gathering of the politicians who ran the US government was an irresistible draw for anyone with a beef – which in the late 1960s seemed like just about everybody.

Regardless of the tenor of the times, conservative old Mayor Daley – the personification of a 'square' if there ever was one – was planning a grand convention. Word that protesters would converge on Chicago sparked authorities' plans to crack the head of anybody who got in the way of Daley's show. Local officials shot down all of the protesters' requests for parade permits, despite calls by the press and other politicians to uphold the civil right of free assembly.

Enter Abbie Hoffman, Jerry Rubin, Rennie Davis, Tom Hayden, Bobby Seale and David Dellinger. They called for a mobilization of 500,000 protesters to converge on Chicago, and their plans steadily escalated in the face of city intransigence. As the odds of confrontation became high, many moderate protesters decided not to attend.

When the convention opened, there were just a few thousand young protesters in the city. But Daley and his cronies spread rumors to the media to bolster the case for their warlike preparations. Some of these whoppers included claims that hippie girls would pose as prostitutes to give the delegates venereal disease and that LSD would be dumped into the city's water supply.

The first few nights of the August 25-30 convention saw police staging midnight raids on hippies and protesters attempting to camp in Lincoln Park. The cops went on massive beating sprees, singling some individuals out for savage attacks. Teenage girls were assaulted by cops who shouted, 'You want free love? Try this!' Journalists, ministers and federal Justice Department officials were appalled.

The action then shifted to Grant Park, across from the Conrad Hilton (now the Chicago Hilton and Towers), where the main presidential candidates were staying. A few thousand protesters held a rally, which was met by an overwhelming force of 16,000 Chicago police officers, 4000 state police officers and 4000 members of the National Guard armed with tear-gas grenades, nightsticks and machine guns

When some protesters attacked a few officers, the assembled law enforcers staged what investigators later termed a police riot. Among the low-lights: cops shoved bystanders through plate-glass windows and then went on to beat them as they lay bleeding amid the shards; police on motorcycles ran over protesters; police chanted 'Kill, kill, kill!,' swarmed journalists and attempted to do just that; and when some wounded conventioneers were taken to the hotel suite of presidential candidate Gene McCarthy, cops burst through the door and beat everybody in sight.

The next night Mayor Daley went on national TV and attempted to defend the mayhem with an outright lie. He said he knew of plans to assassinate all the visiting presidential candidates. In reality, what Daley and the police did was play right into the hands of the most extreme of the protesters, who had hoped to provoke just such a sorry spectacle.

The long-term effects of the riots were far greater that anyone could have guessed. The Democratic candidate for president, Hubert Humphrey, was left without liberal backing after his tacit support of Daley's tactics, and as a result Republican Richard Nixon was elected president. Chicago was left with a huge black eye for decades. Once the most popular host to the hugely lucrative political conventions, it saw none return for almost 30 years, until 1996. The stories of police brutality, coupled with reports of rampant corruption in the department, led to decade-long changes that made the Chicago police force more racially balanced than it had ever been; it emerged as one of the most professional departments in the country.

Lyndon Johnson's attorney general refused to prosecute any of the protesters for conspiring to riot in Chicago. But in 1969 President Nixon ordered just such prosecutions, even though the actions of those charged may well have helped elect him. The 'Chicago Seven' trial became a total farce; the accused used it as a platform for protest, and aging judge Julius Hoffman showed a Daley-like tolerance for their antics by sentencing them to prison for contempt of court. However, on the central charges of inciting riots, all seven were acquitted.

1989	2001
Richard M Daley elected mayor	MTV's *Real World* comes to Chicago, met with protestors

The Sears Tower – which had shared tallest American building honors with the World Trade Center – hastily closed its observation deck. It soon reopened, but with airport-style X-ray machines and security devices installed on the ground floor. Other less lofty sites followed suit. The Chicago Board of Trade, fearing the financial havoc that could be wreaked by a well-timed bomb, began restricting visitors to its observation deck. The Chicago Mercantile Exchange did the same. For weeks after September 11, just going to work in the Loop felt a little like a brave and reckless act. By the end of October, a no-fly zone encircled the Loop. The no-fly zone was lifted after a couple of weeks, but then reinstated in March 2003 after a good deal of campaigning by Mayor Daley. Shortly after this, Daley closed down Meigs Field.

2002	2003
Plans for new Soldier Field unveiled, immediately hailed as 'the mistake by the lake'	Outgoing governor George Ryan commutes all of Illinois' death row inmates' sentences

Neighborhoods

Neighborhoods

You're ready to dive into Chicago, and we're right there with you. We've taken Chicago's dozens of neighborhoods and smooshed them into eleven action-packed areas, bursting at the seams with sights, shops, restaurants and adventure.

We start in the Loop, the city's historic heart, before heading across the Michigan Ave bridge to Near North and the Magnificent Mile. From there, we'll promenade up Michigan Ave through the tony Gold Coast, finding our footing on Clark for a speedy trip through historic Old Town and trendy Lincoln Park. Party-friendly Lake View comes next on our northward trek, followed soon thereafter by scruffy Uptown and European Andersonville. We head west from there, dropping by hip Wicker Park/Bucktown and Ukrainian Village. The West Side is our next port of call, and while we're in the area, we swing by vibrant Pilsen. Following Roosevelt back into the booming South Loop and Near South Side, we'll continue our southward momentum and wrap up the journey in South Chicago.

ITINERARIES

One Day

Start your high-speed day with a laid-back breakfast at the Original Pancake House (p138), followed by a quick cab ride down to the Art Institute (p62). Walk off the art-buzz in your head afterwards with a short stroll through Grant Park to Buckingham Fountain (p63) for a photo op. Walk to the Berghoff (p128) for lunch, and then take a cab up to Michigan Ave for some top-tier window shopping. Dinner is deep-dish pizza at the nearby Giordano's (p134), followed by sunset drinks way, way up on the 96th floor of the John Hancock Center's Signature Lounge (one floor up from the Signature Room, p137). If you're feeling jazzy, take a cab to the Green Mill (p179) afterwards. If not, take in a play at the Lookingglass Theatre (p170) just down the street from the Hancock. Then its back to the hotel for some well-deserved slumber.

Three Days

Spread the stops mentioned above out over two days, and spend your second afternoon on the water, taking the Chicago Architecture Foundation's riverboat tour (p60). Afterwards, take the Blue Line to Wicker Park (p81), where you can go shopping for souvenirs along Milwaukee and Damen. Dinner that night can go one of two ways – soulful and spicy at Soul Kitchen (p149), or outer-space fusion at the futuristic Mod (p149). No matter how good your dinner, you'll have the blues by the time your cab pulls up at Buddy Guy's Legends (p178) afterwards. Day Three is a sleep-in day, followed by a late-morning visit to one of the Museum Campus (p90) institutions. Have lunch in the Loop (p61), then spend the rest of the day investigating the neighborhood of your choice. Wherever you find yourself for dinner, follow it up with a movie at the classic old Music Box Theater (p173).

One Week

Tackle the three day itinerary, pampering yourself along the way with a visit to one of Chicago's many spas or bathhouses (p188). Make time for a Cub's game (p184) or, if sports aren't your thing, spend a day gallery-hopping in River North (p69) or the West Loop (p87). Relax in Lincoln Park (p74) and visit the superb (and free!) African exhibit at the Lincoln Park Zoo (p75). In your Chicago travels, you're bound to fall in love with one of the dozens of neighborhoods here. City-sponsored walking tours (p60) are a great way to get to know the city like a native. Or let a Chicago Greeter (p60) take you on a free, personalized guided tour you won't soon forget.

ORGANIZED TOURS

Sightseeing Bus Tours

American Sightseeing (☎ 312-251-3100) departs from the Palmer House Hilton and other downtown hotels. The buses are of the big air-conditioned and tinted-glass variety, which means that you're definitely insulated from the sights you see. They run two-hour tours of north and south Chicago neighborhoods starting at $20. American Sightseeing operates the same tours under the Gray Line brand name as well.

The **Chicago Trolley Co** (☎ 773-648-5000; www.chicagotrolley.com) runs year-round tours in 'San Francisco-style' vehicles and red double-decker buses. Their 13-mile guided tour takes you through downtown and Near North, it covers all the major sights and, best of all, you can hop on and off to your heart's content. Tours start at $10. Call to find out the stop closest to you.

Sightseeing Boat Tours

Chicago has two main boat-tour companies offering similar 90-minute tours of the river and lake for similar prices. The guides are often perfunctory, offering bad jokes and limited information. Be aware that passing through the locks to and from the lake can take up a fair part of the tour. Boat tours run from May to November.

Mercury Chicago Skyline Cruises (Map pp282–3; ☎ 312-332-1353) departs from the southeast corner of the Michigan Ave Bridge; tours start at $17. **Wendella Sightseeing Boats** (Map pp280–1; ☎ 312-337-1446; www.wendellaboats.com) departs from the northwest corner of the Michigan Ave Bridge, tours start at $16. Both Mercury and Wendella operate essentially the same tour and both also offer other tours and night cruises.

Shoreline Sightseeing (Map pp280–1; ☎ 312-222-9328; www.shorelinesightseeing.com) runs tours of Lake Michigan and the Chicago River and also acts as a water taxi, shuttling riders between Navy Pier, the Shedd Aquarium and the Sears Tower. Tours start at $10; water taxi rides at $6. Printed translations of the tour narration are available in 12 languages including French, Spanish, German, Polish, Arabic, Japanese and Hindi.

If you're looking for a tour of Chicago's skyline with a little more muscle, **Seadog Cruises** (Map pp280–1; ☎ 312-822-7200; www.seadogcruises.com) is happy to assist. Its 2000+HP speedboats will zip you through a 30-minute lake tour, or take it slower with a 75-minute architecture tour along the river. Tours start at $16.

Odyssey Cruises (Map pp280–1; ☎ 800-947-9367; www.odysseycruises.com) operates a sleek cruise boat that looks like a huge yacht. Two-hour cruises, which sail throughout the year, include a meal and music. Glamour doesn't come cheap, and the company suggests that you should dress up for the experience. Brunches and lunches start at $36, dinners at $81. A two-hour moonlight cruise during the summer costs $31 and leaves at midnight.

The **Spirit of Chicago** (Map pp280–1; ☎ 866-211-3804; www.spiritcruises.com) offers slightly downscale lunch and dinner cruises (wear what you want), departing year-round except when the lake is frozen. Lunch cruises start at $38, dinner cruises at $75 and various party cruises (no chow) begin at $27. The boat offers lots of open space on deck for enjoying the view.

Mystic Blue Cruises (Map pp280–1; ☎ 888-330-4700) offers a slightly hipper (read: younger) take on the lakefront tour, with lunch, midday, dinner, cocktail and moonlight tours, starting at $22.

When the wind blows, which is most of the time, the 148ft **Windy** (Map pp280–1; ☎ 312-595-5555), a four-masted gaff topsail schooner, plies the lake from May to September. The class B tall ship is the only certified four-masted traditional sailing vessel in the US. Passengers can play sailor by helping to raise and lower the sails. A better deal is to play skipper by trying your hand at the wheel. With only the sound of the wind in your ears, the *Windy* is the most relaxing way to see the skyline from offshore. Ninety-minute tours start at $25.

Special Interest Tours

Sure, the tourist boat companies run architecture tours. Those in the know, though, make a beeline for the cruises run by the **Chicago Architecture Foundation** (CAF; ☎ 312-922-3432; www.architecture.org). The foundation operates two offices where the staff are ready to answer questions – the John Hancock Center (p71) and the Santa Fe Center (Map pp282–3; 224 S Michigan Ave).

The 90-minute CAF boat tours are lead by CAF volunteers and depart daily from early May through October, from the southeast corner of the Michigan Ave Bridge and the Chicago River. Tickets cost $25.

The CAF also runs more than 50 walking tours of the city and suburbs. Two of the most popular are the Historic Skyscrapers walking tour, which departs at 10am daily, and the Modern Skyscrapers tour, departing at 1:30pm daily. Both start at the Santa Fe Center and cost $12. The Hancock Center office also dispatches a tour of N Michigan Ave at 11am Friday, Saturday and Monday; it costs $12 and lasts about two hours.

CAF also operates bus tours of Chicago, Prairie Ave, Hyde Park, Oak Park and other areas. During the summer it offers architectural bike tours. Call for schedules. One of the best deals is CAF's El tours of the Loop on summer Saturdays. These are free – call for details.

Another set of highly recommended tours are those run by city's Department of Cultural Affairs. **Chicago Neighborhood Tours** (☎ 312-742-1190; www.chgocitytours.com) hits a different neighborhood every Saturday morning, and all the tours are lead by local experts. Tours include many neighborhoods ignored by more mainstream tour companies. To attend the $25 tours, be at the Chicago Cultural Center (p62) at 9:30am for the 10am bus departure.

The city is also behind another worthwhile, almost too-good-to-be-true endeavor. **Chicago Greeter** (☎ 312-744-8000; www.chicagogreeter.com), based out of the Chicago Cultural Center (see earlier), pairs visitors with a local volunteer who will take guests on an informal, free two-hour tour around town. One week's notice required.

Black CouTours (☎ 773-233-8907; www.blackcoutours.com) offers 2½-hour bus tours that focus on African American history in Chicago with a generous dash of soul. This is an excellent way to see parts of the South Side ignored by major tours. Tickets start at $25. Daily departures happen at 9am, noon and 3pm. Make sure you confirm pick-up/departure points when booking.

Chicago With Children

Chicago is a kid's kind of place. Here are the city's sights that will have them screaming (in a good way).

Sears Tower Skydeck (p65) Fantastic views and special kid-friendly history exhibits make this a sky-high treat.

'The Picasso' statue (p115) Adults can ponder the meaning of it all while kids whoop it up sliding down the ramp built into the sculpture's base in the Loop .

Grant Park (p63) Erupting fountains, proximity to trains, and lots of room to run make this a beloved park for youngsters.

Navy Pier fountains and rides (p68) A Ferris wheel, a carousel, and a thousand joyful ways to get soaked.

Chicago Children's Museum (p67) The only problem you'll face on a visit to this educational playland on Navy Pier is making your kids leave come closing time.

John Hancock Center Observatory (p71) Their noses will be stuck to the glass for hours.

Field Museum of Natural History (p91) Where you'll discover everything from dinosaurs to lost civilizations.

Shedd Aquarium (p93) The top-notch collection of fish and marine mammals makes for a whale of a good time.

Adler Planetarium (p91) Where little astronomers are stars.

Paddleboat Rides on North and South Ponds in Lincoln Park (p74) Water fights optional.

Lincoln Park Zoo (p75) The new African exhibit includes an entire room full of cockroaches.

Chicago's beaches (p84) The pint-sized waves are perfect for pint-sized swimmers.

Peggy Notebaert Nature Museum (p76) Where the butterflies frolic freely.

Museum of Science and Industry (p108) This huge museum will leave even the most energetic child happily spent after a few educational hours.

Chicago Supernatural Tours (☎ 708-499-0300; www.ghosttours.com) offers five-hour tours daily in summer and on weekends the rest of the year. The ghoulish itinerary takes in murder sites, cemeteries, supposedly haunted houses and all sorts of other places with some kind of spiritual connection (at least in the minds of the tour leaders). Tours cost $35.

Horse-drawn carriages depart from the Water Tower day and night throughout the year. These attract lots of suburban teens who are in town for a prom and want to smooch. Rates start at $35 for a minimum of 30 minutes; each half-hour thereafter costs another $35. Drivers will hope for a tip, whether they give witty commentary or leave you to your romance. You can choose a route or let the driver pick one for you. Carriages can be reserved in advance through **JC Cutters** (☎ 312-664-6014; www.jccutters.com).

Untouchable Gangster Tours (☎ 773-881-1195; www.gangstertour.com) leads comic tours through gangland Chicago daily; tickets cost $24. Confirm pick-up/departure points when booking.

THE LOOP & GRANT PARK

Eating p125; Shopping p189; Sleeping p215

Caffeine junkies needing a morning fix can skip the latte when they come to the Loop; the surging energy of the city's historic heart is enough to get anyone's pulse racing. The Loop breathes electricity, with the clattering roar of the El trains echoed in the tumultuous tides of office-bound workers. Orange-vested newspaper hawkers wade into traffic, fishing for sales from executives barking into cell phones. And above the melee, a towering forest of steel and stone soaks in the first rays of the sun.

The vital signs of the Loop – named for the El tracks which encircle it – weren't always so strong. The 1970s and 1980s saw many of the Loop's theaters and restaurants flee to the Near North, Gold Coast and other neighborhoods. A disastrous effort that turned State St into a pedestrian mall in 1979 proved a 15-year failure that primarily benefited exhaust-belching buses. Most of the remaining entertainment venues in the area closed or moved. At night the streets needed only a few urban tumbleweeds to complete the bleak tableau.

But during this same period the city doggedly kept trying to resuscitate the area. Tax breaks were offered to developers, and State St eventually was attractively remodeled with new street lamps, El entrances and other classical details, and reopened to traffic.

Now that the new Loop theater district has further helped to revive the neighborhood, developers have hit upon innovative schemes for some of the older office buildings. Previously, these architecturally significant buildings would have been torn down because their small floors, low ceilings and other details make them unsuitable for modern offices. Now, however, developers have realized that those small floors are perfect for residences and hotels. As part of this trend, the number of people living in the Loop and its environs has grown by 37% in 10 years.

Grant Park, the green playspace that forms a leafy buffer between the Loop and Lake Michigan shares the Loop's story of grand starts and big slips. Like the Loop, the park has gotten plenty of loving attention from city's budget office in the past decade, though, turning once-seedy areas into blooming examples of urban planning.

Transport

El All lines converge in the Loop; find your destination and take your pick.

Bus 56 runs along Milwaukee Ave from Wicker Park into the Loop; 151 comes down Michigan Ave from the lakefront in the north; 156 travels along LaSalle St from River North.

Metra Randolph St Station for the north loop; Van Buren St Station for the south.

Parking There is an underground pay lot on Michigan Ave at Washington St and another at Van Buren St. Warning: if you park at a meter along S Columbus Dr, be aware that each meter covers two spaces. If there's no meter at your spot, you likely need to feed the closest one.

Orientation

Wacker Dr (and the Chicago River beyond it) serves as the north and west boundaries of the Loop. The busy Congress Pkwy cuts across the south end of the neighborhood. When looking for an address in the Loop, pay close attention to the compass designation that kicks it off; both Madison (the dividing line for the city's north/south addresses) and State (the dividing line for Chicago's east/west addresses) are located here. If you arrive at your destination, and your hotel has become a Burger King, chances are good that you've swapped an N for an S or an E for a W.

Grant Park acts as a long buffer between the Loop on the west and Lake Michigan to the east. The park is girded by three main north–south thoroughfares, the busy Lake Shore Dr S, Columbus Dr and, on the Loop edge, S Michigan Ave. Millennium Park sits in the northwest corner of the park. The summer parades for Chicago's ethnic communities often pass through the park, running along S Columbus Dr between E Balbo Dr in the south and E Monroe in the north.

Top Five Loop & Grant Park

- Tracking down the Loop's **architectural wonders** (p61).
- Cooling off on a hot day in the mists of the **Buckingham Fountain** (p63).
- Enjoying the beer, er, history at the **Berghoff** (p128).
- Taking in the colorful chaos of the **Mercantile Exchange** (p63).
- Sliding down the **Picasso** (p115).

ART INSTITUTE OF CHICAGO

Map pp282–3

☎ 312-443-3600; www.artic.edu/aic/; 111 S Michigan Ave; adult/senior/student & child $10/6/6, free Tue; ⏱ 10:30am-4:40pm Mon, Wed-Fri, until 8pm Tue, 10am-5pm Sat & Sun

One of the world's premier museums, the Art Institute of Chicago has the kind of celebrity-heavy collection that routinely draws gasps from patrons. Grant Wood's stern *American Gothic*? Check. Edward Hopper's lonely *Nighthawks*? Uh huh. Georges Seurat's *A Sunday Afternoon on La Grand Jatte* (you know, the one that Cameron freaked out over in *Ferris Bueller's Day Off*...)? You bet.

Many of the iconic works that have become part of popular culture – through spoofs in movies, cartoons, and advertising – live in the Art Institute. The museum's collection of impressionist and postimpressionist paintings is second only to collections in France, and the number of surrealist works – especially boxes by Joseph Cornell – is also tremendous.

In the galleries you'll find African and ancient American art; American art from the 17th century onward; ancient Egyptian, Greek and Roman art; architecture; Chinese, Japanese and Korean art, beginning 5000 years ago; European decorative arts since the 12th century; European painting and sculpture from 1400 to 1800; 19th-century European painting; photography; prints and drawings; textiles; furniture; and 20th-century painting and sculpture.

Don't even think of coming to Chicago without spending at least two hours in the museum. And when you do come, sit down with one of the excellent, free museum maps to plan a route that will take you directly to the styles and periods that turn you on. Simply wandering through the museum floor by floor will have your feet crying foul before you even make it to the Renaissance. Even a 'greatest hits' tour will reveal some fantastic, unexpected finds, so don't be afraid to be choosy.

The main entrance is the original 1893 Allerton Building, where Adams St meets Michigan Ave. The steps themselves become one of the city's prime rendezvous points on fair days.

The modern 1977 Rubloff Building, accessed via the Columbus Dr entrance, houses the School of the Art Institute, where the number of pierced body parts far exceeds the student body. The Rice Building was added in 1988.

The museum's good café and restaurant are open for lunch daily and stay open until 7pm Tuesday.

CHICAGO CULTURAL CENTER

Map pp282–3

☎ 312-346-3278; 78 E Washington St; admission free; ⏱ 10am-7pm Mon-Wed, 10am-9pm Thu & Fri, 10am-5pm Sat, 11am-5pm Sun

Think you're just going to swing by the Visitor Information Center and grab some of their free maps and brochures? Think again. Exhibitions, beautiful interior design and free concerts by up-and-coming Chicago musicians all make the block-long Chicago Cultural Center an easy place to enter and a difficult place to leave. The exhibitions on three floors change frequently; take a moment as you enter on either Randolph or Washington Sts to find out the schedule of events.

Excellent **building tours** (☎ 312-742-1190; tours free; ☽ 1:15pm Tue-Sat) leave from the Randolph St lobby. Free lunchtime concerts take place every weekday at 12:15pm.

GRANT PARK Map pp282–3

Over the years the park often called 'Chicago's front yard' has suffered deprivations more befitting a backyard. Through much of the 20th century, commissioners bowing to the tyranny of the auto allowed Lake Shore Dr, Columbus Dr and Congress Pkwy to be developed into major thoroughfares, robbing the park of many of its best open areas. (Every year the huge Taste of Chicago festival closes Columbus Dr and Congress Pkwy for two weeks, and the world doesn't come to an end.)

Somnolent care from the Chicago Park District saw the entire place give way to weeds, dead trees and other neglect. The sad situation changed dramatically in the early 1990s, when Soldier Field won its bid to host the opening ceremonies for the 1994 World Cup. Realizing that thousands of impressionable visitors would stroll through Grant Park on their way to the stadium, the city began an ambitious program to spruce up the place.

Hundreds of new trees have since been planted, sidewalks have been replaced and Buckingham Fountain has been repaired. Now looking much better, Grant Park makes an excellent place both to visit and to travel through on your way to and from the Museum Campus.

Kate Sturges Buckingham, a very wealthy widow, gave the magnificent **Buckingham Fountain** (flows 10am-11pm May 1-Oct 1) to the city in 1927 in memory of her brother, Clarence. She also wisely left an endowment to maintain and operate the fountain. It's twice the size of its model, the Bassin de Latone at Versailles. The central fountain is meant to symbolize Lake Michigan, with the four water-spouting sea creatures representing the surrounding states. The fountain presents a subtle show rather than randomly spraying its 1.5 million gallons. Like so much in life, the spray begins small. Each successive basin fills, stimulating more jets. At the climax the central fountain spurts up to its full 150 feet. The crowd sighs in awe and is thankful that smoking is allowed. The fountain climaxes once an hour, and mood lighting (colored lights timed to match the fountain's 'moods') comes

Trading Floors

Part modern dance and part compulsive gambling, life on Chicago's trading floors makes for riveting theater. Hands fly, shouts ring through the air and a few shoving matches break out in these chaotic scenes, as traders compete to buy or sell commodities and options for the best price. When a split-second's miscalculation can cost $10,000 or more, the stakes are as high as the energy levels. These people take caffeine to relax.

The two main futures trading organizations in Chicago both have free viewing areas overlooking their high-tech trading floors. The swarms of costumed traders surrounded by acres of flashing, ringing sci-fi technology makes for an utterly surreal sight, like an economist's remake of a Fellini film. Even if you understand none of the spectacle unfolding beneath you, the scene is absolutely unforgettable.

Unfortunately, since the September 11 attacks, both of Chicago's trading floors have begun limiting access to viewing areas. As of this writing, the **Chicago Board of Trade** (Map pp282–3; ☎ 312-435-3590; 141 W Jackson Blvd at LaSalle St; admission free; ☽ 9:30am-12:30pm Mon-Fri) was open to groups by appointment only. Depending on the national terror alert levels, you'll likely have better luck at the **Chicago Mercantile Exchange** (Map pp282–3; ☎ 312-930-8249; 10-30 S Wacker Dr; admission free; ☽ 8:30am-3:15pm Mon-Fri). Call ahead to both for updates.

You can meet the traders after work (usually starting about 3pm), when they begin the energetic decompression from their incredibly high-pressure jobs at the legendary **Alcock's Inn** (Map pp282–3; ☎ 312-922-1778; 411 S Wells St). Some of the patrons are newly rich and others newly broke, but most of them are drunk.

on at 8pm; the best time to experience the full melodic effect is 9pm.

At the four corners of the gravel expanse that surrounds the fountain, pavilions have toilets and sell refreshments.

Up until 200 years ago, much of the land in northern Illinois was prairie, a vast undulating expanse that bloomed with a rainbow of wildflowers through the growing season. Early settlers who crossed it said it was like sailing in an ocean of color. With farming and development, this delicate ecosystem died out, as nonnative plants muscled their way into the region. In 1985 artist Chapman Kelley received permission to plant the 1.5-acre **Wildflower Works** near the Daley Bicentennial Plaza with native wildflowers. With a team of dedicated volunteers, Kelley found seeds for the long-forgotten plants. More than 15 years later, the Illinois wildflowers are much better established. From April through October a constantly changing panoply of flowers in all shapes and sizes takes its turn on Kelley's stage. Take some time here to wander around, listen to the bumblebees and imagine the flowers in front of you stretching as far as the eye can see.

Edward Kemeys' bronze **lions** have become Chicago icons since they began flanking the entrance to the Art Institute in 1894. Tucked away in a garden on the northwest side of the Institute sits British sculptor Henry Moore's **Large Interior Form**, a bronze statue that bears Moore's trademark smooth, rounded contours and half-human, half-blob appearance.

Augustus Saint-Gaudens' **Sitting Lincoln**, Chicago's second sculpture of Abraham Lincoln, the 16th US president, contrasts with the artist's more animated study in Lincoln Park. In this statue President Lincoln shows the isolation of his office as he sits alone in a chair.

Architect Daniel Burnham's observation that no one had ever personified the Great Lakes inspired Lorado Taft to create **Fountain of the Great Lakes**, a large bronze work, in 1913. Partially hidden by surrounding shrubs, it's worth seeking out. Here's the artist's description of what the five conch-shell-holding women are up to: 'Superior on high and Michigan on the side both empty into the basin of Huron, who sends the stream to Erie, whence Ontario receives it and looks wistfully after.' This progression duplicates that of the Great Lakes.

The **Bowman and the Spearman** by Ivan Mestrovic consists of two 17ft-high bronze figures of Native Americans. Installed in 1928, they symbolize the struggle between Indians and Whites as the latter moved west and settled there. Mestrovic depicted the figures in the act of using their weapons, which are left to the imagination of the viewer. Originally much closer together, they were separated by the 1956 intrusion of Congress Pkwy, which destroyed the grand steps that once led to a plaza beyond.

The **Theodore Thomas Memorial** shows a 15ft bronze woman straddling a globe and listening to a chord on her lyre. This 1923 work by Albin Polasek honors the founder of the Chicago Symphony Orchestra.

Replanting is restoring the diversity of native and imported trees that once grew in the park. The following species are listed in ascending order of size; the original designers of the park intended for the trees to become gradually larger as the rows progressed away from open spaces.

The small flowering crab apples blossom throughout May and are later covered with fruit. The small, thorny hawthorns that flower in May are native to the area. Honey locusts, another native species, are used to line streets because they seem impervious to salt, dogs, barbecue embers and other urban hazards.

When the park was built, its designers planted elms, long considered the most graceful of shade trees. More than 75% of the original 3000 elms have died from Dutch elm disease. Their replacements are hybrid American elms – less graceful but much more resilient.

Buckingham Fountain, Grant Park (p63)

The **Stock Exchange Arch** is a relic amputated from the great building when it was demolished in 1972. The *AIA Guide to Chicago* calls it the 'Wailing Wall of Chicago's preservation movement.'

The park's **Rose Gardens** contain 150 varieties best viewed from mid-June to September.

To watch Chicagoans at a favorite pastime, stop by **Hutchinson Field**, where scores of amateur league softball games are played each summer.

MILLENNIUM PARK Map pp282–3

A new 24-acre extravaganza, Millennium Park occupies a prime location on Michigan Ave between Randolph and Monroe Sts. Originally slated to open with the millennium, the park got off to an embarrassingly slow start when the original contractor – a chum of Mayor Daley's – went $100 million over budget, missed various deadlines, and was eventually fired. The sailing has been smoother since, and the park now boasts a number of completed attractions. The stately curved colonnades and fountain on the northwest end – a replica of the Greek-inspired structure that stood here until 1953 – is a godsend for the city's wedding portrait photographers. (Those looking to make it into the background of a couple's special moment need only wait a few minutes on sunny days for a blushing bride and groom to come along). The **McCormick-Tribune Ice Rink** (55 N Michigan Ave; Oct-Mar) allows skaters to meditate on the beauty of the Loop's skyline as they dodge careening children.

The park's most eye-catching attribute, though, is the **Gehry Bandshell**, a huge outdoor music pavilion designed by Frank Gehry, the trendsetting architect responsible for the Guggenheim Museum in Bilbao, Spain. The freaky curved ribbons of stainless steel peeling back from above the bandshell have already raised the ire of conservative Chicagoans, but the acoustics are supposed to be superb, projecting sound all the way to the back of the 30,000-capacity venue. Another new addition is the long-windedly named **Joan W & Irving B Harris Theater for Music & Dance** (☎ 312-629-8696; www.madtchi.com; 205 East Randolph Dr), located behind the bandshell. The 1500-seat theater will be a high-profile home for a dozen non-profit arts groups.

The melding of city finances and local artistry is also on view at the **Riverwalk Gateway** (Map pp282–3), Chicago's largest work of public art. For it, artist Ellen Lanyon created 28 glazed, fired panels that relate key moments in Chicago's river-centric history. The 6in by 9in panels depict everything from the 1673 trampings of explorers Marquette and Jolliet, to flag-toting waterskiers celebrating the reduction of river pollution in 2000.

SEARS TOWER Map pp282–3

☎ 312-875-9696; www.the-skydeck.com; 233 S Wacker Dr; adult/child/senior $9.50/6.75/7.75; 10am-10pm May-Sept, 10am-8pm Oct-Apr, last ticket sold 30 min before closing

It's no longer the world's tallest building (the title goes to Malaysia's Petronas Towers), but there's no doubt that the Sears Tower has become a symbol of Chicago. It boasts the kind of stats that make good grade-school presentations: 43,000 miles of phone cable, 2232 steps to the roof, enough concrete to build an eight-lane highway 5 miles long.

Much of what's inside the 110-story, 1454ft building is mundane office space. But the lure of the world's highest observation deck draws more than 1.5 million people a year. The Skydeck entrance is on the Jackson Blvd side of the block-size building. Your journey to the top starts with a walk through an airport-style metal detector, followed by a slow elevator ride down to the waiting area where visitors queue for tickets. A sign will tell you how long you'll have to wait to get to the top. On busy days it can be an hour or longer, so this is a good time to confirm the visibility – before you invest your time and money. Even days that seem sunny can have upper-level haze that limits the view. On good days, however, you can see for 40 to 50 miles, as far as Indiana, Michigan and Wisconsin.

After buying your ticket, you'll have to sit through *Over Chicago*. The syrupy narration and dated aerial footage of Chicago in the film may seem endless, but after the 15-minute presentation, you're cleared for takeoff. The 70-second elevator ride will definitely have your ears popping.

Once on the Skydeck, you're bound to think the view was worth the price paid in money and patience. The entire city stretches below, and you can take the time to see exactly how Chicago is laid out. Sunsets can be quite stunning, and the emergence of lights at twilight is charming. Interesting, kid-friendly exhibits on Chicago history wrap around the interior walls, serving as an ideal distraction for those suffering from an unexpected onset of vertigo.

NEAR NORTH & NAVY PIER

Eating p125; Shopping p189; Sleeping p215

The Loop may be where Chicago fortunes are made, but the Near North is where those fortunes are spent. The song of Near North is a heady choir of salespeople's greetings, excited shoppers cooing and the crackle of luxury goods being swaddled in paper. All of it backed by the steady beat of cash registers opening and closing.

The epicenter of it all is the upscale shopping haven of N Michigan Ave, also known as the Magnificent Mile. This is a prime place to see Chicago's old money leading their armies of personal assistants in commando raids on the racks at Chanel. You don't have to be a millionaire to enjoy the Magnificent Mile though, the whole area – from the Tribune Tower on the south end to the historic Water Tower on the north – glows with a kind of majestic, fairy-tale warmth. This is especially true from mid-November through January, when the **Magnificent Mile Lights Festival** (see City Calendar p13) strings zillions of little lights in the trees lining N Michigan Ave.

In the River North area, west of State St, art is the big business. What was once a grimy, noisy assortment of warehouses, factories and association headquarters has become Chicago's most prestigious gallery district– a bastion of high ceilings, hardwood floors, and expensive paintings and sculpture.

The area east of Michigan Ave is called Streeterville in honor of one of the city's great characters, George Wellington Streeter. Streeter and his wife were sailing past Chicago in the 1880s, purportedly on their way from Milwaukee to the Caribbean when they ran aground on a sandbar near what is today Chicago Ave and Lake Shore Dr. Streeter built a little causeway to the mainland and convinced developers to dump excavated dirt on the site. Soon the area had grown to several acres, and Streeter seceded from the city and Illinois.

Various efforts to evict Streeter and a band of loyal squatters ended in the courts in 1918. Streeter lost. Today Streeterville contains some of Chicago's most valuable property, much of it home to hotels, expensive high-rise condos and offices. The almost-complete River East Center is being built on several blocks east of Columbus Dr along Grand Ave. The huge project includes hotels, movie theaters, and – you guessed it – more shops.

Orientation

Near North is surrounded on three sides by water – the lake to the east, and branches of the Chicago river to the south and west. Chicago Avenue crops the neighborhood neatly across the top. River North, conveniently, has easy access to the Kennedy Expressway. Grand Ave serves as a good east–west thoroughfare for navigating the bottom end of Near North. State St bisects the area on the north–south axis.

Navy Pier juts out into Lake Michigan on the eastern edge of the Near North neighborhood. You can hoof it here from Michigan Ave in about 15 minutes. To get to Navy Pier by car, take the Grand Ave exit from Lake Shore Dr. A free shuttle trolley runs daily between the pier and the Grand Ave El stop on the Red Line.

ANTI-CRUELTY SOCIETY Map pp280–1
159 W Grand Ave
Stanley Tigerman, the architect of this building, is known for his witty creations. He meant for the facade facing LaSalle St to resemble a basset hound. Tigerman's parking garage at 60 E Lake St in the Loop looks like an old Bentley.

BEING BORN SCULPTURE Map pp280–1
Ohio & Ontario Sts
Like the Loop, the Near North area contains a number of public sculptures. Commissioned by the tool and die industry, *Being Born* is a 1983 stainless steel sculpture by Virginio Ferrari. It symbolizes both precision, with its two fitted rings, and economic growth, with its open outer ring. Lots of Chicagoans have had the opportunity to contemplate this particular piece, for it sits at the confluence of Ohio and Ontario Sts where they meet the entrance to the Kennedy Expressway.

CHICAGO CHILDREN'S MUSEUM
Map pp280–1
☎ 312-527-1000; www.chichildrensmuseum.org; Navy Pier; admission $7, free Thu after 5pm; ☺ 10am-5pm Tue, Wed & Fri-Sun, to 8pm Thu
The target audience of this attraction will love the place. Designed to challenge the imaginations of kids aged toddler through 10, the colorful and lively museum near the main entrance to Navy Pier gives its wee visitors enough hands-on exhibits to keep them climbing and creating for hours.

Among the favorite exhibits, Dinosaur Expedition explores the world of paleontology. The game show 'Face to Face' teaches the young ones how not to grow up to be jerks by cautioning against prejudice and discrimination. Designing your own flight of fancy is the goal at the build-your-own-airplane Inventing Lab. And Waterways lets kids get wet just when they've finally dried out from the Navy Pier fountains. Hint: come in the afternoon to avoid the crowds.

CHICAGO SUN-TIMES Map pp280–1
401 N Wabash Ave
With all the appeal of an aluminum can, the headquarters of the *Sun-Times*, the most-read paper in the city, does not lure admirers, but it does boast a nice outdoor plaza which overlooks the river and the Loop skyline from the east side of the building. Trees, lawns you can sit on and many, many benches make

Transport
El Red Line to Grand for the Mag Mile's south end and River North; Red Line to Chicago for the Mag Mile's north end.

Bus 151 runs along N Michigan Ave; 156 is a good north–south bet through River North; 65 travels along Grand Ave to Navy Pier.

Parking The further you get away from the Mag Mile, the more common the metered parking. Parking at Navy Pier is costly – $11 an hour. Instead, look for signed lots west of Lake Shore Dr near the pier and take a free shuttle to the pier.

this a wonderful spot to rest your weary dogs on a decent day. A branch of the ubiquitous McDonald's and a small grocery store provide on-site sustenance.

HOLY NAME CATHEDRAL Map pp280–1
☎ 312-787-8040; 735 N State St; admission free; ☺ 7am-7pm
It's ironic that in a town with so many grandiose churches, the Chicago archdiocese would call this modest Gothic church home. It's even more ironic when you consider that the archdiocese has had to close some of its most beautiful churches because of declining membership in some parishes.

Built in 1875 to a design by the unheralded Patrick Keeley, the cathedral has twice been remodeled in attempts to spruce it up. The latter effort in fact covered up bullet holes left over from a Capone-era hit across the street (see the boxed text Capone's Chicago p80). The cathedral does provide a quiet place for contemplation, unless the excellent choirs are practicing, in which case it's an entertaining respite. Open most of the day, it holds frequent services.

MEDINAH TEMPLE Map pp280–1
600 N Wabash Ave
The Medinah Temple was built in 1912 by the Shriners, who chose a flamboyant Moorish design for their festival hall. The temple was threatened with destruction in the late 1990s by rapacious developers coveting its locations. After an outcry from preservationists in 2000, a typically Chicago deal was cut – the Temple's terra-cotta–bedecked exterior survived, but developers converted the interior to – of all things – a Bloomingdale's home furnishings store.

Top Five Near North & Navy Pier

- Facing death – and fantastic views – on the **Navy Pier ferris wheel** (p68).
- Checking out the black-and-white photos at **Catherine Edelman** (p69) in River North.
- Scarfing up handfuls of sticky, sweet CaramelCrisp from **Garrett Popcorn** (p193).
- Meandering through the aisles of **Paper Source** (p194), dreaming up art projects.
- Spending a week's wages on a jaw-droppingly beautiful room with a bathtub view at the **Peninsula** (p221).

NAVY PIER Map pp280–1

☎ 312-595-7437; www.navypier.com; 600 E Grand Ave; admission free; ☺ 10am-10pm Sun-Thu, 10am-midnight Fri & Sat, shorter hours Sep-May, individual restaurants and attractions may have different hours

Chicago's most-visited tourist attraction, Navy Pier will absolutely blow the minds of children under 12. The pier's collection of high-tech rides, hands-on fountains, kid-focused educational exhibits, fast-food restaurants and trinket vendors will transport your child into the kind of overstimulated, joyful state you haven't witnessed since you finally gave in and got them the puppy for their birthday last year.

For the childless, Navy Pier's charms are more modest. The views out over the city from the pier are spectacular, and the stomach-curdling ride on the gigantic Ferris wheel is a must. Also, a myriad of themed boat tours depart from the Pier's southern side. The pier isn't all about rides and cotton candy, however. Many of the over seven million visitors to the pier each year actually come here on business – much of the eastern end of the structure consists of exposition space managed in conjunction with McCormick Place. It's a hoot to watch the crowds of laminate-badge-toting convention-eers fighting surly suburban pre-teens for a table in the pier's McDonalds.

The 150ft **Ferris wheel** ($5 per ride) is much more exciting than any Ferris wheel has a right to be. This is due partly to the dizzying heights of the thing, but also because of the almost non-existent security precautions (make sure the small gate separating you from the tarmac far below is properly shut!). As long as you don't suffer from acrophobia, though, the ride will be one of your best memories of Chicago. The **carousel** ($4 per ride) is another classic, with

bobbing, carved horses and organ music. Kids will be clamoring to ride the **Time Escape 3-D** (☎ 415-495-7000; www.timeescape.com; adult/child/senior $10/8/8) a futuristic, virtual roller-coaster ride that takes visitors back in time to Chicago's dinosaur-filled past, and forward 300 years into its zippy future. The flashing, shaking ride lasts 15 minutes, and will likely leave more of an impression on kids than their parents.

A variety of acts appears through the summer at the **Skyline Stage** (☎ 312-595-7437), a 1500-seat rooftop venue with a glistening white canopy. See the Entertainment chapter for details on the IMAX Theater (p173) and the Chicago Shakespeare Theater (p169).

Some of Navy Pier's free amusements include the fountains at the entrance to the pier. It's as much fun to watch the cavorting kids as the fountain itself; scores of water jets squirt at unpredictable intervals, and every-one's encouraged to get wet. The upper-level **Crystal Gardens fountains** feature delightful water jets that appear out of nowhere and lazily arc over the heads of the unsuspecting.

If you're looking for further diversions, a flo-tilla of competing tour boats lines the dock. For the skinny on what's available, see Organized Tours p59. In summer **Shoreline Sightseeing** (☎ 312-222-9328) runs a water taxi between Navy Pier, the river near the Sears Tower and the Shedd Aquarium.

RIVER ESPLANADE Map pp280–1
Chicago River waterfront, btwn N Michigan Ave & N Fairbanks Ct

The developers looking to cash in on River East Center were given a mandate by the city – for the proposed shopping area to go through, the company would have to leave the River Esplanade to the Chicago Park District. It was a good deal for both parties, and the River Esplanade makes an excellent place to take a break from your hectic days of unwinding. Beginning with the oddly pro-portioned curving staircase at the northeast tower of the Michigan Ave Bridge, the land-scaped walkway extends east along the river past the Sheraton Hotel.

Every hour on the hour, from 10am to 2pm and again from 5pm to midnight, the espla-nade's **Centennial Fountain** shoots a massive arc of water across the river for 10 minutes. The entire exercise is meant to commemorate the labor-intensive reversal of the Chicago River in 1900, which tidily began sending all of the city's wastes downriver rather than into the lake. (Chicago's neighbors downstate, as you can guess, do not go out of their way to celebrate this feat of civil engineering.)

RIVER NORTH GALLERIES

Unlike the ragtag galleries of Pilsen, or the up-and-comers in the West Loop, River North galleries tend to show money artists for a money clientele. The atmosphere here is still welcoming, though, and the gallery owners are happy to let normal folk like you and me wander through their showrooms. You can get a gallery map at any of the galleries to help you find artwork to your liking. The **Douglas Dawson Gallery** (Map pp280–1; ☎ 312-751-1961; 222 W Huron; 10am-5:30pm Mon-Fri, 10am-5pm Sat) specializes in Asian, African and American tribal art, with a focus on African ceramics. The contemporary art at the **Jean Albano Gallery** (Map pp280–1; ☎ 312-440-0770; 215 W Superior St; 10am-5pm Tue-Fri, 11am-5pm Sat) includes paintings, drawings, and interesting textile works. **Robert Henry Adams Fine Art** (Map pp280–1; ☎ 312-642-8700; 715 N Franklin; 10am-5pm Tue-Fri, noon-5pm Sat) is a friendly, two-floor gallery specializing in works by pre-WWII American impressionist, regionalist and modernist painters. The first gallery to arrive in River North back in the mid-'70s (when it looked more like the West Loop does today), **Zolla-Lieberman Gallery** (Map pp280–1; ☎ 312-944-1990; 325 W Huron St; 10am-5:30pm Tue-Fri, 11am-5:30pm Sat) continues to show very cool contemporary art by established and emerging artists. If you love photography, drop by **Catherine Edelman** (Map pp280–1; ☎ 312-266-2350; 300 W Superior St; 10am-5:30pm Tue-Sat), where the works range from traditional landscapes to mixed-media photo-based collages.

RORA MOSAIC Map pp280–1
Erie St and Chicago River north branch

Artist Ginny Sykes' *Rora* symbolizes the Chicago River. The mosaic of glass tile is worth a look if you're in the area already.

SMITH MUSEUM OF STAINED GLASS WINDOWS Map pp280–1
☎ 312-595-5024; Navy Pier; admission free; as for Navy Pier

The owners of Navy Pier don't care much about promoting this free, impressive attraction, but visitors who wander along the lower-level terraces of Festival Hall will discover the country's first museum dedicated entirely to stained glass. Many of the 150 pieces on display were made in Chicago (a stained glass hub in the late 1800s, thanks to the influx of European immigrants), and most hung at one point in Chicago churches, homes and office buildings. Even if you think stained glass is something for blue-haired grandmas, you should make a point of coming by: the articulately explained collection ranges from typical Victorian religious themes to far-out political designs (the Martin Luther King Jr one is especially noteworthy). And fans of Louis Comfort Tiffany will rejoice to find 13 of his works hanging here.

TRIBUNE TOWER Map pp280–1
435 N Michigan Ave

Colonel Robert McCormick, eccentric owner of the Chicago *Tribune*, collected – and asked his overworked reporters to send – rocks from famous buildings and monuments around the world. All 138 of these are now embedded around the base of the Tribune Tower. In 1999 the *Tribune* added a moon rock brought back by the Apollo 15 mission; look for it on the right side of the building.

GOLD COAST

Eating p125; Shopping p189; Sleeping p215

In its most pristine reaches, the Gold Coast outshines even its gilded name, the well-heeled historic mansions here glinting with an un-self-conscious wealth. When you stroll through the neighborhood, especially around Astor St, you'll take in some of the most beautiful old homes in Chicago, if not the country. With a little imagination, you can almost see the late-19th-century moguls who settled the area, brandishing diamond-tipped canes at each other and cradling their tiny dogs on the carriage rides into their Loop offices.

Today, those magnates would have to fight their way to the curb through the throngs of *House and Garden* devotees clinging to the iron gates and drooling. This being Chicago, though, the Gold Coast's historic enclaves like Astor St weren't always so revered. Time has

Transport

El Red Line to Clark/Division for the northern reaches; Red Line to Chicago for the southern areas.

Bus 151 runs along N Michigan Ave; 70 runs along Division St before swooping south to the Newberry Library; 66 swings by the Museum of Contemporary Art.

Parking Resident-only streets stymie street parking. Try LaSalle St for unmetered parking, or let a restaurant valet find you a spot for around $10.

moved on here, and a great number of the beautiful old mansions disappeared 50 years ago to make room for high-rise, high-cost apartments along the lake. So it goes in the Gold Coast. Despite the area's upper-class leanings, the atmosphere is anything but sedate. Teens on gas-powered scooters zoom up the paths alongside Lake Shore Dr, past crowds of beach volleyball players gathering for a lunchtime match. At night, young professionals mix and mingle at Museum of Contemporary Art socials, shifting the party to the singles bars around State and Division Sts as the hour grows later.

The further you move away from the lake, the less rarefied the Gold Coast's air. The extreme example being the Cabrini-Green housing projects on the outer western edge of the Gold Coast at Division and Larrabee Sts. A shorthand for public housing gone awry, the Cabrini-Green apartments look as if a war has been fought (and lost) among their bombed-out towers. Fire-scarred and heartrendingly bleak, the projects are being slowly demolished, the remaining residents relocated far away to the Chicago suburbs. True to Gold Coast form, developers have already draw up plans for the luxury townhouses that will eventually sweep across the valuable 70-acre plot of land. Driving by the smoldering wreck today, it's hard to imagine anyone living there. But in a sign of things to come, the first Cabrini-Green Starbucks has already opened for business.

Orientation

The Gold Coast is just north of Near North and south of Lincoln Park (the park in this case, not the neighborhood). Streetwise, the area stretches languidly along Lake Shore Dr, running up to North Ave in the north and down to Chicago Ave in the south. Astor St is tucked into the northeast corner of the Gold Coast, one block in from the lake. The most hectic parts of the neighborhood are in the south along the posh Michigan Ave and Oak St shopping areas. The Cabrini-Green neighborhood reaches along Division St, between Orleans and Larrabee Sts.

860-880 N LAKE SHORE DR Map pp278–9

The International Style of high-rises got its start with this Mies van der Rohe work. Built from 1949 to 1951, the twin towers were the manifestation of designs Mies first put forward in 1921. The idea of high-rises draped only in a curtain of glass and steel was so radical at the time that psychologists speculated about the impact of living in a transparent home. Check out the buildings from the lakefront path early in the morning for maximum effect.

1340 N STATE ST Map pp278–9

The sexual revolution perhaps started in the basement 'grotto' of this otherwise unremarkable 1899 mansion, which belonged to *Playboy* impresario Hugh Hefner in the 1960s and '70s. Later a dorm for the School of the Art Institute (imagine the pickup lines!), it was gutted in 1993 and turned into four very staid but very expensive condos.

1550 N STATE ST Map pp278–9

French elegance came to Chicago in a manner as humble as Napoleon's ego with this 1912 apartment house, which once boasted a mere one unit per floor.

ARCHBISHOP QUIGLEY PREPARATORY SEMINARY Map pp278–9

☎ 312-787-8625; 831 N Rush St; admission free;
Ⓥ 11am-3pm Mon-Sat May-Sep, noon-2pm other times
Built in 1919 in a flamboyant Gothic style, the stunning Archbishop Quigley Preparatory Seminary holds the magnificent Chapel of St James, which was ambitiously modeled after the grand 13th-century Sainte-Chapelle in Paris, Louis IX's palace chapel. With 45,000 panes of glass in its impressive array of stained-glass windows, the Chicago version certainly comes close to the original. Local choral groups sometimes perform in the chapel, definitely a recommended and ennobling treat.

ASTOR ST

In 1882 Potter and Bertha Palmer were the power couple of Chicago. His web of businesses included the city's best hotel and a huge general merchandise store later sold to a clerk named Marshall Field. When they relocated from Prairie Ave north to a crenellated castle of a mansion at what's now 1350 N Lake Shore Dr, the Palmers set off a lemming-like rush of Chicago's wealthy to the neighborhood around them. The mansions along Astor St reflect the grandeur of that heady age.

Originally four, now three, the 1887 homes at Nos **1308–1312** (Map pp278–9) feature a lovely sculptured quality that extends to the turrets, gables and dormers. The architect, John Wellborn Root, was so pleased with his efforts that he moved into No **1310** (Map pp278–9). Once one home, now several apartments, the 1887 mansion at No **1355** (Map pp278–9) represents the full flower of Georgian revival. Note the alternating skulls and animal heads above the windows.

While he was still working for Louis Sullivan, a 19-year-old Frank Lloyd Wright designed the large but only 11-room **Charnley-Persky House** (Map pp278–9; ☎ 312-573-1365; 1365 N Astor St) and he proclaimed with his soon-to-be-trademarked bombast that it was the 'first modern building.' Now home to the National Society of Architectural Historians, the house is sometimes open for tours. Call for times and prices. A late arrival on the street, the 1929

Astor St, Gold Coast

Russell House (Map pp278–9; 1444 N Astor St) is art deco French at its most refined. The 1880 mansion that serves as the **Archbishop's Residence** (Map pp278–9; 1555 N State St) spans the entire block to Astor. Built in the Queen Anne style that later became known generically as 'Victorian,' this comfortable place looks like it would provide solace to any archbishop pondering the sins of the flock.

FOURTH PRESBYTERIAN CHURCH
Map pp278–9

☎ 312-787-4570; 126 E Chestnut St; admission free

This 1914 church belongs to one of the city's wealthiest congregations. It brings to mind a bunch of dons in some old Gothic school guzzling port and eyeing the choirboys. Lurid fantasies aside, the church provides a welcome break from the commercial blocks and offers a reminder of the not-so-long-ago times when low-rise mansions dominated the neighborhood. Occasional organ recitals take place in the splendid sanctuary.

INTERNATIONAL MUSEUM OF SURGICAL SCIENCE Map pp278–9

☎ 312-642-6502; www.imss.org; 1524 N Lake Shore Dr; adult/senior & student $6/3, free Tue; ☾ 10am-4pm Tue-Sat

Home to an eclectic collection of surgery-related items, the Museum of Surgical Science features such a poorly marked assortment of medical items that at first the museum seems like nothing more than a place to escape a vicious lake squall. But start exploring and you'll soon be rewarded with fascinating thematic displays, such as the one on bloodletting, the act of bleeding patients to death to 'cure' them. The undeniable gems of the collection are the 'stones,' as in 'kidney stone' and 'gallstone.' All of the spectacularly large specimens were passed by patients who may have wished instead for a good bloodletting.

JOHN HANCOCK CENTER Map pp278–9

☎ 312-751-3681; www.hancock-observatory.com; 875 N Michigan Ave; observatory adult/child/senior $9.75/6/7.75; ☾ 9am-11pm

The world's tallest 'mixed-use' building (meaning that it contains both residential and commercial space), the Hancock is the third-tallest building in Chicago, at 1127ft. Much less popular than the Sears Tower's Skydeck, the Hancock's viewing platform benefits from having shorter lines and no sappy film. The friendly employees guide you to the

Neighborhoods – Gold Coast

fast – 23mph – elevators for the 40-second ride to the 94th floor. In many ways the view here surpasses the one at the Sears, and the screened, outdoor area lets you listen in on the sounds of the city. When you're that far above the street, there's something almost lyrical about the dull roar of traffic punctuated by jackhammers and sirens.

However pleasant the view from the top, locals shake their heads sadly at the suckers who pay to make the ascent. The elevator ride to the Hancock's 96th-floor Signature Lounge, one floor up from the Signature Room restaurant (p137), they're quick to point out, is free. Why shell out $10 to go stand around on some windblown viewing deck when the same money could get you a glass of wine, a comfy seat, and almost identical views a few floors higher? They've got a point. The lounge's elevators are to the right of the cashier's desk for the observatory.

Top Five Gold Coast

- Practicing your beach-bum moves at **Oak St Beach** (p84).
- Getting high on a 'Gold Coast Martini' at the **Signature Lounge** (above the Signature Room, p137) on the 96th floor of the John Hancock Center.
- Checking out the cool collages by Barbara Kruger at the **Museum of Contemporary Art** (p72).
- Pondering a play at **Lookingglass Theatre** (p170) in their new Water Works location.
- Watching bespectacled patrons pore over impossibly large, ancient books at the **Newberry Library** (p72).

MUSEUM OF CONTEMPORARY ART
Map pp278–9

☎ 312-280-2660; www.mcachicago.org; 220 E Chicago Ave; adult/senior & student $10/6, free after 5pm Tue; ☼ 10am-8pm Tue, 10am-5pm Wed-Sun

Covering art from 1945 forward, the MCA uses extensive piece descriptions to alleviate a lot of the head-scratching, 'what the hell is it?' befuddlement that tends to accompany encounters with modern art. The museum boasts an especially strong minimalist, surrealist, and book-arts collection, but the works here span the modern art gamut, from Jenny Holzer's LED *Truisms* to Joseph Beuys' austere *Felt Suit*. The permanent collection includes art by Franz Kline, René Magritte, Cindy Sherman and Andy Warhol, with displays arranged to highlight the blurring of the boundaries between painting, photography, sculpture, video and other media. The MCA also regularly hosts dance, film, and speaking events from an international array of contemporary artists. Puck's at the MCA, a café overlooking Lake Michigan (see p137), attracts crowds with its fine views of the sculpture garden and lake beyond, as well as its creative food.

NEWBERRY LIBRARY Map pp278–9

☎ 312-943-9090; www.newberry.org; 60 W Walton St; admission free, must be 16 or older; ☼ 10am-6pm Tue-Thu, 9am-5pm Fri & Sat

Humanities nerds and those trying to document far-flung branches of their family tree will have a field day at this research library. Entry requires a library card, but one-day passes are available for curious browsers. Once inside, you can pester the patient librarians with requests for help in tracking down all manner of historical ephemera. (The collection is non-circulating, though, so don't expect to take that first edition of the King James Bible home with you.) The Newberry also often features interesting special exhibits, as well as a bookstore where you can pick up such treatises as *Buffy the Vampire Slayer and Philosophy* and cool vintage Chicago travel posters. Free tours of the impressive building take place 3pm Thursday and 10:30am Saturday .

ST BENEDICT FLATS Map pp278–9
42-50 E Chicago Ave

The St Benedict Flats offer an unusual glimpse of French Second Empire architecture.

WASHINGTON SQUARE Map pp278–9
Btwn N Clark St, N Dearborn St, W Delaware Pl, W Walton St

This rather plain park across from the Newberry Library has had a colorful and tragic history. In the 1920s it was known as 'Bughouse Square' because of the communists, socialists, anarchists and other -ists who gave soapbox orations here.

In the 1970s, when it was a gathering place for young male prostitutes, it gained tragic infamy as the preferred pickup spot of mass-murderer John Wayne Gacy. Gacy took his victims back to his suburban home, where he killed them and buried their bodies in the basement. Convicted on 33 counts of murder (although the actual tally may be higher), he was executed in 1994.

Delaware Pl and Walton, Clark and Dearborn Sts border the park.

WATER TOWER Map pp278–9
806 N Michigan Ave

Believe it or not, the 154ft Water Tower, a city icon and focal point of the Mag Mile, once dwarfed all the buildings around it. Built in the late 1860s, the Water Tower and its associated building, the **Pumping Station** (aka the Water Works) across the street, were constructed with local yellow limestone in a Gothic style popular at the time. This stone construction and lack of flammable interiors saved them in 1871, when the great Chicago fire roared through town.

The complex was obsolete by 1906, and only public outcry saved it from demolition three times. Whether Oscar Wilde would have joined the preservationists is debatable: when he visited Chicago in 1881, he called the Water Tower 'a castellated monstrosity with salt and pepper boxes stuck all over it.' Restoration in 1962 ensured the tower's survival, and today it houses the **City Gallery** (312-742-0808; ☉ 10am-6:30pm Mon-Sat, 10am-5pm Sun), showcasing Chicago-themed works by local photographers. The Pumping Station across the street houses a Visitor Information Center (p253).

LINCOLN PARK & OLD TOWN
Eating p125; Shopping p189; Sleeping p215

If you've lost track of a Midwestern fraternity brother or sorority sister, chances are good you'll find them living happily in Lincoln Park. Ground zero for Chicago's yuppie population, the neighborhood bustles with Banana Republic-wearing residents walking dogs, Rollerblading and pushing babies around in $300 strollers. Local curmudgeons will grouse about Lincoln Park being a soulless victim of gentrification, but the area has some undeniable charms, including great restaurants, cute boutiques, and the Clark St record-store corridor, where the city's music illuminati pick up tomorrow's hits.

Lincoln Park also has the park itself, a well-loved playland. The park, almost 50% larger than Central Park in New York, offers Chicagoans a chance to celebrate summer with paddleboat rides (aka raucous water fights) on North Pond, and commiserating visits to the polar bears at the Lincoln Park Zoo.

South of Lincoln Park, Old Town had a free-spirited past in the 1960s as the epicenter of Chicago's hippie culture. Artists, long-hairs and other freaks flocked to Old Town to tune in, turn on and drop their money on cool black-light posters and bongs from head shops on Wells St. Falling into disrepair in the 1970s, Old Town made a comeback in the 1980s and now is one of the North Side's most expensive places to buy property. Visitors won't find too much in the way of sights, but Old Town outranks its more lively neighbors when it comes to comedy – improv bastion Second City is here, as is Zanies, Chicago's best stand-up club.

Orientation

The streets of Lincoln Park are clogged with all manner of high-end SUVs – if you drive here, you'll likely know the area inside-out by the time you find parking. Lincoln Park is a huge neighborhood, stretching from the park on the east side all the way over to Racine Ave on the west. Armitage Ave runs along the southern end of the neighborhood; Diversey Pkwy serves as Lincoln Park's northern boundary. Oz Park, whose corner abuts Lincoln Park at its intersection with Geneva Tce, is one of the area's landmarks, as is DePaul University. You'll find DePaul spreading out from the intersection of Sheffield Ave and Fullerton Pkwy.

Old Town is much smaller than Lincoln Park, running from approximately Armitage Ave in the north, Halsted St in the west, and North Ave to the south. The bottom edge of the park forms Old Town's eastern flank.

Transport

El Brown, Purple or Red line to Fullerton or the Brown or Purple Line to Armitage for Lincoln Park; Brown or Purple Line to Sedgwick, or the Red Line to Clark/Division for Old Town.

Bus 76 runs along Diversey Pkwy, 74 spans Fullerton, 72 cuts through Old Town along North Ave.

Parking Lincoln Park is a headache. If you're stuck for spots, consider heading out to the meters along Diversey Harbor. Old Town has plenty of cars competing for its plentiful meters. Try the pay garage at Piper's Alley, at North Ave and Wells St.

CHICAGO HISTORICAL SOCIETY

Map pp276–7

☎ 312-642-4600; www.chicagohistory.org;
1601 N Clark St; adult/child/senior $5/1/3, free Mon;
☺ 9:30am-4:30pm Mon-Sat, noon-5pm Sun

The history of the Lincolns, Capones, Daleys and other notables gets some attention here, but this well-funded museum focuses on the average person. The role of the commoner in the American Revolution sets the tone for the humanistic exhibits. One, titled 'Fort Dearborn and Frontier Chicago,' shows how settlers and Indians changed each other's lives. The Pioneer Court offers hands-on demonstrations in the intricacies of making candles, weaving blankets and knitting clothes. None of the work was easy.

Much of the 2nd floor is devoted to Chicago's development and history, with displays that explore the roles of immigration and industry, as well as the problems of slums and the lives of the rich. Special exhibitions – the museum's strong point – cover such diverse topics as how bungalows allowed almost every family to afford a home, and Chicago's role in the birth of gospel music. The Big Shoulders Cafe serves tasty soups and sandwiches, and the bookstore is excellent.

CRILLY COURT Map pp276–7

Off Eugenie St

The facades of the 1890-vintage apartments of Crilly Court are charming stone variations of Queen Anne architecture. The backs of the properties have surprising wrought-iron porches right out of the French Quarter in New Orleans. The house at 1710 Crilly Court is the earliest known site associated with the gay and lesbian civil rights movement in the US. In 1924 and 1925 Henry Gerber lived in the house, founding the country's first ever gay civil rights organization during his residency.

DEPAUL UNIVERSITY Map pp276–7

☎ 773-325-7000; 2320 N Kenmore Ave

DePaul University is charming or ugly, depending where you are. The campus stretches east and west of the El south of Fullerton Ave. Chalmers Place is a scholarly square east of the El. The row houses were built for a seminary that has since been absorbed by DePaul.

West of the Fullerton El stop, the Academic Center and the University Center were built in 1968 and 1978, respectively, in an architectural style that's aptly named 'brutalism;' both monstrosities look like they're meant to

be last redoubts in case of urban assault. The 1992 library marks a new and vastly improved era of DePaul design. Notice how the architects have tried to camouflage some of the Academic Center.

ELKS VETERANS MEMORIAL Map pp276–7

☎ 773-528-4500; 2750 N Lakeview Ave; admission free;
☺ 9am-4pm

The Elks Club, once a hugely popular men's social club, has fallen on hard times all over the US, but during its heyday it built this impressive memorial to honor members killed at war.

FREDERICK WACKER HOUSE

Map pp276–7

1838 N Lincoln Park West

The Frederick Wacker House offers a rare glimpse at how Chicago's houses looked before the 1871 fire. This one was built right afterward – the flames roared through here – but just before the arrival of laws that banned wood structures in the area devastated by the fire.

HENRY MEYER HOUSE Map pp276–7

1802 N Lincoln Park West

The Henry Meyer House is another wooden example built during the same brief window of opportunity as the Wacker House (see above). Imagine whole blocks of these homes and you'll start to get an idea of the horror of the fire.

LINCOLN PARK Map pp276–7

The neighborhood gets its name from this park, Chicago's largest. Its 1200 acres stretch for 6 miles, from North Ave north to Diversey Pkwy, where it narrows along the lake and continues until the end of Lake Shore Dr. The park's many lakes, trails and paths make it an excellent place for recreation. Cross-country skiing in the winter and sunbathing in warmer months are just two of the activities Chicagoans enjoy in Lincoln Park. Many buy picnic vittles from the markets on Clark St and Diversey Pkwy.

Most of Lincoln Park's pleasures are natural. Some of the joys of the park include sculptor Augustus Saint-Gaudens' **Standing Lincoln**, which shows the 16th president deep in contemplation right before he delivers a great speech. Saint-Gaudens based the work on casts made of Lincoln's face and hands while Lincoln was alive. The statue stands in its own garden east of the Chicago Historical Society.

Near the southeast corner of LaSalle Dr and Clark St, the **Couch Mausoleum** is the sole reminder of the land's pre-1864 use: the entire area was a municipal cemetery. Many of the graves contained hundreds of dead prisoners from Camp Douglas, a horrific prisoner-of-war stockade on the city's South Side during the Civil War. Removing the bodies from the designated park area proved a greater undertaking than the city could stomach, and today if you start digging at the south end of the park you're liable to make some ghoulish discoveries.

From a little dock in front of pretty **Cafe Brauer**, a 1908 Prairie School architectural creation, you can rent two-person paddleboats and cruise the South Pond, south of the zoo. A more bucolic cruise can be had on the North Pond, which doesn't have the zoo crowds. Rent boats from the little boathouse east of where Deming Place meets the park. The rental season at both ponds is roughly May through September.

Just north of the zoo are two other worthy sights that keep zoo hours. Near the zoo's north entrance, off Stockton Dr, is the **Lincoln Park Conservatory** (☎ 312-742-7736; admission free), two gardens first planted in 1891. These bloom year-round under 3 acres of glass. The 1887 statue **Storks at Play**, outside the conservatory, has enchanted generations of Chicagoans.

The **Alfred Caldwell Lily Pool**, created in 1937, is an important stopover for migrating birds. The stonework resembles the stratified canyons of the Wisconsin Dells. When not overrun with people, the pool is a magical setting, especially in winter. Planted with native Midwestern species, it's at the north end of the zoo near Fullerton Ave.

LINCOLN PARK ZOO Map pp276–7

☎ 312-742-2000; www.lpzoo.com; 2200 N Cannon Dr; admission free; ⏰ 9am-5pm, until 7pm May-Sep

The free zoo is one of Chicago's most popular attractions, and its appeal only increased with the 2003 opening of the Regenstein African Journey. The naturalistic African walk-through is a cutting-edge example of zoo exhibits done right – the human visitors are allowed to get surprisingly close to animals who swim, hop and crawl in remarkably lifelike environments. Adults will love the cuddly, perpetually puzzled looking meerkat, and kids will scream with disgusted glee at the entire room filled with hissing cockroaches.

The rest of the zoo – which opened in 1868 – is fairly typical. **Farm-in-the-Zoo**, the place where many urbanites first learn that milk comes from cows instead of cardboard containers, features a full range of barnyard animals in a faux farm setting just south of the zoo. Frequent demonstrations of cow milking, horse grooming, butter churning and other chores take place.

The exhibits don't make any bones about the ultimate fate of most livestock. For instance, those cute piglets head to the slaughterhouse only four to six months after birth.

The exhibits for the lions and other big cats, elephants, monkeys, and sea lions are fine but unremarkable. And the cramped penguin habitat borders on the depressing. Still, free is a very good price, and if you come during colder months, you'll have many of the exhibits to yourself. You can easily reach the zoo from most parts of the park; there are entrances to it on all sides. Drivers be warned: parking is among the worst in the city.

MOODY CHURCH Map pp276–7

☎ 312-943-0466; www.moodychurch.org; 1630 N Clark St

Directly across from the Chicago Historical Society stands the hulking Moody Church, a non-denominational church started by 19th-century missionary DL Moody. Moody, who also founded the Moody Bible Institute in the Gold Coast, was the Billy Graham of his age – a charismatic preacher who took his literal interpretations of the Bible to audiences around the world. The church, which can hold almost 4000 worshippers, was built in 1925. Tours available by request.

OZ PARK Map pp276–7

Btwn Geneva Ave, Webster Ave, Halsted St

Oz Park is celebrating its name thanks to the generous donations of the neighborhood's rich. The *Tin Man* stands at the northeast corner of the park, wondering which passersby might have a heart for him, while a yellow brick sidewalk stretches from that same corner into the park. Those neighborhood dollars also bought Oz the best playground in the city.

PEGGY NOTEBAERT NATURE MUSEUM Map pp276–7

☎ 773-755-5100; www.naturemuseum.org; 2430 N Cannon Dr; adult/child/senior $7/4/5; free Thu; 🕙 9am-4:30pm Mon-Fri, 10am-5pm Sat & Sun

This wonderful hands-on museum allows you to do everything from walking among fluttering butterflies to engineering your own river system. Other exhibits show how many different wild animals live in urban Chicago, both inside and outside. A computer lab allows visitors to solve environmental problems, and kids are given free reign to explore, scamper and climb while they learn.

Butterfly room, Peggy Notebaert Nature Museum

ST CLEMENT'S CHURCH Map pp276–7

☎ 773-281-0371; 646 W Deming Pl

Istanbul's Hagia Sophia inspired the restored Byzantine mosaics that grace the dome of St Clement's Church, a Catholic church built in 1918. When the University of Notre Dame football team loses, Sunday mass is a sea of red eyes in this parish, which caters to young, single college grads. The church sits on a street lined with gracious mansions with extra-wide front lawns.

ST MICHAEL'S CHURCH Map pp276–7

☎ 312-642-2498; 1633 N Cleveland Ave

Believe it or not, St Michael's Church was once the Sears Tower of its day. From 1869 until 1885, the Catholic church reigned as the tallest building in Chicago. Built in 1869 by German Catholics, the church was largely destroyed in the 1871 Chicago fire, and completely rebuilt two years later. The Romanesque interior – with its fantastic stained glass – is open to the public.

LAKE VIEW

Eating p125; Shopping p189; Sleeping p215

Okay, so the name of this inland neighborhood is a little off. But you know what? No one who lives here is complaining. The twenty- and thirtysomethings inhabiting the three overlapping Lakeview 'hoods of Wrigleyville, Boys Town and the Belmont area are too busy checking each other out to notice some dumb lake anyway.

Wrigleyville – named for star attraction Wrigley Field – has become a magnet for singles, who frolic and cruise in the ridiculous number of bars and restaurants that line Clark and Southport. The tenor of the neighborhood is much like that of the stadium it surrounds: well-mannered by day with an impish dose of carousing by night. Yuppies looking for more bang for their apartment buck have been abandoning their Lincoln Park condos for Wrigleyville over the past five years. But unlike the hyper-gentrified neighborhoods to the south, Wrigleyville has managed to handle the influx of cell phones and SUVs and still retain its color and atmosphere (read: high-alcohol tolerance).

Transport

El Red Line Addison stop for Wrigleyville; Brown and Red Line Belmont stop for Belmont and Boys Town.

Bus 152 traces Addison St; 22 follows Clark St; 8 runs along Halsted St.

Parking In a word: nightmare. Especially in Wrigleyville, where side streets are resident-only. Take the train or bring a really good book-on-tape to listen to as you try to find parking.

You don't need a map to know you've arrived in the predominantly gay section of Lake View known as Boys Town. If the rainbow flags don't tip you off, the abundance of hot, well-dressed men will. Just south of Wrigleyville, the well-heeled hub of Chicago's gay community bustles on Broadway St during the day and gets hedonistic on Halsted St at night. Boys Town is also the place to come if you accidentally left those fur-lined handcuffs at home; the shops here are known for their quirky, fun and sex-friendly vibe.

Though the crowds may be straighter, the shopping scene is equally wild in Belmont, just west of Boys Town. This is the youngest-feeling of Lake View's neighborhoods and the stores here cater to every lifestyle whim of local goths, punks, and hipsters. Whether you need hair dye, a Fender Telecaster, or a vintage Siouxsie Sioux and the Banshees t-shirt, you can count on the endearingly attitude-heavy emporiums here to come through for you.

For all its copious energy, Lake View has little in the way of historic sights or cultural attractions. When you come here, be sure to bring your credit cards.

Orientation

Lake View begins at Diversey Pkwy and stretches from the lake to Ashland Ave, with Irving Park Rd cropping the neighborhood in the north. Wrigleyville occupies the top half of the area, its bars and restaurants are clustered on Southport Ave, south of Irving Park Rd, and on Clark St, south of Addison St. Boys Town is further south and closer to the lake than Wrigleyville; its two main drags are Halsted and Broadway Sts. The charms of the Belmont area, handily, are located on Belmont Ave, where it meets Clark St.

ALTA VISTA TCE Map pp272–3
Btwn Byron & Grace Sts

Chicago's first designated historic district is worthy of the honor. Developer Samuel Eberly Gross re-created a block of London row houses on Alta Vista Tce in 1904. The 20 exquisitely detailed homes on either side of the street mirror each other diagonally, and the owners have worked hard at maintaining the spirit of the block. Individuality isn't dead, however: head to the back of the west row and you'll notice that every house has grown to the rear in dramatically different fashions.

WRIGLEY FIELD Map pp272–3
☎ 773-404-2827; 1060 W Addison St

This legendary baseball park draws plenty of tourists, who pose year-round under the classic neon sign over the main entrance. Baseball fanatics can take a 90-minute stadium **tour** (☎ 800-843-2827; tours $15) on select weekends during the baseball season. Reservations are required for the tour, which takes visitors through the clubhouse, dugouts

and press box. If you don't have time for a tour, or can't get tickets for a game, stroll over to Sheffield Ave on game day and chat with the guys who hang around, waiting for a ball to be hit out of the park. Notice, too, how the owners of the surrounding three-flats have turned their rooftops into bleachers (an enterprising maneuver that has never sat well with Cubs owners). See the Sports chapter for details on attending a Cubs game (p184).

Top Five Lake View

- Watching the clouds dawdle across the ceiling of the **Music Box Theater** (p173) before a movie.
- Raising a toast to a local alt-country band at **Schubas** (p177).
- Shopping for retro Cubs shirts at **Strange Cargo** (p201).
- Joining the sports fans cutting work and taking in a day game at **Wrigley Field** (p77).
- Egging on the frantic geniuses at **ImprovOlympic** (p169).

The Man Who Saved the Lakefront

When Chicagoans frolic at the lakefront's vast expanse of beaches and parks, they should thank Montgomery Ward, founder of the department stores bearing his name, who led an impassioned crusade to save the shore from development.

For two decades beginning in 1890, Ward invested a good chunk of his fortune in legal battles to block various projects that would have used a little bit of the shoreline here and a little bit there until all that would have separated the city from the lake was a wall of buildings. Although he was up against the three forces that have shaped the city – greed, power and corruption – Ward steadfastly defended Chicago's original charter, which stipulated that the lakefront should remain 'forever open, clear and free.' Although his many critics thought of him as a populist dilettante, Ward saw the parks as a 'breathing spot' for the city's teeming masses.

After Ward's death in 1913, many others continued fighting for his cause. They had their work cut out for them, as a steady stream of politicians viewed developing the empty real estate of the lakefront and beaches as 'progress.' For example, during the 1960s Mayor Richard J Daley and his cronies hatched schemes that would have put huge overpasses and cloverleaves at both Oak St Beach and 57th St Beach. Fortunately, both schemes died after massive protest.

ANDERSONVILLE & UPTOWN

Eating p125; Shopping p189

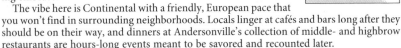

Andersonville comes out of nowhere. On your way up to this northern neighborhood, you'll pass generic street after generic street, middling blah neighborhoods filled with dollar stores and ugly apartments. And just when you think you've run out of cool Chicago – boom! – that's when Andersonville's oasis of charming shops, fun bars, and top-notch eateries envelop you in a welcoming embrace.

The vibe here is Continental with a friendly, European pace that you won't find in surrounding neighborhoods. Locals linger at cafés and bars long after they should be on their way, and dinners at Andersonville's collection of middle- and highbrow restaurants are hours-long events meant to be savored and recounted later.

You can blame some of that Euro-feel on the Swedes, who started building homes here when Andersonville was little more than a cherry orchard. Their legacy continues today in many of the stores, like the butter-lovin' Swedish Bakery (p148). But the Swedes are only partly responsible for the distinct flavor of Andersonville. The blocks surrounding Clark St from about Argyle St through Bryn Mawr Ave have become popular with young professionals. The once-low rents attracted graphic artists and other creative types in the 1980s and '90s. Many lesbians have found a home among the widely varied residents, and rainbow flags commonly flutter alongside the blue and yellow flags of Sweden. The shopkeepers and condo owners may still routinely sweep their sidewalks each day, as per Swedish tradition, but these broom-wielding businesspeople are as likely to be Lebanese or gay as they are the stolid older Nordic residents.

Uptown, the scrappy neighborhood to the south of Andersonville, has a fascinating history with Al Capone and the mob (see the boxed text p80). And before there was Hollywood, there was Uptown. Charlie Chaplin lived here in 1915 when the area was the epicenter of moviemaking in the country. This ragtag area also hides a surprising nook of gorgeous Prairie School homes around Hutchinson St. If you can't make it down to see Frank Lloyd Wright's Robie House (p109) on the South Side, cruise through here to see some amazing work by those he influenced.

Uptown's most recent contributions to the city have been the kind you eat with chopsticks. A myriad of hole-in-the-wall Asian eateries along Argyle St have earned this area the name 'Little Saigon' and made it a mecca for fans of Vietnamese food. Unlike settled Andersonville, Uptown has some rough spots – keep an eye out at night.

Transport

El The Red Line to Berwyn, six blocks east of Clark St, for Andersonville; take the Red Line to Argyle for Argyle St; the Red Line's Lawrence Ave is good for trips to lower Uptown; Red Line to Sheridan for Graceland Cemetery.

Bus 151 runs along Sheridan Rd; 22 travels along Clark St; 80 covers Irving Park Rd; 78 stretches along Montrose Ave.

Parking Meter and on-street parking available in Andersonville and Uptown, though big concerts at the Aragon in Uptown can make things hairy.

Orientation

Most of the bars, restaurants, and shops in Andersonville are along N Clark St, above W Foster Ave. The Lakewood-Balmoral neighborhood sits just east of there, between N Broadway and N Glenwood Ave. Rosehill Cemetery is tucked into the northwest corner of Andersonville.

The exact boundaries of Uptown change depending on who you're talking to, and tend to evaporate entirely if you're talking to image-conscious realtors. In general, Uptown begins below W Foster, reaching as far south as W Irving Park Rd, as far west as N Ashland Ave, and east to Lake Michigan. The 'restaurant row' section of Argyle St is between N Broadway St and N Sheridan Rd.

ARGYLE ST Map p274

Btwn N Broadway St & N Sheridan Rd

Like Andersonville, the neighborhood around Argyle St seems to appear out of nowhere. As you come around the corner from Broadway onto Argyle, suddenly everything – from the stores to the restaurants to the car-detailing shops – is decked out in Laotian, Vietnamese, and Cambodian script. Even the El train station is topped with a pagoda and painted in the auspicious colors of bright green and red. Many of the residents of the area came here as refugees from the Vietnam war, and their presence has solved Chicago city planner's worries about how to reverse the declining fortunes of this Uptown enclave. The storefronts are all filled now (though the area still looks a little scruffy). The several blocks of Argyle St make a good stopover for lunch, or for a half-hour's wandering and window-shopping.

ESSANAY STUDIOS Map p274

1333-1345 W Argyle St

Back before the talkies made silent film obsolete, Chicago reigned supreme as the number one producer of movie magic in the US. In those days Essanay churned out silent films with soon-to-be household names like WC Fields, Charlie Chaplin and Gilbert M Anderson (aka 'Bronco Billy,' the trailblazing star of the brand-new Western genre and co-founder of Essanay). Filming took place at the studio, but it also ventured out into surrounding North Side neighborhoods. At that point, getting the product out the door and into theaters was more important than producing artful, well-made films, so editing was viewed somewhat circumspectly. As a result, it was not uncommon in the early Essanay films to see local Chicago children performing unintentional cameos, or bits of familiar neighborhoods poking into the edge of 'California' mesas. Essanay folded in 1917, about the time that many of their actors were being lured to the bright lights of a still-nascent Hollywood. These days, the building belongs to St Augustine College, but the company's terra-cotta Indian head logo remains above the door at 1345.

GRACELAND CEMETERY Map p274

☎ 773-525-1105; 4001 N Clark St; 🕑 8am-4:30pm

Why go to Memphis to see ostentatious memorials to the dead when you can go to Graceland right in Chicago? The local version is in much better taste and is the final resting place for some of the biggest names in Chicago history. Most of the notable tombs lie around the lake, in the northern half of the 121 acres. Buy a 25¢ map at the entrance to navigate the swirl of paths and streets.

Many of the memorials relate to the lives of the dead in symbolic and touching ways: National League founder William Hulbert lies under a baseball; hotelier Dexter Graves lies under a work titled *Eternal Silence*; and George Pullman, the railroad car magnate who sparked so much labor unrest, lies under a hidden fortress designed to prevent angry union members from digging him up.

Daniel Burnham, who did so much to design Chicago, gets his own island. Photographer Richard Nickel, who helped form Chicago's nascent preservation movement and was killed during the demolition of his beloved Chicago Stock Exchange Building (the 1972 accident was unrelated to the demolition), has a stone designed by admiring architects. Other notables interred here include architects John Wellborn Root, Louis Sullivan and Ludwig Mies van der Rohe (whose sleek, modern tombstone perfectly mirrors his architecture), plus retail magnate Marshall Field and power couple Potter and Bertha Palmer.

HUTCHINSON ST DISTRICT Map pp272–3

Standing in marked contrast to some of Uptown's seedier neighborhoods, the Hutchinson St District is a proud, well-maintained area perfect for a genteel promenade. The homes here were built in the early 1900s, and represent some of the best examples of Prairie-style residences in Chicago. Several of the homes along Hutchinson St – including the one at **839 Hutchinson St** – are the work of George W Maher, famous student of Frank Lloyd Wright. Of special note are the homes at **817 Hutchinson St** and **4243 Hazel St**.

Top Five Andersonville & Uptown

- A game of Scrabble and a fine Belgian ale at the **Hop Leaf** (p165).
- Diving into a bag of velvety rich cookies from the **Swedish Bakery** (p148) and washing them down with tiny cups of free coffee.
- Thirty plays in sixty minutes at Neofuturists' **Too Much Light Makes the Baby Go Blind** (p170).
- Ogling the Prairie-style homes on **Hutchinson St** (p79).
- Celebrating the anniversary of Prohibition's repeal at the classy, historic **Green Mill** (p179).

LAKEWOOD-BALMORAL

These residential blocks draw their name from the two streets they are centered on: Lakewood and Balmoral Aves. You can explore this area when you're walking to and from the El. The houses here all date from the turn of the 20th century. Quite large, they were built as single-family homes for upper-middle-class families who often employed Swedish servants. Among the variety of designs: **5222 N Lakewood Ave** (Map p274), which looks like something out of *Hansel and Gretel*; **5347 N Lakewood Ave** (Map p274), an example of the Craftsman style that emphasized careful detailing; and **St Ita's Church** (Map p274; 1220 W Catalpa Ave), which is in the 13th-century French Gothic style.

Capone's Chicago

Chicagoans traveling the world often experience an unusual phenomenon when others ask where they're from. When they answer 'Chicago,' the local drops into a crouch and yells something along the lines of 'Rat-a-tat-a-tat, Al Capone!' Although civic boosters bemoan Chicago's long association with a scar-faced hoodlum, it's an image that has been burned into the public consciousness by television shows such as *The Untouchables*, movies and other aspects of pop culture.

Capone was the mob boss in Chicago from 1924 to 1931, when he was brought down on tax evasion charges by Eliot Ness, the federal agent whose task force earned the name 'The Untouchables' because its members were supposedly impervious to bribes. (This wasn't a small claim, given that thousands of Chicago police and other officials were on the take, some of them raking in more than $1000 a week.)

Capone came to Chicago from New York in 1919. He quickly moved up the ranks to take control of the city's South Side in 1924. He expanded his empire by making 'hits' on his rivals. These acts, which usually involved bullets shot out of submachine guns, were carried out by Capone's lieutenants. Incidentally, Capone earned the nickname 'Scarface' not because he ended up on the wrong side of a bullet but because a dance-hall fight left him with a large scar on his left cheek.

The success of the Chicago mob was fueled by Prohibition. Not surprisingly, the citizens' thirst for booze wasn't eliminated by government mandate, and gangs made fortunes dealing in illegal beer, gin and other intoxicants. Clubs called 'speakeasies' were highly popular and were only marginally hidden from the law, an unnecessary precaution given that crooked cops usually were the ones working the doors. Commenting on the hypocrisy of a society that would ban booze and then pay him a fortune to sell it, Capone said: 'When I sell liquor, they call it bootlegging. When my patrons serve it on silver trays on Lake Shore Drive, they call it hospitality.'

It's a challenge to find traces of the Capone era in Chicago. The city and the Chicago Historical Society take dim views of Chicago's gangland past, with nary a brochure or exhibit on Capone or his cronies (though the CHS bookstore does have a good selection of books). Many of the actual sites have been torn down; what follows are some of the more notable survivors.

Capone's Chicago Home (7244 S Prairie Ave) This South Side home was built by Capone and mostly used by his wife Mae, son Sonny and other relatives. Al preferred to stay where his vices were. The house looks almost the same today.

Maxwell St Police Station (Map pp286–7; 943 W Maxwell St, two blocks west of Halsted St) This station exemplified the corruption rife in the Chicago Police Department in the 1920s. At one time, five captains and about 400 uniformed police were on the take here.

City Hall (Map pp282–3; 121 N LaSalle St) This building was the workplace of some of Capone's best pals. During William 'Big Bill' Thompson's successful campaign for mayor in 1927, Al donated well over $100,000.

Holy Name Cathedral (Map pp280–1; 735 N State St) Two gangland murders took place near this church. In 1924, North Side boss Dion O'Banion was gunned down in his floral shop (738 N State St) after he crossed Capone. In 1926 his successor, Hymie Weiss, died en route to church in a hail of Capone-ordered bullets emanating from a window at 740 N State.

St Valentine's Day Massacre Site In perhaps the most infamous event of the Capone era, seven members of the Bugs Moran gang were lined up against a garage wall and gunned down by mobsters dressed as cops. After that, Moran cut his losses and Capone gained control of Chicago's North Side vice. The **garage** (Map pp276–7; 2122 N Clark St) was torn down in 1967 to make way for a retirement home, and residents there claim they sometimes hear ghostly noises at night. A house used as a lookout by the killers stands across the street (2119 N Clark St).

Green Mill (Map p274; 4802 N Broadway St) This tavern was one of Capone's favorite nightspots. During the mid-1920s the cover for the speakeasy in the basement was $10. You can still listen to jazz in its swank setting today (see p179).

Mt Carmel Cemetery Capone is now buried in this cemetery in Hillside, west of Chicago. He and his relatives were moved here in 1950. Al's simple gray gravestone, which has been stolen and replaced twice, is concealed by a hedge. It reads 'Alphonse Capone, 1899-1947, My Jesus Mercy.' Capone's neighbors include old rivals Dion O'Banion and Hymie Weiss. Both tried to rub out Capone, who returned the favor in a far more effective manner.

ROSEHILL CEMETERY Map p274

☎ 773-561-5940; Bryn Mawr & Western Aves

The entrance gate to Chicago's largest cemetery is worth the trip alone. Designed by WW Boyington, the same architect who created the old Water Tower on Michigan Ave, the entry looks like a fantastical cross between high Gothic and low Disney. Through the gates, you'll find the graves of many Chicago bigwigs, from Chicago mayors to a US vice president to meat man Oscar Mayer. You'll also discover some of the weirdest grave monuments in the city, including a postal train and an enormous carved boulder from a Georgia Civil War battlefield. More than one ghost story started here; keep an eye out for vapors as night falls.

Rosehill Cemetery

SWEDISH-AMERICAN MUSEUM CENTER Map p274

☎ 773-728-8111; 5211 N Clark St; adult/child $4/2;
🕑 10am-4pm Tue-Fri, 10am-3pm Sat & Sun

The permanent collection at this small storefront museum focuses on the lives of the Swedes who originally settled Chicago. In that sense it reflects the dreams and aspirations of many of the groups who have poured into the city since it was founded. At the museum, you can check out some of the items people felt were important to bring with them on their journey to America. Butter churns, traditional bedroom furniture, religious relics and more are all included in the collection.

UPTOWN THEATRE Map p274

4816 N Broadway; www.uptowntheatrechicago.com

When it opened in 1925, this grand movie theater cheerily billed itself as 'an acre of seats in a magic city.' Among its other magical amenities, Chicago's largest theater boasted a space-age 'freezing and air-washing' plant and a 10,000-pipe organ which the theater owners giddily described as being able to produce 'effects of the sublimest beauty or most humorous imitation of the animal kingdom.' A matinee at the 4381-seat Spanish Baroque Revival behemoth was a rite of passage for many Chicago children. It closed in 1981, but the landmark building is currently slated for a $30 million renovation and reopening as the Uptown Theatre and Center for the Arts.

WICKER PARK/BUCKTOWN & UKRAINIAN VILLAGE

Every Chicago hipster worth their jean jacket has a personal story about how they were almost killed in Wicker Park a decade ago. Those stories – from an era when prostitution, gangs and drive-by shootings defined the area – are recounted with the same sort of nostalgic pride that a grandparent uses to explain that they had to ride cows to school in the olden days. For the days of stray bullets are over, and Wicker Park and Bucktown have shot to the top of the list of happening neighborhoods in Chicago.

Just try to make your way along Milwaukee Ave near Damen Ave on a Friday night, and you'll get a sense for the riotous popularity of the neighborhood. Even in these tough economic times, the clubs and bars here are packed, during the weekend techno dance parties, indie rock concerts and cool author readings all happen within 30 feet of each other. And on any given day, dozens of hip shoe stores, resale shops, boutiques, bookstores, restaurants and salons hold court, providing Chicagoans with the necessary fuel for the modern urban lifestyle.

The neighborhood's transition from slumland to Starbucks didn't happen overnight, though, and there were some memorable snags along the way. In 2001, MTV brought the cast of its reality show *The Real World* to Chicago, renting a Wicker Park loft for the photogenic group. The cameras began rolling, and all seemed to be going according to plan when neighborhood residents, fearing that exposure from the show would speed gentrification, began showing up outside the apartment to protest. What started as a halfhearted, tongue-in-cheek resistance movement soon escalated, and by the time the cast left town there had been eleven arrests and multiple reports of vandalism.

All the hubbub would have been slightly bewildering to the generations of working class Central European immigrants who originally lived in simple wood-frame residences here. Some of the descendants of those original Wicker Park occupants have found a home in Ukrainian Village, just to the south of Wicker Park. This mostly residential, largely working-class area is closer in feel to the Wicker Park/Bucktown of yore (though without quite as many drug dealers or gang members). It's also home to many of the artists and post-college hipsters who were priced out of Wicker Park.

As Wicker Park's more down-to-earth cousin, Ukrainian Village may not be showing up in style magazines, but it's well worth a visit. Especially Division St, on the very north end of the neighborhood, where you'll find an irresistible array of breakfast joints, cutting-edge record stores, one-of-a-kind shops and underground bars. For more on Bucktown shops and Wicker Park's historic homes, see the Walking Tour chapter (p117).

Transport

El Blue Line to Damen Ave for Wicker Park/Bucktown; Blue Line to Division for Ukrainian Village.

Bus 50 runs up Damen Ave; 72 runs along North Ave; 70 travels along Division St.

Parking Meter and free on-street parking at a premium in Wicker Park/Bucktown; widely available in Ukrainian Village.

Orientation

All roads lead to Wicker Park/Bucktown. Or at least three of them do, anyway: Wicker Park is centered at the perpetually packed intersection of N Milwaukee, N Damen and W North Aves. Bucktown stretches north along Damen Ave from the Bloomingdale Ave train bridge. The triangular park itself is a block and a half south of North Ave on Damen. The area's beautiful old homes are immediately northwest of the park, straddling either side of North Ave.

Ukrainian Village is south of Wicker Park. Its northern boundary is the colorful Division St, though most of its sights are located on W Chicago Ave.

WICKER PARK/BUCKTOWN

Eating p125; Shopping p189

FLAT IRON BUILDING Map p275
1579 N Milwaukee

The warren of galleries, studios and workshops in this landmark building have been responsible for a sizable percentage of the artistic zaniness that has long made Wicker Park such a magnet for creative types. Keep an eye on telephone poles around the area for flyers detailing the latest shows and gallery open houses taking place within. (For information on the Around the Coyote Arts Festival, which takes place here every year, see the City Calendar p12)

NELSON ALGREN HOUSE Map p275
1958 W Evergreen Ave

In this house, a three-flat one block south of the park, writer Nelson Algren created some of his greatest works about gritty life in the neighborhood. Algren won the 1950 National Book Award for his novel *The Man with the Golden Arm*, set on Division St near Milwaukee Ave. You can't go in to the house on Evergreen, but you can admire it from the street.

POLISH MUSEUM OF AMERICA Map p275
☎ 773-384-3352; 984 N Milwaukee Ave; adult/senior & student $2/1; ◑ 11am-4pm Fri-Tue

If you don't know Pulaski from a pierogi, this is the place to get the scoop on Polish culture. The museum is the oldest ethnic museum in the US, and while you won't find high-tech 3D virtual rollercoaster rides or IMAX screens, you will get a chance to learn about some of the Poles who helped shape Chicago's history. (Pulaski, by the way, was a Polish hero in the American Revolution).

ST MARY OF THE ANGELS CHURCH
Map p275
☎ 773-278-2644; 1850 N Hermitage Ave

With a dome modeled on St Peter's in Rome, the huge St Mary of the Angels dominates both

Louis Sullivan–designed home, Wicker Park

Bucktown and the view from the Kennedy Expressway. Built with money from Polish parishioners prodded by a zealous pastor, the church features angels on the parapet, in the nave and possibly in the heavens above as well.

Certainly the church is blessed, as proven by its ability to cheat death. Only 60 years after its completion in 1920, its maintenance costs – which had gone through the holey roof – and its declining membership made it a prime candidate for an early demise. But a grassroots campaign arose to save the church, drawing support from the community and people across the city. In 1992 the repairs, which cost more than the original construction bill, were completed, and the invigorated parish has drawn many new members.

WICKER PARK Map p275
Intersection of N Damen Ave & W Schiller St
Sure, Chicago invented the zipper and a handful of other useless bric-a-brac. The city's true legacy, though, will be in a strange softball game invented here. Aptly named, 16-Inch Softball uses the same rules as normal softball, but with shorter games, a bigger, squishier ball and a complete lack of gloves or mitts on the fielders. They've been playing it here for over 75 years, and there's even an online Hall of Fame (www.chi16in-halloffame.com). Wicker Park is a prime place to see the uniquely Chicago sport played by die-hard fanatics. And for

travelers suffering withdrawal from the pooch left at home, Wicker Park's dog park is a great way to get in some quality canine time.

UKRAINIAN VILLAGE
Eating p125; Shopping p189
SAINTS VOLODYMYR & OLHA CHURCH Map p275
☎ 312-829-5209; 739 N Oakley Blvd
Liturgical differences led the traditionalists at St Nicholas (see below) to build the showy Saints Volodymyr & Olha Church in 1975. It makes up for its paucity of domes – only five – with a massive mosaic showing the conversion of Grand Duke Vladimir of Kiev to Christianity in AD 988.

ST NICHOLAS UKRAINIAN CATHOLIC CATHEDRAL Map p275
☎ 773-276-4537; 2238 W Rice St
The cathedral is the less-traditional of the neighborhood's main churches. Its 13 domes represent Christ and the Apostles. The intricate mosaics – added to the 1915 building in 1988 – owe their inspiration to the Cathedral of St Sophia in Kiev.

UKRAINIAN INSTITUTE OF MODERN ART Map p275
☎ 773-227-5522; www.uima-art.org; 2320 W Chicago Ave; admission free; ⌚ noon-4pm Wed, Thu, Sat & Sun
The 'Ukrainian' in the name is somewhat of a misnomer, as this bright white storefront showcases local artists regardless of ethnicity (along with a host of works by people of Ukrainian descent). The space has earned a reputation for putting together some of the best exhibits in Chicago. Shows here range from playfully pretty to perplexingly cerebral works, done in a host of media.

Top Five Wicker Park/ Bucktown & Ukrainian Village

- Shopping for vintage clothes along **Milwaukee Ave** (p202).
- Costa Rican burritos and an oatmeal shake at **Irazu** (p150).
- Pouring over all the weird, wonderful local comics and magazines at **Quimby's** (p212).
- Boutique browsing along **Damen** (p202).
- A late breakfast on one of the cool places on **Division St** (p148).

Get Your Beach On

The Gold Coast's Oak St Beach is just one of the sandy expanses that stretch along the lake, making Chicago the Miami of the Midwest (if only for a few months each year). The city's best beaches, from north to south:

Loyola Beach (Map pp270–1) which runs for more than eight blocks from North Shore Ave to Touhy Ave, features an upscale wooden playgrounds for kids. It's fairly close to the Chicago International Hostel and the Loyola El stop.

Montrose Beach (Map pp270–1) is a great wide beach with a curving breakwater. The Montrose Harbor bait shop sells ice for coolers. There's ample parking, but the walks to the beach can be long. To get there by bus, take No 146 or No 151.

Fullerton Beach (Map pp276–7) fills with Zoo day-trippers and Lincoln Parkers. The narrow beach can get jammed on weekends, but a five-minute walk south from Fullerton yields uncrowded vistas.

North Ave Beach (Map pp276–7) is the closest thing Chicago has to a Southern California beach. Countless volleyball nets draw scores of beautiful people wearing the latest skimpy, neon-hued thongs. The steamship-inspired beach house contains a seasonal café. A short walk out on the curving breakwater anytime of the year yields postcard views of the city from a spot that seems almost a world apart.

Oak St Beach (Map pp278–9) lies at the north end of Michigan Ave, less than five minutes from the Water Tower. The hulking Lake Shore Dr condos cast shadows in the afternoon, but this popular beach remains packed.

Ohio St Beach (Map pp280–1), nestled between Lake Shore Dr and Navy Pier, is convenient for those who want a quick dip or a chance to feel some sand between sweaty toes.

12th St Beach (Map pp284–5, hidden east of Meigs Field and south of the Adler Planetarium, makes a great break from the myriad sights of the Museum Campus. Its out-of-the-way location gives the narrow enclave an exclusive feel.

57th St Beach (Map pp288–9), just across Lake Shore Dr from the Museum of Science and Industry, features an expanse of clean, golden sand.

Jackson Park Beach (Map pp288–9), a bit further south of 57th St beach, contains a stately, recently restored beach house with dramatic breezeways. This beach, next to the yacht harbor, has a charm lacking at the beaches with more modern – and mundane – facilities.

WEST SIDE

The scene outside the moniquemeloche gallery in the West Loop is about what you'd expect from one of Chicago's hottest art districts. Mod ladies pick at fussy salads on the patio of Follia, just named Chicago's best new restaurant. A couple of black-clad guys in punishing German eyewear discuss post-minimalism over a microbrew at the Fulton Lounge. And a man in rubber boots stands across the street, meditatively hosing blood out of the back of his truck.

Wait just a second there...

But yes, you saw it right. In the West Loop, one of the West Side's up-and-coming neighborhoods, the city's meatpackers and gallery owners exist side-by-side. As weird as it all seems at times, it works. The incongruous pairing of blue collar and black turtleneck is typical for many of the neighborhoods on Chicago's West Side, a patchwork of hard-to-define neighborhoods that includes Little Italy, Greektown and the West Loop, as well as the notoriously rough neighborhoods like Lawndale and Garfield Park further out.

The constant in the West Side is change. In Little Italy (which deserves the diminutive name, consisting as it does these days mostly of Taylor St), the main agent of change is the University of Illinois, Chicago. The school has teamed up with the city and developers to put in new housing throughout the sometimes-iffy neighborhood. As the UIC has been remaking the neighborhood – so has it been remaking itself. The infamous recipient of one of the ugliest campuses known to humankind (see University of Illinois, Chicago p86), the university has been healing some old architectural wounds with an extensive remodeling plan.

North of Little Italy, Greektown offers little in the way of sights. Gustatory tourists, though, will revel in the flavors here; the area has enough Greek tavernas and cafés to make Zeus feel at home. No matter how triumphant your *tsatsiki*, though, it can't compare with the amazing dish of greens they've cooked up at the Garfield Park Conservatory. When, in 1994, the Conservatory announced plans to do a top-to-bottom renovation of the disintegrating facilities there, it seemed laughable. Ten years later, the long-shot plan of revitalizing one of the country's biggest plant houses in one of the city's worst neighborhoods has been an unmitigated success.

Safety is definitely a consideration when visiting many sites on the West Side. The areas discussed here are OK during the day, and some are OK at night as well. Individual cautions, as well as transportation options, are covered in each neighborhood section. If you have a car, you can cover the entire area in an afternoon.

Orientation

No two ways about it, the West Side is huge. And we're only covering a small portion of it here. If you don't have a car, the distances between neighborhoods are painfully vast. Walking is also impeded by annoying obstructions like Highway 290, which makes an easy stroll between Greektown and Little Italy all but impossible. Unless you're a talented long-distance runner, use cabs to get from place to place.

The West Loop area is the northernmost of the West Side neighborhoods we cover. Its main arteries are W Randolph and W Washington Sts, with Halsted St cutting north–south along its eastern edge. Greektown lives just three blocks south on Halsted from where Halsted meets W Washington. If you just keep heading south on Halsted, you'll pass the smoggy, traffic clogged roundabouts of Highway 290, and find the northeastern edge of the UIC campus. Hull House is just a block south, and Taylor St, the main thoroughfare for Little Italy, is one long block south from Hull House. Again, taking a cab through these areas will save you a lot of time, and prevent you from walking through some sketchy neighborhoods on Taylor St near Halsted.

Transport

El Green Line to Clinton for the West Loop; Blue Line to Clinton for Greektown; Blue Line to Polk for Little Italy; Green Line to Conservatory-Central Park Dr for Garfield Park Conservatory.

Bus 20 runs Loop-bound along Washington St, returns along Monroe St; 8 travels along Halsted St.

Parking West Loop free parking is plentiful, especially in the afternoon; Greektown parking can be tough to find but valets abound; Little Italy is fine for free on-street parking.

WEST LOOP

Eating p125

BATCOLUMN Map pp286–7

600 W Madison St

Artist Claes Oldenburg – known for his gigantic shuttlecocks in Kansas City and oversized cherry-spoon in Minnesota – delivered this simple, controversial sculpture to Chicago in 1977. The artist mused that the 96ft bat 'seemed to connect earth and sky the way a tornado does.' Hmm... See it for yourself in front of the Harold Washington Social Security Center.

CHICAGO FIRE DEPARTMENT ACADEMY Map pp286–7

☎ 312-747-7239; 558 W DeKoven St

Rarely has a public building been placed in a more appropriate place: the fire department's school stands on the very spot where the 1871 fire began – between Clinton and Jefferson Sts. Although there's no word on whether junk mail still shows up for Mrs O'Leary, the acad-emy trains firefighters so they'll be ready the next time somebody or some critter kicks over a lantern (see the boxed text Don't Look at Me – It Was the Cow p48). If you call in advance on weekdays, you might be able to watch some training exercises.

HAYMARKET RIOT MONUMENT

Map pp286–7

1300 W Jackson Blvd

On May 4, 1886, striking factory workers held a meeting at Haymarket Square, at Randolph, between Halsted and Des Plaines Sts west of the Loop. Toward the end of the meeting a mob of police appeared, things quickly degenerated into chaos, and a bomb exploded, killing one policeman and wounding several others. Police began to fire shots into the dispersing crowd, and by the end of the day, six more policemen had been shot and killed (most shot down accidentally by other policemen) and sixty others were injured. Despite the fact that the identity of the bomb-thrower was never known, eight anarchist leaders were convicted of inciting murder, and four were hanged for the crime (a fifth was sentenced, but committed suicide in his cell).

Public sentiment worldwide favored the striking workers, who were demanding an eight-hour workday and were the victims of efforts by the factory owners and their police lackeys to discredit them.

In memory of the seven dead cops, a statue was erected on the spot some years later: a stilted officer standing with arm upraised, commanding peace 'in the name of the people of Illinois.' The statue has since had a history almost more violent than the event it commemorates. Thieves made away with the plaques at its base several times, and shortly after the turn of the 20th century a bus driver rammed it, claiming to be sick of seeing it every day. In 1928 it was moved several blocks west, to Union Park, where it stood peacefully until the uproarious 1960s, when it was blown up twice. Repaired yet again, the statue has found a home in the courtyard of the Chicago Police training center. Stop at the duty desk and say you're there to see the statue. The men convicted of the bombing have become martyrs for the contemporary anarchist and labor activist movements; the monument near their graves at the **Forest Home Cemetery** (Map pp286–7; ☎ 708-366-1900; 863 S Des Plaines Ave, Forest Park) is a popular pilgrimage site.

OLD ST PATRICK'S CHURCH Map pp286–7
☎ 312-648-1021; www.oldstpats.org; 700 W Adams St
A Chicago fire survivor, this 1852 church is the city's oldest and one of its fastest-growing, thanks to the strategies of its politically connected pastor, Father Jack Wall. Old St Pat's is best known for its year-round calendar of social events for singles, including the enormously popular World's Largest Block Party, a weekend-long party with big-name rock bands where Catholic singles can flirt with each other. (No less an authority than Oprah has proclaimed the block party the best place to meet one's match.) The social programs have boosted Old St Pat's membership from four (yes, four) in 1983 to thousands two decades later. The domed steeple signifies the Eastern Church; the spire signifies the Western Church. Call to find out when the church is open so you can see the beautifully restored Celtic-patterned interior, which was originally built by parishioners well over a century ago.

Old St Patrick's Church

UNITED CENTER Map pp286–7
☎ 312-455-4650; www.unitedcenter.com; 1901 W Madison St
Built for $175 million and opened in 1992, the United Center arena is home to the Bulls and the Blackhawks (see p184) and is the venue for special events such as the circus. The statue of an airborne Michael Jordan in front of the east entrance pays a lively tribute to the man whose talents financed the edifice. The center, surrounded by parking lots, is OK by day but should be avoided at night – unless there's a game, in which case squads of cops are everywhere in order to ensure public safety. **Tours** (☎ 312-455-4650 ext 244; tours $20; 15 person minimum) wind their way through the concourse, press box and scoreboard control room.

UNIVERSITY OF ILLINOIS AT CHICAGO Map pp286–7
☎ 312-996-7000
UIC used to be a much more interesting place to visit for all the wrong reasons. Noted Chicago architect Walter Netsch created a design that provoked extreme protests when it opened. Netsch proclaimed that it was his goal to re-create the sense of wonder one feels when exploring an Italian hill village, but the realities of Netsch's design were unremittingly grim. Imagine a maximum security prison without the barbed wire and you have the right idea. By the mid-1980s the whole ugly place was falling

apart and despised by its 30,000 students and faculty. In 1990 a massive rebuilding program began to eradicate much of Netsch's hill town. His voice of protest was lone.

The **University Center Housing & Commons** (700 S Halsted St), an attractive undergraduate dorm that welcomes people onto the campus, became the first major building to break with the past. In the last decade the campus has become a pleasant place to go to school, but there's no reason to make a special trip there. However, if you don't go to the campus, it might just come to you. It has jumped south of Roosevelt Rd in a big way, in the process gobbling up the historic Maxwell St Market and many other surrounding blocks.

The **Jane Addams Hull House** (☎ 312-413-5353, 800 S Halsted St; admission free; ⏰ 10am-4pm Mon-Sat, noon-5pm Sun) has a much warmer reputation than Netsch's work. In 1889, at age 29, Jane Addams founded Hull House to provide day-care facilities, a kindergarten, an employment bureau and many other social services to masses of exploited and hopeless Eastern European immigrants. She also provided space where the burgeoning labor unions could meet. She won the Nobel Peace Prize for her efforts in 1931. She died in 1935, but Hull House continues her work at locations around the city.

UIC has preserved Addams' house, along with the 1905 dining hall where neighborhood residents could come for hot meals. A 15-minute slide show on the second floor of the dining hall details Addams' work. Displays document the struggle for social justice waged by Hull House and others in the first half of the 20th century.

WEST LOOP GALLERIES

The residents and realtors are still battling for naming rights to this area of meat processors, cool galleries, and chic restaurants. Some say West Loop; others West Loop Gate. And a small number of loft-dwellers just call it home. Either way, the neighborhood galleries – which radiate out from Peoria and Washington Sts– show the kind of maverick, risk-taking art that the established River North galleries won't touch.

You can wander from gallery to gallery all day, but our picks for the best stops include **Gallery 312** (Map pp286–7; ☎ 312-942-2500; 312 N May St; ⏰ 11am-5pm Tue-Sat), one of the largest of the West Loop galleries, and one of the most creative. Check out the finger puppets in their tiny gift store. Located on one of the busiest meatpacking streets in the neighborhood, **moniquemeloche** (Map

pp286–7; ☎ 312-455-0299; 951 W Fulton St; ⏰ noon-6pm Tue-Fri, 11am-6pm Sat) shows about 50% works by young Chicago artists, while the other half is international. **Bodybuilder & Sportsman** (Map pp286–7; ☎ 312-492-7261; 119 N Peoria St; ⏰ 11am-6pm Tue-Sat) was awarded 'best gallery for emerging artists' status by *Chicago* magazine in 2003. The shows in their small space often blend elements of humor and commentary. Upstairs from Bodybuilder & Sportsman, **Gallery 1R** (Map pp286–7; ☎ 312-738-3915; 119 N Peoria St; ⏰ 1pm-6pm Tue, 11am-6pm Thu-Sat) began as an informal space for art in Pilsen before moving to the West Loop. The art shown here is usually by local students. **Vendanta** (Map pp286–7; ☎ 312-432-0708; 835 W Washington St; ⏰ 10am-6pm Tue-Fri, 11am-5pm Sat) is an energetic force on the young Chicago art scene, and **Donald Young Gallery** (Map pp286–7; ☎ 312-455-0100; 933 W Washington St; ⏰ 10am-5:30pm Tue-Fri, 11am-5:30pm Sat) serves as the West Loop's venerable anchor, showcasing work by well-known artists like Sophie Calle and Dan Flavin.

The West Loop Gallery walking tour (p112) can help navigate through the art on offer here.

Top Five West Side

- Hungrily eyeing the chocolate and vanilla plants in the Sweet House room of the **Garfield Park Conservatory** (p88).
- Stumbling across tomorrow's star artists today in the **West Loop galleries** (p87).
- Keeping a watch for Oprah while digging into a plate of eggs at **Wishbone** (p153).
- Grabbing two Polish dogs from **Jim's Original** (p151) and eating them in your car.
- Taking in a Bulls game at **United Center** (p185).

LITTLE ITALY

Eating p125

PIAZZA DIMAGGIO Map pp286–7

The area south of the Eisenhower Expressway to Roosevelt Rd was a thriving Italian community until the 1950s, when several blows almost killed it. The expressway itself was rammed through the most vibrant part of the neighborhood, the surviving commercial area was demolished for the campus of the University of Illinois at Chicago, and several public housing projects were scattered through what was left. Many people still suspect that the old

Mayor Daley intended the entire scheme as retribution for the schemes of rival politicians.

Perhaps out of sheer stubbornness, the Italian residents hung on, supporting a commercial district on Taylor St. Meanwhile, professionals drawn to the university and the fast-growing Chicago Medical Center to the west discovered the tree-lined streets of the neighborhood. Beginning in the 1970s, gentrification transformed old homes and added new townhouses. And now that the city has spent vast sums beautifying Taylor St, the neighborhood is set to take off.

Although clearly slated for demolition, the remaining blighted housing projects remain a safety concern; visitors to the area should take care to avoid stretches that go from safe to grim in a block. Be extra careful around the blocks between Racine Ave and Loomis St on Taylor St, and in the areas west of Damen Ave and south of Roosevelt Rd.

Taylor St preserves many old Italian family businesses. As part of the city's beautification campaign, a portion of S Bishop St that meets Taylor St has been converted into Piazza DiMaggio, in honor of Joe DiMaggio, the Italian-American baseball star. Directly across the street is the future home of the **National Italian American Sports Hall of Fame**, which is bound to include more on DiMaggio.

GARFIELD PARK
GARFIELD PARK CONSERVATORY
Map pp270–1

☎ 312-746-5100; 300 N Central Park Blvd; admission free; ☷ 9am-5pm

With 4½ acres under glass, the Park District's pride and joy, built in 1907, seemed like a lost cause in 1994. Located far away from the heart of the city, in a neighborhood that tended to scare away visitors, the Conservatory nevertheless began a multi-million dollar restoration campaign. By 2000, it was completed, and the crowds have been pouring in ever since. One of the original designers, Jens Jensen, intended for the 5000 palms, ferns and other plants to re-create what Chicago looked like during prehistoric times. Today the effect continues, all that's missing is a rampaging stegosaurus. The Economic House features a fascinating range of plants that are used for food, medicine and shelter. New halls contain displays of seasonal plants, which are especially spectacular in the weeks before Easter. A children's garden lets kids play with plants that aren't rare or irreplaceable, and a Demonstration Garden was added in 2002 to help answer the questions of the wide-eyed urban gardeners who come here. If you drive, note that the neighborhood is still not the safest.

PILSEN
Eating p125

You won't be in the Windy City for two minutes before a proud resident sidles up to you and explains that, 'You can travel all around the world without ever leaving Chicago.' The best way to respond to these delusional rantings is to nod, smile and back away very, very slowly. For while Chicago boasts a number of thriving ethnic communities, none of them offer the immersive feel of being in another land entirely.

None of them, that is, except for Pilsen. Pilsen is the center of the Latino world in Chicago, and a trip to this convenient neighborhood really is like stepping into the streets of a foreign country. Pilsen thumps with *tejano* and brassy mariachi music, and the streets flow with the sounds of Spanish. The salsas here scald, the moles soothe, and the sidewalks are filled with umbrella'd food carts that tempt passers-by with a rainbow array of cold, pulpy *agua frescas* and spicy-sweet *verduras* (thin slices of melon or cucumber dusted with a chili-powder kick).

Chicago's hipster underground has also been quietly relocating here for the last decade. The area around 18th and Halstead Sts has become a hub for storefront art galleries and painter's spaces. Even the taste-making record label Thrill Jockey has its offices here. (Look for a vintage Mick Jagger poster in a window on 18th St and you've found them.) The mix of MFA-wielding sculptors and

Transport
El Blue Line to 18th St.

Bus 9 travels north–south between Pilsen and Irving Park Rd.

Parking is plentiful on side streets.

recent Spanish-speaking immigrants has been a mostly amiable one, and places like the Jumping Bean give both camps a place to eat, relax and whup each other in games of chess.

The architecture of the neighborhood is another draw. The original Czechoslovakian and Central European settlers here modeled their three-flats and storefronts from the world they'd left behind. In Pilsen, you can also see the city's old vaulted sidewalks, especially along 18th Pl, where one old cottage after another features a front yard several feet below the level of the sidewalks. (The streets were later raised to allow for the construction of sewers.)

Pilsen does have its rough spots, though if you stick to the main drags, you'll be fine. So fine, in fact, that artists and the Latino residents are becoming nervous about the future of their neighborhood. '¡Defienda Pilsen!' ('Defend Pilsen!') graffiti appears on walls from time to time, a call to arms against the gentrification transforming neighborhoods to the north. For now, though, Pilsen exists under developers' radars, and life continues apace in one of Chicago's coolest neighborhoods.

Orientation

The parts of Pilsen you'll be exploring are limited to the corridor of 18th St, between Halsted St on the far east end and Wolcott Ave on the west. Most of the restaurants and stores cluster around 18th St's intersection with Ashland Ave. The Mexican Fine Arts Museum is located in Harrison Park, a five-minute walk west from the bulk of the other attractions. Many of the storefront galleries are on the eastern end of 18th St, where Hwy 90/94 cuts through the neighborhood.

COOPER DUAL LANGUAGE ACADEMY Map pp286–7
1645 W 18th Pl

The exterior wall of the academy is the canvas for a 1990s tile mosaic that shows a diverse range of Mexican images, from a portrait of farmworker advocate Dolores Huerta to the Virgin of Guadalupe. Each summer art students add more panels.

MEXICAN FINE ARTS CENTER MUSEUM Map pp286–7
☎ 312-738-1503; www.mfacmchicago.org; 1852 W 19th St; admission free; ☀ 10am-5pm Tue-Sun

Founded in 1982, this vibrant museum has become one of the best in the city. Housed in a renovated field house in Harrison Park, the gleaming exhibit space tackles a bewilderingly complex task (summing up a thousand years of Mexican art and culture), and pulls it off beautifully. The art here ranges from classical-themed portraits to piles of carved minibus tires. The turbulent politics and revolutionary leaders of Mexican history are well represented, including works about Cesar Chavez and Emiliano Zapata. A truly wonderful find. The museum also sponsors readings by top authors and performances by musicians and artists. And if you are in town during the fall, be sure to check out the exhibits and celebrations relating to November 1, the Day of the Dead, a traditional Mexican holiday that combines the festive with the religious. The events take place for a month on either side of the day.

PILSEN UNDERGROUND GALLERIES

Few of them answer their phones, most are only open on Saturdays, and almost all of them are located in the 'curator's' living room. However unconventional their working methods, Pilsen's galleries play a vital role in the city's art scene. This is where young artists have their debuts, and where established artists can display genre-bending, conceptual pieces that would never be allowed in the pristine 'white cubes' of West Loop or River North galleries. The galleries tend to be open from noon to 5pm on Saturday only, and most will have a sign out front explaining their hours and instructions for entry ('Ring our doorbell' is a common one).

Some of the more established spaces include **SixFourFive** (Map pp286–7; ☎ 312-491-1897; 645 W 18th St) and Michael Thomas' **Dogmatic** (Map pp286–7; ☎ 312-492-6698; 1822 S Des Plaines St), both of which have been pushing boundaries (and buttons) in the Chicago art world for years. Newcomer **Unit B** (Map pp286–7; ☎ 312-491-9384; 1733 S Des Plaines St) shows paintings and photos in its bright space. **Bucket Rider** (Map pp286–7; ☎ 312-421-6933; 565 W 18th St) displays conceptual pieces in a split-level space. A recent memorable show turned the entire place into a life-size dollhouse.

ST ADALBERT CHURCH Map pp286–7
1650 W 17th St

This 1914 church features 185ft steeples, and is a good example of the soaring churches built by Chicago's ethnic populations through thousands of small donations from parishioners, who would cut family budgets to the bone to make their weekly contribution. The rich ornamentation in the interior of this Catholic church glorifies Polish saints and religious figures.

ST PIUS CHURCH Map pp286–7
1901 S Ashland Ave
The Poles had St Adalbert's; the Irish had St Pius, a Romanesque Revival edifice built between 1885 and 1892. Its smooth masonry contrasts with the rough stones of its contemporaries. Catholics of one ethnic group never attended the churches of the others, which explains why this part of town, with its concentration of Catholic immigrants, is thick with steeples.

THALIA HALL Map pp286–7
1807 S Allport St
Named for the Greek muse of comedy, who casts a bemused gaze from a spot in the arch over the entrance, Thalia Hall brought out the bohemian side of the Czech immigrants, who

used it for theater and music productions. Socialists also used it as a rallying place back in the late 1800s; some of the Haymarket Riot testimony centered on meetings held here, and the rabble-rousing anarchist Emma Goldman preached to the assembled masses from the stage. Its interior theater was modeled after that of the Old Opera House in Prague. Sadly, the building hosts little more than pigeons these days.

Top Five Pilsen

- Gulping down a strawberry *agua fresca* from one of the innumerable food carts along **18th St** (p153).
- Tearing into the al pastor pork at **Nuevo Leon** (p154).
- Learning about the Mexican avant-garde at the awesome **Mexican Fine Arts Center Museum** (p89).
- Spending a Saturday in strangers' living rooms on a tour of Pilsen's **underground galleries** (p89).
- Losing a game of chess to a local master at **Cafe Jumping Bean** (p154).

SOUTH LOOP & NEAR SOUTH SIDE

The Chicago crane, a species that once thrived throughout the city, now resides primarily south of the Loop. No, we're not talking about shorebirds here. These are the 100ft tall building cranes, the kind whose presence means only one thing for a neighborhood: dramatic change is coming.

And it is. The South Loop – which includes the lower ends of downtown and Grant Park along with the historic Printer's Row and Dearborn Park neighborhoods – started the trend in the 1980s. During that time, the South Loop's beautiful, derelict old buildings became homes and super-convenient launching pads for Chicago's downtown workers. Suddenly, the area was alive again. Booming. And the ongoing renovations of the Museum Campus area added further polish onto a newly gleaming neighborhood.

Developers' eyes then turned southward, towards the Black, poor neighborhoods just inland from the Field Museum, Soldier Field, and McCormick Place convention center. Chicago's early millionaires like Marshall Field and George Pullman built their stately mansions along Prairie Ave here in the late 1800s. But when they packed up for the Gold Coast a decade later, the rest of Chicago's money moved with them. By the 1950s, the Near South Side had turned into a bleak zone of boarded up storefronts and dangerous streets.

That era for the Near South Side officially ended in 1993, when Mayor Daley surprised everyone by moving from Bridgeport to the Near South Side townhouse development called Central Station. And now the city's wealthy are following his example and flocking to a neighborhood that's been ignored for the last five decades.

The sudden influx of wealthy Whites into a formerly impoverished area makes for a very surreal scene. The steel skeletons of high-rise lofts and luxury condos have sprouted up everywhere, but essentials like grocery stores, cafés and restaurants haven't yet followed.

It gives the Near South Side the feel of a play caught between acts – one set already disappearing as another hastily takes its place.

A few sections of the Near South Side, though, have remained constant through the decades of change. The Prairie Ave historic district still offers an intimate look at the glorious homes that set the tony tone here a hundred years ago. And Chinatown continues to bustle day and night – as it has for years – with the Chicagoans who flock to the ethnic enclave for bubble teas, dim sum, and heaping bowls of spicy noodles.

Orientation

The blocks here are long, and, for the time being anyway, uncongested. The South Loop extends between Congress Pkwy in the north and Roosevelt Rd in the south. Printer's Row and Dearborn Park are both part of the South Loop, while the plethora of developments south of Roosevelt Rd fall under the Near South Side jurisdiction. The Museum Campus is located along Lake Shore Dr, on the strip's eastern edge. S Michigan Ave – a far more sedate version of its charmingly opulent cousin to the north – connects the Loop to the Prairie Ave Historic District. Highway 55 runs across the southernmost edge of the Near South Side.

Transport

El Green, Orange and Red Lines to Roosevelt for Printer's Row or Museum Campus/Soldier Field; Red Line to Cermak-Chinatown for Chinatown.

Metra Roosevelt Rd stop for Museum Campus/Soldier Field; 18th St for Prairie Ave Historic District; McCormick Place North Building for McCormick Place.

Bus 29 to Printer's Row; 12 to Museum Campus/Soldier Field; 4 to Prairie Ave Historic District; 21 to Chinatown.

Parking The Museum Campus boasts plenty of lot parking; meter parking available but scarce in South Loop and readily available in Near South Side.

SOUTH LOOP

Eating p125; Shopping p189; Sleeping p215

ADLER PLANETARIUM Map pp284–5

☎ 312-922-7827; www.adlerplanetarium.org; at the end of Solidarity Dr; adult/child/senior $13/11/12, discount for Chicago residents, free Mon & Tue Jan-Feb & mid-Sep–late Dec; ⊙ 9am-6pm Sat-Wed, 9am-9pm Thu-Fri, shorter hours Sep-Apr

The first planetarium built in the western hemisphere, the Adler Planetarium & Astronomy Museum has seen visitor numbers soar in recent years. From the entrance to the Adler, visitors descend below the 1930 building, which has 12 sides, one for each sign of the zodiac. In the newest wing, a digital sky show re-creates such cataclysmic phenomena as supernovas. Interactive exhibits allow you to simulate cosmic events such as a meteor hitting the earth (this one is especially cool). The original planetarium does a good job planning special events around celestial occurrences, be they eclipses or NASA missions. In the Sky Theater a mechanical Zeiss projector can create huge varieties of nighttime sky effects.

The Adler does a commendable job of involving visitors in astronomy, with live video links to various telescopes around the world and research facilities that are totally accessible to visitors. The sky-show programs

last about 50 minutes. The whole place can be easily covered in less than two hours. A cafeteria serves all the usual stomach-filling burgers and sandwiches.

Near the entrance to the Adler, a **12-foot sundial** by Henry Moore is dedicated to the golden years of astronomy, from 1930 to 1980, when so many fundamental discoveries were made using the first generation of huge telescopes. About 100 yards west in the median, the bronze **Copernicus statue** shows the 16th-century Polish astronomer Nicolaus Copernicus holding a compass and a model of the solar system.

FIELD MUSEUM OF NATURAL HISTORY Map pp284–5

☎ 312-922-9410; www.fieldmuseum.org; 1400 S Lake Shore Dr; adult/child/senior & student $10/5/7, some exhibits extra, discount for Chicago residents, free Mon & Tue Jan-Feb & mid-Sep–late Dec ⊙ 9am-5pm, last admission 4pm

With over 70 PhD-wielding scientists and 20 million artifacts, you know things are going to be hopping at the Field Museum. The big attraction here is the *Tyrannosaurus rex* named Sue, a 13ft-tall, 41ft-long beast who menaces the grand space with ferocious aplomb. Sue, the most complete *T. rex* ever discovered, takes its name from Sue Hendrickson, the fossil-hunter who found the 90%-complete skeleton in South Dakota in 1990.

The head honchos at the Field know how large dinosaurs loom in the grade-school imagination, which is why Sue is just one of many dinosaur-related exhibits here. You can also watch staff paleontologists clean up fossils, learn about the evolution of the massive reptiles, and even learn about *Homo sapiens'* evolutionary ties to the extinct beasts. The Dinosaur Hall contains a range of real and replica skeletons of the beasts who measure their age in the tens of millions. While the Dinosaur Hall is set to close for remodeling in 2004, exhibits, including Big Sue, will remain on show.

A clever blend of the fanciful with a large amount of Field artifacts, the 'Inside Ancient Egypt' exhibit re-creates an Egyptian burial chamber on three levels. The mastaba (tomb) contains 23 actual mummies and a reconstruction of the one built for Unis-ankh, the son of the last pharaoh of the Fifth Dynasty, who died at age 21 in 2407 BC. The bottom level, with its twisting caverns, is especially worthwhile. Those reeds growing in the stream are real.

Other displays worth your time include 'Underground Adventure,' a vast exhibit exploring the habitats of animals and insects that live underground, and 'Life Over Time,' where animatronic exhibits actually make learning about single-celled organisms fun.

MERRILL C MEIGS FIELD Map pp284–5

Just south of the Adler Planetarium, the once-busy commuter airport Meigs Field now lies silent. Mayor Daley had long lobbied for the closing of the airport, suggesting with increasing vehemence that the valuable real estate should be converted into a park. After meeting continued resistance from the

Top Five South Loop & Near South Side

- Soaking in the atmosphere and music at the **Velvet Lounge** (p179).
- Satisfying your inner shutterbug at the **Museum of Contemporary Photography** (p92).
- Slurping noodles out of a fresh pineapple at **Joy Yee's** (p156).
- Communing with the pipsqueak (well, sort of) Beluga whales at the **Shedd Aquarium** (p93).
- Making scary faces at Sue, the *Tyrannosaurus Rex*, in the **Field Museum of Natural History** (p91).

airfield's users, Daley plowed ahead in a controversial incident described in the History chapter under the heading King Richard the Second's Reign Continues (p44). But the anger has already died down over the incident, and it's only a matter of time before Meigs becomes green again. The nearby Burnham Park yacht harbor completes this increasingly bucolic picture.

MUSEUM OF CONTEMPORARY PHOTOGRAPHY Map pp284–5

☎ 312-663-5554; www.mocp.org; 600 S Michigan Ave; admission free; ☽ 10am-5pm Mon-Fri, to 8pm Thu, noon-5pm Sat

Located in one of the many buildings of Columbia College, this museum focuses on American photography since 1959. Once primarily a venue for student work, it has won widespread support as the only institution of its kind between the coasts. The permanent collection includes the works of Debbie Fleming Caffery, Mark Klett, Catherine Wagner, Patrick Nagatani and 500 more of the best photographers working today. Special exhibitions augment the rotating permanent collection.

OLMEC HEAD NO 8 Map pp284–5

Near the Field Museum, the city has installed Olmec Head No 8. Over 7ft tall, it's a copy of one of the many amazing stone carvings done by the Olmec people more than 3500 years ago in what is now the Veracruz state of Mexico. No one has been able to figure out how the Olmec carved the hard volcanic rock.

PRINTER'S ROW

Chicago was a center for printing at the turn of the century, and the rows of buildings on Dearborn St from Congress Pkwy south to Polk St housed the heart of the city's publishing industry. By the 1970s the printers had left for more economical quarters elsewhere, and the buildings largely emptied out, some of them barely making it on the feeble rents of obscure nonprofit groups.

In the late 1970s savvy developers saw the potential in these derelicts, and one of the most successful gentrification projects in Chicago began. The following describes some of the notable buildings in the area as you travel from north to south.

A snazzy renovation of the **Mergenthaler Lofts** (Map pp284–5; 531 S Plymouth Court), the 1886 headquarters for the legendary linotype company, included the artful preservation of a diner storefront. The **Pontiac Building** (Map pp284–5; 542 S Dearborn St), a classic 1891 design by Holabird & Roche, features the same flowing masonry surfaces as the firm's Monadnock Building, to the north.

A massive and once-windowless wreck, the 1911 **Transportation Building** (Map pp284–5; 600 S Dearborn St) enjoyed a 1980 restoration that assured that the neighborhood had arrived. The **Second Franklin Building** (Map pp284–5; 720 S Dearborn St), a 1912 factory, shows the history of printing in its tiled facade. The roof slopes to allow for a huge skylight over the top floor, where books were hand-bound, for this building existed long before fluorescent or high-intensity lamps did. The large windows on many of the other buildings in the area serve the same purpose.

Once the Chicago terminal of the Santa Fe Railroad, the 1885 **Dearborn St Station** (Map pp284–5; 47 W Polk St) used to be the premier station for trains to and from California. Today it merely sees the trains of parent-propelled strollers from the Dearborn Park neighborhood, built on the site of the tracks to the south.

SHEDD AQUARIUM Map pp284–5

☎ 312-939-2438; www.shedd.org; 1200 Lake Shore Dr; pass to all exhibits adult/child & senior $21/15, aquarium-only ticket adult/child & senior $8/6, discount for Chicago residents; ☼ 9am-6pm, shorter hours Sep-May

The world's largest assortment of finned, gilled, amphibious and other aquatic creatures swims within the marble-clad confines of the John G Shedd Aquarium. Though it could simply rest on its superlative exhibits – beluga whales in a four million-gallon aquarium anyone? – the Shedd makes a point of trying to tie concepts of ecosystems, food webs and marine biology into its presentation of super-cool animals. Permanent exhibits include the multilevel Oceanarium, which mimics ocean conditions off the northwest coast of North America. The beluga whales inside are remarkably cute creatures that come from the pint-size end of the whale scale. Their humped heads and natural 'smiles' make them look eerily human. You'll also see Pacific white-sided dolphins, harbor seals, and sea otters. Don't linger only on the main floor – you can go underneath the cement seats and watch the mammals from below through viewing windows. The 'Wild Reef' exhibit will have sharkophiles and sharkophobes equally entranced; over a dozen sharks cut through the waters in a simulation of a Philippines reef ecosystem. And the 'Amazon Rising' exhibits offers a captivating look at a year in the Amazon River and rain forest. Some of the newer and special exhibits sell out early in the morning; consider buying tickets through the website beforehand to ensure entry.

The stretch of grass on the lake between the Shedd and the Adler may be the setting for more amateur and postcard photos than any other place. One look toward the skyline will show you why: the view is good year-round; on clear days in winter, when the lake partially freezes and steam rises off the buildings in the Loop, it verges on the sensational.

JOHN G. SHEDD AQUARIUM

SOLDIER FIELD Map pp284–5

South of the Field Museum is Soldier Field. Built from 1922 to 1926, the oft-renovated edifice has been home to everything from civil rights speeches by Martin Luther King Jr to Chicago Fire soccer games. It got its latest bursting-at-the-seams look in a controversial 2003 makeover.

SPERTUS MUSEUM Map pp284–5

☎ 312-922-9012; www.spertus.edu; 618 S Michigan Ave; adult/child $5/3, free Fri; ☾ 10am-5pm Sun-Wed, 10am-7pm Thu, 10am-3pm Fri

An excellent small museum devoted to 5000 years of Jewish faith and culture, the Spertus boasts an equally excellent corps of volunteers. The museum's exhibits juxtapose aspects of Jewish life and religion to convey the diversity of both. The Zell Holocaust Memorial – the country's first permanent museum exhibition of its kind – features oral histories from survivors who immigrated to Chicago, as well as the names of Chicagoans' relatives who died.

The museum mounts well-curated special exhibitions that cover topics as diverse as Biblical images in classical art and Jewish humor in the US. The basement is devoted to a children's area called the ARTiFACT Center, where kids can conduct their own archeological dig for artifacts of Jewish life.

THADDEUS KOSCIUSKO MEMORIAL

Map pp284–5

Western end of median btw Adler Planetarium & Shedd Aquarium

Near the western end of the median, the Thaddeus Kosciusko Memorial honors the Polish general who fought on the winning side of the American Revolution and then returned to help his nation's fight for freedom. This and the Copernicus statue inspired the city to rename the street Solidarity Dr in 1980 to honor the Lech Walesa-led movement in Poland.

NEAR SOUTH SIDE

Eating p125; Shopping p189; Sleeping p215

CHINATOWN

To experience the full charm of Chinatown, wander its streets and browse in its many varied small shops, especially in the retail heart of the neighborhood, on Wentworth Ave south of Cermak Rd. Other interesting parts include Cermak Rd itself and Archer Ave just to the north. The neighborhood is one of the city's most vibrant, and its affluent residents are developing land in all directions even as more immigrants continue to arrive.

The Cermak-Chinatown El stop on the CTA Red Line is just to the east of the action. East of the stop itself is a dicey area dominated by a housing project. But the busy streets of Chinatown itself tend to be safe.

The **On Leong Building** (Map pp284–5; 2216 S Wentworth Ave) once housed various neighborhood service organizations and some illegal gambling operations that have led to spectacular police raids. It now houses the Chinese Merchants Association. Built in 1928 and also known as the Pui Tak Center, the grand structure is a fantasy of Chinese architecture that makes good use of glazed terra-cotta details. Note how the lions guarding the door have twisted their heads so they don't have to risk bad luck by turning their backs to each other.

On much of the rest of Wentworth you'll find a blend of typical Chicago and Chinese architecture. The characteristic arch near Cermak Rd was added in the 1970s, and amateur political scientists can study the 'Four basic values of a nation' inscribed on the back of it. The continually growing **Chinatown Square** (Map pp284–5; Archer Ave at Cermak Rd) dates from 1992 and features some of the area's best restaurants.

HILLARY RODHAM CLINTON WOMEN'S PARK Map pp284–5

Fronting on Prairie Ave, with the Glessner House to the north and the Clarke House to the west (see Prairie Ave Historic District p95), the 4-acre park is named for former first lady, now US Senator Hillary Rodham Clinton, who grew up in suburban Park Ridge and calls herself a lifelong Cubs fan (though that slipped her mind when she also pledged her loyalty to both the Mets and the Yankees in her successful bid to become a New York senator). Since Clinton dedicated the park in 1997, landscapers have added a French garden, fountain and winding paths. As bright as its future looks, the park has a notorious past. The Fort Dearborn massacre, in which some Native Americans rebelled against the incursion of white settlers, is thought to have occurred on this very spot on August 15, 1812.

MCCORMICK PLACE Map pp284–5

☎ 312-791-7000; www.mccormickplace.com; 2301 S Lake Shore Dr

Called the 'mistake by the lake' before the new Soldier Field renovation stole the title, the McCormick Place convention center is an economic engine that drives up profits for the city's hotels, restaurants, shops and airlines. 'Vast' isn't big enough to describe it, nor 'huge,' and 'enormous' doesn't work, so settle for whatever word describes the biggest thing you've ever seen. The 2.2 million sq ft of meeting space spreads out over three halls, making this the largest convention center in the country.

The East Building (now called Lakeside Center) interrupts the sweep of the lakefront. The oldest part of today's complex, it was completed to replace the original fireproof McCormick Place, which burned down in 1967. The *Chicago Tribune* played a disgraceful role in the original building's construction, with its owner Col Robert R McCormick using all of his hefty political weight to get it built on the lake. (Politicians who opposed the project were threatened with investigative stories.)

The North Building, a barn of a place, accrued huge cost overruns during its construction in 1986. The newest addition, the South Building, was finished in 1997. The best of the lot, it features the Grand Concourse, a bright and airy hall linking all the buildings.

It's easy to get a cab to and from McCormick Place. A great insider's tip is the 23rd St Metra train station, hidden in the lowest level of the North Building. Trains to and from the Randolph St and Van Buren St Stations, in the Loop, stop often during rush hour. Midday Monday through Saturday, they depart from Randolph St at 20 minutes past the hour and take seven minutes to reach McCormick Place. Parking can be a hike from the buildings and is expensive. The main entrance to McCormick Place now lies on Martin Luther King Jr Dr, just north of the Stevenson Expressway.

NATIONAL VIETNAM VETERANS ART MUSEUM Map pp284–5

☎ 312-326-0270; 1801 S Indiana Ave; adult/child $5/4; ☺ 11am-6pm Tue-Fri, 10am-5pm Sat, noon-5pm Sun

Opened in 1996, the National Vietnam Veterans Art Museum displays the art of Americans who served in the military during the war in Vietnam. Spread over three floors in an old commercial building, it features a large and growing collection of haunting, angry, mournful and powerful works by veterans.

Cleveland Wright's *We Regret to Inform You* is a heartbreaking look at a mother in her kitchen at the moment she learns of her son's death. Joseph Fornelli's sculpture *Dressed to Kill* comments on the role of the average grunt in Vietnam. Some 58,000 dog tags hang from the ceiling, a haunting reminder of the Americans who died in the war. A small café here serves snacks.

PRAIRIE AVE HISTORIC DISTRICT

By 1900 Chicago's crème de la crème had had enough of the scum de la scum in the nearby neighborhoods. Potter Palmer led a procession of millionaires north to new mansions on the Gold Coast. The once-pristine neighborhood, which lined Prairie Ave for several blocks south of 16th St, fell into quick decline as one mansion after another gave way to warehouses and industry. Thanks to the efforts of the Chicago Architecture Foundation, a few of the prime homes from the area have been carefully restored. Streets have been closed off, making the neighborhood a good place for a stroll. A footbridge over the train tracks links the area to Burnham Park and the Museum Campus.

House on Prairie Ave

The **John J Glessner House** (Map pp284–5; ☎ 312-326-1480; 1800 S Prairie Ave; tours adult/child $11/7, free Wed; ☺ tours 1pm & 3pm Wed-Sun) is the premier survivor of the neighborhood. Famed American architect Henry Hobson Richardson took full advantage of the corner site for this beautiful composition of rusticated granite. Built from 1885 to 1887, the L-shaped house, which surrounds a sunny southern courtyard, got a hundred-year jump on the modern craze for interior courtyards. Much of the home's interior looks like an English manor house, with heavy wooden beams and details. More than 80% of the current furnishings are authentic, thanks to the Glessner family's penchant for family photos.

Tours of the Glessner House include the nearby **Henry B Clarke House** (Map pp284–5; 1827 S Indiana Ave), the oldest structure in the city. When Caroline and Henry Clarke built this imposing Greek Revival home in 1836, log cabins were still the rage in Chicago residential architecture. The sturdy frame paid off, because during the past 160 years the house has been moved twice to escape demolition. The present address is about as close as researchers can get to its somewhat undefined original location. The interior has been restored to the period of the Clarkes' occupation which ended in 1872.

Generally, you can't visit the following houses, but you still can admire them from the outside. Modeled after 15th-century French châteaus, the **William K Kimball House** (Map pp284–5; 1801 S Prairie Ave) dates from 1890 to 1892. Both it and the Romanesque **Joseph G Coleman House** (Map pp284–5; 1811 S Prairie Ave) next door now serve as the incongruous headquarters for the US Soccer Federation. Limestone puts a glitzy facade on the brick **Elbridge G Keith House** (Map pp284–5; 1900 S Prairie Ave), an early 1870 home that is now home to the **Woman Made Gallery** (☎ 773-489-8900), a space dedicated to promoting works by women artists.

SECOND PRESBYTERIAN CHURCH
Map pp284–5

☎ 312-225-4951; 1936 S Michigan Ave; call for hours
Designed by James Renwick, the architect of St Patrick's Cathedral in New York and Washing-ton DC's original Smithsonian Institution build-ing, the 1874 church is a neo-Gothic limestone celebration accented by Tiffany stained glass.

WILLIE DIXON'S BLUES HEAVEN
Map pp284–5

☎ 312-808-1286; 2120 S Michigan Ave; admission $10 incl tour; ☉ noon-2pm Mon-Sat, reservations required
From 1957 to 1967, this humble building was the home of the legendary Chess Records, a temple of blues and a spawning ground of rock and roll. The Chess brothers, two Polish Jews, ran the recording studio that saw – and heard – the likes of Muddy Waters, Bo Diddley, Koko Taylor and others. Chuck Berry recorded four Top 10 singles here, and the Rolling Stones named a song '2120 S Michigan Ave' after a recording session at this spot in 1964. (Rock trivia buffs will know that the Stones named themselves after the Muddy Waters song 'Rolling Stone.')

Today the building belongs to Willie Dix-on's Blues Heaven, a nonprofit group set up by the late blues great who often recorded at the studios to promote blues and preserve its legacy. A gift store is open in front, while the old studios are upstairs. There are many artifacts on hand as well.

More often than not visitors will meet AJ Tribble, Blues Heaven docent and Willie Dixon's nephew. During summer, concerts happen at 6pm every Thursday in the open space next door to the building.

Neighborhoods – South Loop & Near South Side

Chinatown (p94)

SOUTH CHICAGO

A complete history of the rise and fall of the various empires of Chicago's far South Side (including Bronzeville, Bridgeport, Hyde Park, Kenwood and Pullman) reads a little like a Wagner opera. Powerful leaders, decadent wealth, palaces, paupers, epic battles, grand ideas, supernatural destruction and ignominious defeats. From the dark history of Chicago's massive slaughterhouses to the blinding dawn of the nuclear age on a Hyde Park squash court, the personalities of the South Side have long served as a guiding force in the city's fortunes, and, to some extent, the country's destiny.

That era, for the most part, is over. This part of town, south of the Stevenson Expressway and east of the Dan Ryan Expressway, has had a tough time since WWII. Whole neighborhoods have vanished, with crime and blight driving residents away. The construction of the vast wall of housing projects along the east side of the Dan Ryan Expressway created huge impoverished neighborhoods where community ties broke down and gangs held sway.

But the news isn't all bad. Armchair historians will find some intriguing traces of the South Side gone by. Bronzeville – home to a Black artistic renaissance in the 1940s and 50s that rivaled Harlem – boasts a handful of worthwhile sights. Irish Bridgeport, former site of the infamous stockyards and the 1968 Democratic Convention debacle, is a must for fans of Mayor Daley. Pullman (see the boxed text p108) offers a rare look at a capitalists' utopian dream. Kenwood's historic homes look better than ever, and the gargoyle-filled Gothic campus of the University of Chicago in Hyde Park offers visitors more Nobel-lauded brainiacs per square inch than any other place on Earth.

The slow pace and lack of things to do means that South Chicago shouldn't be at the top of anyone's tourist agenda. But if you find yourself curious about Chicago's powerful past, there's plenty here to discover.

Orientation

You'll need a car for a visit to Bronzeville and Bridgeport. Conveniently, Highway 90/94, the Dan Ryan Expressway, offers a high-speed route to both neighborhoods. Bronzeville's main drag is S Martin Luther King Dr (though some of the historic sites are three blocks to the west along S Indiana Ave). Bridgeport is just west of Bronzeville, on the other side of Highway 90/94. When you see Comiskey Park you'll know you're almost there. The Bridgeport neighborhood runs between 31st St in the north and 43rd St in the south.

For Hyde Park and Kenwood, skip the highway and take Lake Shore Dr, exiting at 57th Dr (also the Museum of Science and Industry exit). Kenwood is located immediately north of Hyde Park, between S Drexel Blvd to the west, E Hyde Park Blvd to the south, and the lake to the east.

Transport

El Green Line to 35th St/Bronzeville/IIT for Bronzeville or IIT; Red Line to Sox/35th for Bridgeport.

Bus 1 runs down Michigan Ave to Bronzeville; 8 travels along Halsted St in Bridgeport; 6 runs from State St in the Loop to 57th St in Hyde Park.

Metra 53rd St station for Kenwood; 57th St station for Hyde Park.

Parking Bronzeville has plenty of on-street parking, as does Bridgeport (except for when the White Sox are playing); finding a space in Kenwood isn't a problem, but Hyde Park can be tight. Free parking is available on the street and in University parking lots after 4 pm weekdays and all day on weekends. If you're really stumped in Hyde Park, look south of the Midway Plaisance.

Hyde Park is flanked by two huge parks, Washington Park in the west and Jackson Park, where the Museum of Science and Industry is located, to the east. The two parks are connected by the Midway Plaisance, a long green strip of land and accompanying boulevards that run along the south edge of the University of Chicago campus. The intersection of 57th St and S University Ave is a great place to start your explorations of the University of Chicago campus.

BRONZEVILLE
HISTORIC BUILDINGS

Once home to Louis Armstrong and other notables, Bronzeville thrived as the vibrant center of Black life in the city from 1920 to 1950, boasting an economic and cultural strength that matched that of New York's Harlem. Shifting populations, urban decay and the construction of the wall of public housing along State St led to Bronzeville's decline. The same forces that led to the neighborhood's decline can make visiting the area a cautious endeavor. Plan to come with a car during the daytime; it's best to totally avoid the area at night.

Examples of stylish architecture from the past can be found throughout Bronzeville, but note that some of the buildings are in miserable shape and aren't worthy of more than an inspection of the exterior. You can see some fine old homes along two blocks of Calumet Ave between 31st and 33rd Sts, an area known as 'The Gap.' The buildings here include Frank Lloyd Wright's only row houses, the **Robert W Roloson Houses** (Map pp270–1; 3213-3219 S Calumet Ave).

One of scores of Romanesque houses that date from the 1880s, the **Ida B Wells House** (Map pp270–1; 3624 S Martin Luther King Dr) is named for its 1920s resident. Wells was a crusading journalist who investigated lynchings and other racially motivated crimes. She coined the famous line: 'Eternal vigilance is the price of liberty.'

Gospel music got its start at **Pilgrim Baptist Church** (Map pp270–1; ☎ 312-842-5830; 3301 S Indiana Ave), originally built as a synagogue from 1890 to 1891. It has a classic exterior that only hints at the vast and opulent interior.

The **Supreme Life Building** (Map pp270–1; 3501 S Martin Luther King Dr), a 1930s office building, was the spot where John H Johnson Jr, the publishing mogul who founded *Ebony* magazine, got the idea for his empire, which also includes *Jet* and other important titles serving African Americans. Behind the porcelain-metal exterior panels lies a classic decorative facade.

In the median at 35th St and Martin Luther King Jr Dr, the **Victory Monument** (Map pp270–1) was erected in 1928 in honor of the Black soldiers who fought in WWI. The figures include a soldier, a mother and Columbia, the mythical figure meant to symbolize the New World.

Pig Problems

In *The Jungle*, Upton Sinclair described the Chicago stockyards this way: 'One could not stand and watch very long without becoming philosophical, without beginning to deal in symbols and similes, and to hear the hog-squeal of the universe.'

These were slaughterhouses beyond compare. By the early 1870s they processed more than one million hogs a year and almost as many cattle, plus scores of unlucky sheep, horses and other critters. It was a coldly efficient operation. The pigs themselves became little more than a way to turn corn into a denser, more easily transportable substance that was thus more valuable.

The old saying – that once the animals were in the packing houses, everything was used but the squeal – was almost true. Some bits of pig debris for which no other use could be found were fed to scavenger pigs, who turned the waste into valuable meat. But vast amounts of waste were simply flushed into the south branch of the Chicago River, and it then flowed into the lake. Beyond the aesthetic and health problems that ensued, the packers had to contend with other consequences of their pollution.

Meat processed in Chicago was shipped in ice-packed railroad cars to the huge markets in the East. The ice was harvested from lakes and rivers each winter and then stored for use all year long. But ice that was taken from the Chicago River returned to its stinky liquid state as it thawed over the meat on the journey east, thus rendering the carcasses unpalatable. The packers finally had to resort to harvesting their ice in huge operations in unpolluted Wisconsin.

ILLINOIS INSTITUTE OF TECHNOLOGY

Map pp270–1 ☎ 312-567-3000; 3300 S Federal St

A world-class leader in technology, industrial design and architecture, IIT owes much of its world-famous look to legendary architect Ludwig Mies van der Rohe, who fled the Nazis in Germany for Chicago in 1938. From 1940 until his retirement in 1958, Mies designed 22 IIT buildings that all reflect his tenets of architecture, which combine simple metal frames painted black with glass and brick infills. The star of the campus and Mies' undisputed masterpiece is **SR Crown Hall** (3360 S State St), appropriately home to the College of Architecture. The building, close to the center of campus, appears to be a transparent glass box floating between its translucent base and suspended roof. At night it glows from within like an illuminated jewel.

(Continued on page 107)

1 Scene from Chicago Marathon
2 One of Chicago's finest 3 Wave
Swinger ride, Navy Pier (p68)
4 Cubs fan, Wrigley Field (p77)

1 City on the lake 2 City on the river 3 Museum of Science and Industry (p108), Hyde Park 4 PK Wrigley statue, the Loop

1 *Chicago River cruises (p59)*
2 *Detail on a building, Chinatown*
3 *Detail on Marshall Field & Co building (p191), the Loop*
4 *Wrigley Building (p39), Near North*

1 Frank Lloyd Wright's Robie House (p109), Hyde Park 2 Art gallery, Pilsen (p89) 3 Museum of Contemporary Art (p72), Gold Coast 4 Art gallery, Near North (p69)

1 Butterfly in the Peggy Notebaert Nature Museum (p76), Lincoln Park 2 Vendor outside Wrigley Field 3 Lincoln Park (p74) 4 ImprovOlympic (p169), Lake View

1 Caton St (p117), Wicker Park
2 Mexican Fine Arts Center
Museum (p89), Pilsen 3 Quimby's
(p212), Wicker Park 4 Church,
Ukrainian Village

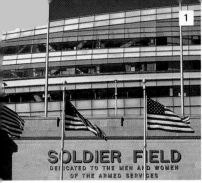

1 Soldier Field (p94), South Loop
2 Tombs of Potter Palmer and William Goodman, Graceland Cemetery (p79), Uptown 3 Adler Planetarium (p91), South Loop
4 Illinois Institute of Technology (p98), Bronzeville

1 *Lincoln Park (p74)* 2 *Old St Patrick's Church (p86), West Loop* 3 *In the Loop* 4 *Street musicians, Gold Coast*

(Continued from page 98)

BRIDGEPORT

UNION STOCKYARDS GATE Map pp270-1
850 W Exchange Ave

Bridgeport is more important for its historical role in the city than for its ability to draw tourists. The stockyards were once a major attraction, but they are long closed and their land is being rapidly covered by new warehouses and industry. The traditional home of Chicago's Irish mayors (this is where the Daley dynasty grew up), Bridgeport remains an enclave of descendants of Irish settlers. A few Chinese and Hispanic people have moved in, but many African Americans, who live to the south and east, feel that they're not welcome here. While a number of residents say that Bridgeport is more tolerant now than in its past, it will probably never live down its role in the 1919 race riots, when neighborhood thugs went on a killing spree after a Black youth on a raft floated too close to a 'White' beach.

Halsted St from 31st St south to 43rd St is Bridgeport's rather uninteresting main drag. Most of the neighborhood lies west of the huge train embankment that itself is west of Comiskey Park. However, Bridgeport extends north of the park all the way to Chinatown and makes for a good walk after a game if you're in a group and don't stray east of the Dan Ryan Expressway.

A tiny vestige of the stockyards stands just west of the 4100 block of S Halsted St. The Union Stockyards Gate was once the main entrance to the vast stockyards where millions of cows and almost as many hogs met their ends each year. The value of those slaughtered in 1910 was an enormous $225 million. Sanitary conditions were eventually improved from the hideous levels documented by Upton Sinclair (see the boxed text p98), although during the Spanish-American war, American soldiers suffered more casualties because of bad cans of meat from the Chicago packing houses than because of enemy fire.

KENWOOD

KEHILATH ANSHE MA'ARIV-ISAIAH ISRAEL TEMPLE Map pp288-9
☎ 773-924-1234; 1100 E Hyde Park Blvd;
call for opening times

Also called KAM Synagogue, this is a domed masterpiece in the Byzantine style. Its acoustics are said to be perfect.

S WOODLAWN AVE

The beautiful neighborhood just north of Hyde Park is best toured by car. A mix of middle-class and wealthy Whites and Blacks, including some famous names, make their homes in the many large and imposing mansions.

Many classic homes old and new line the gracefully shaded Woodlawn Ave, including the **Isidore Heller House** (Map pp288-9; 5132 S Woodlawn Ave), an 1897 Frank Lloyd Wright house with the characteristic side entrance. The house at **4944 S Woodlawn Ave** (Map pp288-9) was once home to Muhammad Ali. The bodyguards around the 1971 **Elijah Muhammad House** (Map pp288-9; 4855 S Woodlawn Ave) indicate that Nation of Islam leader Louis Farrakhan currently lives here.

HYDE PARK
Eating p125; Shopping p189

DAVID & ALFRED SMART MUSEUM OF ART Map pp288-9
☎ 773-702-0200; http://smartmuseum.uchicago.edu;
5550 S Greenwood Ave; admission free; 10am-4pm Tue-Fri, 11am-5pm Sat & Sun

Named after the founders of *Esquire* magazine, who contributed the money to get it started, the official fine arts museum of the university opened in 1974 and expanded in 1999. The 8000 items in the collection include some excellent works from ancient China and Japan and a colorful and detailed Syrian mosaic from about AD 600. The strength of the collection lies in paintings and sculpture contemporary to the university's existence. Auguste Rodin's *Thinker* occupies a thoughtful place (hey, it's the Smart museum), as do works by Arthur Davies, Jean Arp, Henry Moore and many others.

DUSABLE MUSEUM OF AFRICAN AMERICAN HISTORY Map pp288-9
☎ 773-947-0600; www.dusablemuseum.org;
740 E 56th Place; adult/child/senior & student; $3/1/2, free Sun; 10am-5pm Mon-Sat, noon-5pm Sun

In a peaceful part of Washington Park, this museum features more than 100 works of African American art and permanent exhibits which cover African Americans' experiences from slavery through the civil rights movement. The museum, housed in a 1910 building, takes its name from Chicago's first permanent settler, Jean Baptiste Pointe du Sable, a French-Canadian of Haitian descent (see History p45).

Neighborhoods – South Chicago

MUSEUM OF SCIENCE AND INDUSTRY Map pp288–9

☎ 773-684-1414; www.msichicago.org; 5700 S Lake Shore Dr; adult/child/senior $9/5/7.50; ☺ 9:30am-4pm Mon-Fri, 9:30am-5:30pm Sat & Sun, shorter hours Sep-May

This overstimulating museum will defeat even the most rambunctious six-year-old. (If you're older than six, give in now, as you don't stand a chance). Nine permanent exhibits thoroughly examine everything on earth, from cerebral concepts like the passage of time to basic questions about the origins of breakfast cereal. Visitors can climb through a German U-boat captured during WWII and press their noses against the window of the Apollo 8 command module. Some of the museum's most famous exhibits are also its simplest. The 'Human Body Slices' exhibit consists of a man and a woman who died in the 1940s – their bodies cut in half-inch sections then pressed between pieces of glass. Eeew, we know. But amazing all the same.

Top Five South Chicago

- Grokking the cool (but kind of gross) **body slices** (p108) at the Museum of Science and Industry.
- Bookstore hopping along **E 57th St** (p213) in Hyde Park.
- Scoping those clean Prairie School lines at the **Robie House** (p109).
- Crashing out with a good book in the old-fashioned, Harry Potter-esque **William Rainey Harper Memorial Library** (p110).
- Wandering through a fallen utopia in **Pullman** (p108).

The main building of the museum served as the Palace of Fine Arts at the landmark World's Columbian Exposition in 1893, which was set in the surrounding Jackson Park. When you've had your fill of space capsules, coal mines, and Zephyrs at the museum, the park makes an excellent setting to recuperate.

Pullman

George Pullman's dream community turned into a nightmare when idealism ran headlong into capitalism in 1894. The millionaire rail-car manufacturer started this namesake town in 1880 in order to provide his workers with homes in a clean and wholesome environment. He built houses, apartments, stores, a hotel and churches, all of which were meant to return 6% on his investment.

Pullman earned kudos from both industrialists and social activists. The town's careful design was based on French models and featured an aesthetic that was unknown in workers' housing then or now. But the 1893 depression hit Pullman's luxury rail-car business hard. The firm laid off some workers and cut the pay of others. Rents and prices in Pullman's town stayed high, however, to ensure the 6% profit.

Worker resentment grew and resulted in the Pullman strike of 1894. Violent clashes between the strikers and thugs hired by Pullman were finally settled when federal troops were sent in to force the strikers back to work. It was another turning point for the American labor movement, which had been fueled by the 1886 Haymarket Riot.

Pullman died a bitter man in 1897. The following year, the Illinois Supreme Court ordered the company to sell the town except for the factories. The sale of the town's properties was completed by 1907, and the neighborhood has experienced ups and downs since then. The last part of the complex finally closed for good in 1981.

The southern part of Pullman, where the higher-paid craftsmen and managers lived, has been largely bought up by people determined to preserve it. North Pullman, with simpler housing for laborers, is only now being appreciated for its underlying architectural qualities.

Visit Pullman in the daytime so you can appreciate the buildings. Start with the **Hotel Florence** (11111 S Forrestville Ave), a striking Queen Anne building that is currently undergoing restoration.

The **Colonnade Apartments** (112th St at Champlain Ave), four matching curved 1892 apartment buildings, surround the former market hall. The tiny bachelors' apartments upstairs were obviously not intended for men who expected company.

A rambling complex with varied rooflines, the **Pullman Administration Building and Clock Tower** (111th St at Cottage Grove Ave) is solidly French in conception. A fire in 1998 nearly destroyed the building. The state of Illinois is moving forward – albeit at a glacial pace – with plans to restore the complex and create a railroad museum.

If you're driving, take I-94 south to the 111th St exit. Pullman is a half-mile west. By Metra, go to 111th St station. The **Historic Pullman Foundation** (☎ 773-785-8901; www.pullmanil.org; 11141 S Cottage Grove Ave; ☺ noon-2pm Sun-Fri, 11am-2pm Sat) offers information on the complex and leads occasional walking tours as well. Call for info.

Frank Lloyd Wright's Robie House

ROBIE HOUSE Map pp288–9

☎ 773-834-1847; 5757 S Woodlawn Ave; adult/child & senior $9/7; ⏱ tours 11am, 1pm & 3pm Mon-Fri, continuous tours 11am-3:30pm Sat & Sun

This masterpiece is the ultimate expression of Frank Lloyd Wright's Prairie School style; it makes the otherwise charming surrounding houses look like so many dowdy old aunts. The long, thin Roman bricks and limestone trim mirror the same basic shape of the entire house. The long and low lines, which reflect Midwest topography, are ornamented solely by the exquisite stained- and leaded-glass doors and windows.

The materials used to construct the house were as revolutionary as the design. Poured concrete forms the basis of many of the floors and balconies, while steel beams support the massively overhanging roof – a radical concept for residential construction. Tours of the interior take in the entire house, save the upper floor and servants' quarters. Note that Wright, a control freak if there ever was one, used built-in furniture, windows and other details to prevent the owners from messing with his interior design vision. A gift shop with books and other mementos operates in the garage.

A Bomb Is Born

At 3:53pm on December 2, 1942, Enrico Fermi looked at a small crowd of men around him and said, 'The reaction is self-sustaining.' The scene was a dank squash court under the abandoned football stadium in the heart of the University of Chicago. With great secrecy, the gathered scientists had just achieved the world's first controlled release of nuclear energy. More than one sigh of relief was heard amid the ensuing rounds of congratulations. The nuclear reactor was supposed to have been built in a remote corner of a forest preserve 20 miles away, but a labor strike had stopped work. The impatient scientists went ahead on campus, despite the objections of many who thought the thing might blow up and take a good part of the city with it. Places such as Los Alamos in New Mexico and Hiroshima and Nagasaki in Japan are more closely linked to the nuclear era, but Chicago is where it began.

UNIVERSITY OF CHICAGO Map pp288–9

☎ 773-702-1234; 5801 S Ellis Ave

Some universities collect football championships. The University of Chicago collects Nobel Prizes – 74 to the year 2002. In particular, the economics department has been a regular

109

winner, with faculty and former students pulling in 22 prizes since the first Nobel for economics was awarded in 1969. Merton Miller, a U of C economics faculty member and a Nobel winner, explained the string of wins to the *Sun-Times*: 'It must be the water; it certainly can't be the coffee.'

The university's classes first met on October 1, 1892. John D Rockefeller was a major contributor to the institution, donating more than $35 million, which he called 'the best investment I ever made in my life.' The original campus was constructed in an English Gothic style. Highlights of a campus tour include the **Rockefeller Memorial Chapel** (5850 S Woodlawn), the exterior of which will send sculpture-lovers into paroxysms of joy – the facade

bears 24 life-size and 53 smaller religious figures, with even more inside. The **William Rainey Harper Memorial Library** (1116 E 59th St) is another must-see. The long row of arched, two-story windows bathe the 3rd-floor reading room with light and an almost medieval sense of calm. The **Bond Chapel** (1050 E 59th St) is equally serene. Built in 1926, the exquisite 300-seat chapel is the harmonious creation of the architects, sculptors, woodcarvers and glassmakers who worked together on the project.

On Ellis Ave, between 56th and 57th, sits the 1968 Henry Moore bronze sculpture, **Nuclear Energy**, marking the spot where Enrico Fermi and company started the nuclear age (see the boxed text p109).

Walking Tours

Walking Tours

WEST LOOP GALLERY WALK

Tucked between meatpacking plants and warehouses, the galleries of the West Loop are the beachhead for contemporary art in Chicago. The scene in the neighborhood is like nowhere else in the city. Loop-bound bike messengers zip through the rutted streets, dodging chicken-laden semis and beef-toting forklifts, as art patrons carefully make their way over loading docks on their way from one gallery to the next.

Though the galleries here may be less established than their River North peers, the lower rents mean that young galleries can afford to have larger showrooms and take bigger chances on up-and-coming and controversial artists. So lace up your walking shoes and set that black beret at a rakish tilt – it's time to explore art, Chicago-style.

The West Loop, located between the Clinton and Ashland stops on the Green line, is awkward to reach via public transportation. If you don't mind the seven-block walk east along Lake St from the Ashland stop, go for it. If you'd rather save your energy for rigorous art-contemplation (our recommendation), take a cab. Regardless, we'll start our tour on May St between Fulton and Grand, at **Gallery 312 1** (p87).

Walk Facts

Start Taxi direct to Gallery 312, or Green Line to Ashland, walk east seven blocks on Lake St, making a left on May St
End Taxi from Checker Cab offices, or walk up Washington St to S Clinton St. Left on S Clinton walk to Clinton stop on El
Distance 0.9 miles
Duration 2 hours

You'll have to be buzzed in here; if nothing happens the first time you ring the doorbell, give it a second go. (The curators are likely on the phone or downstairs in the gallery.) After wending your way through the labyrinth of hallways, you'll slip into one of the best places for art in the West Loop. Gallery 312's interconnected rooms showcase intriguing, non-stuffy contemporary art from local artists. Whether it's made from Astroturf, computer chips or roe-bound-stones, the work here is well crafted and thought provoking.

When you're done at Gallery 312, head back down May St and make a left on Fulton St. This is one of the main streets for meatpacking and meat-sorting factories in the city, and if you're here before 3pm, you'll likely see hordes of men in white butcher coats, standing out front of the businesses, overseeing the arrival and departure of the day's meat. Look in the windows of **Morlen Sinoway Atelier 2** (☎ 312-432-0100; 1052 W Fulton) and **Function + Art 3** (☎ 312-243-2780; 1046 W Fulton) as you pass. If you see anything that catches your eye, stop in. Otherwise, continue up Fulton. At the intersection of Fulton and Morgan, you can see the anchor of the neighborhood, the multistory Fulton Market Cold Storage (motto: 'WE BOX LOOSE MEAT'). Note as well, the neighbor at 1044 – the lofts with their high-end barbecue grills on the balconies are a sign of yuppie things to come in the neighborhood.

On the south side of the street is the next stop, **moniquemeloche 4** (p87). That's Monique sitting at the desk. Her multilevel gallery has been here since 2001, showcasing Chicago and international artists in a variety of media. Meloche, who also curates traveling shows, is a great resource for local art and artists – ask her about any special one-offs that might be going down while you're in town.

Outside again, look to your left. The restaurant **Follia 5** (☎ 312-243-2888; 953 W Fulton) next door serves artful Italian food; their pizzas are a good way to stop rumbling stomachs. If you're full, head east again on Fulton, passing the European furnishings store **Casati 6** (☎ 312-421-9905; 949 W Fulton) and making a right on Sangamon St. You'll pass under the El tracks at Lake St, and continue south, making a left on Randolph St and right on Peoria St.

Peoria is the West Loop's art hive – the phrase 'Peoria Street galleries' has become almost synonymous with West Loop art. Start on the east side of the street at 119 Peoria, the home of **Bodybuilder and Sportsman 7** (p87). You'll have to ring the doorbell for admittance. Hike up one floor, and follow the signs to the gallery. Run by School of the Art Institute of Chicago grad Tony Wight, the space stole the name (and the sign) from the one-time sporting goods shop they used to occupy. Wight, though dead serious about art, uses his small gallery with scuffed floors to show paintings, drawings and video works that tend to poke holes in the over-inflated art world. You'll find an even more renegade approach to art upstairs in **Gallery 1R 8** (p87). Formerly run as a 'stray gallery' in Pilsen, this tiny space is the newest comer on the West Loop scene. Their works tend to be by students and other artistic troublemakers.

Head back onto Peoria, and walk across the street. This is where you'll be glad you had that pizza from Follia. No fewer than six galleries live in the 118 N Peoria St complex.

Flamingo (p114)

On the ground floor, you'll find one of the best – the expansive, concrete-floored **Rhona Hoffman 9** gallery (☎ 312-455-1990). Upstairs, though, are a whole host of other worthwhile options, including the photo-oriented **Flatfilegalleries 10** (☎ 312-491-1190) and the top-notch **Aron Packer Gallery 11** (☎ 312-226-8984), whose multimedia group shows are always a treat.

At this point, your head is likely an artistic blur. Which is good, as you're almost done. Walk south down Peoria and cross Washington St. You'll be turning right here to head to one of the grand galleries in the West Loop, **Donald Young Gallery 12** (p87). Donald Young handles some of the biggest names in contemporary art, including Bruce Nauman, Sol LeWitt, and Richard Serra. A trip here is a little like a visit to a free museum.

From Donald Young, double back up Washington to the final art stop: 835 W Washington, the home of **Vendanta 13** gallery (p87). One of the movers and shakers in the lesser-known modern art world, Vendanta shows works ranging from beautiful, haunting paintings, to cartoony political drawings. Vendanta shares a building with several other galleries as well, including **Thomas McCormick 14** (☎ 312-226-6800) and **Kraft Lieberman 15** (☎ 312-948-0555).

Back out on the street, you have a very important decision to make. The **Checker Taxi 16** (☎ 312-243-2537) dispatching office is immediately to your left at 845 Washington. You can hop into one of the cabs waiting out front and head off to your next adventure. Or you can settle into a delicious southern meal at **Wishbone 17** (p153), an Oprah-approved hot spot two blocks west. The choice is yours. (Hint: Wishbone has seats just as comfortable as the taxis, and their biscuits are far more filling than any food for thought your cabdriver might offer).

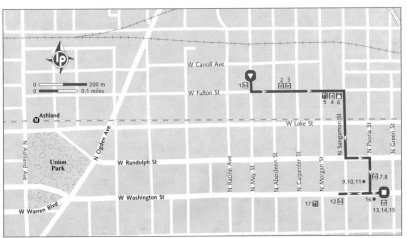

LOOP SCULPTURE WALK

You'd think the horrible Chicago weather would discourage anyone from leaving *anything* outside all winter. But nope – in true can-do, world-be-damned spirit, Chicago has dozens of top-notch pieces of sculpture decorating the plazas, courtyards and entryways of the Loop year-round. Where does all the money come from to buy and maintain the art, you ask? Good question. In 1967 the arrival of the Picasso sculpture at what's now the Richard J Daley Civic Center began a veritable sculpture frenzy that culminated in the city council 'Percent for Art' decree in 1978, when the

Walk Facts

Start Blue Line to LaSalle
End Blue, Brown, Green, Orange Line to Clark
Distance 2.1 miles
Duration 1½ hours

powers that be decided that new or renovated public buildings had to set aside a certain percentage of building funds to acquire and display art for the public.

It was a rare case of bureaucratic genius, and this walking tour will take you by some of the fruits of that decree, including world-class works by Alexander Calder, Pablo Picasso and Joan Miró.

We start our tour down in the southern reaches of the Loop. Exit the LaSalle St station and walk west to S Financial Pl. At 1 Financial Pl, you'll find **San Marco II 1**. Inspired by the four horses that grace the facade of St Mark's Basilica in Venice, artist Ludovico de Luigi created this stone sculpture on the plaza. Walk north up Financial Pl, making a right onto W Van Buren St, a left on S Clark St, and a right onto Jackson Blvd.

If the fierce and somewhat emaciated figure of Ludovico's horse has reminded you that you haven't eaten yet today, you can duck into Wendy's at Jackson and Clark for some fries.

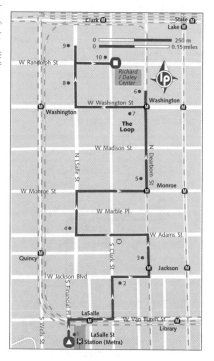

Feeling appropriately nourished? Good, as our next artwork stands before us. **The Town-Ho's Story 2**, in the lobby of 77 W Jackson, is by artist Frank Stella, and is named for a chapter in *Moby Dick*. The 20ft-tall artwork looks like it was wrenched from the bottom of the Cook County landfill, and it attracted, ahem, *attention* as soon as it was unveiled. One employee in the building (which houses the EPA among other federal bodies) waited all of six days after the sculpture was dedicated before circulating a petition asking for the work to be removed, claiming that 80% of EPA employees objected to the work, and that the 'pile of junk' made the government look bad. The petition garnered over six hundred signatures in a matter of days, but the *Story* remains the same.

Continue east on Jackson, turning left onto Dearborn. Alexander Calder's soaring steel sculpture **Flamingo 3**, on S Dearborn St between Adams St and Jackson Blvd, provides some much-needed relief to the stark facades of the federal buildings around it. Calder dedicated the sculpture in October 1974 by riding into the Loop on a bandwagon pulled by 40 horses, accompanied by a circus parade. Note the cement blocks on the outskirts of the plaza that prevent car-bombers from driving into the square – utilitarian sculptures of a far more recent vintage than Calder's work.

From here, we make a left on Adams, walking two blocks to the corner of LaSalle St, where **Chicago Fugue 4** resides. The 28ft-tall bronze piece is located in the lobby of the 190 N LaSalle St building. Its artist, Brit Anthony Caro was an assistant to Henry Moore, and has pieces of his work in museums around the world.

Walk north up LaSalle, turn right onto Monroe St, walk two blocks, and then make a left on Dearborn. Russian-born artist Marc Chagall loved Chicago, and donated this grand 1974 mosaic, called **The Four Seasons 5**, on the Dearborn St side of Bank One Plaza in 1974. Using thousands of bits of glass and stone, the artist portrayed six scenes of the city in hues reminiscent of the Mediterranean coast of France, where he kept his studio. Chagall continued to make adjustments, such as updating the skyline, after the work arrived in Chicago.

Keep moving northward on Dearborn across Washington St, where we'll check

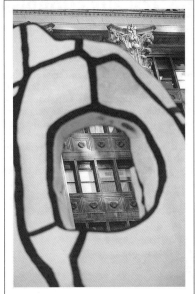

Monument with Standing Beast

out another of Chicago's classic sculptures, **'the Picasso' 6**. Officially it's untitled, but Chicagoans soon adopted their own no-nonsense name for the huge work in front of the Daley Center. Picasso was 82 when the work was commissioned. It was made to the artist's design specifications at the US Steel Works in Gary, Indiana, and erected in 1967. When Chicago tried to pay Picasso for the work, he refused the money, saying the sculpture was meant as a gift to the city. Bird, ape, dog, woman – you decide. The base makes a great slide for kids.

Across Washington St from Daley Plaza, you'll find Joan Miró's **Chicago 7**. Miró hoped to evoke the 'mystical force of a great earth mother' with this 40-foot sculpture, made with various metals, cement and tile in 1981. Continue along Washington for a block, turning right on LaSalle. Look up over the entrance to 120 N LaSalle for **Arts and Science of the Ancient World: The Flight of Daedalus and Icarus 8**. This large 1991 glass mosaic by School of the Art Institute alumnus Roger Brown above the entrance shows dad and son escaping the labyrinth of the Minotaur. The lobby houses the second installment in the mosaic series, *Arts and Sciences of the Modern World: LaSalle Corridor with Holding Pattern*, which features a more contemporary take on flight. The building is the most recent skyscraper in Chicago by local architect Helmut Jahn (see the boxed text p41).

Walk north up LaSalle, across Randolph St, to 160 N LaSalle, our next stop. Two-and-a-half stories tall, Richard Hunt's 1993 welded stainless steel **Freeform 9** decorates the facade of the Illinois State Office Building.

Double back on LaSalle and head east to 100 W Randolph St. Our final stop is at **Monument with Standing Beast 10**, created in 1984 by French sculptor Jean Dubuffet. The fun white fiberglass work looks a little like inflated puzzle pieces and has a definite Keith Haring-esque feel to it. As you can see by the large number of kids crawling around inside the sculpture, this is definitely a hands-on piece of art. Explore to your heart's content, and afterwards, check out the James R Thompson Center right in front of you. For the story on this controversial piece of architecture, see p41.

DAMEN AVE SHOPPING SPREE

Chicago's neighborhoods seem to be in a perpetual state of upward mobility. Just a few years ago, MTV tried to film *The Real World* in Wicker Park, and the ensuing protests by residents over the media corporation's presence in their neighborhood led to a number of arrests. Gentrification has taken its course in Wicker Park and the adjoining community of Bucktown since then though, and the protests of those days feel like a distant memory. Today, the neighborhood is a commercial zone where some of the city's hottest fashion boutiques and cool little stores have set up shop. The following walk will take you up and down Damen Ave, in the heart of Bucktown. Note: men may want to skip ahead to the part of the tour that begins ' If you happen to have a suffering spouse or significant other in tow...'

The start of the tour is the Damen Ave El stop, where you'll disembark and hit the ground running. Speaking of... If you've been feeling like your feet need some new fashions, make your first stop **City Sole/Niche 1** (p211). If your budget is under $100, head straight to the City Sole section of the store, where the more affordable fashions live. Looking to go crazy? Have a go at Niche's selection of shoes by European designers. The staff in both wings of the sizable store pout like fashion models, but they're helpful.

With your shoebox(es) bagged and ready to go, it's time to cross the street. In other parts of town, this is a relatively simple operation, but this intersection is legendary for getting tourists turned around. To make it to the east-side sidewalk on Damen is simple enough, just cross to in front of the Soul Kitchen restaurant. Now here's where the fun begins. You'll have to cross over Milwaukee Ave, then cross North Ave, just to make it back to Damen. Made it? Good.

Heading up Damen on the east side of the street, the first stop will be **p45 2** (p212). This small gallery is about as far from the Gap as you can get, philosophically and fashion-wise. All the clothes here are envelope-pushing designs from up-and-coming fashionistas. In Chicago, p45 serves as a convenient predictor for what is going to be worn around town by everyone in six months. Their jewelry is almost entirely created by local designers, making it a unique place to pick up a gift for a girlfriend back home.

On the same block, but several storefronts to the north, **Clothes Minded 3** (p211) offers less over-the-top women's fashions than p45, and the prices are much more down-to-earth as well. This is the perfect shop for basic cute tops and casual wear.

Keep going on Damen across Wabansia Ave, and you'll hit **Tangerine 4** (p212), a pretty, high-ceilinged space that ranks among the friendliest of the Bucktown boutiques. Lines they carry include Laurie B and Nanette Lepore.

That's four stores down, and just five more to go. If you happen to have a suffering spouse or significant other in tow, this is the point to set them free. A block west of Damen on Armitage Ave is one of the city's best coffeehouses/bars, the **Map Room 5** (p166). The coffee is good there, the beers are excellent and the fashion talk is kept to an absolute minimum, making it a great place to jettison whiny tag-alongs who don't share your love of shopping. You can plan a rendezvous at the Damen El Stop in an hour or so, and continue on your way.

Women who wear sizes 12 to 28 looking for a hip, stylish clothes beyond the dreadful collections of the corporate 'plus-size' retail chains, should head up Damen to **Vive La Femme 6** (p213), a one-of-a-kind boutique that also sells bags and accessories. Otherwise, cross Damen a little south of Vive La Femme, and begin the walk southward, down the west side of the street.

The first store on our southerly route is the wee **Saffron 7** (p212). See it there on the right? Duck in for classic-cut evening wear and accessories, along with jewelry, shawls, and bath and beauty products. Owner Padmaja designs the clothes herself, and she's happy to talk abut them.

Further south, you'll find the answer to the eternal question 'What the hell am I supposed to bring to a baby shower?' The coolest kids' store in Chicago, **Red Balloon 8** (p212) offers classic children's toys and clothes. And if you're anything like us, you'll end up walking out with some cool goodies for yourself as well. At this point your shopping load is likely becoming burdensome. Take a right on Armitage and run your bags over to the Map Room, dropping the packages off with your SO while you grab a cappuccino to go. Retrace your steps to Damen and continue south along the avenue.

The first of our remaining two stops is **Apartment No 9 9** (p202), a chic men's store that caters to sophisticated twenty- and thirty something Chicago metrosexuals. The pants and shirts are the last word in men's designers, and the shaving kits, complete with brush and lather mug, make good gifts.

And just when you thought your credit card couldn't take anymore, we hit **Climate 10** (p211). A store with absurdly cute cards, stationery, funny books, and other essentials. Browse to your heart's content, and don't forget to pick up a 'wish you were here' postcard for all the poor suckers back at home.

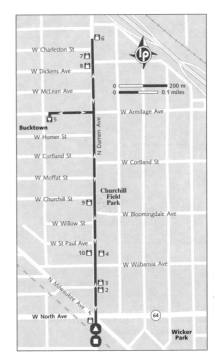

WICKER PARK HOMES WALK

Known now as a mecca for hip clothes and urban accessories, Wicker Park also has a rich history and a number of absolutely stunning old homes. After the great fire, Chicago forbade the building of wood homes within city limits. At the time, Wicker Park was far beyond the municipal boundaries, and builders were free to use timber to their hearts' content. The result you see today is what many of Chicago's well-off residential neighborhoods looked like before the fire. When you've shopped till you've dropped, and you're ready for a little R&R strolling on some of the city's most beautiful streets, look no further than Wicker Park.

From the Damen El stop on the CTA Blue Line, walk two blocks northwest on Milwaukee Ave to Caton St. Turn left and begin the tour. You'll notice that the neighborhood gets gentrified the moment you leave shabby Milwaukee Ave. At **2138-2156 W Caton St 1**, you'll see an 1891 minidevelopment of five large homes, each with a different exterior design and theme. Among the variations: No 2142, Queen Anne; No

Walk Facts

Start Blue Line to Damen
End Blue Line to Damen
Distance 0.8 miles
Duration 1 hour

2146, Swiss; No 2152, Renaissance. The stone-and-brick home at No 2156 used to belong to Norwegian Ole Thorp, who built the houses. This street used to be a private road called Columbia Place, with gates on both ends to keep out the riffraff.

The large 1891 turreted house at **2159 W Caton St 2** is a good example of Queen Anne style. At the intersection of Caton and Leavitt Sts, cross Leavitt.

To make the upscale apartment flats at **1644** and **1658 N Leavitt St 3** fit in with nearby mansions, builders used high-quality materials such as limestone and cut glass and included ornately

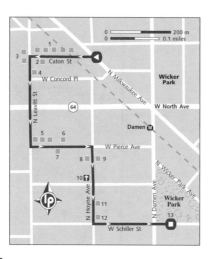

carved wooden details. If you pause here long enough, the El train will come roaring by. The noise from the train is one of the reasons rents in apartment buildings like 1644 Leavitt stay reasonable.

Head south on Leavitt St for one block. The 1893 mansion at **2156 W Concord Pl 4** features a proud conical tower and an interesting curved front.

Continue south on Leavitt St; cross North Ave and turn east (left) on Pierce Ave. The three similar houses at **2146, 2150** and **2156 W Pierce Ave 5** date from 1890. Note how the limestone at 2150 has held up better than the sandstone at 2156 and 2146.

See all that woodwork on **2138 W Pierce Ave 6**? You'd never guess that the original owner, John D Runge, owned a wood-milling firm. Notice the Masonic insignia under the eaves of the dormer. The 1899 house at **2135 W Pierce Ave 7** includes more detail (in pressed metal, wood and brick) than the eye can soak up. The side porch overlooking a garden was a popular detail in the neighborhood. Note the polychromatic paint job.

At the end of the block, turn south (right) onto Hoyne Ave. Tastes of the day obviously favored sculpted figures of women, as seen on the 1886 house at **1520 N Hoyne Ave 8**, which was built for a Russian lumber baron. The porch of the 1895 turreted Queen Anne house at **1521 N Hoyne Ave 9** features wood carved to resemble lace. The **Wicker Park Lutheran Church 10** (N Hoyne Ave at LeMoyne St) was built in 1906 with granite salvaged from an upscale Levee District brothel.

Ripe for restoration, the 1879 Italianate house at **1417 N Hoyne Ave 11** includes a typical side porch. The proud French Second Empire mansion at **1407 N Hoyne Ave 12**, dating from 1879, features a cast-iron porch.

Turn east (left) on Schiller St and proceed one block; cross Damen Ave. The 1891 house at **1941 W Schiller St 13** is a prime example of Queen Anne architecture in all of its styling. It's been beautifully restored.

After your tour, rest up across the street in Wicker Park.

Detail on a house designed by Louis Sullivan, Wicker Park

Walking Tours – Wicker Park Homes Walk

UNIVERSITY OF CHICAGO WALK

One of the country's powerhouse research institutions, the University of Chicago boasts a beautiful English Gothic campus located in Hyde Park. This walk will take you around campus to some of the highlights. When viewing the classic old buildings, keep looking up for the stone menageries of critters, fairies, monsters and other creatures that are carved into cornices, rooftops, entrances and windows.

Walk Facts

Start Metra to 59th St
End Metra to 59th St
Distance 1.4 miles
Duration 1 hour

Start at Frank Lloyd Wright's masterful **Robie House 1** (p109). Walk a half-block south down Woodlawn Ave to **Ida Noyes Hall 2** (1212 East 59th St). Built as a women's dormitory in 1916, the building has hosted concerts from jazz greats like Miles Davis, and now serves as the visitors center. Note the woman's head carved into the entry arch. Inside, the lobby, lounge and library are richly detailed. Campus life on the U of C takes a backseat to scholastic endeavors, with distractions like coffee shops and bars few and far between. Those that do exist tend to be hidden away in campus buildings, such as the nice pub you'll find in the basement here.

Cross Woodlawn Ave to **Rockefeller Memorial Chapel 3** (5850 S Woodlawn Ave). Named for industrialist John D Rockefeller, who coughed up the funds to establish the university in 1890, this wondrous space hosts frequent musical performances in the acoustically rich, soaring interior. University officials sent themselves off on junkets to England to ensure the authenticity of the chapel, which was completed in 1928. Head inside for a beautiful moment of calm.

Turn west (right) on 59th St, then turn right again into the courtyard just past Foster Hall. **Foster, Kelly, Green & Beecher Halls 4** (5844–5848 S University Ave), the first women's halls, were built in 1893 and 1899. Foster Hall features a pack of gargoyles on the turret overlooking the midway.

Continue north, walking between Walker Museum (actually used for classrooms), on the left, and the modern Pick Hall, on the right. Cross the main quad to reach **Eckhart Hall 5** (1118 E 58th St). One of the last Gothic buildings built on campus, it was completed in 1930. The carved details honor the resident physics, astronomy and mathematics departments.

Pass into Hutchinson Court through the arched entrance to the left of Eckhart, and you'll reach the tower group. Dominated by **Mitchell Tower 6** (1135 E 57th St), which is modeled after Oxford's Magdalen College, these four 1903 buildings are linked by interior cloisters. The tower, which was the first purely aesthetic building at the university, contains 10 bells, whose cacophonous chimes delight some and annoy others.

Exit Hutchinson Court by walking to the west, then turn right into **Hull Court 7**. This area includes (in clockwise order starting at Culver Hall, on the left) the 1897 anatomy, zoology and biology buildings. Look for the griffins atop zoology. The pond was once stocked with exotic fish.

Continue north through **Cobb Gate 8**. A university architect actually felt his style was cramped on campus, so he donated this ceremonial entryway in 1900 and let loose with his ornamental passions. The gargoyles struggling on the climb to the top are said to represent undergraduate students.

Turn west (left) and face north to see the **Joseph Regenstein Library 9** (1100 E 57th St). Walter Netsch, the architect whose notions

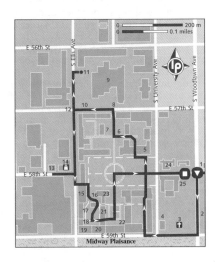

119

University of Chicago (p214)

of an Italian hill village led to some perverse creations at the University of Illinois at Chicago (most of which have since been torn down because of their unpopularity), built this in 1970. The vertical grooves and slit windows are supposed to help the library fit in with the classic structures to the south. In a very U of C touch, the library contains a cafeteria, so students won't have to waste precious research time walking elsewhere to eat. The bright-colored buildings behind the Regenstein are some of the newest additions to campus, the **Palevsky Residential Commons 10**. The vibrant hues on the dorms are part of deliberate attempts the U of C has tried to make things a little less stodgy around campus.

From here, walk west along 57th St to Ellis Ave, turn right and walk a half-block north to the 1967 bronze Henry Moore sculpture **Nuclear Energy 11** (p109). A human skull and a mushroom cloud come together in this work, which sits on the exact spot where Enrico Fermi and company started the nuclear age. (See the boxed text, p109.)

Turn back south and go to the corner of 57th St and Ellis Ave, where you'll come to **Snell-Hitchcock Hall 12** (5709 S Ellis Ave). The usual ornamental English posies are dispensed with on this 1902 men's dormitory, in favor of corncobs and other prairie flora. The hall is on the National Register of Historic Places for its contributions to the Prairie Style school of architecture.

Continue south to the corner of 58th St and Ellis Ave, turn right and walk a half-block west to the **Cummings Life Science Center 13** (920 E 58th St). A huge brick-and-limestone building and the tallest on campus, this 1973 structure features 40 brick chimneys climbing the walls to provide ventilation for the many labs within.

Walk back to the corner of 58th St and Ellis Ave. At the **University Bookstore 14** (970 E 58th St), you can get a cup of coffee, or buy a T-shirt to remember your visit forever.

Across the street you'll find **Cobb Hall 15** (5811 S Ellis Ave), the university's oldest building, which opened its classrooms and offices in 1892. The architect, Henry Ives Cobb, designed the next 18 buildings constructed on campus. The 4th-floor Renaissance Society holds frequent art shows.

Walk diagonally southeast through the cloister joining Swift Hall and **Bond Chapel 16** (1050 E 59th St). Built in 1926, this exquisite 300-seat chapel is the harmonious creation of the architects, sculptors, woodcarvers and glassmakers who worked together on the project. Look for the lute player on the cornice.

Exit the chapel and turn right into the courtyard. The classics quad includes (in counterclockwise order starting at Cobb Hall) **Gates-Blake 17** and **Goodspeed Halls 18** (1892), the **classics building 19** (1915), **Wieboldt Hall 20** (1928) and **Frederick Haskell Hall 21** (1896). Characters from Aesop's fables decorate the classics building, while images of noted authors adorn Wieboldt.

Pass through the archway between Wieboldt and Haskell to get to the **William Rainey Harper Memorial Library 22** (1116 E 59th St). The massive 1912 twin-towered building presents a grand facade both to the campus and the midway. The long row of arched, two-story windows bathe the 3rd-floor reading room with light.

Walk north to **Swift Hall 23** (1025 E 58th St), the 1926 home of the Divinity School. Its prominent position on campus signifies the importance of religion in education. In the basement there's a decent coffee shop.

Continue north to the center of the traffic circle. Turn east (right) and walk along 58th St to the **Chicago Theological Seminary 24** (1178 E 58th St), on your left. The redbrick 1926 buildings provide a Tudor contrast to the university. The cloisters invite contemplation, and the beautiful Hilton Memorial Chapel invites prayer. Across the street stands the **Oriental Institute Museum 25** (☎ 773-702-9507; 1155 E 58th St; admission free), which houses one of the world's best collections of Near Eastern antiquities (many of which were discovered by U of C archaeologists). Continue west to Robie House to complete the campus tour.

HISTORIC LOOP ARCHITECTURE WALK

The Loop abounds with important, beautiful and interesting architecture. Just by walking its streets for about half a day, you can trace the development of modern architecture in Chicago, the US and worldwide. This tour will focus on the landmark buildings in the Loop from 1885 to 1914. For more information on the architects and buildings, check out the Architecture chapter (p35).

Let's start at the **Reliance Building 1** (p37). This building, a Burnham and Root creation, was finished in 1895. Home of the Burnham Hotel since 1999, the building's owners have gone to considerable lengths to reproduce parts of the interior as they were at the turn of the 20th century, including the decorative metal elevator grills, marble-clad ceiling and walls, and mosaic floor. Head on in for a look.

Kitty-corner from the Reliance Building is **Marshall Field & Co 2** (p37), at the intersection of State and Washington. Marshall Field's mercantile strategy was to 'dazzle the customer with opulence.' And one kind of customer appealed to him above all: women. In the late 1800s, unescorted women shoppers were frowned upon, but Field welcomed them warmly, and Field was actually the first Chicago retailer to add women's bathrooms to his store. This building was built in stages, starting in 1892 and ending in 1914.

Continuing on, walk east on Washington St to the **Chicago Cultural Center 3** (p37). Built in 1897, the building started its life as the Chicago Library. The impressive hodgepodge of Greek, Roman and European architectural details became all the rage in the city after 1893, when Daniel Burnham designed scores of structures similar to this one for the Chicago-hosted World's Columbian Exposition. Duck inside and check out the famous stained-glass domes, and rooms modeled on the Doge's Palace in Venice and Athens' Acropolis.

Let's turn right (south) and walk along Michigan Ave to the intersection of Madison and the **6 N Michigan 4** building. From his corner office in this building, Montgomery Ward fumed as he saw developers encroaching on Grant Park (see the boxed text, p77). The 1899 structure, designed by Hugh MG Garden and Richard E Schmidt, has changed a lot from the way it looked when it was the center of Ward's operations, but many charming terra-cotta details, such as reliefs of plants and animals, still exist – albeit under layers of grime.

Head west on Madison two blocks, stopping to admire the Louis Sullivan–designed metalwork facade on **Carson Pirie Scott & Co 5** (p39). In many ways, this building, completed in 1906, is the finest example of the Chicago School of architecture in the city. Across State St, at 7 W Madison, is another Chicago School masterpiece, the **Chicago Building 6** (p38). Constructed in 1905 as the Chicago Savings & Trust, the building now houses young artists in its role as School of the Art Institute of Chicago dorms.

Continue south down State St to Monroe, where we'll cut through the **Palmer House Hilton 7**. Head up the escalator into the lobby and prepare to begin drooling immediately. This sumptuous space was created by Holabird and Roche, the same folks behind our previous stop. When it was built in 1905, the hotel was the largest in the world. Find the Wabash Ave exit, and walk south one block to Adams. Make a left here, and walk towards the Art Institute. Along the way, you'll pass the remodeled liquor warehouse, which comprises the Adams-facing portion of the **Symphony Center 8,** home of the Chicago Symphony Orchestra.

When you hit the **Art Institute 9** (p37), stop for a second and take in the classical design details from 1893. This portion of the building was very much of the time, built the same year that the World's Columbian Exposition was bringing a mania for re-interpreted antiquity to the city's architectural scene. Continue down Michigan to the **Santa Fe Center 10** (p38). This Daniel Burnham–designed building is the home of the Chicago Architecture

Marshall Field & Co building (p37)

An El of a Tour

For $1.50 you can see Chicago in its glory and despair and get an up-close tour of many of the city's most interesting neighborhoods. From your (usually) climate-controlled car on the El, you'll enjoy a vantage point that's impossible from the street. You can see how neighborhoods have grown and declined while tracing the city's history. Any of the lines pass interesting sights, but the following tour on the Orange and Brown Lines will give you the most varied experience.

Start by boarding an Orange Line train at **Clark**, which is part of the bulbous glass monster known as the James R Thompson State of Illinois Center. At **State**, the next stop, look right. Next to the Chicago Theater is the Page Brothers Building, with a cast-iron facade. Before the great fire in 1871, most of the Loop's buildings resembled this one.

The train turns south and runs above Wabash Ave. Through the upper-floor windows of buildings on both sides, you can catch myriad glimpses of urban life that are denied pedestrians. This is one of the busiest stretches of the Loop tracks, which opened in 1897 to unite the various elevated lines built by several different companies. The tracks have survived several proposals through the years to replace them, their longevity mostly thanks to a lack of public funding for the construction of anything better.

As you leave the Loop, you penetrate what was once known as the Levee District, a notorious area populated from about 1890 to 1910 by prostitutes, gamblers and other vice-seekers. Around **Roosevelt** you'll see the residential development called Central Station, which the mayor calls home. This is one of the many vast projects that are now transforming the area. After the tracks split, the Orange Line heads southwest and traverses acres of vacant land once used for railroad yards servicing the hundreds of daily passenger trains that made Chicago the rail transit hub of the country.

Continuing southwest, the line is hemmed in by the Stevenson Expressway and the Chicago River. Past **35th St/Archer** the tracks climb to their highest point for the best view of the skyline from anywhere on the El system. Just before **Western**, look left to see a relic from the city's days as a major meat processor. The cattle ramps and holding pens look out of place today.

After **Kedzie** the line overlooks block after block of tidy bungalows before it reaches Midway Airport, where the planes take off above the trains. At **Midway**, which is the end of the line, cross the tracks and return downtown.

When you reach the Loop, the train will turn left, heading west, and stop at the **Library** station. Two pioneer office towers flank Dearborn St, to the right of your train. On the east side of the street, the Fisher Building dates from 1896. Look for the terra-cotta fish and other seashore critters decorating the exterior. On the west side is the world-famous Monadnock Building. One block west of the Fisher and Monadnock Buildings on Clark St, the Chicago Metropolitan Correctional Center, built in 1975, cuts its unique angle to the left of the tracks. The building houses people awaiting trial for federal crimes; believe it or not, its 5-inch-wide plastic windows allowed a few inmates to escape before bars were added on the inside.

Get off when you reach **Clark** and cross over the tracks to board a Brown Line train. One of Chicago's most famous views occurs right as the trains leave the Loop and cross the Chicago River. The most delightful station out of a mostly dreary lot in the Loop is **Quincy**. Originally built in 1897 and restored by the city in 1988, it shows what all the stations once looked like.

Between **Chicago** and **Armitage** there used to be seven stations; now there is only one. This run gives a stark illustration of the disparities in wealth in the city. To the east is the Gold Coast, one of the nation's wealthiest neighborhoods; to the west is Cabrini-Green, one of the poorest. Notice how upscale developments are hemming the low-income housing projects in on all sides.

The sharp turns at Halsted St, a daily annoyance to thousands of standing commuters, are a legacy of the free-enterprise roots of the El system. During the line's construction in the 1890s, the German farmers in the area held out for higher prices for their land. Instead of negotiating, the then-private El company simply went around them.

Beginning at **Armitage**, the tracks run north through gentrified Lincoln Park. After **Belmont** the line heads west and offers some of the most varied views in the city. The distant lakefront, numerous vintage buildings and industrial water towers all combine for constantly changing urban panoramas.

West of the **Western** stop, which serves the old Lincoln Square German neighborhood, the line descends to ground level. There's a nice crossing of the Chicago River before the tracks terminate at **Kimball**, in Albany Park. From here you can explore the neighborhood, which has many Middle Eastern and Asian shops, or you can return to the Loop. Alternatively, take a No 81 Lawrence Ave CTA bus east to the **Lawrence** El stop on the Red Line. From here you can ride south past Wrigley Field back to the Loop.

Foundation. Head into the lobby to check out the vast well of light Burnham built into the structure – you'll see it repeated in the Rookery, later in the tour.

Stroll two blocks further on S Michigan Ave, to the **Auditorium Building 11** (p37). Louis Sullivan and Dankmar Adler collaborated on this fantastic 1889 building. It is thought that Frank Lloyd Wright likely drafted some of the interior details, as he was working in Sullivan's office during the period in which the building was designed. Roosevelt University has taken over what was originally a hotel portion of the building.

Turn right onto Congress Pkwy, walking the length of the Auditorium Building, before turning right up Wabash Ave and making your first left onto W Van Buren St. Two blocks on, we find the **Fisher Building 12** (p38). This timeless Chicago classic was born in 1896 and absolutely glows in the afternoon sun. Look for all the aquatic details added to the facade, a play on the name of the building's owner, Lucius Fisher.

Make a right-hand turn onto Dearborn St and walk north. That thick-based building you see beside you is the **Monadnock Building 13** (p38). You'll know if there are any architects nearby, as they'll be staring at the structure in a near-religious reverie. This important building was groundbreakingly tall when it was built in 1891. Ah, how times have changed.

Let's continue up to Dearborn and Adams Sts, stopping at 140 S Dearborn, home to the 1893 **Marquette Building 14** (p37). There are more of the beautiful stained-glass panels you see above the entrance located inside the lobby. The final stop on our tour is also one of the most gorgeous. Two blocks east of the Marquette building off of Adams is the **Rookery 15** (p37). The original design by Burnham and Root, with its load-bearing walls of granite and brick, surrounds a spectacular atrium space that was remodeled in 1907 by Frank Lloyd Wright. The light in here is heavenly, and when you bask in the architectural details inside, try to imagine the building without the pools of light. That's the way it was from the 1940s onward, when the building managers covered over the skylights with tar paper and paint. It wasn't until the building's new owner took over in 1988 that the sun was allowed to shine through again.

Eating

Eating

In a recent interview, the TV talk show host Jay Leno proclaimed Chicago his favorite city to visit. The reason, he went on to explain, was the city's food. And what, of all the four-star epicurean destinations in the Windy City, was Mr Leno's top recommendation?

His answer, which immediately endeared him to every last non-vegetarian man, woman and child in Chicago, was Mr Beef.

Yes, *that* Mr Beef. The no-frills sandwich joint on Orleans, where the apex of culinary sophistication is not spilling too much sauce on your pants before you leave. The reason that answer earned Leno so many points with locals was because it contained a distinctly Chicagoan perspective about food. Which can be neatly summarized in three rules:

1) The neighborhood places are almost always the best places
2) Price does not always correlate with value
3) When in doubt, go for the beef.

There are exceptions of course. Chicago loves to eat well and eat broadly; your average Chicagoan would have no problem explaining the difference between sashimi and Szechwan, tandoori and Thai. But there's also an inherent reluctance to embrace the next big dish or food style out of New York simply because it's new. Or from New York.

This is why Chicago restaurants are some of the best in the world. Because whether they're a hole-in-the-wall or a rooftop bistro, new restaurants here have to prove themselves both capable *and* neighborly. It's a tough balancing act, and, as you might suspect, turnover rates in the Chicago restaurant world are high.

The veterans that do stick around, though, are guaranteed to be worth your time. And the fledgling places striving to be the next Frontera Grill, Charlie Trotter's or Tru make Chicago a reliably hopping restaurant town. So get out there and enjoy.

Just make sure, at some point in your visit, to go for the beef.

Opening Hours

Despite the late hours some restaurants keep, Chicagoans tend to have dinner between 6:30am and 8:30pm. Lunch falls from 11:30am to 2pm, and breakfast tends to be served from 8pm to 10am. That beloved creature, brunch, is an amorphous meal that essentially lasts from whenever you wake up on Saturday and Sunday until about 5pm.

Like tipping for counter-service, there are no hard and fast rules for opening hours in Chicago. The mid-level and budget places usually open around 10am and stay open until around 11pm. Chains, fast-food restaurants and coffee shops get an even earlier start, opening their doors to the harried public around 7am or 8am. Quite a few of the high-end restaurants in Chicago don't serve lunch and close on Sunday or Monday: this seems to be what you do when you're a classy Chicago eatery. In the listings we've noted with each venue where hours stray from the standard as well as any closed days, but if you're going out of your way, it's best to call ahead. Good news for night owls is that Chicago is a late-night diners' paradise. Along with family-style diners like the Golden Apple, an impressive number of smaller restaurants will keep the kitchen open past midnight, especially on weekends.

How Much

In the following restaurant write-ups, we've indicated the range in prices on single entrées rather than entire meals. The phrase 'mains $8-$23' means that, between the lunch and the dinner menu, the cheapest entrée you'll find costs $8, and the most expensive $23. Lunch entrées in Chicago restaurants are usually 40% cheaper than the same entrée served after the sun goes down.

For an average sit-down lunch in Chicago, including tip and a drink, expect to pay about $12 per person. Dinner, including drink and tip, will likely be about $30 per person. Eating ethnic foods like Indian, Thai, Chinese or Ethiopian will save you money. As will checking out our 'cheap eats' category. At these good-food-on-a-budget restaurants, you can have lunch for under $8 and dinner for under $15.

Booking Tables

Here's a good rule of thumb: if you would feel uncomfortable wearing a T-shirt to the restaurant in question, that is a good sign you should probably call ahead and ask about reservations. This is much more true on weekends than midweek. And some places won't take a reservation for parties of less than four or five. But it will save you much aggravation and time spent nursing appetizers at the restaurant's bar if you call ahead to see.

And once you have your reservation, keep it. Or call and cancel as soon as you know you're not going to make it. Some of the fancier restaurants have adopted your dentist's policy of charging a 'no-show' fee for their MIA guests. That fee can be as much as $50. Yeeowch.

Top Five Eat Streets

Good restaurants in Chicago have a magnetic ability to attract other quality eateries. Here are five streets with an embarrassment of dining riches.

- **Randolph St, West Loop** (p152) Sumptuous food in grand, eye-catching settings.
- **Devon Ave, Far North** (p157) More naan than you can shake a tandoori skewer at in this Indian and Pakistani restaurant row.
- **Southport Ave, Lake View** (p142) A burgeoning hotspot for fun, unpretentious dining.
- **Clark St, Wrigleyville** (p142) Between the buffalo-sized burgers, top-notch Thai and supreme sashimi, if you can't find it here, you're not looking hard enough.
- **Division St, Ukrainian Village** (p149) This hipster's dining paradise includes several of the best brunch places in town.

Tipping

If, at the end of your meal, you thought the service was fine, tip a minimum of 15% of the pre-tax bill. If the service was great, take that number up to 20%. Indifferent or hostile waitstaff deserve whatever pittance you feel like leaving. (If the service was truly abysmal, discuss it with the manager – not only will the waiter get a stern dressing-down later, but you might get your bill reduced for your pain and suffering). Many restaurants add the tip into the bill for parties of six or more.

At cafés or *taquerias* where you order food and drinks at the counter, the tipping etiquette is a little less clear (though a tip jar will always be prominently displayed). If you order food that someone then brings to your table, it's common practice to drop about 10% of your total in the tip jar. If you're getting food or drinks to go, no tip is expected.

Valet parkers should get anywhere from $2 to $5 when they return your car to you (assuming the car is in the same shape it was when you surrendered it to them).

Take Out & To Go

With so many parks in Chicago, picnics are going to be a high priority during your visit (if you're here in winter, you can picnic in the car with the heater on). You can pick up groceries and drinks at the ubiquitous Jewel (☎ 800-539-3561) stores. Whole Foods (Map pp280–1; ☎ 312-932-9600; 50 W Huron St) has top-notch produce and a health-conscious selection of organic foods and baked goods. If you want to do less assembly work, try the deli counter at the incomparable Bari (see p150), or pick from the high-class, pre-cooked delicacies at Charlie Trotter's To Go (see p137).

If you're looking for snacks fresh off the vine, the city sponsors farmers markets all over Chicago from May to October. Loop locations include Federal Plaza on Tuesdays and Daley Plaza on Thursdays. The markets attract growers from around the region and offer opportunities to try everything from asparagus in May to rhubarb in October. Visit the Chicago farmers markets website – www.ci.chi.il.us/SpecialEvents/FarmersMarketCalendar.html – for a complete schedule.

Eating

THE LOOP & GRANT PARK

The Loop restaurant scene is all about business. In the morning, office workers sprint through the Dunkin' Donuts or Starbucks to grab something to scarf at their desks. At lunchtime, the speedy tableau unfurls again, with paper pushers waiting in lines to get a Caesar salad or a ham-on-rye at upscale soup and sandwich places like Boudin or the Corner Bakery. The power dining begins at night, as the executive bigwigs who spent the days negotiating mergers and takeovers slide into steak-house booths to seal the deal. Loop restaurants mirror these trends, providing a myriad of cheap, quick chains and sumptuous expense-account perennials.

BERGHOFF Map pp282–3 *German & American*
☎ 312-427-3170; 17 W Adams St; mains $8-20;
🕑 closed Sun; Blue, Red Line to Jackson

The building and this historic restaurant both date from 1898. The first place in Chicago to serve a legal drink at the end of Prohibition, the Berghoff is currently the only restaurant in town with its own carpentry shop that employs full-time workers who maintain the antique woodwork and furniture. (The Berghoff also boasts the city's first liquor license, on display in the dining room.) The menu carries old-world classics such as sauerbraten and schnitzel, but it also features lighter treats such as swordfish and Caesar salad.

Charlie Trotter's Restaurant (p137)

The quick and efficient waiters serve a huge crowd of regulars, plus day-trippers from the 'burbs. The adjoining Stand Up Bar has changed little in a century, although women have been admitted for the past 40 years. Sandwiches ($7) are served from a buffet line at lunch, and frosty mugs of Berghoff beer, direct from the Wisconsin brewery, still line the bar.

EVEREST Map pp282–3 *French*
☎ 312-663-8920; 40th fl One Financial Plaza, 440 S LaSalle St; mains from $30; 🕑 dinner only, closed Sun & Mon; Blue Line to LaSalle

If you're celebrating an anniversary or other romantic milestone while you're in Chicago, this is your chance to score some *major* points. The 40th-floor views and unfailingly attentive, tuxedo-clad waiters set the scene for a meal your significant other will be talking about for years. The food is French, with a slant toward the Alsace region, home of chef Jean Joho, who also runs Brasserie Jo (see p130). Great value: the three-course pre-theater prix-fixe menu is just $49 per person (seatings at 5:30pm only). Reservations essential.

ITALIAN VILLAGE Map pp282–3 *Italian*
☎ 312-332-7005; 71 W Monroe St; mains $9-28; 🕑 La Cantina Enoteca & Vivere closed Sun; Blue Line to Monroe

There are three restaurants under one roof here. The namesake Village looks a bit like a Disney set, with twinkling lights and storefronts that evoke the feeling of a southern Italian hill town. The very traditional red-sauce menu includes old-style cuisine such as *mostaccioli* pasta with sausage. If you're part of a couple you can cozy up in the private booths (but you can't reserve these in advance so you'll have to hope your timing is right). La Cantina Enoteca is a casual supper club that serves regional specialties such as cannelloni and seafood. A few distinctly American steaks make the cut here as well. Vivere, at the high end of the Village in both price and cuisine, boasts more than 1500 bottles in its wine cellar. The menu features high-minded interpretations of standards such as veal scallopini, joined by unusual numbers such as bass-filled squid-ink pasta.

MILLER'S PUB Map pp282–3 *American*
☎ 312-645-5377; 134 S Wabash Ave; mains $8-24; 🕑 to 4am; Brown, Green, Orange, Purple Line to Adams

A photo of your favorite dead celebrity can probably be found somewhere on the walls at this Loop institution next to the Palmer

House. Miller's has been serving remarkably tender and candy-sweet ribs for decades. The rest of the menu includes the usual upscale bar staples – salads, burgers and the like. The exceptionally late closing time makes this a popular choice with the post-theater crowd and office workers burning the midnight oil.

NICK'S FISHMARKET Map pp282–3 _Seafood_
☎ 312-621-0200; One First National Bank Plaza, W Monroe St; mains $16-43; 🕑 closed lunch Sat, closed Sun; Blue Line to Monroe

Nick's doesn't escape its office surroundings so much as serve as an extension of them, offering a convenient spot for business lunches and dinners. Even if you're not wooing a client, Nick's is worth a visit. Grab a quick meal upstairs in Nick's Grill, or head down to the main attraction – the dim, cozy confines of Nick's dining room. Long known for its traditional dishes – lobster thermidor, king crab, pepper steak etc – Nick's has been branching out under chef José Bernal, goosing familiar seafood entrées with Asian flavors. Drinkers will enjoy the 10 kinds of martinis on offer, as well as the sizable wine list.

PALM Map pp282–3 _Steak & Seafood_
☎ 312-616-1000; Swissôtel Chicago, 323 E Wacker Dr; mains $18-125; bus 157

Not picking up the check tonight? Then head to Palm's for the best lobster you've ever had (about $20 a pound). Given that these crustaceans average about 5lb, you can see why you'll want to be sitting on your wallet and brimming with thanks at check time. Equally costly New York strip steaks are also about the best ever.

RUSSIAN TEA TIME Map pp282–3 _Russian_
☎ 312-360-0000; 77 E Adams St; mains $15-28; Brown, Green, Orange, Purple Line to Adams

You've got to like a place where the menu starts with detailed, seven-step instructions on how to drink a shot of vodka properly (Step 6: Say 'Oh Khorosho!' – 'It feels good!' Step 7: Repeat process in 10 to 15 minutes). Clearly there's more than tea flowing here. The czar-worthy menu includes borscht, _pelmeni_ (dumplings), beef stroganoff and more. Russian folk songs complete the mood.

TRATTORIA NO 10 Map pp282–3 _Italian_
☎ 312-984-1718; 10 N Dearborn; mains $14-27; 🕑 closed lunch Sat, closed Sun; Blue Line to Washington

This bustling Italian restaurant's location just a couple blocks from the Loop theater district

makes it an ideal candidate for filling your belly pre-play. The simple menu provides exceptionally flavorful takes on familiar items like ravioli (try the asparagus tip, aged _bufala_ mozzarella and sun-dried tomato filling) and risotto. If you're in a hurry, the servers will help you get out the door fast; if not, lingering is warmly condoned.

Cheap Eats
BURRITO BUGGY Map pp282–3 _Mexican_
☎ 312-362-0199; 206 W Van Buren St; mains $4-7; 🕑 lunch only; Brown, Green, Orange, Purple Line to LaSalle

This quickie lunch option – a favorite with traders from the Chicago Stock Exchange – serves the biggest, weirdest burritos you've ever encountered. The barbecue chicken burrito includes tangy chicken alongside corn, cilantro, cheese and mashed potatoes(!). Amazingly, it works. The jerk chicken burrito is equally delicious.

GOLD COAST DOGS
Map pp282–3 _American_
☎ 312-578-1133; 17 S Wabash Ave; mains $3-6; 🕑 to 6pm; Brown, Green, Orange, Purple Line to Madison

Get your dog char-grilled and to go at this run-down temple to the legendary Chicago hot dog. 'Chicago dogs' come with the proper sides here: onions, relish, mustard, hot peppers, celery salt and a warm pickle spear. Not in the mood for a dog? The burgers are tops as well. The atmosphere in the restaurant, which shares space with a fast-food chain, is enough to make you lose your appetite though – get the dog and take a hike.

JACOBS BROS BAGELS
Map pp282–3 _Bagels_
☎ 312-922-2245; 53 W Jackson Blvd; mains $1-4; 🕑 lunch only; Blue Line to Jackson

Chicago is not much of a bagel town, making this convenient outpost of Jacobs Bros all the more noteworthy. The bagels here are almost as substantial as the surrounding 6ft-thick walls of the Monadnock Building (one of Chicago's first skyscrapers).

SOPRAFFINA MARKET CAFFE
Map pp282–3 _Italian_
☎ 312-726-4800; 222 W Adams St; mains $6-10; 🕑 lunch only, closed Sat & Sun; Brown, Purple, Orange Line to Quincy

Fast-food Italian with panache, the fresh cuisine here includes a bevy of salads such as chickpea, wheat berry and portobello mushroom and *giardiniera* (hot peppers). You can also order sandwiches, pasta and super-thin-crust pizza. This branch of the local chain also serves filling breakfasts.

Top Five the Loop & Grant Park

- Barbecue chicken burritos with mashed potato filling at **Burrito Buggy** (p129).
- The intoxicating elevator ride to the dining area of **Everest** (p128).
- Beer and sauerkraut after work at the **Berghoff** (p128).
- Settling into **Miller's Pub** (p128) for a 3am steak.
- Toasted garlic bagel and a little historic architecture at **Jacobs Bros Bagels** (p129).

NEAR NORTH & NAVY PIER

The area north of the Chicago River has some of the best dining options in the city. Whether you're eating tapas or Thai, Near North leans towards creative presentations and lively atmosphere. This is also Chicago's pizza mecca; pizza-lovers up for the challenge could hit Chicago's top five pizza restaurants without having to leave the neighborhood. Now *that's* amore!

Navy Pier...well...it's about what you'd expect. Plenty of chains whose culinary achievements mostly center on their dexterity with a deep-fat fryer. There is one seafood standout on the pier worth exploring, however.

Near North

BANDERA Map pp280–1   American
☎ 312-644-3524; 535 N Michigan Ave; mains $10-25; Red Line to Grand

Looking up at the ugly entry to this 2nd-story restaurant on Michigan Ave, you'd have no idea what a gem awaits inside. The red-bedecked Bandera has the comfortable, retro feel of an expensive supper club, but without the snooty waiters (and at half the price). American classics predominate here, such as meatloaf, grilled fish and rotisserie chicken. Portions are large, and the food is complemented by live jazz starting nightly around 7pm. When you've shopped till you've dropped, this is the place to come pick yourself back up again.

BEN PAO Map pp280–1   Chinese
☎ 312-222-1888; 52 W Illinois St; mains $9-17; closed lunch Sat & Sun; Red Line to Grand

Chinese food reaches new heights under the inspiration of Rich Melman; the high-ceilinged dark interior, with its circular bar, is one of the most chic Asian restaurants in town. The menu – which lands Ben Pao on 'Best Of' lists every year – features many twists, including five-spice shrimp satay, lemon-crusted chicken and Hong Kong spicy eggplant.

BICE Map pp280–1   Italian
☎ 312-664-1474; 158 E Ontario St; mains $13-26; Red Line to Grand

This import from Milan provides an excellent opportunity to savor the delicately spiced foods of northern Italy without the jet lag. Risottos are superb, as are the creamy pastas. At the outdoor tables you can keep your eyes on the sidewalk crowd and ignite the jealousy of the passing rabble by letting your tongue linger on the homemade gelato. Inside, the stylish art deco decor makes a good backdrop for the stylish patrons.

BRASSERIE JO Map pp280–1   French
☎ 312-595-0800; 59 W Hubbard St; mains $9-30; dinner only; Blue Line to Merchandise Mart

This huge, open place serves wonderful food from Alsace, the French region near Germany where owner Jean Joho was born. From the signature beer specially brewed by a local microbrewery to the hot and fresh baguettes, all the details are right. Try the great *choucroute* (smoked meats and sausages on sauerkraut) or the shrimp in a bag. The service is as bright and cheery as the decor. Wear a fancy hat on Thursday and get a free *chapeau au chocolat* desert.

CAFE IBERICO Map pp280–1   Spanish
☎ 312-573-1510; 739 N LaSalle St; meals $15-30; Brown Line to Chicago

Happy diners look like kids in a candy store as they ponder their little plates of tapas here. Among the choices: *salpicon de marisco* (seafood salad with shrimp, octopus and squid), *croquetas de pollo* (chicken and ham puffs with garlic sauce) and *vieiras a la plancha* (grilled scallops with saffron). Finish it off with flan. Most of the small dishes average $4.50. Iberico's sangria is a force to be reckoned with, and in the summer the entire front room will be packed wall-to-wall with Loop workers knocking back pitchers of the stuff.

CARSON'S Map pp280–1   *Barbecue*
☎ 312-280-9200; 612 N Wells St; mains $15-28;
Brown Line to Chicago

Huge piles of fall-off-the-bone, baby-back pork ribs are the speciality at this Chicago classic, a potential gold mine for cardiologists with cash-flow problems. The decor here is dated, but you'll be gazing at your sauce-covered fingers anyway. Coleslaw, fries and rolls accompany the main attraction.

CYRANO'S BISTROT Map pp280–1   *French*
☎ 312-467-0546; 546 N Wells St; mains $9-19;
😊 closed Sun & Mon; Blue Line to Merchandise Mart

This popular casual French restaurant is named for the famous Cyrano of Bergerac, the hometown shared by chef and owner Didier Durand. A very cheerful place, Cyrano's serves a menu of southern French favorites, including numerous roasted meats (and, in a bow to local culinary obsessions, a few pasta dishes as well). A few tables line the street and make a good place to sip one of the many wines while watching the afterwork hordes march home. The $13 lunch special is a four-course marvel that's served all at once.

Cheezburger! Cheezburger!

Only the dimmest of rubes tries to order fries at the Billy Goat Tavern (Map pp280–1; ☎ 312-222-1525; lower level of 430 N Michigan Ave), a cathedral of grease, smoke and rousing conversations that also qualifies as a tourist attraction. John Belushi brought national fame to this place with his skit on Saturday Night Live. Among the memorable lines: 'No fries – chips!' and 'No Coke – Pepsi!'

Local fame stems from its subterranean position between the *Sun-Times* and *Tribune*. Legions of photos of dead writers and columnists line the walls; any link between their demises and a steady diet of beer, burgers and cigarettes must be coincidental. One such legendary patron was *Tribune* columnist Mike Royko. On weekdays a few families attired in Cubs clothing sometimes visit, but they're soon chased away by the after-work hordes of drunken journalists, carousing ad execs and no-nonsense laborers. It warms the heart to see a suburban family cowering next to some beer-swilling, smoke-blowing galoot. But beware: the tourists get their revenge on the weekends, when they own the place. Prices are dirt cheap, but if you like your burger to have the distinctive taste of meat, order a double.

DAO Map pp280–1   *Thai*
☎ 312-337-0000; 230 E Ohio St; mains $6-9;
Red Line to Grand

A classic Thai restaurant in a neighborhood lacking in good dining options, Dao is popular with lunching workers. Although the prices are low, the ambience here is a cut above your usual bare-bones Thai eatery, with traditional Thai decorations lending the room a touch of exotic class. Service at all times is quick and cheerful, and all dishes can be made vegetarian on demand.

ERAWAN Map pp280–1   *Thai*
☎ 312-642-6888; 729 N Clark; mains $12-38;
😊 closed lunch Sat & Sun; Red Line to Chicago

An ornate, four-star take on Thai food, Erawan sweats the small stuff, from intricately carved garnishes to food presentations that will have you reaching for your camera. The three-course, prix-fixe lunch menu for $20 is a great introduction to the work of chef Art Lee, who pushes Thai flavors and textures into otherworldly directions.

FOGO DE CHAO Map pp280–1   *Brazilian*
☎ 312-932-9330; 661 N LaSalle St; lunch $25, dinner $40; 😊 closed lunch Sat & Sun; Brown Line to Chicago

For those of you who've always dreamed of having Brazilian *gauchos* (cowboys) serve you a never-ending array of meat from a trolley cart, well, we have some good news. And the rest of you will probably like Fogo de Chao as well. This all-you-can-eat meaty import from Brazil revolves around heaps and heaps of well-seasoned lamb, chicken, pork loin and steak. The wonderful dishes here are served in a novel way: diners are issued laminated discs on entry – turn it green side up, and servers dressed as *gauchos* will hurry to your table to fill your plate with whatever meats you desire. Other perks include mashed potatoes, fried bananas and unlimited trips to the well-stocked salad bar.

FRONTERA GRILL Map pp280–1   *Mexican*
☎ 312-661-1434; 445 N Clark St; mains $14-25;
😊 closed Sun; Red Line to Grand

Once you've eaten here, you'll never be able to look at the so-so stuff most places pass off as Mexican food again. Chef-owner Rick Bayless has achieved celebrity status with his fresh variations inspired by south-of-the-border fare. His unusual pepper sauces are worth rolling around your palate like a fine wine. Hot tortillas made on-site hold tacos *al carbón*, which are filled with charred beef and grilled green onions. *Chiles rellenos* (stuffed poblano peppers) await converts to their succulent richness. The place is always mobbed, so expect to wait; reservations are only taken for five or more. See also the listing for Topolobampo (p133).

GENE & GEORGETTI

Map pp280–1   *American*
☎ 312-527-3718; 500 N Franklin St; mains $15-35;
🕙 closed Sun; Brown Line to Merchandise Mart
For once, a place touting itself as one of Frank Sinatra's favorite restaurants can back up the claim, which should tell you everything you need to know about this classic steak house, more than half a century old. Out of place in the city, the wooden building looks like it would be more comfortable on a two-lane road in some farm town. Old-timers, politicos and crusty regulars are seated downstairs. New-timers, conventioneers and tourists are seated upstairs. The steaks are the same on both levels: thick, well aged and well priced.

GREEN DOOR TAVERN

Map pp280–1   *American*
☎ 312-664-5496; 678 N Orleans St; mains $6-14;
🕙 closed Sun; Brown Line to Chicago
The 1872 building housing this veteran bar and grill is one of the oldest structures north of the river. The Green Door Tavern has been around almost as long, serving up great burgers, sandwiches, salads and a few pasta dishes. The walls here are completely covered with ancient photos, signs and memorabilia. If you're in the mood for simple but well cooked food in a lively, entertaining old-Chicago setting, this is the place for you.

JOE'S SEAFOOD, PRIME STEAK & STONE CRAB
Map pp280–1   *American*
☎ 312-379-5637; 60 E Grand Ave; mains $12-24;
🕙 closed lunch Sun; Red Line to Grand
A Chicago restaurateur imported Joe's Stone Crab from Miami Beach and gave it a distinctly local spin, not the least of which is the 'Prime Steak &' in the name. The signature item here in this well-appointed, masculine-feeling restaurant is stone crab – the succulent arthropods are flown in daily from the Gulf of Mexico. The crabs, which may be unavailable in summer months, can run up to $100. The key lime pie here has been known to elicit tears of joy in more sensitive diners.

LEONA'S Map pp280–1   *American*
☎ 312-867-0101; 646 N Franklin St; mains $9-34;
Brown Line to Chicago
'We refuse to serve pretentious appetizers out of thimbles. Mangia!' So goes the motto at this reliable local chain, where filling meals of pizza, sandwiches, steak and ribs dominate. This outpost of Leona's, which has remained a family business for the last 53 years, is located right under the El tracks, near many of the River North galleries.

NAHA Map pp280–1   *New American*
☎ 312-239-4030; 500 N Clark St; mains $14-27;
🕙 closed Sun; Red Line to Grand
The gray finished-concrete floors and subdued color palette help put the focus where it should be – on the food. Chef Carrie Nahabedian draws from her Armenian roots in crafting popular entrées as roast mint and lemon-marinated leg of lamb, and halibut with fennel pollen and herbs. Creative salads are another speciality of the house. Don't miss the heirloom tomato and homemade ricotta cheese salad if it's in season. Ask for a table along the south wall for better people-watching opportunities – the power-brokering going on at Naha is a savory meal all its own.

NOMI Map pp280–1   *French*
☎ 312-239-4030; 800 N Michigan Ave; mains $10-55;
Red Line to Chicago
Named for its stately position on North Michigan Avenue, NoMi has been setting Chicago foodies' hearts afire since opening in 2001. Located on the 7th floor of the new Park Hyatt hotel, the sleek, minimalist restaurant is worth a visit for its views over the Magnificent Mile alone. Acclaimed chef Sandro Gamba's knack for combining French fare with Asian flair is evident in dishes ranging from roasted Chilean sea bass to frog leg risotto. Reserve a window table around sunset – it's one of the most romantic experiences the city has to offer. Reservations required.

PASHA Map pp280–1   *French & Italian*
☎ 312-397-0100; 642 N Clark St; mains $12-30; 🕙 to 4am, dinner only (kitchen closes at 3am), closed Mon; Red Line to Grand
The only restaurant in Chicago to feature a bar in the ladies, Pasha is known for doing things a little differently. Pasha is both restaurant and club, with diners separated from dancers by sinuous wrought-iron railings. The interior – a pastiche of 21st-century industrial and opulent

styles from Russia and the Middle East – gets progressively louder as the night goes on, and the kitchen is known for creative French-Italian cuisine such as shrimp and strawberry risotto and veal medallions with artichoke hearts and white wine.

ROSEBUD ON RUSH Map pp280–1 *Italian*
☎ 312-266-6444; 720 N Rush St; mains $14-38; Red Line to Chicago

Huge portions of familiar Italian standards dominate the tables at this outpost of the Rosebud empire (see the Little Italy section p133). The prices, quality and weight of the doggie bags are all high. Specialities include veal in its many forms. You'll be unlikely to find enough energy to sing 'Chicago' as you and a companion attempt to plow your way through the Festivale di Sinatra con Amore, a massive meal for two that seems to include half the menu.

SHAW'S CRAB HOUSE
Map pp280–1 *Seafood*
☎ 312-527-2722; 21 E Hubbard St; mains $10-50; ⚘ closed lunch Sat & Sun; Red Line to Grand

If you're just going to hit one fish place in Near North, come to Shaw's. Their beautiful old dining room feels like a step back in time to the Jazz Age. Oysters and crab are the way to go here; to find out what's best and freshest, ask one of the friendly and efficient servers. The crab-cake appetizer and the key lime pie make good bookends to the meal. The adjoining Blue Crab Lounge, which has live music several nights a week, is the casual adjunct to the main restaurant.

SPAGO Map pp280–1 *New American*
☎ 312-527-3700; 520 N Dearborn St; mains $10-28; ⚘ closed Sun; Red Line to Grand

Things have calmed down quite a bit here since the glitterati-filled first year of the Los

---

Angeles restaurant's Chicago outpost. These days, the vibe in the open-kitchen eatery is still energetic but crowds tend to be here more for chef Francois Kwaku-Dongo's food than for the scene itself. The entrées – like chinois chicken salad and sautéed salmon with green lentils – come from the California fusion palette, which blends techniques and cuisines from every continent.

SUSHISAMBA RIO Map pp280–1 *Fusion*
☎ 312-595-2300; 504 N Wells; mains $15-30; Brown Line to Merchandise Mart

The Japanese-Brazilian-Peruvian restaurant has an eye-popping interior, complete with year-round rooftop dining with views over the city and a simulated Amazon River running under glass. A DJ spins records on the mezzanine, and patrons can avail themselves to drinks from Chicago's only caipirinha bar (caipirinha is a Brazilian spirit made from sugar cane). Oh, the food? Sushi rolls, miso-marinated sea bass, and small flash-fried crabs, which you eat like oversized popcorn. Dress like you're heading to a chic nightclub, and you'll fit right in.

TOPOLOBAMPO Map pp280–1 *Mexican*
☎ 312-661-1434; 445 N Clark St; mains $16-33; ⚘ closed Sun; Red Line to Grand

Part of the same operation as Frontera Grill, this is where chef Rick Bayless lets his creativity flow unfettered by cost restrictions. Compared to its rollicking neighbor, Topolobampo's mood seems downright serious, as diners sample combinations of flavors most people never knew existed. The menu changes nightly; be prepared for a memorable experience. Reservations required.

TRU Map pp280–1 *French*
☎ 312-202-0001; 676 N St Clair St; dinner $80-135; ⚘ dinner only, closed Sun; Red Line to Grand

Gale Gand (of the Food Network's *Sweet Dreams*) and Rick Tramonto opened one of the city's best restaurants in 1999. The food is French, but with a sense of humor. Starters include a trademark staircase of caviar, with a variety of the little fish eggs waltzing down the steps. The eclectic and ever-changing menu also features a cheese course that's one of the best in the US and renowned deserts, such as the heavenly roasted pineapple carpaccio. Expect flawless service in the all-white dining room. Menus include an all-vegetable version ($90) and a chef's special collection ($135).

Top Five Near North & Navy Pier

- Time traveling with crabs at **Shaw's Crab House** (p133).
- A big pitcher of sangria and a tiny plate of garlicky potatoes at **Cafe Iberico** (p130).
- Affordable Mexican adventuring at the **Frontera Grill** (p131).
- Learning the tricks of the cab-driving trade at **Mike's Rainbow Restaurant** (p134).
- Clowning around with Rick Tramonto's *amuse bouche* at **Tru** (p133).

WILDFIRE Map pp280–1 · American
☎ 312-787-9000; 159 W Erie St; mains $11-23;
⏰ dinner only; Brown Line to Chicago

A huge grill, rotisserie and wood-burning oven roast shrimp, prime rib, steak and ribs at this haven for barbecuers with snow-covered grills. Prices for the generous portions average about $18 – not bad for this comfortable and welcoming place. In the best tradition of Chicago smoke-filled rooms (where dubious political deals are cut), you'll emerge smelling of smoke, but at least it's barbecue rather than cigar.

Navy Pier

The none-too-great dining options at Navy Pier include an assortment of contrived theme restaurants as well as chains like McDonald's. If you're planning a sojourn here, save your eating for spots further west, although kids will no doubt be satisfied with the offerings.

RIVA Map pp280–1 · Seafood
☎ 312-644-7482; 700 E Grand Ave, on Navy Pier;
mains $11-37; bus 66

The high-class option for Navy Pier victuals, Riva combines Italian with seafood. The latter is fitting, given Lake Michigan laps a few feet away. Needless to say, the menu features plenty of calamari and various fresh grilled fish dishes (the tuna is especially good). The inflated prices buy great views of the lake and city skyline.

Cheap Eats

BIG BOWL Map pp280–1 · Asian
☎ 312-951-1888; 60 E Ohio St; mains $8-12;
Red Line to Grand

Big bowls of Asian noodles – more than 30 varieties – are the speciality here, all made with fresh ingredients and a kicking array of sauces. The choices include wheat noodles with shrimp, black beans and snow peas, and barbecued chicken and noodles in broth. The interior is modern and stylish, with huge booths in the shape of – you guessed it – big bowls.

BOSTON BLACKIES Map pp280–1 · American
☎ 312-938-8700; 164 E Grand Ave; mains $5-12;
Red Line to Grand

The gregarious old guys playing dollar poker up front (you use dollar bills as the playing cards, betting on the serial numbers) set the tone at Blackies. Platters of burgers and sandwiches are made with top-notch ingredients. The cheddar oozes out like volcanic magma under the chives and bacon bits on the potato skins ($6).

GINO'S EAST Map pp280–1 · Pizza
☎ 312-943-1124; 633 N Wells St; mains $7-25;
Brown Line to Chicago

In the great deep-dish pizza wars going on right now in Chicago, Gino's is easily one of the top three heavies. And they encourage their customers to do something neither Pizzeria Uno nor Giordano's would allow: customers at Gino's have been covering over every available surface (except for the actual food) with graffiti. The pizza is something you'll write home about: the classic stuffed cheese and sausage pie oozes countless pounds of cheese over its crispy cornmeal crust.

GIORDANO'S Map pp280–1 · Pizza
☎ 312-951-0747; 730 N Rush St; mains $8-26;
Red Line to Chicago

The founders of Giordano's, Efren and Joseph Boglio, claim that they got their winning recipe for stuffed pizza from – aww – their mother back in Italy. If you want a slice of heaven, order the 'special,' a stuffed pizza containing sausage, mushroom, green pepper and onions. We think it's the best deep-dish pizza in Chicago.

MIKE'S RAINBOW RESTAURANT
Map pp280–1 · American
☎ 312-787-4499; 708 N Clark St; mains $3.50-8;
⏰ to 1am; Red Line to Chicago

From the number of taxi cabs parked out front, you'd think this old-school diner doubled as a dispatching service. But the cabbies hanging out here are off-duty, attracted by the low, low prices and friendly vibe of the Near North institution. Big breakfasts come with real hash brown potatoes and are available throughout the day.

MR BEEF Map pp280–1 · American
☎ 312-337-8500; 660 N Orleans St; mains $4-7;
⏰ lunch only, closed Sun; Brown Line to Chicago

A local classic, the $4.50 Italian beef sandwiches come with long, spongy white buns that rapidly go soggy after a load of the spicy beef and cooking juices has been ladled on. Past a sign marked 'Classy Dining Room,' you'll find a decidedly unclassy porch with picnic tables and an odd selection of movie posters on the wall. The pictures of Jay Leno aren't fake – he comes here every time he's in town.

PITA PAVILION Map pp280–1   *Mediterranean*
☎ 312-335-9018; 8th flr Chicago Place, 700 N Michigan Ave; mains $5-10; ⏰ lunch only; Red Line to Grand

On crummy days, the atrium winter garden atop Chicago Place can be one of the brightest places to eat lunch, amid palm trees and burbling fountains, with a great view up and down the Magnificent Mile. The pick of the food court here has to be the Pita Pavilion, which serves a great falafel pita sandwich for $4. The other cuisine choices are mall food-court standards.

PIZZERIA UNO Map pp280–1   *Pizza*
☎ 312-321-1000; 29 E Ohio St; mains $8-26; Red Line to Grand

Ike Sewell supposedly invented Chicago-style pizza here on Dec 3, 1943, although his claim to fame is hotly disputed by other claimants. This well-worn building has been gussied up to resemble the franchised branches, but the pizza still tastes best here. A light, flaky crust holds piles of cheese and an herb-laced tomato sauce. The pizzas take a while, but stick to the pitchers of beer and cheap red wine to kill time and avoid the salad and other distractions, so you can save room for the main event. The $18 classic lands on the table with a resounding thud and can feed a family of four.

THAI STAR Map pp280–1   *Thai*
☎ 312-951-1196; 660 N State St; mains $6-12; Red Line to Chicago

This survivor sparked the affordable Thai food rage of the early 1980s. Now its legions of competitors have closed, and it continues to soldier on with excellent and inexpensive food served on plywood tables in a charmless corner location. Palate-scorching curries are the specialty; none cost more than $6. Once your eyes are watering, you're less likely to notice the lack of decor. BYOB.

GOLD COAST
The Gold Coast's restaurants consist mostly of mid- to high-end eateries intent on providing a pleasant meal without the DJ booths and special effects that mark the scene in hipper neighborhoods. Steak, heavy and rare, is on the menu here, and many of the city's power players come here to seal nefarious deals over a table-sized porterhouse. The main eat street is Rush St, though some of the area's more interesting picks are located a little off the beaten path.

BISTRO 110 Map pp278–9   *French*
☎ 312-266-3110; 110 E Pearson St; mains $10-28; Red Line to Chicago

One of the first bistros to set up shop in Chicago, Bistro 110 has aged well over its nearly two decades in operation. The lively space still feels fresh and modern, and the service is as friendly and attentive as ever. Don't leave here without trying the Robuchon lamb, which is roasted and braised for 20 hours before reaching your table. The spicy pepper steak in cognac cream sauce is equally memorable. In town over the weekend? The New Orleans-style jazz brunch is a great way to spend your Sunday.

CRU CAFE & WINE BAR
Map pp278–9   *French*
☎ 312-337-4001, 888 N Wabash Ave; mains $12-24; ⏰ to 1am; Red Line to Chicago

Choose among no less than 500 bottles at this sleek wine bar. The well-dressed patrons speak in lots of European accents, some of them even authentic. In summer you can idle away hours people-watching from the outdoor tables. In winter you can gather with a full-bodied red around the roaring fireplace inside. The food ranges from sandwiches to salads to quiche, none of it cheap: a club sandwich is $17. The late-night cheese platters seem a world removed from the late-night weenies you can get elsewhere.

Mr Beef (p134)

Eating – Gold Coast

GIBSON'S Map pp278–9 *Steak House*

☎ 312-266-8999; 1028 N Rush St; mains $20-80;
closed lunch Mon-Thu; Red Line to Clark/Division

It's a scene seven nights a week at this local original. Politicians, movers, shakers and the shaken-down compete for prime table space in the buzzing dining area. The bar is a prime stalking place for available millionaires. As for the meat on the plates, the steaks are as good as they come, and the seafood is fresh and expensive.

LE COLONIAL

Map pp278–9 *French-Vietnamese*
☎ 312-255-0088; 937 N Rush St; mains $13-24;
Red Line to Chicago

A colonial outpost of the New York original, Le Colonial re-creates the feel of a swank Vietnamese restaurant during the French era of the 1950s. Fortunately, there's no malaria, and the food shows more imagination than the French exhibited during their rule. The delicately seasoned offerings include warm salads and several seafood and duck dishes. The upstairs bar, with the greenery and languidly turning fans, achieves an atmospheric charm that will have you reaching for a tonic.

MK Map pp278–9 *New American*

☎ 312-482-9719; 868 N Franklin St; mains $12-36;
Brown Line to Chicago

The exposed brick walls hint at mk's industrial past, but this dining hotspot is nothing if not civilized. Chef Michael Kornick wows the mostly business crowds with artfully presented dishes such as seared ahi tuna, roast rack of lamb, and sautéed veal sweetbreads. The desserts are equally scrumptious; pastry chef Mindy Segal has received deserved acclaim for her banana brioche bread pudding and amazing peach and wild huckleberry *crostada*. Noise levels here on weekends hinder confidential tête-à-têtes, but those looking for imaginative culinary creations paired with excellent people-watching opportunities won't go home disappointed.

MORTON'S Map pp278–9 *Steak House*

☎ 312-266-4820; 1050 N State St; mains $19-75;
dinner only; Red Line to Clark/Division

With a clubby ambience and prime service, Morton's has remained Chicago's premier steak house long enough for scores of competitors to arrive on the scene. The meat here is aged to perfection and displayed tableside

Gone to the Dogs

Nobody knows how the classic Chicago hot dog evolved, but it's definitely become a unique creation you won't find anywhere else in the US. More than just a wiener and a bun, a Chicago dog contains a vast array of condiments and flavorings. When done right, it should defy easy consumption, with various ingredients flopping out all over the place and juices and sauces oozing in all directions.

For the record, a Chicago hot dog begins with an all-beef hot dog, preferably a local Vienna brand. Some places steam them, others boil and a few grill. Which method is best is a matter of great debate. However cooked, the 'tube steak' is then laid into a fresh poppy-seed bun. Now the fun begins. A traditional dog will have all of the following toppings, although local variations exist:

- Diced onions, white or yellow
- Diced tomatoes
- Sliced cucumbers, possibly slightly pickled
- Shredded iceberg lettuce
- Diced green bell pepper
- Pepperoncini (Italian hot and pickled peppers)
- Sweet relish, usually a virulent shade of green
- Bright yellow mustard
- Catsup (although some would say 'never!')
- Celery salt

The result? Part salad, part hot dog. It's not hard to find a good Chicago hot dog; several hundred joints throughout the city peddle different varieties. Start by looking for the big Vienna Beef signs. You'll know you've found a promising spot if it contains a few distinctly un-fancy Formica tables and a long counter for ordering. The following three places are all recommended:

- Gold Coast Dogs (see p129)
- Hot Doug's (Lake View, p146)
- Wiener Circle (Lincoln Park, p142)

before cooking. See that half a cow? It's the 48oz double porterhouse. Smaller – but still quite dangerous if dropped on your toe – are the fillets, strip steaks and other cuts. The immense baked potatoes could prop up church foundations. Try the hash browns, superb versions of a side dish all too often ignored. Expensive reds anchor the wine list.

PJ CLARKE'S Map pp278–9 *American*

☎ 312-664-1650; 1204 N State St; mains $8-23;
Red Line to Clark/Division

Hungry for some companionship? PJ Clarke's is an upscale restaurant/pub where Chicago's straight, thirtysomething singles come to eyeball one another. Both classy and cozy, PJ Clarke's specializes in comfort foods with high-end twists, like the Béarnaise Burger or the Teriyaki Skirt Steak sandwich.

PUCK'S AT THE MCA

Map pp278–9   *New American*
☎ 312-397-4034; 220 E Chicago Ave; mains $6-14; ☺ lunch only, closed Mon; Red Line to Chicago
Located in the Museum of Contemporary Art, this outlet of the irrepressible Wolfgang Puck features strictly contemporary cooking, with dishes that fuse Asian and Mediterranean cuisine. The changing menu features lots of marinated seafood and salads, as well as a few hot items. A deli counter offers sandwiches and more to go. In summer, dine out back on the MCA's patio, one of the city's great hidden gems.

PUMP ROOM Map pp278–9   *American*
☎ 312-266-0360; Ambassador East hotel, 1301 N State St; mains $11-38; Red Line to Clark/Division
Book yourself into Booth One at this legendary spot and you'll have something in common with the pantheon of celebrity customers whose photos line the walls. Famous since the 1940s, this Pump Room continues its tradition of understated elegance. Real VIPs, or just lucky poseurs, sit in Booth One, a see-and-be-seen throwback to a previous, glamorous era. There's a dress code, which means you'll be well-attired for the cheek-to-cheek dancing that takes places most nights after dinner. Veal porterhouse and grilled sea bass head up the American menu.

SIGNATURE ROOM AT THE 95TH

Map pp278–9   *American*
☎ 312-787-9596; John Hancock Center, 875 N Michigan Ave; mains $12-39; Red Line to Chicago
Near the top of the Hancock Center – no points for guessing the correct floor – this large room offers stunning views on clear days. Given that diners spend more time looking out the windows than looking at their plates, you'd think the kitchen wouldn't trouble itself over the food, but the fish, steak and pasta dishes are quite good. The lunch buffet ($14), served Monday to Saturday, can be a fine deal, especially if you satisfy your view cravings here as opposed to buying a ticket to the Hancock observation deck. Families come for the Sunday brunch; cheapskates get the same soul-stirring views for the price of a (costly) beer, one flight up in the Signature Lounge.

Charlie Trotter's *by Ryan Ver Berkmoes*

I was standing on Armitage Ave, admiring the grape leaves growing over the arbors next to the entrance to **Charlie Trotter's Restaurant** (Map pp276–7; ☎ 773-248-6228; www.charlietrotters.com; 816 W Armitage Ave) when one of the valet parkers appeared at my elbow and asked me if I would like a menu. 'Sure,' I said. A short time later, the valet returned with a creamy sheet of paper listing the night's lineup. 'Please,' he said with a gentle and sincere smile, 'enjoy your evening.'

Despite the utter lack of evidence that I, a grubby guidebook writer lurking on the sidewalk, would ever have the means to spend an evening in Charlie Trotter's rarefied air (roughly $175 per person), a valet had anticipated my needs and sought out what I desired. Menu in hand, I departed with a big smile on my face.

Making people smile – that's the goal of the thirtysomething Trotter, who modestly says his dream is to run the finest restaurant in the world. It's a goal he's meeting. He's won a slew of culinary honors, including James Beard Foundation awards and the Grand Award from the *Wine Spectator*, which has named Charlie Trotter's the best restaurant in the world for wine and food.

Part of the allure is the surprise that awaits each night. There is no regular menu, no signature dish. Rather, an ever-changing lineup of offerings varies according to the seasons and the ingenuity of Trotter and his artful staff. The kitchen's creations cater to the eye as much as the palate. Architects could learn from the complex constructions of food and sauces.

Diners choose between the $100 prix-fixe vegetarian menu and the $125 grand menu. The wine selection spans a 45-page list and a 40,000-bottle cellar. A grand menu in late 2003 included extravagant entries such as 'Terrine of Skate with Marinated Radish, Shellfish Gelee & Saffron Infused Yellow Taxi Tomato Broth,' and 'Grilled Arkansas Rabbit Loin with Rillette, Cumin, Chanterelle Mushrooms & Spicy Date Puree.'

On better-dressed days I've had some splendid meals at Charlie Trotter's. For each meal I booked weeks in advance, and you should, too. Make that months in advance, if you want the kitchen table, where four people can enjoy a close-up view of the action. The restaurant takes reservations four months out.

Should you not dine at the restaurant, you can always partake of some other part of the growing Trotter empire. Trotter has put out a long list of cookbooks and launched the upscale takeaway **Charlie Trotters To Go** (Map pp276–7; ☎ 773-868-6510; 1337 West Fullerton Ave), where even those on the tightest budgets can buy a taste of heaven.

Eating – Gold Coast

Eating – Lincoln Park & Old Town

Top Five Gold Coast

- Swinging with the New Orleans-style jazz brunch at **Bistro 110** (p135).
- Ordering up a skillet o' joy at the **Tempo Cafe** (p138).
- Keeping winter at bay with homemade chili from the **Lo-cal Locale** (p138).
- Putting away a Dutch Baby at the **Original Pancake House** (p138).
- A glass of red and a seat outside at **Cru Cafe & Wine Bar** (p135).

Cheap Eats

FOODLIFE Map pp278–9 *Food Court*
☎ 312-335-3663; mezzanine level Water Tower Place, 835 N Michigan Ave; mains $5-9; Red Line to Chicago

At this high-concept food court, you pick up a magnetic card on the way in, and the staff reserve you a table. Then you wander around and choose items from the stir-fry, Mediterranean, Mexican, salad or rotisserie bars. Your meal gets tallied up on the card, and you pay on the way out. A fun refuge from the Water Tower shopping hordes.

JOHNNY ROCKETS Map pp278–9 *American*
☎ 312-337-3900; 901 N Rush St; mains $6-14; Red Line to Chicago

This faux '50s diner, on the back side of the vast 900 N Michigan mall, features a kitchen, eating area and servers all clad in white. Kids like the spot, and folks rave about the burgers.

LO-CAL LOCALE Map pp278–9 *American*
☎ 312-943-9060; 912 N Rush St; mains $4-6; Red Line to Chicago

A budget haven in the midst of the Gold Coast's ritziest shopping, this spot has fiercely loyal customers and strong ideas about making things fresh, from scratch. The homemade chili here will keep the cold Chicago winds at bay, and the calzones, veggie burgers and funky burritos (try the Cajun with turkey sausage and red beans and rice) are equally good. This place also has the creamiest, chocolatiest frozen yogurt anywhere. Cash only.

ORIGINAL PANCAKE HOUSE
Map pp278–9 *Breakfast*
☎ 312-642-7917; 22 E Bellevue Pl; mains $5-10; lunch only; Red Line to Clark/Division

Follow your nose to this quaint little cash-only breakfast chain, tucked into a quiet alcove of its busy Near North neighborhood. *Chicago* magazine awarded the OPH Best Breakfast, and it's easy to see why. With 20 different kinds of pancakes (including the formidable, basketball-sized Dutch Baby) and a myriad of egg dishes, the Original Pancake House stands head and shoulders above most Gold Coast breakfast options.

TEMPO CAFE Map pp278–9 *American*
☎ 312-943-3929; 6 E Chestnut St; mains $6-13; 24hr; Red Line to Chicago

Bright and cheery, this 24-hour upscale diner brings most of their meals to the table the way they're meant to be served – in a skillet. Their omelette-centric menu includes all manner of fresh veggies and meat, as well as sandwiches, soups and salads. The scene here after the bars close is chaotic and fun.

Tempo Cafe

LINCOLN PARK & OLD TOWN

It's a great time to be opening a restaurant in Lincoln Park, where the trendy locals make dining out an integral part of their busy social calendars. Halsted and Lincoln are the two streets for culinary window shopping in the neighborhood; on both streets the restaurants tend to be loud, energetic affairs. Having DePaul University in the neighborhood helps keep the roster of cheap eats booming, even as the commercial rents here continue to shoot skyward.

The restaurant scene in Old Town is a quieter version of Lincoln Park. Dining here is casual and un-trendy, appealing mostly to thirty- and fortysomethings in the neighborhood. If you're undecided where to eat come dinner time, just walk up Wells St and let your nose be your guide.

Lincoln Park

BACINO'S Map pp276–7 *Pizza*
☎ 773-472-7400; 2204 N Lincoln Ave; mains $7-20; Brown, Red Line to Fullerton

This local chain specializes in the stuffed variation of Chicago-style pizza. A very thin crust on the top allows still another layer of cheese to be piled on even higher. The stuffed spinach model – the most popular choice – contains plenty of useful iron to fuel your grueling tourism schedule.

CAFE BA-BA-REEBA! Map pp276–7 *Spanish*
☎ 773-935-5000; 2024 N Halsted St; mains $16-30; Brown, Red Line to Armitage

If you plan on kissing anyone after dinner, make certain they've dined with you at this delightfully ersatz tapas joint where the garlic-laced sauces may have you surreptitiously licking the plates. The menu changes daily but always includes some spicy meats, marinated fish and a potato salad that will forever have you lambasting the gloppy American version. Plates cost about $6 apiece and you should plan on putting away at least three of these per person. If you want a main event, order one of the nine paellas ($12 a person) as soon as you get seated in one of the many rooms – they take a while to prepare.

CAFE BERNARD Map pp276–7 *French*
☎ 773-871-2100; 2100 N Halsted St; mains $18-23; Brown, Red Line to Armitage

This fun veteran has been peddling simple French food for decades – since the times when this was a solid blue-collar neighborhood and French meant something you tried on a date. The tables are intimate, the atmosphere romantic and the French bistro classics well prepared. Try the pork loin *au poivre* (with pepper). Out back is the Red Rooster Cafe & Wine Bar – a great post-meal stop (see p162).

JOHN BARLEYCORN MEMORIAL PUB
Map pp276–7 *American*
☎ 773-348-8899; 658 W Belden Ave; mains $6-16; Brown, Red Line to Fullerton

This windowless tavern that dates from the 1890s stays perpetually young. The toast of Lincoln Park's post-collegiate masses, the vast comfort-food menu offers burgers, tuna melts, potato skins and the like. Outdoor seating started in the side garden and has spread right around to the front. The beer selection is good, but this is really more eatery than bar. Note: avoid the oversize poseur in Wrigleyville.

KING CRAB Map pp276–7 *Seafood*
☎ 312-280-8990; 1816 N Halsted St; mains $17-31; Brown, Red Line to Armitage

The prices and the sartorial demands on the customers are modest at this simple place that's popular with people seeing shows at the nearby Steppenwolf and Royal George theaters. The generous portions of seafood include treats such as grilled prawns, blackened tuna and oysters from the notable raw bar. The restaurant's namesake is always available, but the price varies with the market.

O'FAMÉ Map pp276–7 *American*
☎ 773-929-5111; 750 W Webster Ave; mains $6-18; Brown, Red Line to Armitage

This popular sit-down restaurant started as a take-out business (now tucked into the eatery's eastern edge). Thin-crust pizza and ribs are popular with the neighborhood diners and Steppenwolf theatergoers. Want to stage your own play? You can get picnic versions of everything from the gleaming white-tile take-out area and enjoy them in Oz Park, across the street.

RJ GRUNTS Map pp276–7 *American*
☎ 773-929-5363; 2056 N Lincoln Park West; mains $7-14; bus 22

The very first of the now-ubiquitous Lettuce Entertain You stable of restaurants, RJ Grunts came on the scene in the 1970s, when Lincoln Park emerged as the young singles' neighborhood of choice. Now, as then, the huge fruit and vegetable bar and the burgers are the mainstays. This is a fun post-zoo lunch spot; even the pickiest kids (and parents) will find something to love here.

ROSE ANGELIS Map pp276–7 *Italian*
☎ 773-296-0081; 1314 W Wrightwood Ave; mains $7-15; ☾ dinner only, closed Mon; Brown, Red Line to Fullerton

It must be something they put in the tortellini: you'll see nothing but smiles on diner's faces in this vegetarian-friendly Italian restaurant. The three rooms here all feel like a friend's living room (though the bruschetta and thin-crust pizzas will likely outshine anything your pals have ever concocted).

TILLI'S Map pp276-7 *Fusion*
☎ 773-325-0044; 1952 N Halsted St; mains $9-18; Brown, Red Line to Armitage

This comfy restaurant has an eclectic menu (the Thai barbecue salmon is great) that mixes ingredients from all over the globe. Diners are in their late 20s and early 30s, and the young professional crowd gets loud and boisterous on weekend nights, especially on winter evenings, when everyone basks and drinks by the floor-to-ceiling fireplace. During the week, things are much calmer, and Tilli's becomes a favorite for the Lincoln Park new-mom scene.

VIA CARDUCCI Map pp276-7 *Italian*
☎ 773-665-1981; 1419 W Fullerton; mains $7-20; ☽ dinner only; Brown, Red Line to Fullerton

The simple, southern Italian dishes regularly draw complex moans of delight from diners at this small Lincoln Park gem. Red-checkered tablecloths complement the Baroque murals on the walls, and the food leans towards thick tomato-based sauces and amazing sausages (not to mention generous portions – you'll likely be enjoying leftovers from your dinner for lunch the following day).

VINCI Map pp276-7 *Italian*
☎ 312-266-1199; 1732 N Halsted St; mains $9-19; ☽ closed Mon; Red Line to North/Clybourn

The Steppenwolf brass nameplate on one of the tables here show you that this rustic Italian restaurant knows which side its crusty bread is buttered on. Vinci offers much more than proximity to the city's famous stage, though. The dishes here are well-crafted spins on Italian favorites, like the fungus-friendly grilled polenta with portobello and *cremini* mushrooms in a porcini mushroom broth, and a grilled duck breast with a balsamic vinegar sauce.

> ## Top Five Lincoln Park & Old Town
>
> - Chillingly good desserts at **Oberwies Dairy** (p141).
> - The curses, the blessing of **Wiener Circle** (p142).
> - Table-made guacamole at **Adobo Grill** (p140).
> - Sampling the non-snaily delights at **Escargot** (p140).
> - Getting messy with a plate of ribs at **Twin Anchors** (p141).

Old Town

ADOBO GRILL Map pp276-7 *Mexican*
☎ 312-266-7999; 1610 N Wells; mains $10-19; ☽ closed lunch Mon-Fri; Brown Line to Sedgwick

Like Rick Bayless at Topolobampo, Adobo chef Paul LoDuca takes Mexican foods and flavors to another dimension at his lively eatery near Second City. The yummy guacamole appetizer is made table-side, and the dishes that follow it are no less extraordinary. Try the trout steamed in corn husk or the tender chicken breast in an Oaxacan black mole sauce. Thirsty? The margaritas are predictably good, but Adobo also has over 80 sipping tequilas on hand.

BISTROT MARGOT Map pp276-7 *French*
☎ 312-587-3660; 1437 N Wells St; mains $7-20; Brown Line to Sedgwick

A visit to Bistrot Margot is like a visit to a little Parisian corner bistro in one of the remoter districts. Roast chicken, steak and *frites*, mussels and other coastal shellfish highlight the classic menu. The interior mixes dark wood with bright tiles and red booths, and the busy crowd adds to the atmosphere. It's a good idea to make reservations for the popular Sunday brunch.

ESCARGOT Map pp276-7 *French*
☎ 312-642-5858; 1962 N Halsted; mains $14-27; ☽ dinner only, closed Mon; Brown Line to Armitage

Local food critics have been swooning over young maestro chef Eric Aubriot's latest, a restaurant that offers complex flavors and inventive preparations without the sky-high price tags that usually come with French fare. Snag a table in the sunroom overlooking busy Halsted, and soak in the sensory overload of seasonal dishes like mushroom ravioli or sautéed monkfish. The springtime tones in the dining room compliment the festive, convivial atmosphere.

FIREPLACE INN Map pp276-7 *American*
☎ 312-664-5264; 1448 N Wells St; mains $12-27; ☽ kitchen open until 1:30am Fri & Sat; Brown Line to Sedgwick

This local classic has been serving up Chicago-style baby-back ribs for over 35 years. Steaks, burgers and seafood round out the menu. The steak fries are perfectly crisp on the outside and tender on the inside. Blue-cheese lovers will want to spring for the extra charge for that dressing on the side salad. The two-level dining room is heavy with wood – almost as much as the namesake fireplace burns up in a night. When the snow is blowing off the lake and the sidewalks are piling up with drifts, you can warm your cockles here. (But you can also air them out in summer at the garden tables.)

HEAT Map pp276–7 *Japanese*
☎ 312-317-9818; 1507 Sedgwick; mains $14-100;
✪ closed lunch Tue, closed Sun; Brown Line to Sedgwick

This tiny, minimalist restaurant prepares the most meticulously fresh sashimi in Chicago. How fresh is it? Customers can pick a live fish from the restaurant's tank and, a few slices later, enjoy their still-twitching dinner. Though some of the live fish run up to $80 per pound here, less fanfare-requiring menu items average about $16. Connoisseurs of Japanese food on a limited budget should try the $25 lunch, one of Chicago's great value meals.

¡SALPICÓN! Map pp276–7 *Mexican*
☎ 312-988-7811; 1252 N Wells St; mains $16-25;
✪ dinner only Mon-Sat; Red Line to Clark/Division

Another favorite among Chicago's high-end Mexican restaurants, Priscilla Satkoff's place have elevated *ceviche* (raw fish marinated in lime juice) and *chiles rellenos* (stuffed poblano peppers that are batter-fried) to an art. Many other items come slathered in heavenly mole. The festive interior features high ceilings and bold colors. Create bright colors in your head by trying some of the 60 tequilas, including some rare, oak-barrel-aged numbers.

TOPO GIGO Map pp276–7 *Italian*
☎ 312-266-9355; 1516 N Wells St; mains $9-23;
Brown Line to Sedgwick

Roasted peppers and grilled zucchini on the antipasto table are just some of the treats that await at this faithful adaptation of a Roman trattoria, an excellent choice for a relaxing evening of delicious Italian food. The linguini Cinque Terre also scores big points.

TWIN ANCHORS Map pp276–7 *American*
☎ 312-266-1616; 1655 N Sedgwick St; mains $8-18;
Brown Line to Sedgwick

Twin Anchors is synonymous with ribs, and Chicagoans can get violent if you leave their city without sampling some of Twin Anchors' baby-backs. The meat drops from the ribs as soon as you lift them. Choose among fries, onion rings and baked potatoes for sides. This spot doesn't take reservations, so you'll have to wait outside or around the neon-lit 1950s bar, which sets the tone for the whole place. An almost-all Sinatra jukebox completes the '50s supper-club ambience. (Actually, the

restaurant itself dates from 1932.) To avoid a really long wait, drop by midweek.

Cheap Eats
CHICAGO BAGEL AUTHORITY
Map pp276–7 *Bagels*
☎ 773-248-9606; 953 W Armitage Ave; mains $2-6;
Brown, Red Line to Armitage

This lively little spot makes a good stop for a fast breakfast and lunch. The bagels are fine plain or decked out in sandwich fixings.

FRESH CHOICE Map pp276–7 *American*
☎ 312-664-7065; 1534 N Wells St; mains $6-9;
Brown Line to Sedgwick

If you're feeling a little burned out on the hot dogs, steaks and mozzarella-laden pizzas, this healthy spot is a great place for a light meal or a vitamin-packed fruit smoothie. Grab an oven-baked sub and sit at the sidewalk tables, or treat your weary body to a salad and a fresh-squeezed carrot juice or a wheatgrass cocktail.

NOOKIES, TOO Map pp276–7 *American*
☎ 773-327-1400; 2114 N Halsted St; mains $6-12;
Brown, Red Line to Armitage

You can cleanse your previous night's sins with the oat-bran pancakes at this popular brunch spot or choose from a full complement of eggs, waffles and sandwiches. The fresh-squeezed orange juice is pricey but worth it if your taste buds are already awake.

OBERWEIS DAIRY Map pp276–7 *Ice Cream*
☎ 773-665-8364; 1528 W Fullerton Ave; mains $3-7;
bus 9

Routinely rated as the best ice cream in Chicago, the Oberweis serves up shakes that couldn't be thicker or creamier if they were squeezed directly from the cows on the Oberweis family-owned farms. Which, come to think of it, they are. Sundaes and suspiciously rich sugar-free frozen yogurt are also available.

OLD JERUSALEM
Map pp276–7 *Middle Eastern*
☎ 312-944-0459; 1411 N Wells; mains $5-9; Brown line to Sedgwick

The schwarma and falafel are both fantastic at this friendly, 27-year-old Old Town joint. Looking for something leafy? Try the Greek salad, served with Lebanese flatbread. The atmosphere is bare-bones; get it to go and have a feast in Lincoln Park.

PASTA BOWL Map pp276–7   *Italian*
☎ 773-525-2695; 2434 N Clark St; mains $6-13; bus 22

The music is loud and the decor basic at this affordable neighborhood pasta joint. The sauces here are top notch; the pesto reeks of garlic and the Bolognese is redolent with basil. The meatball sub is also excellent, and the prices are just a fraction higher than Subway across the street.

VIENNA BEEF FACTORY STORE &
DELI Map pp276–7   *American*
☎ 773-235-6652; 2501 N Damen; mains $3-6;
😊 lunch only, closed Sun; bus 50

You've eaten them all around town, now come to the source. The out-of-the-way Vienna Beef factory is the source for the majority of hot dogs sold in Chicago, and their workers' deli is one of the freshest places to try the famous creations. Hot dog haters can nosh on corned beef sandwiches or potato pancakes. And Vienna fans can pick up a case of the dogs at the on-site store to share with loved ones at home.

WIENER CIRCLE Map pp276–7   *American*
☎ 773-477-7444; 2622 N Clark St; mains $3-6;
😊 24hr; Brown, Red Line to Diversey

'Order now or get the fuck out!' screams the apron-clad man behind the counter while an addled patron tries to comply. It's 4:30am at this Lincoln Park equivalent of a roadhouse, and the scene has reached its frenetic peak. Wiener Circle is both infamous and revered in Chicago; the place where verbal abuse is a cheerful sport and where the kitchen kicks out some of the best char-grilled hot dogs money can buy.

Pizzeria Uno (p135)

LAKE VIEW

Like Lake View itself, the restaurant scenes vary as you move from block to block. Boys Town, on Halsted St north of Belmont Ave, has stylish eateries catering to all tastes and preferences. The Belmont Ave area contains a huge variety of restaurants whose quality – but not prices – match that found closer to the center of town. The Belmont El stop is central to much of the area. Scores of moderate and budget-priced eateries serve food from around the world on Clark St, roughly from Belmont Ave to a little north of Wrigley Field. Some aim their menus squarely at the undiscriminating tastes of suburban day-trippers. Others offer imaginative food at excellent prices. The CTA Belmont and Addison stops are close to either end of the strip.

The name on everybody's lips these days, though, is Southport. The once-quiet Lake View road has turned into a mecca for restaurants and clubs. The stretch of Southport from Belmont Ave north to Irving Park Rd is particularly hopping. Take the CTA Brown Line to the Southport stop to put yourself in the heart of the action.

ADDIS ABEBA Map pp272–3   *Ethiopian*
☎ 773-929-9383; 3521 N Clark St; mains $8-15;
Red Line to Addison

A nice change from the fare at the mobs of sports bars in the area, the heaping portions of Ethiopian food here include lots of legumes, grains, spices and vegetables. Everything comes atop *injera*, large and spongy flat bread that you tear pieces from to scoop up all the stewed goodness.

ANDALOUS Map pp272–3   *Moroccan*
☎ 773-281-6885; 3307 N Clark St; mains $9-16;
Brown, Red Line to Belmont

There's much more than couscous on the menu at this cheerful Moroccan bistro, which offers numerous veggie options. The *meknes tagine* is a charming concoction of lemony chicken sautéed in onions.

ANN SATHER Map pp272–3   *American*
☎ 773-348-2378; 929 W Belmont Ave; mains $5-15;
Brown, Red Line to Belmont

In the early 1980s local marketing genius Tom Tunney took a longtime neighborhood coffee shop and gave it a trendy and quirky ad campaign that emphasized its good, basic food. Young professionals now flock here for platefuls of reasonably priced chow served in stylishly friendly surroundings. At night Swedish standards such as meatballs and potato sausage join American classics like salmon and meat loaf. Famous for breakfast are Ann Sather's warm and gooey cinnamon rolls, worth a trip in themselves.

ARCOS DE CUCHILLEROS

Map pp272–3   *Spanish*
☎ 773-296-6046; 3445 N Halsted St; ☒ closed Mon; mains $7-17; Red Line to Addison

This comfy place avoids the upscale hype of some of the other tapas joints. The owners come from Madrid, and they have faithfully replicated one of that city's family cafés, with a long bar, narrow room and dark wood furniture. Small plates of classics such as sautéed lima beans, chickpea croquettes and tortilla *española* (a cold egg and potato omelette) average $7 each. Don't keep track of how many pitchers of tangy sangria you drink; just keep ordering.

BANANA LEAF Map pp272–3   *Thai*
☎ 773-883-8683; 3811 N Southport Ave; mains $7-13; bus 80

Inside a suitably leafy and lush room you choose from a lengthy Thai menu that is refreshingly free of the designer touches now commonplace elsewhere. Thai noodles, curries and basil dishes run about $8. At dessert, bananas come fried, roasted or steamed.

COOBAH Map pp272–3   *Latin*
☎ 773-528-2220; 3423 N Southport Ave; mains $7-16; ☒ closed lunch Mon-Fri; Brown Line to Southport

This hopping Latin restaurant and bar in the hot Southport corridor serves up spicy tamales and sweet plantains along with some of the best mojitos in Chicago. Despite the fever pitch of the place on weekend nights (DJs start spinning at 10pm), servers remain attentive and friendly. Try the Coobah pancakes (buttermilk pancakes with cinnamon butter and rum maple syrup) at the weekend brunch.

CULLEN'S Map pp272–3   *American*
☎ 773-975-0600; 3741 N Southport Ave; mains $7-19; bus 152

Bar chow predominates at this welcoming tavern connected to the Mercury Theatre. Lots of wood and tile evoke a classic Chicago watering hole, though this place dates from more recent times. Baked artichoke appetizers, marinated tuna sandwiches and juicy burgers are typical of the fare. The beer list is long and interesting.

DELEECE Map pp272–3   *New American*
☎ 773-325-1710; 4004 N Southport Ave; mains $5-25; ☒ closed lunch Mon-Thu; bus 80

At this upscale café that was once a grocery store, the aromas wafting from the kitchen have an international appeal. Poblano peppers and cilantro add a Mexican touch, ginger chimes in for Asia and olive oil speaks for the Mediterranean. Prices reflect the grocery-store roots, but the soup is definitely not canned. The staff get praise for being able and affable. Deleece has become a popular Sunday brunch spot.

DUKE OF PERTH Map pp272–3   *Scottish*
☎ 773-477-1741; 2913 N Clark St; mains $5-14; bus 22

This genuine Scottish pub offers various Scottish delights like haggis, which may well drive you to drink any or all of the vast number of single malts on offer. However, punters from all around drop in for the excellent fish and chips (all-you-can-eat for $7 Wednesday and Friday). The beer garden is a good refuge.

ERWIN Map pp272–3   *New American*
☎ 773-528-7200; 2925 N Halsted St; mains $16-$19; ☒ closed Mon; Brown, Red Line to Diversey

'Comfort food' is the trendy term for the kind of rib-sticking fare that Midwestern moms have served for decades. When Mom's not around to heat up the stove, your average Joe might resort to the supermarket's frozen food section for his comfort. High-class Joes – or at least those with sophisticated palates – resort to Erwin. Dishes on the ever-changing menu feature American ingredients but combine food styles from around the world in imaginative ways. Bring Mom (especially to the delightful Sunday brunch).

HI RICKY Map pp272–3   *Asian*
☎ 773-388-0000; 3730 N Southport Ave; mains $7-9; bus 152

The long, inexpensive menu travels through Vietnam, Indonesia, Thailand and China. Satays are the stars and come with prawn chips and an array of sauces. A sampler of all eight satay varieties is only $9. Other items include noodles, soups and stir-fries, all served in a bright and cheerful setting.

JACK'S ON HALSTED

Map pp272–3 *New American*
☎ 773-244-9191; 3201 N Halsted St; mains $13-25;
closed lunch Mon-Sat; Brown, Red Line to Belmont

Special of the day? It's always fun food served in an eclectic dining room by highly personable staff. The menu hops around the world, stopping off for American classics like steak or Cajun and then moving on for Italian, French and Asian, with a number of good vegetarian choices along the way. You can wash down every course with the many fine American wines. Be sure to save room for dessert. Sunday brunch is worthy of special occasions.

LE LOUP Map pp272–3 *French*
☎ 773-248-1830; 3348 N Sheffield Ave; mains $14-19;
Brown, Red Line to Belmont

Those in the know are constantly wondering why this place isn't mobbed. Let them figure it out, as you enjoy the friendly service and exceptional French fare at this low-key spot. The name means 'the wolf,' and you'll happily wolf down classics such as the $9 blue-cheese salad and the $16 cassoulet, made with white beans, duck and sausage. The dining area is small and intimate. The adjoining garden, lushly planted with flowers and trees, comes alive in the summer.

MATSUYA Map pp272–3 *Japanese*
☎ 773-248-2677; 3469 N Clark St; mains $6-16;
Red Line to Addison

The wooden boat in the window hints at the sushi-dominated menu here, one of the best value places on the Japanese dining scene. The sushi offerings include standards such as California rolls down to the square-shaped Osaka-style sushi. The rest of the menu plumbs unusual depths (sample item: octopus marinated in bean paste). Less adventurous types will be happy with the teriyaki-marinated grilled fish.

MENAGERIE Map pp272–3 *New American*
☎ 773-404-8333; 1232 W Belmont; mains $12-25;
Brown, Red Line to Belmont

Brought to you by former chefs from Bistro 110 and Green Dolphin Street, this newcomer mixes art with its artful dishes, serving up imaginative seafood and steak dishes in a gallery-like setting. The international wine list includes over a dozen by the glass.

MIA FRANCESCA Map pp272–3 *Italian*
☎ 773-281-3310; 3311 N Clark St; mains $10-25;
Brown, Red Line to Belmont

Diners jam the large room at one of the most popular small, family-run Italian bistros in the city. A buzz of energy swirls among the closely spaced tables, topped with white tablecloths, and the arrangements of fresh flowers. The kitchen is open on one side, allowing full view of your food's preparation. The frequently changing handwritten menu features earthy standards with aggressive seasoning from southern Italy. Other treats include wafer-thin pizzas and the often-overlooked staple of Italian kitchens: polenta. Service can be harried because of the clamoring crowds.

MONSOON Map pp272–3 *Indian*
☎ 773-665-9463; 2813 N Broadway; mains $12-30;
dinner only, closed Mon; Brown, Red Line to Diversey

The French-trained Indian chef here spent time at the Peninsula Hotel before helming the kitchen at this beautiful, upscale Indian restaurant. The space is gorgeous, with an open kitchen offering diners an up-close view of the work that goes into making the Darjeeling tea–smoked chicken, tandoori rib-eye steak and shrimp *pakoras* so delicious.

MOTI MAHAL Map pp272–3 *Indian*
☎ 773-348-4392; 1031 W Belmont Ave; mains $8-13;
Brown, Red Line to Belmont

It doesn't look like much from the outside and actually looks worse inside, but it serves excellent Indian food. Everybody working here learned to cook in India, and it shows. The various legume curries are spiced just right. The mixed grill combines a lot of everything – curries, *tikkas* and more – and tops the price list at $13. You'll find it next to impossible to spend more per person. The drink selection is BYOB, which gives you infinite choice and keeps the costs down even more.

Eating – Lake View

OUTPOST Map pp272–3 · *New American*
☎ 773-244-1166; 3438 N Clark St; mains $14-19;
Red Line to Addison

During the 1930s the China Clipper flying boats of Pan American World Airways linked the world to the US on routes spanning the globe. Journeys were made in segments, stopping at company outposts in the Pacific and the Atlantic. Ted Cizma, the son of one of Pan Am's former flight attendants, has teamed up with his partners to create a warm, casual and chic restaurant that draws inspiration from the clippers' many ports of call. Dishes offered on the constantly changing menu have included plantain fritters and grilled tuna and New Zealand venison. The room is decorated with maps showing the clipper routes.

PAT'S PIZZA Map pp272–3 · *Pizza*
☎ 773-248-0168; 3114 N Sheffield Ave; mains $7-22;
Brown, Red Line to Belmont

Thyme is a key ingredient of the sausage here, and combined with a few other toppings, it makes for a great thin-crust combo pizza. A frequent winner of Chicago *Tribune* competitions (which means that the *Sun-Times* regularly dumps on it), Pat's is a family place that still seems a bit overwhelmed by the huge changes in the neighborhood. If you're not here for a thin-crust, skip it.

PINGPONG Map pp272–3 · *Asian*
☎ 773-281-7575; 3322 N Broadway; mains $7-13;
☷ to midnight, dinner only; Brown, Red Line to Belmont

This sexy, modern restaurant spices their mix of Japanese, Thai, and Chinese food with a healthy dose of house music. The food is un-greasy, carefully spiced and surprisingly affordable; the hip clientele who wait patiently for one of the few tables in this small space know good value when they see it.

PS BANGKOK Map pp272–3 · *Thai*
☎ 773-871-7777; 3345 N Clark St; mains $7-18;
☷ closed Mon; Brown, Red Line to Belmont

The shrimp curries burst with hot, plump shrimp at this spot, one of Chicago's best Thai restaurants. The various fish tanks hint at the long list of seafood dishes, many of them the elaborate kind found at banquets in Thailand. The chicken satay, which leads the lengthy menu, comes with an excellent peanut sauce.

STREGA NONA Map pp272–3 · *Italian*
☎ 773-244-0990; 3747 N Southport Ave; mains $8-15;
bus 80

That hallmark of late-20th-century restaurant design – exposed brick – is the dominant element of the dining room here, which opens onto the street. Locals twirl the typical Italian fare around their forks with glee. The name comes from a witch in Italian children's stories.

TANGO SUR Map pp272–3 · *Steak House*
☎ 773-477-5466; 3763 N Southport Ave; mains $11-27;
☷ closed lunch Mon-Sat; bus 80

This BYOB Argentine steak house smells great and serves classic skirt steaks and other beefy options. Not in the mood for steak? Then kidneys await. Not in the mood for meat? Go elsewhere. Tables outside expand the seating from the very small and spare interior. This may be the only smoke-free steak place in town.

TUSCANY Map pp272–3 · *Italian*
☎ 773-404-7700; 3700 N Clark St; mains $10-29;
Red Line to Addison

A branch of the well-known original on Taylor St in Little Italy, this Tuscany has a wood-burning pizza oven and a real grill to prepare the various steaks on the menu. The menu draws its inspiration from northern Italy; look for creamy risottos and rosemary-flavored grilled meats. Although rather hoity-toity by Clark St standards, this place is still very casual.

YOSHI'S CAFE Map pp272–3 *Japanese*
☎ 773-248-6160; 3257 N Halsted St; mains $16-26; closed Mon; Brown, Red Line to Diversey

Yoshi and Nobuko Katsumura preside over one of the most innovative casual places in town. The changing menu focuses on low-fat dishes with a Japanese flair. The kitchen treats all ingredients with the utmost respect, from the salmon and other seafood options to the tofu in the vegetarian dishes. Try to save room for the group dessert, which includes a little bit of everything on the menu. The service is every bit as good as the food.

Cheap Eats

CHICAGO DINER Map pp272–3 *Vegetarian*
☎ 773-935-6696; 3411 N Halsted St; mains $5-11; Red Line to Belmont

This vegetarian diner has been serving items such as barbecue *seitan*, wheatmeat and tofu stroganoff for over twenty years now. The hipster staff are friendly, and the powerful coffee comes from local roaster Intelligentsia. In the morning, breakfast tofu omelettes are a hit. At night, entrées feature varying amounts of grains and veggies. Vegans take note: even the pesto for the pasta can be had without a lick of cheese.

HOT DOUG'S Map pp272–3 *American*
☎ 773-348-0326; 2314 W Roscoe St; mains $2-5; lunch only, closed Sun; bus 50

The gourmet sausages served here by owner Doug may be on the forefront of a Chicago hot dog revolution. With specialities ranging from blueberry-merlot-venison to sesame-ginger-duck, the food at this friendly place has food reviewers dragging out their superlatives. On Saturday, Doug offers fries cooked in thick duck fat (you have to ask for them).

ORANGE Map pp272–3 *American*
☎ 773-549-4400; 3231 N Clark St; mains $5-11; lunch only, closed Mon; Brown, Red Line to Belmont

When you drive down Clark St on a Saturday and see a place with lines of people winding out the door, you'll know you've come across Orange. Serving kooky dishes like French toast kebabs and jelly donut pancakes, alongside more traditional breakfast staples, Orange is the first thing many Chicagoans want to see in the morning.

PENNY'S NOODLE SHOP
Map pp272–3 *Asian*
☎ 773-281-8222; 3400 N Sheffield Ave; mains $5-9; Brown, Red Line to Belmont

Despite several other excellent Asian choices within a few blocks, this place attracts crowds most hours of the day and night. You'll see people waiting outside in all weather, good and bad. Maybe these hapless hordes are drawn by the place's minimalist decor, low prices or – no doubt – the cheap, tasty noodle soups ($6 average). Penny's is BYOB, so stock up on drinks before you get here.

PICK ME UP Map pp272–3 *American*
☎ 773-248-6613; 3408 N Clark; mains $6-9; 3pm-3am Mon-Fri, 24hr Sat & Sun; bus 22

This colorful after-hours hub for the city serves a tasty, oddball array of things like 'sam-mitches' and 'pizzadillas' to a post-bar (and later) crowd. Designed to look like the inside of a crooked house out of a children's book, the Pick Me Up features brightly painted walls and a cacophonous collection of old signs and advertisements. The coffee's strong and the filling entrées are way more interesting than your standard diner fare.

SHIROI HANA Map pp272–3 *Japanese*
☎ 773-477-1652; 3242 N Clark St; mains $5-12; closed lunch Sun, Brown, Red Line to Belmont

Every large city, if it's lucky, has its Shiroi Hana – the dirt-cheap sushi place where the food is consistently good, if not overwhelming. Lunch is a particularly sweet deal, with most sushi costing just $1.20 per piece.

VILLAGE TAP Map pp272–3 *American*
☎ 773-883-0817; 2055 W Roscoe St; mains $6-12; bus 50

This neighborhood tavern does everything well: food, drink and atmosphere. And that's the problem – it can get crowded on Friday and Saturday night. Otherwise, it's a real winner. The friendly bartenders give out free samples of the ever-changing and carefully chosen lineup of Midwestern microbrews. The kitchen turns out some great burgers, veggie burgers and chicken sandwiches, and the spiced pita chips are a nice touch. Out back the beer garden contains a fountain; inside the tables enjoy good views of the TVs for ball games. There are board games available so you and your friends can make your own fun.

ANDERSONVILLE & UPTOWN

Though Andersonville started with the Swedes, the food here has expanded in much more cosmopolitan directions. Modern takes on French, Korean, Middle Eastern and Belgian abound on Clark St. Thankfully, one artifact of the neighborhood's Nordic past survives: the must-see Swedish Bakery, where butter and sugar flow like water. Getting up to Andersonville's main drag is best accomplished by car or cab. If you're taking the El, head to the Red Line Berwyn stop.

The star of Uptown's dining scene is Asian Argyle St. Even the Argyle El Station sports an Asian motif in this neighborhood full of restaurants and shops run by people from Southeast Asia. Families in search of the American dream are always opening someplace new on Argyle St. The same holds true on the adjoining blocks of Broadway and Sheridan Rd (three blocks east of Broadway). The restaurants here serve piping hot soup and huge portions of noodles at *very* affordable prices. Bring a big appetite.

Andersonville

ANDIE'S Map p274 *Mediterranean*
☎ 773-784-8616; 5253 N Clark St; mains $7-14;
Red Line to Berwyn
The larger Reza's next door may draw the yuppie hordes, but discerning Andersonville locals flock to Andie's for smooth, garlicky hummus and more. A recent remodeling has turned the dining room into a Mediterranean showplace. The cooking occurs in an open kitchen, and smells of grilling meat, eggplant and the world's best lentil soup fill the air.

JIN JU Map p274 *Korean*
☎ 773-334-6377; 5203 N Clark St; mains $7-16;
☾ dinner only; Red Line to Berwyn
One of a handful of 'nouveau Korean' restaurants in town, Jin Ju throws a culinary curveball by tempering Korean food to Western tastes. The minimalist, candlelit interior of Jin Ju echoes softly with downbeat techno, and the stylish thirtysomethings who come here enjoy entrees like *haemul pajon* (a fried pancake stuffed with seafood) and *kalbi* (beef short ribs). In keeping with the current rage for drinks ending in 'tini', the restaurant offers a scrumptious 'sojutini', made with *soju*, a Korean spirit distilled from sweet potatoes.

LA TACHE Map p274 *French*
☎ 773-334-7168; 1475 W Balmoral Ave; mains $12-26;
☾ dinner only; Red Line to Berwyn
This art deco-ish space offers a sweet elegance and reasonably priced, high-end bistro fare to a rapidly growing fan base. The kitchen maestro here is Dale Levitski, known for making breakfast place Orange such a success. The veal cheeks here are wonderful, as is the odd-sounding chicken marengo, a chicken dish served with garlicky crawfish, mushrooms and a poached egg. Looking for a romantic restaurant on the North Side? You've just found it.

TOMBOY *New American*
☎ 773-907-0636; 5402 N Clark St; mains $15-23;
Red Line to Berwyn
You might wonder about the name here until you realize that Andersonville is a favorite neighborhood of Chicago's lesbian community. Tomboy, with its white tablecloths and exposed brick walls – prepares artful and filling dishes, including a number of meat-free pasta dishes, plus carnivorous items like filet mignon with Gorgonzola cream sauce. An eclectic wine list rounds out the menu.

Uptown

HAI YEN Map p274 *Vietnamese-Chinese*
☎ 773-989-0712; 1007 W Argyle St; mains $5-25;
☾ closed Wed; Red Line to Argyle
Many of the dishes at this warm Argyle St eatery require some assembly, pairing shrimp, beef or squid with rice crepes, mint, Thai basil, and lettuce. For an appetizer, try the *goi cuon*, fresh rolls of vermicelli rice noodles along with shrimp, pork and carrots. The *bo bay mon* comes with seven (yes, seven) different kinds of beef. Order sparingly, or ask for some help from your server – like the *bo bay mon*, many of the dishes are large enough to feed an army.

THAI PASTRY Map p274 *Thai*
☎ 773-784-5399; 4925 N Broadway; mains $5-10;
Red Line to Argyle
A favorite at lunch with workers from Uptown and Andersonville, this unpretentious Thai restaurant is a find. Though the front of the restaurant is dedicated to the sweets that the name implies, the bulk of the inviting space is dedicated to full lunches and dinners. The pad Thai is excellent, and the spot-on curries arrive still simmering in a clay pot.

Eating – Andersonville & Uptown

Top Five Andersonville & Uptown

- Pad Thai with treats at **Thai Pastry** (p147).
- A romantic night out at **La Tache** (p147).
- Devouring everything in sight at the **Swedish Bakery** (p148).
- Stopping by **Hai Yen** (p147) for a feast fit for a Vietnamese king.
- Washing down the *kim chee* with a sojutini at **Jin Ju** (p147).

Cheap Eats

KOPI, A TRAVELER'S CAFE

Map p274   *Coffeehouse*
☎ 773-989-5674; 5317 N Clark St; mains $5-8;
Red Line to Berwyn

An extremely casual coffeehouse with a pile of pillows on the floor in the window, Kopi stocks a large range of travel books, and serves sandwiches and desserts to its lefty clientele. On the bulletin board you'll find ads from people looking for trekking partners for Kazakhstan or looking to unload last year's rock-climbing gear.

SWEDISH BAKERY Map p274   *Bakery*
☎ 773-561-8919; 5348 N Clark St; cookies $1;
☺ closed Sun; Red Line to Berwyn

You get free coffee in amazingly small cups here, but that's the only thing minimalist about the place, with its butter-laden breads, cookies and pastries. Everything is astoundingly good here. Are you in Andersonville? Come here now.

WICKER PARK/BUCKTOWN & UKRAINIAN VILLAGE

Wicker Park and Bucktown hang somewhere between artist haunt and high-priced loft land, and their restaurants match this schism. Along Milwaukee Ave in Wicker Park you'll find a $2 taco joint next to a chi-chi place where $2 won't even cover the tip for the restaurant's valet parking. Bucktown's main eat street, Damen Ave, rolls the two disparate worlds into one – boasting a number of eateries that sell high-end takes on low-end comfort food. It will likely be a few years yet before the Wicker Park/Bucktown area fully comes into its own, food-wise. In the meantime, the mish-mash of new and old, cheap and pricey is delightful (and delicious). Grab the Blue Line to Damen to start your eating adventures.

Over the past two years, Ukrainian Village has become one of the hot new places for restaurant openings. Especially along Division St near Damen, young restaurateurs have been setting up shop with some encouraging results. The same is true on the eastern edge of the neighborhood, along Chicago Ave near Halsted St. This chunk of town is called West Town, and with the success of places like Flo and the West Town Tavern, it's become an oasis of good eats in a somewhat dingy neighborhood. Cars or cabs are the best way to navigate Ukrainian Village, though the Chicago Blue Line stop will take you close to some of the best options in West Town.

Wicker Park/Bucktown

FORTUNATO Map p275   *Italian*
☎ 773-645-7200; 2005 W Division; mains $12-28;
☺ closed lunch Mon-Sat; Blue Line to Damen

This of-the-moment Italian restaurant is tops with thirty- and fortysomethings who have been following chef Jennifer Newberry on her trek through a number of Chicago restaurants. From the taste of things here – ravioli stuffed with braised oxtail or wood-grilled fillet of trout – she's found a great home.

LE BOUCHON Map p275   *French*
☎ 773-862-6600; 1958 N Damen Ave; mains $12-23;
☺ dinner only, closed Sun; Blue Line to Damen

Classic French food at nonclassic prices makes for a winning combination at this quaint little spot. Neighborhood types who know a good deal when they see it often pack Le Bouchon to feast on all the standards from France. The lyonnaise salad is a winner. Other faves on the short menu range from escargot to chocolate *marquisse* (a chocolate mousse without the egg whites). Want to see the tiny kitchen? Head to the bathroom – it's on the way.

MERITAGE CAFE & WINE BAR

Map p275   *New American*
☎ 773-235-6434; 2118 N Damen Ave; mains $24-30;
☺ dinner only; Blue Line to Damen

The wine list is almost as long as the gaze down the nose you get from the haughty help at this ode to the Pacific Northwest. But if you're ready for this kind of scene, you'll be rewarded with some really good regional American food featuring lots of fish like salmon, plus mushrooms and game from the forest and various Asian influences. The former corner bar has been renovated just enough to let the light in while still preserving the Victorian character of the building. The covered and heated patio allows you to eat outside in all but the worst weather.

MIRAI SUSHI Map p275 *Japanese*
☎ 773-862-8500; 2020 W Division St; mains $9-19; ⏲ dinner only; Blue Line to Damen

This high-energy restaurant has an even higher-energy lounge upstairs, both packed with happy, shiny Wicker Park residents enjoying some of the freshest sushi in the area. From the trance-hop electronic music to the young, black-clad staff, Mirai is a place where connoisseurs of sashimi and *maki* gather to throw back a few cocktails between savory bites of yellowtail and shitake tempura. Nonsmokers rejoice: chef Jun Ichikawa doesn't allow cigarettes anywhere near his kitchen on the main floor. Smokers should head upstairs or grab a sidewalk table out front.

MOD Map p275 *New American*
☎ 773-252-1500; 1520 N Damen; mains $15-25; ⏲ closed lunch Mon-Sat; Blue Line to Damen

The white, retro-futuristic decor here looks just like what sci-fi freaks in the '50s dreamed restaurants would look like in 2030. Hypermodern plastic furniture and plastic inflatable lighting abound, and the staff glide around in uniforms from rave clothing store Softcore down the street. The fusion food is similarly outside-the-box, using locally grown produce and meats from boutique farms in dishes that are sometimes normal (cornflake crusted catfish) and sometimes a little weird (spring nettles), but usually excellent.

NORTHSIDE Map p275 *American*
☎ 773-384-3555; 1635 N Damen Ave; mains $7-13; Blue Line to Damen

The clientele at this sweet spot are mostly Lincoln Park transplants – 29 year-old money managers and their marketing major girlfriends. It's no wonder why they're here – the covered, plant-filled atrium gives diners a touch of summer no matter how cold it is outside, the cheeseburgers and other pub grub are well cooked and the apple pie is amazing.

SILVER CLOUD Map p275 *American*
☎ 773-489-6212; 1700 N Damen Ave; mains $7-16; Blue Line to Damen

This bar and grill doesn't win with every dish – the Tater Tots, no matter how fun sounding, taste like they came from your grade-school cafeteria. But the atmosphere, all dark-woody and glowing, is exceedingly comfortable. The mood changes on weekends, when the place fills with an amiably loud crowd of young professional twentysomethings.

SOUL KITCHEN Map p275 *Southern*
☎ 773-342-9742; 1576 N Milwaukee Ave; mains $10-26; Blue Line to Damen

The tangerine and olive walls and leopard-skin motif set the mood at this hipster hangout. Big, bright dishes drawn from the South come to the table with plenty of spices and eclectic accents. The Jamaican jerk chicken skewers are flavorful, while the pecan-coated catfish is sweet and crunchy. Other interesting touches include the collard greens seasoned with cilantro and barbecued lamb with mango sauce. Wrap everything up with cinnamon-spiced coffee.

SPRING Map p275 *New American*
☎ 773-395-7100; 2039 W North Ave; mains $15-28; ⏲ dinner only, closed Mon; Blue Line to Damen

The seafoody entrées at this award-winning place come to your plate by way of Asia, with chef Shawn McClain lovingly dressing up lobster, grouper, halibut and scallops in mouthwatering soy glazes, hot and sour broth and fresh wasabi. The restaurant – which used to be a bathhouse – looks a little like an Ikea showroom; simple, modern lines and muted colors set the tone.

Ukrainian Village
FLO Map p275 *Southwestern*
☎ 312-243-0477; 1434 W Chicago Ave; mains $5-14; ⏲ closed Mon; Blue Line to Chicago

The southwestern-flavored dishes at this twenty something brunch favorite have textures and flavors like fantastic short stories – delicious enough to devour in one sitting, but so well-crafted you want to make them last as long as possible. Think you've had a breakfast burrito before? Not until you've eaten here. Art on the walls is by local artists, and the cheerful staff keep the coffee flowing.

LEO'S LUNCHROOM Map p275 _American_
☎ 773-276-6509; 1809 W Division St; mains $6-13;
closed Mon; Blue Line to Division

When Wicker Park and Ukrainian Village artists roll out of bed on weekends, they roll directly to Leo's and then stay here all day. The place is run-down, but the mid-end comfort cuisine (biscuits and gravy or pumpkin pancakes for breakfast, spinach salad with goat cheese and salmon over pasta for lunch and dinner) is priced to move. Grab a seat in the deck out back when the sun is out. Cash only.

MILK AND HONEY Map p275 _New American_
☎ 773-395-9434; 1920 W Division; mains $6-10;
lunch only; Blue Line to Division

A bright, stylish space for an excellent breakfast or lunch, Milk and Honey has become the hang-out _du jour_ for discerning Ukrainian Village hipsters. Most of the dishes are prepared from scratch by co-owner Carol Watson, and the menu also includes a long list of salads.

Taqueria El Milagro (p154)

SMOKE DADDY RHYTHM & BAR-B-QUE Map p275 _Barbecue_
☎ 773-772-6656; 1804 W Division St; mains $6-16;
Blue Line to Division

This is a great example of the bar/restaurant/ club fusion places that are opening in some of the hipper parts of town. Top-notch ribs emerge from the huge wood-fired pit. The sweet-potato fries on the side win raves, and non-carnivores can enjoy barbecued veggies. Live blues and jazz acts play on a small stage every night. Watch for blues singer Lenny Linn. You can hang onto the bar as you ponder the interesting aprons hanging on the wall.

WEST TOWN TAVERN
Map p275 _New American_
☎ 312-666-6175; 1329 W Chicago Ave; mains $10-19;
dinner only; Blue Line to Chicago

People in Chicago can't stop talking about this place, an unpretentious, inventive restaurant where the food is far more interesting than the name lets on. Conversations bounce off the exposed brick walls and tin ceiling in the handsome dining area, as friends catch up over plates of pork chops with wild rice and skillet-roasted mussels.

Cheap Eats
ALLIANCE BAKERY Map p275 _Bakery_
☎ 773-278-0366; 1736 W Division; mains $5-7;
closed dinner Sun; Blue Line to Division

The staff are friendly and the sandwiches awesome at this small, independent bakery. Best of all, if you get lunch here, a dessert bar item comes with your meal. Just looking for a pick-me-up after a tough day of shopping? The huge double-fudge chunk walnut brownie should do the trick.

BARI FOODS Map p275 _Deli_
☎ 312-666-0730; 1120 W Grand Ave; mains $4-7;
lunch only; Blue Line to Grand

You'll find the best meats Chicago has to offer in this Italian grocery. If you have a car and plan to picnic, drop by Bari and pick up a sub or two (or three – there's always breakfast tomorrow, right?) along with a nice bottle of Italian red.

IRAZU Map p275 _Costa Rican_
☎ 773-252-5687; 1865 N Milwaukee; mains $4-10;
closed Sun; Blue Line to Western

This unbelievably cheap hole-in-the-wall would be one of Chicago's best values at three times the price. The Costa Rican burritos are plump with chicken, black beans and fresh avocado, and the sandwiches contain a Costa Rican 'mystery sauce' that should be patented. Try the oatmeal shake here; it's like drinking a cold oatmeal cookie (that's a good thing). Cash only.

JAMBALAYA Map p275 *Cajun*
☎ 773-289-3678; 1653 N Damen; mains $6-12; Blue Line to Damen

Run by a New Orleans native, this tiny sandwich shop has been winning converts around Chicago with its Louisiana-style crawfish, catfish and shrimp po' boys. The service can be slow, but the crispy, crunchy Creole sandwiches are worth the wait. Cash only.

MARGIE'S Map p275 *Ice Cream*
☎ 773-384-1035; 1960 N Western Ave; mains $6-11; ⏰ to 1am; Blue Line to Western

This ice cream parlor on the outer northwest edge of Wicker Park has been making and selling their own luscious sundaes, splits and cones since 1921. It's been almost a long since the crowded place remodeled; the tables are few here, and waits of a half-hour or more are common. Once you get a seat, you can forestall the inevitable with a burger or sandwich, or just throw yourself into the cold, creamy main course.

MIKO'S Map p275 *Italian ice*
☎ 773-645-9664; 1846 N Damen Ave; drinks $2-4; ⏰ May-Oct; Blue Line to Damen

Pause on a hot day for some cool homemade Italian ice at this seasonal fave. You can sit under the large oak tree in front and enjoy fruit flavors such as lemon, raspberry and peach.

PONTIAC CAFE Map p275 *American*
☎ 773-252-7767; 1531 N Damen Ave; mains $6-14; Blue Line to Damen

This café resides in an old gas station that's been converted into a restaurant whose outside seating serves as Wicker Park's favorite gathering spot on warm days. Expect interesting sandwiches on *panini* and good whole-grain salads.

TECALITLAN Map p275 *Mexican*
☎ 312-384-4285; 1814 W Chicago Ave; mains $3-12; Blue Line to Chicago

One of the best burritos in the world is here; weighing more than a pound and costing less than $5, the *carne asada* (charcoal-grilled

beef) burrito with cheese is not just one of the city's best food values, it's one of the city's best foods. Add the optional avocado and you'll have a full day's worth of food groups wrapped in a huge flour tortilla. For a tasty, greasy change, ask to mix the *carne asada* with pork. The many other Mexican staples on the menu are all cheap and good.

Worth a Trip

Though you'll have to do a little looking to find the following two West Side joints, both Jim's and Lula are a must for any gustatorial tourist exploring the tastes of Chicago.

Jim's Original (Map pp286–7; ☎ 312-733-7820; 700 W O'Brien St; mains $3-5; ⏰ 24hr) Recently relocated to O'Brien St since the demise of its historic home in the Maxwell St Market, Jim's has been serving up the definitive Chicago hot dog since 1939. Your food choices are the classic Chicago Polish sausage or the classic Chicago pork chop sandwich, both always served with free fries. Drive here; the neighborhood feels a little sketchy.

Lula Cafe (Map pp286–7; ☎ 773-489-9554; 2573 N Kedzie Blvd; mains $8-22; ⏰ closed Tue; Blue Line to Logan Square) When the hipsters from Logan Square have something to celebrate, they come to this friendly, upscale cafe. Even the muffins here are something to drool over, and that goes double for lunch items like pasta *yiayia* (bucatini pasta with Moroccan cinnamon, feta and garlic) and dinners such as olive-oil marinated rib-eye steak with braised kale.

WEST SIDE

The West Side is vast, and we've narrowed things down by focusing on the three close-in neighborhoods of the West Loop, Greektown and Little Italy. Of the three, the burgeoning West Loop area is the most exciting. The West Loop has long been associated with food, thanks to the large number of meatpackers operating here. But it's only been in the last 10 years that the Randolph St corridor running though the center of the area has become a dining destination.

The proximity of the United Center helps fill the neighborhood's copious tables on game day. But even when the Bulls aren't holding court, patrons come out en masse to the high-end restaurants here. Because the cost per square foot has been so low until recently, owners have been able to let their imaginations roam, teaming with interior decorators and architects to produce such fantastical spaces as Red Light and Marché.

That trend is abating as rental costs increase (and the economy festers), but you will still find innovative restaurateurs throwing open their doors and kitchens to a hungry city here. To get to the West Loop, a cab or car is a must, as the closest El stops on the Green and Blue lines are relatively far away from the action.

The areas of Little Italy and Greektown, though less hip than the West Loop, make for a fun night of dining, offering well-honed recipes from Greek and Italian kitchens. Greektown is easily reached on the El, but you'll need a cab or car to get to Little Italy. Some of the areas around Taylor St are dicey.

West Loop

MARCHÉ Map pp272–3 *French*
☎ 312-226-8399; 833 W Randolph St; mains $12-30;
☽ closed lunch Sat-Sun; Green Line to Clinton
Forward-looking French food in an eye-catching, futuristic setting. Favored by those en route to the United Center, Marché has a wide-ranging menu, the ingredients are top-notch and the service is highly proficient. The chocolate trio for dessert defies a description that won't leave you drooling.

RED LIGHT Map pp286–7 *Asian*
☎ 312-733-8880; 820 W Randolph St; mains $17-22;
☽ closed lunch Sat & Sun; Green Line to Clinton
Red Light serves up fare that isn't anything like the fortune-cookie standard. In fact, mention 'sweet and sour pork' to the waiters and their attitudes might just freeze you right out the door. Roasted duck and rock shrimp are a few of the stars amid the fresh ingredients. Whole Taiwanese crispy catfish has emerged as a signature item. The entire restaurant glows like a lit-up jewel box at night; this is one beautiful space.

THYME Map pp286–7 *Fusion*
☎ 312-226-4300; 464 N Halsted St; mains $16-31;
☽ dinner only; Blue Line to Grand
Thyme's chef-owner John Bubala moved just a few blocks north from his former kitchen at the noted Marché and opened up this spot in a neighborhood where you once went to sell

your blood. The food is just as inventive as at Marché, with the menu nabbing ideas and influences from around the globe. On weekends you may have to dine early or late to find a table in the heaving dining room. Better yet, hope for a warm summer night and dine in the verdant garden.

ONESIXTYBLUE

Map pp286–7 *New American*
☎ 312-850-0303; 160 N Loomis St; mains $19-30;
☽ dinner only, closed Sun; Green Line to Ashland
Though Michael Jordan is a co-owner at this sleek fave, you won't find anything remotely sporty about it. High-end French cuisine carried off with a smile has been the trademark of this place since its opening five years ago. The pepper-crusted ahi tuna is a slam dunk, as is the lengthy wine list.

Greektown

PARTHENON Map pp286–7 *Greek*
☎ 312-726-2407; 314 S Halsted St; mains $7-16;
Blue Line to UIC-Halsted
This veteran has anchored Greektown for three decades. The amount of *saganaki* set ablaze here may be a principal factor in global warming. The yelps of 'Opaa!' as the cheese ignites reverberate off the walls of the small dining area. Greeks returning to the city from their suburban retreats have made this place a favorite. All the usual suspects are present, and the lamb comes in many forms.

SANTORINI Map pp286–7 *Greek*
☎ 312-829-8820; 800 W Adams St; mains $12-20;
Blue Line to UIC-Halsted
Fish, both shelled and finned, honor the legacies of Greek fishermen at this popular spot, where fresh whole fish is prepared and served in a tableside display. The boisterous room manages to seem cozy, thanks in part to the large Aegean fireplace. Everything, from the bread to the baklava, goes down swimmingly. Portions are huge, which encourages convivial sharing.

Little Italy

MARIO'S Map pp286–7 *Italian Ices*
1068 W Taylor St; drinks $2; ☽ May-Oct; Blue Line to UIC-Halsted
At this cheerfully tacky institution, super Italian ice keeps the crowds coming in the months when there's no ice on the streets.

ROSEBUD Map pp286–7 *Italian*

☎ 312-942-1117; 1500 W Taylor St; mains $14-22; Blue Line to Polk

Rosebud is not only the beginning of a movie but also the beginning of an empire of Italian restaurants in the city. Massive piles of prime pasta, such as lip-shaped *cavatelli*, come with one of the finest red sauces in town. The high-quality cuisine means that even those with reservations can wait an hour or more. So what's the problem? Have some good red wine and settle in for some people-watching – you're bound to see several folks who regularly turn up in bold type in the local gossip pages.

TUFANO'S VERNON PARK TAP

Map pp286–7 *Italian*

☎ 312-733-3393; 1073 W Vernon Park Pl; mains $8-14; closed Mon; Blue Line to Polk

Still family-run after three generations (it opened in 1930), Tufano's serves up the kind of old-fashioned Italian food that has become trendy again. Spaghetti and meatballs and other rib-sticking classics are good, filling and cheap. The blackboards carry a long list of daily specials, which can include such wonderful items as pasta with garlic-crusted broccoli. Amid the usual celebrity photos on the wall you'll see some really nice shots of Joey Di Buono and his family and their patrons through the decades.

Cheap Eats
ARTOPOLIS BAKERY & CAFE

Map pp286–7 *Greek*

☎ 312-559-9000; 306 S Halsted St; mains $6-14; Blue Line to UIC-Halsted

Like a good Greek salad, this one has many ingredients: one of the city's top bakeries (many of the nearby Randolph St joints get their bread here), which sells oozing baklava for $1.50; a café/bar that opens onto the street, with tables along the front; and a food bar with classics like spinach pie, which you can eat in or take out.

CONTE DI SAVOIA Map pp286–7 *Italian*

☎ 312-666-3471; 1438 W Taylor St; mains $4-8; Blue Line to Polk

This large grocery sells everything an Italian cook could hope for, including scores of imported rarities and fine wines. The deli counter will make real *paisani* swoon and sells various lunch items you can eat at simple tables inside and out.

LOU MITCHELL'S Map pp286–7 *Breakfast*

☎ 312-939-3111; 565 W Jackson Blvd; mains $5-9; lunch only; Blue Line to Clinton

Immediately west of the Loop and close to Union Station, this great coffee shop draws hordes who line up to eat elbow to elbow. What draws them? Breakfast dishes that are some of the best in town. Whether it's omelettes hanging off the plates, fluffy flapjacks, crisp waffles or anything else on the long menu, you can expect perfect preparation with premium ingredients. Cups of coffee are bottomless, just like the charm of the staff, who hand out free treats to young and old alike.

MR GREEK GYROS Map pp286–7 *Greek*

☎ 312-906-8731; 234 S Halsted St; mains $4-7; 24hr; Blue Line to UIC-Halsted

Although there's no sign of Mrs, Ms or Mr Greek, 'the Mr' is a classic gyros joint with good prices. While the fluorescent lighting and plastic decor may be lacking in charm, the gyros have a beauty of their own.

WISHBONE Map pp286–7 *Southern*

☎ 312-850-2663; 1001 W Washington St; mains $5-10; closed dinner Mon; Green Line to Clinton

The perfect corn muffins set the tone for a menu featuring spicy classics such as blackened catfish, fried chicken and baked ham. A big choice of sides includes sweet potatoes that should be a lesson to all the cooks who kill these veggies every Thanksgiving. Breakfasts come with hot, fresh buttermilk rolls. Oprah's Harpo studios are just down the street.

PILSEN

During the months when the weather is not miserably cold, Pilsen could be a side street in Mexico City. Blaring signs in Spanish all but obscure the architecture of this neighborhood, which derives its name from the Czechs who originally lived here 100 years ago. Vendors sell ice cream and especially good rice-pudding pops from carts. Others sell corn on the cob that, once bought, is dipped in melted butter and then rolled in spices. Mariachi music bursts out of stores and apartments. The whole scene makes for good strolling, and the innumerable restaurants make for good eating. The 18th St stop on the CTA Blue Line puts you at the west end of the strip. Because almost all of the food in Pilsen is affordable (even to those on a rice-and-beans budget) we've done away with the Cheap Eats section here.

CAFE JUMPING BEAN
Map pp286–7   *Coffeehouse*
☎ 312-455-0019; 1439 W 18th St; mains $4-9; Blue Line to 18th St

This ramshackle café will make you feel like a regular as soon as you step through the door. The Jumping Bean serves excellent, hit focaccia sandwiches, baked goods and strong coffee to the twenty- and thirtysomething crowd of MFA-wielding artists and local bohemians. Chess and domino games are always breaking out here, and the comfy confines of the place make it an excellent spot for whiling away a couple of hours with a mocha, watching life in Pilsen unfold.

NUEVO LEON Map pp286–7   *Mexican*
☎ 312-421-1517; 1515 W 18th St; mains $7-14; Blue Line to 18th St

This is where the buses come, disgorging dozens of gringo tourists to sample the famed cuisine of Pilsen's most celebrated restaurant. Sounds horrible, right? Wrong. This huge place deserves to be on the bus tours, and the visiting tourists are just a drop in the bucket of local Latino families who crowd in here to dine seven days a week. Superlative versions of tacos, tamales and enchiladas are available, though the dish most likely to blow any meat-eater's taste buds is the *asado de puerco* – tender pork served with homemade flour tortillas.

NUEVO LEON PANDERÍA
Map pp286–7   *Bakery*
☎ 312-243-5977; 1634 W 18th St; cookies $1; Blue Line to 18th St

This Mexican bakery isn't associated with the other famous Nuevo Leon on the block, but the treats here are equally delicious. When you walk in, pick up a silver tray, and tong up cinnamon-encrusted buns, fruit-filled empanadas or Mexican sweet bread, and then take the tray to the counter, where they'll tally your total.

TAQUERIA EL MILAGRO
Map pp286–7   *Mexican*
☎ 312-433-7620; 1923 S Blue Island Ave; mains $4-7; Blue Line to 18th St

Known for cooking up Pilsen's best steak tacos, Taqueria El Milagro also excels in the tamale corn tortilla arts. A recent remodeling has spruced the place up, further enhancing the counter-service restaurant's bright and festive charm. BYOB.

SOUTH LOOP & NEAR SOUTH SIDE

As with the neighborhood itself, the restaurant scene in the South Loop and Near South Side is a work in progress. With the dozens of luxury townhouses and condo projects that have been built here in the last two years, it seems only a matter of time before this area is filled with hot new eateries. How long it will take for them to come, however, is anybody's guess. For now, a few popular pioneers have set up shop along Wabash and Michigan Aves.

The plodding pace of the restaurant scene in the South Loop and Near South Side would do well to take a page from Chinatown's book, where there seem to be more restaurants than storefronts. From the Red Line Cermak-Chinatown stop, it's an easy walk to dim sum, noodles or a refreshing tapioca bubble tea, all of it so affordable that Chinatown has become the cheap eats destination for the South Loop and Near South Side.

South Loop

EDWARDO'S Map pp284–5   *Pizza*
☎ 312-939-3366; 521 S Dearborn St; mains $6-18;
Red Line to Harrison
Edwardo's, a Chicago-based chain, serves justifiably famous stuffed spinach pizza, as well as thin-crust models, sandwiches and salads. Everything is fresh and cheap.

PRAIRIE Map pp284–5   *New American*
☎ 312-663-1143; the Hyatt, 500 S Dearborn St; mains $14-29; Red Line to Harrison
The name here reflects this restaurant's celebration of Midwestern food and ingredients. The dining room, in a prominent ground-floor corner of the Hyatt, has the studied mannerism of Frank Lloyd Wright, with oak chairs that replicate some of Wright's best-known designs. Featured menu items include baby coho salmon, whitefish from Lake Superior and other fishy denizens of the Great Lakes. Corn figures in many dishes, from the chowder to the muffins.

PRINTER'S ROW
Map pp284–5   *New American*
☎ 312-461-0780; 550 S Dearborn St; mains $14-22;
☽ closed lunch Sat, closed Sun; Red Line to Harrison
When he opened this restaurant over 20 years ago, Michael Foley was ahead of two trends: the resurgence of traditional American foods and the revitalization of this Printer's Row neighborhood. Both have long since come to pass, but Foley's restaurant still provides fresh pairings of primarily Midwestern foods. The menu changes with the seasons, but venison direct from the woods and fish direct from the rivers are featured nightly. The smoothly professional service is just what one would expect from a restaurant that has matured without losing an ounce of vitality.

Near South Side
CHICAGO FIREHOUSE
Map pp284–5   *American*
☎ 312-786-1401; 1401 S Michigan Ave; mains $8-25;
☽ closed lunch Sat; Red Line to Roosevelt
An old firehouse that's been beautifully restored, this place offers the kind of traditional tasty fare that would light up the face of any firefighter, albeit at prices that might force the firefighter to take a second job. Ribs and steaks headline the show here, although they're pushed out of the spotlight when local resident Mayor Richard M Daley stops by. Chicago Firehouse also recently added a dine-in wine cellar.

GIOCO Map pp284–5   *Italian*
☎ 312-939-3870; 1312 S Wabash Ave; mains $13-34;
☽ closed lunch Sat & Sun; Red Line to Roosevelt
Restaurateurs Jerry Kleiner and Howard Davis made Randolph St on the West Side one of Chicago's hottest dining areas in the 1990s. Now they've opened a whimsical Italian restaurant in a desolate stretch of the Near South Side that hasn't seen this much action since the 1930s, when almost every building was a speakeasy (including, they'd contend, the home of Gioco). A menu laden with classic Chicago-Italian dishes includes delicate pizzas from a wood-burning oven. Surprises abound, such as the tasty lobster gnocchi.

Chinatown

EMPEROR'S CHOICE

Map pp284–5   *Chinese*

☎ 312-225-8800; 2238 S Wentworth Ave; mains $8-12; Red Line to Cermak-Chinatown

This local veteran has earned a reputation for excellent seafood and service to match. Lobster, the center of the menu, stars in several prix-fixe meals that average $26 per person. The ginger scallops are just as succulent as the name suggests. Feel like some snake? Ask for the special menu for more adventurous diners. But fear not, it doesn't list anything you'd typically call the exterminators for.

JOY YEE'S NOODLE SHOP

Map pp284–5   *Asian*

☎ 312-328-0001; 2159 S China Pl (in Chinatown Square Mall); mains $6-10; Red Line to Cermak-Chinatown

You'd think Joy Yee was giving its ice cold homemade fruit drinks and tapioca bubble teas away for free from the way customers throng this bright restaurant far into the night. Along with the mobbed takeaway drink window, the regular seating area is also packed with diners waiting for their chance to enjoy the big, slurpable bowls of *udon*, chow fun and chow mein noodles. The techno music playing on the stereo is a clear sign that this is not your grandmother's Chinese restaurant.

PHOENIX

Map pp284–5   *Chinese*

☎ 312-328-0848; 2131 S Archer Ave; mains $7-16; Red Line to Cermak-Chinatown

This popular spot rises above the old veterans of Chinatown with excellent, fresh food prepared by chefs direct from Hong Kong. Midday sees an endless parade of dim sum issuing forth on trolleys from the kitchen. On Sunday the parade is lengthier yet. If you're not

coming for dim sum, head elsewhere; the rest of the menu tends towards the bland.

SEVEN TREASURES Map pp284–5 *Chinese*

☎ 312-225-2668; 2312 S Wentworth Ave; mains $5-10; ⓨ to 2am; Red Line to Cermak-Chinatown

The ducks in the window aren't going anywhere, but the frenetic cooks at the woks in the kitchen, which overlooks the sidewalk, compensate for the ducks' inactivity. Who needs a TV food show when you can watch these Cantonese masters slicing, dicing and stir-frying up a storm? When you're tired of just looking, or you're just too hungry, step inside this steamy, bustling family restaurant. All the usual items are here – choose what looked especially good from the street.

THREE HAPPINESS Map pp284–5 *Chinese*

☎ 312-791-1228; 2130 S Wentworth Ave; mains $7-17; Red Line to Cermak-Chinatown

Between 10am and 3pm, sit back as cart after cart bursts from the kitchen carrying steaming arrays of little dim sum treats. The staff may or may not be ready to help you choose, so plunge in and pick a plate. Savvy nibblers angle for tables near the kitchen, where they can get first dibs on the emerging bounty. Everything is tallied on little cards; the meal will rarely add up to more than about $10 a head. Three Happiness also does dinner, but that's not the point. Sunday is the most popular dim sum day – be prepared to line up.

SOUTH CHICAGO

Though the South Chicago neighborhoods of Bronzeville, Hyde Park and Kenwood aren't dining destinations in their own right, they do provide their residents with some excellent food. Home of the University of Chicago, Hyde Park, especially, has some great eats in a college-town atmosphere. The people at the table next to yours may well be debating whether a butterfly flapping its wings in Indonesia really is responsible for global warming. To get to Hyde Park, it's best to have a car, but you can also hop on the Metra train from the Loop Randolph station.

The other attraction on Chicago's South Side is soul food, with fried chicken catfish and juicy collard greens. The soul food places listed below, while not requiring a sizable withdrawal from the bank to pay the bill, will require a car.

Top Five South Loop & Near South Side

- Eating *kung pao* out of a pineapple at **Joy Yee's Noodle Shop** (p156).
- The rattle and roll of the dim sum cart at **Phoenix** (p156).
- Sailing the seafood seas at **Emperor's Choice** (p156).
- Savoring blistered-crust pizza in the sunken dining room at **Gioco** (p155).
- Dinner at **Printer's Row** (p155) before a play.

Getting Curried Away

Between the spice shops, sari stores and Indian restaurants, Devon Ave west of Western Ave is one of the most exotic stretches of Chicago. It's also a damn fine place to get a heaping plate of *saag paneer*, tandoori chicken, garlic naan and other wonders of Indian cooking. The El doesn't come close to this area, so you'll have to drive, take a cab or ride the El to the Red Line's Morse Ave stop and transfer to the No 155 Morse Ave bus.

Indian Garden (Map pp270–1; ☎ 773-338-2929; 2548 W Devon Ave; mains $7–16; bus 155) Items not found on most South Asian menus dominate here. The cooks use wok-like pans and simple iron griddles to prepare a lot of the items. Vegetables go beyond the soggy cauliflower in goopy sauces found at other, less inspired places. Wash it all down with a mango shake.

Udupi Palace (Map pp270–1; ☎ 773-338-2152; 2543 W Devon Ave; mains $5–10; bus 155) This bustling all-vegetarian Indian serves toasty, kite-sized rice crepes stuffed with all manner of vegetables and spices, along with an array of curries. The room gets loud with a twentysomething Anglo hipster and young Indian crowd.

Sabri Nehari (Map pp270–1; ☎ 773-742-6200; 2511 W Devon Ave; mains $6–16; bus 155) Fresh, fresh meat and vegetable dishes distinctly seasoned set this Pakistani place apart from its competitors on Devon. Try the 'frontier' chicken, which comes with a plate of fresh-cut onions, tomatoes, cucumber and lemon, and enough perfectly cooked chicken for two. (The frontier being referred to is Pakistan's mountainous northern frontier). For desert, check out the *kheer*, a creamy rice pudding.

ARMY & LOU'S Map pp270–1   *Soul Food*
☎ 773-483-3100; 422 E 75th St, near Martin Luther King Dr; mains $6–15; ☻ closed Tue; bus 75

If you've never had soul food, start at this warm and welcoming Chicago classic, which rises above the crowd of similar local establishments, many of which are little more than storefronts serving take-out buckets of wings, rib tips and macaroni and cheese. Here you can order fried chicken, catfish, collard greens, sweet-potato pie and all the other classics at prices that are good for your soul. Don't be surprised if you see a few famous Black politicians, led by Jesse Jackson. And don't be surprised if some White politician shows up for a photo op.

CAFFÈ FLORIAN Map pp288–9   *American*
☎ 773-752-4100; 1450 E 57th St; mains $5–10; Metra to 59th St

The menu here traces its heritage back to the original Caffè Florian, which opened in Venice in 1720 and became a meeting place for 'the intelligentsia, with patrons including the most celebrated artists, poets, dramatists, actors, musicians and philosophers of the time,' according to the menu here. The humbler modern version serves lesser mortals, and much of the fare (black-bean nachos, fish and chips) has never graced a tabletop in Venice. But a few Italian items do make the menu, which covers much of the world.

GLADYS' LUNCHEONETTE
Map pp270–1   *Soul Food*
☎ 773-548-6848; 4527 S Indiana Ave; mains $5–$10; ☻ closed Mon; Green Line to 47th

This Bronzeville restaurant has been serving the notable and the common for more than 50 years. The white-aproned waitresses are ageless and their service timeless. The menu bursts with inexpensive soul food and other American standards. You'll find traditional fare at breakfast, but lunch mixes sandwiches with soul food and dinner sees a more extensive soul menu, with items like baked turkey necks and fried catfish.

LEON'S BAR-B-Q Map pp270–1   *Barbecue*
☎ 773-731-1454; 1640 E 79th St; mains $6–14

Since there's no seating inside, you'd better arrive by car and use your vehicle as your dining room. The big slabs of ribs – some of the best in town – come with your choice of sauce, from mild to hot. Just watch your upholstery or, better yet, take a rental car and let Mr Hertz or Ms Avis worry about theirs.

Top Five South Chicago
- Working through a 'garbage' pizza at **Medici** (p158).
- Grabbing a loaf of ciabatta from the **Medici bakery** (p158) for the walk home.
- Lunch in the lot at **Leon's** (p157).
- Keeping an eye (the one not riveted to the fried chicken) peeled for politicians at **Army & Lou's** (p157).
- Downing a 'Monster of the Midway' burger at **Caffé Florian** (p157).

MEDICI Map pp288–9 _American_

☎ 773-667-7394; 1327 E 57th St; mains $6-14;
Metra to 59th St

The world's woes have been solved several times over here, chiefly in the form of thin-crust pizza, sandwiches and salads. Burgers come in myriad choices, with optional toppings. Vegetarians can seek refuge in the veggie sandwich. For breakfast, try the 'eggs espresso,' made by steaming eggs in an espresso machine. After your meal, check the vast bulletin board out front. It's the perfect place to size up the character of the community and possibly find the complete works of John Maynard Keynes for sale cheap. A Medici-run bakery next door now serves fresh-baked bread products.

VALOIS Map pp288–9 _American_

☎ 773-667-0647; 1518 E 53rd St; mains $5-8;
Metra to 53rd St

Feel like you're in the midst of one of those atmospheric National Public Radio segments at this cafeteria where the motto is 'See your food.' Author Mitchell Duneier based his book _Slim's Table_ on regular Valois customers, who run the gamut of Chicago denizens, from number-crunching Nobel Prize-winners to rock-crunching ditch diggers. They've been feasting on the large and tasty portions here for more than 70 years. The standards include long-steamed vegetables, hot beef sandwiches, casseroles and good, fresh biscuits, all of it cheap and hearty. Cash only.

Drinking

Drinking

Top Five Chicago Bar Moments

- Nodding to the beat of underground DJs at **Danny's** (p165).
- Watching movies at hipster heaven **Delilah's** (p161).
- Slurping mussels and downing Belgian beer at the **Hop Leaf** (p165).
- Seeing beer-o-philes panic when forced to choose just one beer from the hundreds on offer at **Quencher's** (p166).
- Winning big-time romantic points for bringing a date to the **Signature Lounge** at the 95th (p137).

Some people blame it on the long winters, others on Midwesterners' innate conviviality. Whatever the reason, Chicago is a bar-happy town, and if you do any socializing in the Windy City, you'll likely step inside a bar or pub at some point.

The sheer variety of bars in the city can make choosing the night's destination a little daunting. The good news is that once you find your favorite spot, you'll have plenty of time to settle in; Chicago bars are open late on weekends, some until 4am.

Chicagoans tend to drink close to home, but there are a few 'destination strips,' bar-rich streets where taxi cabs are constantly headed to deliver more partying patrons. The Damen Ave corridor of Wicker Park/Bucktown is a bar-hoppers Eden, and Lincoln Ave and Halsted St in Lincoln Park are similarly mobbed with hordes of drinkers. The Boys Town area in Lake View is the epicenter of gay nightlife in the city.

In this section, we've only included bars where hanging out is the main attraction. A few listed below may have live music or DJs on the weekends, but the music tends to take a back seat to the sounds of toasts and conversation. If you're looking for the city's best dance floors or stages, head to the Entertainment chapter.

THE LOOP & NEAR NORTH

The bars in the Loop tend to be attached to hotels (and equally attached to charging you $5 for that bottle of Budweiser). Near North is much more interesting, with a selection split between old-school pubs and trendy new places selling *Sex and the City*–style glamour.

BERGHOFF STAND UP BAR Map pp282–3
☎ 312-427-3170; 17 W Adams St;
🕑 11am-9pm Mon-Thu, 11am-9:30pm Fri, 11:30-10pm Sat, closed Sun; Blue Line to Jackson
Adjoining the restaurant, this bar has changed little in a century, although women have been admitted for the past 40 years.

BREHON PUB Map pp280–1
☎ 312-642-1071; 731 N Wells St; 🕑 11am-2am Mon-Fri, noon-3am Sat, noon-2am Sun; Brown Line to Chicago
Forget the gimmicks found in neighboring blocks and experience the real Chicago at this fine example of the corner saloons that once dotted the city. The Brehon purveys 12 kinds of draft beer in frosted glasses to neighborhood crowds perched on the high stools.

CELTIC CROSSING Map pp280–1
☎ 312-337-1005; 751 N Clark St; 🕑 2pm-2am Sun-Fri, 2pm-3am Sat; Red Line to Chicago
The fireplace is imported from Ireland – as are the owners and staff – at this comfy Irish pub. Best of all, the pints of Guinness come in *imperial* pints. That's a little over 3oz more!

CLARK ST ALE HOUSE Map pp280–1
☎ 312-642-9253; 742 N Clark St; 🕑 4pm-4am Mon-Thu, 4pm-5am Fri & Sat, 4pm-2am Sun; Red Line to Chicago
Come here for the neighborhood's best beer selection, which includes a rotating selection of tap beer from some of the best Midwestern microbreweries. Work up a thirst on the free pretzels and cool off in the beer garden out back.

ESPNZONE Map pp280–1
☎ 312-644-3776; 43 E Ohio St; 🕑 11am-midnight Sun-Thu, 11am-1am Fri & Sat; Red Line to Grand
A fantasy land for men whose fantasies consist of watching 20 sports games at once on huge TVs, this bombastic bar features a 'screening room' with a 16ft screen and 'skybox'-style seating.

GREEN DOOR TAVERN Map pp280–1
☎ 312-664-5496; 678 N Orleans St; ⌚ 11am-11pm
Mon & Tue, 11am-midnight Wed & Thu, 11am-1am Fri
& Sat, closed Sun; Brown Line to Chicago
See the review (p132) in the Eating chapter for
details on this old-timey bar.

NARCISSE Map pp280–1
☎ 312-787-2675; 710 N Clark St; ⌚ 5pm-2am Mon-
Fri, 5pm-3am Sat, 7pm-2am Sun; Red Line to Chicago
It's no jeans, no hats and no athletic apparel
at this sumptuous, extravagant spot, one
of Chicago's most beautifully lush lounges.
Order caviar and sip champagne in gilded
splendor while watching the beautiful people
orbit around you.

GOLD COAST
The forty-and-over set have a great time in
these Gold Coast bars.

GIBSON'S Map pp278–9
☎ 312-266-8999; 1028 N Rush St; ⌚ 11am-1am;
Red Line to Clark/Division
Gibson martinis (served with a cocktail onion)
are the namesake speciality at this lively bar attached to Gibson's steak house. See the review
(p136) in the Eating chapter for details. A piano
player begins tickling the ivories at 5pm.

LODGE Map pp278–9
☎ 312-642-4406; 21 W Division St; ⌚ 5pm-4am Sun-
Fri, 5pm-5am Sat; Red Line to Clark/Division
One of those bars that you tend to end up
in by accident, only to have the time of your
life. A Wurlitzer jukebox plays oldies, and the
peanuts are free. The crowd is mostly fortysomethings there to drink until dawn.

LINCOLN PARK & OLD TOWN
The blood-alcohol levels run pretty high in
Lincoln Park's bars, where hard-drinking
yuppies decked out in polo shirts and
Kate Spade bags suck down microbrews
and flirt among themselves to the sounds
of the latest Dave Matthews Band CD. The
bars around DePaul University further
heighten the party-hearty feel of the place,
serving as beer-soaked launching pads for
plenty of awkward conversations the following morning. In Old Town, you'll find
the pace is slower and quirkier.

DEJA VU Map pp276–7
☎ 773-871-0205; 2624 N Lincoln Ave; ⌚ 9pm-4am
Sun-Fri, 9pm-5am Sat; Brown, Red Line to Fullerton
Drinks at this lively 4am bar are half-price on
Sunday. The ebullient mood peaks on Thursday
for live Latin music, and again on the weekends
when DJs spin a mix of techno, alternative and
Latin rhythms. There's a cover Thursday to Saturday, ranging from $3 to $5.

DELILAH'S Map pp276–7
☎ 773-472-2771; 2771 N Lincoln Ave; ⌚ 4pm-2am
Sun-Fri, 4pm-3am Sat; Brown Line to Diversey
From the free artsy movies screened on Saturdays to the non-DJ DJs spinning anything-
goes selections from their personal record
collections, Delilah's is a happy meeting place
for the area's underground scene. Bohemian
sophisticates can choose from a bunch of
high-end single-malts or opt for a $2 beer.

GIN MILL Map pp276–7
☎ 773-549-3232; 2462 N Lincoln Ave; ⌚ 4pm-2am
Mon-Fri, 11am-3am Sat, 11am-midnight Sun; Brown,
Red Line to Fullerton
The slogan here is 'We drink our share and sell
the rest.' They're very friendly about it, too, with
remarkable $2-pint specials on microbrews
some nights. The owners and staff are all fanati-
cal about the Michigan State athletic teams, so
watch what you say about the Spartans.

GOOSE ISLAND BREWERY Map pp276–7
☎ 773-915-0071; 1800 N Clybourn Ave; ⌚ 11am-
1am Mon-Fri, 11am-2am Sat, 11am-midnight Sun; Red
Line to North/Clybourn
Chicago's brewpub features the locally made
Goose Island beers, including the hoppy Honk-
er's Ale and potent XXX Porter. More sporty than
beer-snob tweedy, the brewery has several TVs
and gets packed with fans for Bulls and Cubs
games. The outdoor area is a must in summer.

JOHN BARLEYCORN MEMORIAL PUB
Map pp276–7
☎ 773-348-8899; 658 W Belden Ave;
⌚ 3pm-2am Mon-Fri, 9am-3am Sat, 9am-2am Sun;
Brown, Red Line to Fullerton
John Dillinger used to be a customer here back
in the old days. Now, classical music plays as
projections of art light up the walls, all of which
is happily ignored by the 23 year-olds here to
get drunk. See the review (p139) in the Eating
chapter for details on the worthwhile menu.

Berghoff Stand Up Bar (p160)

KELLY'S Map pp276–7

☎ 773-281-0656; 949 W Webster Ave;
🕐 11am-2am Sun-Fri, 11pm-3am Sat;
Brown, Red Line to Fullerton

DePaul students and fans gather at this classic Chicago bar right under the El – hold onto your glass when a train goes by. Since 1933 – they opened the day after Prohibition ended – the same family has been welcoming all comers with tasty burgers and booze.

LUCILLE'S Map pp276–7

☎ 773-929-0660; 2470 N Lincoln Ave;
🕐 5pm-2am; Brown, Red Line to Fullerton

Instead of stale pretzels and day-old popcorn, how do munchies like bruschetta and prosciutto sound? Lucille's is a rarity – a bar where both the food and the atmosphere are top-notch. The alcoholic offerings include an excellent selection of wines by the glass and a bewildering number of martinis.

MCGEE'S Map pp276–7

☎ 773-871-4272; 950 W Webster Ave; 🕐 11am-2am Mon-Fri, 10am-3am Sat, 11am-2pm Sun; Brown, Red Line to Fullerton

Another DePaul bar in the heart of Lincoln Park, this lively place attracts undergrads and recent grads alike. Stop here if you're feeling nostalgic for your college days.

OLDE TOWN ALE HOUSE Map pp276–7

☎ 312-944-7020; 219 W North Ave; 🕐 noon-4am Sun-Fri, noon-5am Sat; Brown Line to Sedgwick

A wonderful Old Town neighborhood staple from the days before this was a neighborhood, this bar has been the scene of late-night musings since the 1960s – the last time paint was applied. Come by and grab a book from the lending library, drop some quarters in the old-school jazz jukebox and settle in for a few hours of atmospheric merriment.

RED LION PUB Map pp276–7

☎ 773-348-2695; 2446 N Lincoln Ave; 🕐 noon-11pm Mon-Thu, noon-midnight Fri & Sat, noon-10pm Sun; **Brown, Red Line to Fullerton**

A British-style pub run by real Brits, this cozy spot features plenty of UK brews and the best onion rings in the city ($4). The Red Lion also hosts regular author talks and readings.

RED ROOSTER CAFE & WINE BAR
Map pp276–7

☎ 773-871-2100; 2100 N Halsted St; 🕐 5pm-10: 30pm Mon-Thu, 5pm-11:30pm Fri & Sat, 5pm-10pm Sun; Brown, Red Line to Armitage

Connected to Cafe Bernard (p139), this funky little wine bar makes a great stop before or after meals or the theater. Choose among oodles of wines by the glass.

Top Five Coffee Shops

Not every public house in Chicago serves the hard stuff. Whether you need a snack and a caffeinated pick-me-up, or just a comfortable place where you can sit down and read for a few hours, Chicago's coffee shops beckon.

- **Atomix** (Map p275; ☎ 312-666-2649; 1957 W Chicago Ave) This retro-futuristic themed coffee shop in Ukrainian Village is popular with laptop people.
- **Earwax** (Map p275; ☎ 773-772-4019; 1561 N Milwaukee) A funky, sideshow-freak-themed café in Wicker Park that serves veggie food.
- **Intelligentsia Coffee** (Map pp272–3; ☎ 773-348-8058; 3123 N Broadway) Study, gab or work all day in this cozy Lake View outpost of Chicago's hometown coffee roaster.
- **Map Room** (Map p275; ☎ 773-252-7636; 1949 N Hoyne Ave) This comfy Bucktown café gets up with the roosters, and features free live music at night.
- **Uncommon Grounds** (Map pp272–3; ☎ 773-929-3680; 1214 W Grace St) The casual fave in Wrigleyville is great for socializing and also has live acoustic music at night.

STERCH'S Map pp276–7
☎ 773-281-2653; 2238 N Lincoln Ave; ⏰ 3:30pm-2am Sun-Fri, 3:30pm-3am Sat; Brown, Red Line to Fullerton

A genial older crowd of writers and would-be poets hangs out at this convivial bar where there's never a shortage of conversation.

WEED'S Map pp276–7
☎ 312-943-7815; 1555 N Dayton St; ⏰ 4pm-2am Mon-Sat, closed Sun; Red Line to North/Clybourn

The bras hanging from the ceiling like animal pelts set the tone at this bar where beatnik meets bohemia. Weed's is a bar with a thousand strange stories, most of them courtesy of Dada-esque owner Sergio Mayora – whose name has motivated him to run most unsuccessfully for mayor. Spirits stay loose through frequent shots of tequila on the house.

LAKE VIEW

Lake View's bars mirror the distinct neighborhoods it comprises. Wrigleyville, near Wrigley Field, swarms with sports bars, which are mobbed before and after Cubs games. To the west, the Southport corridor

between Addison St and Irving Park Rd is booming with new places targeted at the over-25 set. And in Boys Town, north of Broadway along Halsted, you'll find Chicago's bustling gay nightlife scene.

CLOSET Map pp272–3
☎ 773-477-8533; 3325 N Broadway; ⏰ 2pm-4am Mon-Fri, noon-5am Sat, noon-4am Sun; Red, Brown Line to Belmont

One of the very few lesbian-centric bars in Chicago, the Closet changes mood and tempo at 2am, when the crowd becomes more mixed, the music gets louder and things get a little rowdier.

CULLEN'S Map pp272–3
☎ 773-975-0600; 3741 N Southport Ave; ⏰ 11am-1:30am Mon-Fri, 9pm-2:30am Sat & Sun; bus 152

See the review (p143) in the Eating chapter for the details on this fine tavern. It's connected to the Mercury Theatre, and it's an easy walk to the Music Box movie theater.

DUKE OF PERTH Map pp272–3
☎ 773-477-1741; 2913 N Clark St; ⏰ 5:30pm-2am Mon, 11:30am-2am Tue-Fri, 11:30am-3am Sat, noon-2am Sun; bus 22

See the review (p143) in the Eating chapter for all the details about this excellent pub and beer garden. It boasts almost 80 kinds of single-malt scotch.

GENTRY Map pp272–3
☎ 773-348-1053; 3320 N Halsted St; ⏰ 4pm-2am Sun-Fri, 4pm-3am Sat; Red, Brown Line to Belmont

This stately piano bar serves as a welcome respite for thirty- and forty-year-old gay men tired of the pounding house beats of Boys Town's clubs. Live cabaret music nightly.

GINGER MAN Map pp272–3
☎ 773-549-2050; 3740 N Clark St; ⏰ 3pm-2am Mon-Fri, noon-3am Sat, noon-2am Sun; Brown, Red Line to Diversey

A splendid place to pass an evening, this spot features a huge and eclectic beer selection that's enjoyed by theater types and other creative folks. The G-Man, as it is often called, avoids the overamped Cubs mania of the rest of the strip by playing classical music when the Cubs play at home. There are numerous pool tables in back, and pool is free on Sunday.

GUTHRIE'S Map pp272–3
☎ 773-477-2900; 1300 W Addison St; ☯ 4pm-2am;
Red Line to Addison

A local institution and the perfect neighborhood hangout, Guthrie's remains true to its mellow roots even as the neighborhood goes manic around it. The glassed-in back porch is fittingly furnished with patio chairs and filled with thirty- and fortysomethings. Most tables sport a box of Trivial Pursuit cards.

POPS FOR CHAMPAGNE Map pp272–3
☎ 773-472-1000; 2934 N Sheffield Ave; ☯ 5pm-2am;
Brown, Red Line to Wellington

This refined and classy place makes a perfect spot for a post-theater drink, a celebratory toast or a romantic tête-à-tête. You can choose among 12 champagnes by the glass, 140 more by the bottle and scores of excellent wines as well. The snacks are suitably chichi – pâté and the like – and Pops features live jazz nightly (cover averages $8).

ROSCOE'S Map pp272–3
☎ 773-281-3355; 3354 N Halsted St; ☯ 3pm-2am
Mon-Thu, 2pm-2am Fri, 1pm-3am Sat, 1pm-2am Sun;
Red, Brown Line to Belmont

Affectionately called 'the gay Bennigan's' (the comfortable but generic restaurant) by some of its twenty- and thirtysomething patrons, Roscoe's has a friendly atmosphere, great menu and inviting beer garden.

SOUTHPORT LANES Map pp272–3
☎ 773-472-6600; 3325 N Southport Ave; ☯ 4pm-
1am Mon-Fri, noon-2am Sat, noon-1am Sun; Brown
Line to Southport

This old-fashioned local bar with a good beer selection has undergone a renaissance under the thoughtful management of some upscale types, who oversee the bar itself and an annex with four hand-set bowling lanes. The main bar features an inspirational old mural of cavorting nymphs. Lots of tables populate the sidewalk in summer.

TEN CAT TAVERN Map pp272–3
☎ 773-935-5377; 3931 N Ashland Ave; ☯ 3pm-2am
Sun-Fri, 3pm-3am Sat; bus 9

Pool is serious business at the funky Ten Cat – play takes place on two vintage tables that co-owner Richard Vonachen re-felts regularly with material from Belgium. The ever-changing line-up of eye-catching art comes courtesy of neighborhood artists, and the furniture is a garage-saler's dream. Groups of regulars – most in their 30s – down leisurely drinks at the bar, or, in warm weather, swap pool tales out in the beer garden.

Green Mill (p179)

YAK-ZIES Map pp272–3

☎ 773-525-9200; 3710 N Clark St; ⏰ 11am-2am;
Red Line to Addison

Relive college here with lots of young people wearing sweats and working quickly through pitchers of beer. The TVs show plenty of college sports action, while the frat crowd digs into plates of the popular Buffalo wings and unique parsley-crust pizza.

ANDERSONVILLE & UPTOWN

Andersonville and Uptown have a handful of character-rich, laid-back bars. The area is also a sort of 'Boys Town North,' offering a couple of solid gay-bar options.

BIG CHICKS

☎ 773-728-5511; 5024 N Sheridan Rd; ⏰ 4pm-2am
Mon-Fri, 4pm-3am Sat, 3pm-2am Sun; Red Line to
Argyle

Uptown's Big Chicks has one of the city's most enjoyable bipolar disorders. During the week, the bar is cozily sedate, a place where gay and straight gather to socialize beneath the sizable collection of woman-themed art. Weekends, though, gay men pack the stamp-sized dance floor to boogie until 3am. Sunday at 3:30pm is the bar's legendary free brunch.

HOP LEAF Map p274

☎ 773-334-9851; 5148 N Clark St; ⏰ 2pm-2am
Mon-Fri , 11am-3am Sat, 11am-2am Sun; Red Line to
Berwyn

Owner Michael Roper, using the name of the national beer from his ancestral Malta, has created one of Andersonville's best bars. Highlights here include an intricate original tin ceiling and a jukebox playing classic country and jazz cuts. The beers are artfully selected by Roper, with an emphasis on Belgian and American brews. In 2003, the Hop Leaf opened a kitchen, serving Belgian *frites* and mussels.

SIMON'S Map p274

☎ 773-878-0894; 5210 N Clark St; ⏰ 11am-2am; Red
Line to Berwyn

One of Andersonville's few twentysomething hang-outs, this nautical-themed bar has Pavement playing on the stereo, and a long bar right out of the '50s. The mural on the wall is of the original owner Simon Lundberg and his friends. Lundberg's son now lovingly runs the place.

WICKER PARK/BUCKTOWN & UKRAINIAN VILLAGE

Take the Blue Line to Damen prepared to party. Wicker Park and Bucktown are both open late, and are perfectly set up for a night's worth of bar-hopping. Ukrainian Village is a little rougher and more spread out – cabbing is a good idea.

CHARLESTON Map p275

☎ 773-489-4757; 2076 N Hoyne Ave; ⏰ 3pm-2am
Mon-Sat, noon-2am Sun; bus 50

The resident cats will curl up on your lap at this laid-back Bucktown hangout. Occasional live folk music jibes with the older crowd.

CLUB FOOT Map p275

☎ 773-489-0379; 1824 W Augusta Blvd; ⏰ 8pm-2am
Sun-Fri, 8pm-3am Sat; Blue Line to Damen

This fun bar's cheap drink specials aren't the only sight for sore eyes: the walls here are packed with three decades of musical and pop cultural ephemera. The crowds varies with the eclectic DJ nights – rockabilly one night, '80s the next.

DANNY'S Map p275

☎ 773-489-6457; 1951 W Dickens Ave; ⏰ 7pm-2am
Sun-Fri, 7pm-3am Sat; bus 50

The olive walls of this hipster hang-out are worn from benders past; things rarely get out of hand here. DJs spin relaxed grooves of old soul and downtempo electronica every night. Blessedly TV-free, Danny's is a great place to come for conversation.

GOLD STAR BAR Map p275

☎ 773-227-8700; 1755 W Division; ⏰ 4pm-2am Sun-
Fri, 4pm-3am Sat; Blue Line to Division

This friendly dive is where Irvine Welsh hangs out when he's in Chicago teaching. Join Irvine and the bike-messenger set for cheap drinks and a great jukebox.

LEMMINGS Map p275

☎ 773-862-1688; 1850 N Damen Ave; ⏰ 9pm-4am
Mon-Fri, 2pm-3am Sat, noon-2am Sun; bus 50

This mellow bar features a pool table, good beers on tap and a sign in the window telling local artists how they can get their work displayed in the bar. Lemmings also has one of Chicago's best collection of vintage Schlitz signs from the glory days of crappy beer.

MAP ROOM Map p275

☎ 773-252-7636; 1949 N Hoyne Ave; ☻ 6:30am-2am
Mon-Fri, 7am-3am Sat, 11am-2am Sun;
Blue Line to Damen

Drink locally and think globally at this friendly
corner café/bar where globes line the walls
and a huge map of the world covers the back
wall and ceiling. The Map Room features lots
of local brews and games for whiling away
cold winter days. The volume on the free live
music on weekends is kept to a minimum, so
your conversations can be kept to a maximum.
A great find.

NICK'S Map p275

☎ 312-252-1155; 1516 N Milwaukee Ave; ☻ 4pm-
4am Sun-Fri, 4pm-5am Sat; Blue Line to Damen

This big joint has a friendly, fraternity vibe and a
good collection of beers from around the world.
Weather warm? Hit the beer garden in back.

RAINBO CLUB Map p275

☎ 773-489-5999; 1150 N Damen Ave; ☻ 4pm-2am
Sun-Fri, 4pm-3am Sat; Blue Line to Damen

Ground zero for the city's indie elite during
the week, the boxy, dark-wood Rainbo Club
has an impressive semicircular bar and one
of the city's best photo booths. The service is
slow and the place goes a little suburban on
weekends, but it's otherwise an excellent place
to meet local artists and musicians

QUENCHERS Map p275

☎ 773-276-9730; Fullerton Ave; ☻ 11am-2am Mon-
Sat, noon-1am Sun; bus 74

At the north end of Bucktown, Quenchers is
one of Chicago's most interesting bars. With
over 200 beers from more than 40 nations, it
offers ample opportunities to find that certain
something missing from the swill peddled by
the US brewery giants: flavor. Locals, artisans,
laborers and visiting brew masters enjoy Earle
Miller's hospitality. The prices are the cheapest in
town. Live music can get a little loud, though.

SONOTHEQUE Map p275

☎ 312-226-7600; 1444 W Chicago Ave; ☻ 8pm-2am
Wed-Fri, 8pm-3am Sat; Blue Line to Chicago

The DJs here spin genres of electronica so
hip they don't even have names yet, a perfect

complement to the sleek, next-century space.
This kind of bar would be a snooty disaster
in New York, but absolutely down-to-earth
patrons and reasonable drink prices make it
feel like your corner pub.

Worth a Trip

Chicago has a bunch of worthwhile watering holes
located well off the well-trod drinking path. This is
especially true on Chicago's West and South Sides.
Below are some of the standouts.

Blue Frog Bar & Grill (Map pp284–5; ☎ 312-
943-8900; 676 N LaSalle St; ☻ 11:30am-2am Mon-
Thu, noon-2am Fri, 6pm-3am Sat, closed Sun; Blue
Line to LaSalle) This haven for retro board games
and the people who love them resounds with the
shouts of players winning and losing at 'Operation,'
'Sorry' and a host of other oldies-but-goodies.

Hawkeye's (Map pp286–7; ☎ 312-226-3951;
1458 W Taylor St; ☻ 11am-2am Sun-Fri,
11am-3am Sat; Blue Line to Polk) This Little Italy
institution runs a free shuttle from the United
Center to its doorstep when the Bulls or Blackhawks are playing, making it a good place to come
to celebrate a victory or agonize over a defeat. Its
virtues include a good burger-based menu and fine
seasonal tables outside.

Jimmy's Woodlawn Tap (Map pp288–9; ☎ 773-
643-5516; 1172 E 55th St; ☻ 10:30-2am Mon-Fri,
10:30-3am Sat, 11am-2am Sun; Metra to 55th
St) Some of the geniuses of our age have killed
some brain cells here, one of Hyde Park's few
worthwhile bars. The place is dark and beery, and
a little seedy. But for thousands of University of
Chicago students deprived of a thriving bar scene,
it's home. Hungry? Their Swissburgers
are legendary.

Puffer's (Map pp270–1; ☎ 773-927-6073; 3356
S Halsted St; ☻ 9pm-4am Sun-Fri, 9pm-5am
Sat; Red Line to Sox-35th) A cool pub in staid old
Bridgeport, Puffer's boasts a bright orange facade
and the neighborhood's most amiable clientele,
with folks hanging out, talking and sampling
from the excellent beer selection. A good choice
after a Sox game, it's a 15-minute walk west from
Comiskey Park, er, US Cellular Field.

Drinking – Wicker Park/Bucktown & Ukrainian Village

Entertainment

Entertainment

When Chicago's weekly arts and entertainment paper, the *Reader*, hits the streets every Thursday, there's more than a small risk of someone getting hurt. Not because of poison-pen exposés or yellow journalistic slanderings, mind you. No, the risk caused to the city's populace by the paper is a much more physical one – the four-sectioned thing weighs so much that trying to heft one of them across town could give a grown man a hernia and permanently cripple a small child.

Why does it weigh so much, you ask? Because this is Chicago, and there's at least a pound of goings-on happening every week. Start your weight-lifting regimen now. From theater to dance to experimental musicians playing mic'd hamster wheels, Chicago has so much going on that you'll need all the stamina you can muster just to read about it.

THEATER & IMPROV

They waited on your table at lunch; now see them doing what they *really* love to do. Chicago's actors and playwrights shine every night of the week here, and the lure of potential fame and (somewhat limited) fortune draws young talent to the city's world of companies and acting schools.

Some theater groups have their own venues, others don't. Throughout this chapter we've noted the addresses of those that have regular homes and just the phone numbers (and web addresses) of those that don't. We've also listed a few off-beat venues where the productions are consistently top-notch regardless of who is performing there.

These listings give a small idea of what's being staged. Check the local press – especially the *Reader* – to find out what's hot. If you happen to be in town mid-May, keep an eye peeled for the Chicago Improv Festival (☎ 773-235-8070; www.cif.com), which brings back Chicago's famous comedic names and ensembles for reunion performances on stages throughout the city.

Tickets

Ticket prices for shows range from $10 for small shows to $40 or more for main companies like Steppenwolf. Most average $15 to $25. However, there are a variety of ways to beat these costs. The League of Chicago Theatres (see their website www.chicagoplays.com for Chicago theatre news) operates Hot Tix booths, where same-day tickets to participating shows are sold at half-price. The lineup varies every day, with the best selection available on weekends. Hot Tix sells weekend tickets beginning on Friday, and the booths also offer regular full-price tickets. To find out what's available, go to the Internet site www.hottix.org, which is updated daily, or simply stop by one of the booths.

Hot Tix operates three city locations: in the Loop (Map pp282–3; 78 W Randolph St), at the Visitor Information Center (Map pp278–9; 163 E Pearson St) and at Tower Records (Map pp276–7; 2301 N Clark St). Also, students, children, senior citizens, the disabled, groups and even actors may qualify for special prices from the theaters themselves. Plus, some places offer low-cost preview shows before the official premiere and last-minute deals right before curtain time. The moral of this story? Always check with the box office for any and all deals before plunking down your bucks – even at Hot Tix.

ABOUT FACE THEATRE
☎ 773-784-8565; www.aboutfacetheatre.com
An itinerant ensemble primarily staging serious plays dealing with gay and lesbian themes and issues.

BAILIWICK ARTS CENTER Map pp272–3
☎ 773-883-1090; www.bailiwick.org; 1229 W Belmont Ave; Brown, Red Line to Belmont
This facility boasts two stages that see a constant stream of productions, many of them gay-oriented and many by the resident Bailiwick Repertory.

BLACK ENSEMBLE THEATRE Map p274
☎ 773-769-4451; Uptown Center Hull House, 4520 N Beacon St; Red Line to Wilson
Original works about the lives of African Americans are performed by this established group.

The Palaces of the Loop

Chicago boasts some dreamboat old theaters, all of which have been renovated and reopened in recent years as part of the impressive Loop theater district restoration. The city has posted signs in front of each palatial property detailing the zaniness that went on in each during its heyday. Whether they're showing a Cuban ballet company or a Disney musical, these beauties are worth the price of admission alone.

- **Auditorium Theater** (Map pp282–3; ☎ 312-902-1500; 50 E Congress Parkway)
- **Cadillac Palace Theater** (Map pp282–3; ☎ 312-902-1500; 151 W Randolph St)
- **Chicago Theater** (Map pp282–3; ☎ 312-443-1130; 175 N State St)
- **Ford Center/Oriental Theater** (Map pp282–3; ☎ 312-902-1400; 24 W Randolph St)
- **Shubert Theater** (Map pp282–3; ☎ 312-977-1700; 22 W Monroe St)

Its 2000 staging of *The Jackie Wilson Story* spawned the national touring production.

CHICAGO DRAMATISTS Map p275
☎ 312-633-0630; www.chicagodramatists.org; 1105 W Chicago Ave; Blue Line to Chicago
Using a small, functional theater space, this organization is one of Chicago's best-known incubators for new plays and playwrights.

CHICAGO SHAKESPEARE THEATER
Map pp280–1
☎ 312-595-5600; www.chicagoshakes.com; Navy Pier, 800 E Grand Ave; bus 66
A long-established theater enjoying a beautiful new home out on Navy Pier. As the name implies, the productions are usually adaptations of the Bard's work.

COMEDYSPORTZ Map pp272–3
☎ 773-549-8080; www.comedysportzchicago.com; 2851 N Halsted St; Red, Brown Line to Diversey
The gimmick here is that two improv teams compete with deadly seriousness to make you laugh hysterically. The audience benefits from this comic capitalism, and all the fun is 'G' rated. Alcohol is allowed but it's BYOB.

COURT THEATRE Map pp288–9
☎ 773-753-4472; www.courttheatre.org; 5535 S Ellis Ave; Metra to 55th St
A classical company hosted by the University of Chicago, the Court focuses on great works

from the Greeks to Shakespeare, as well as various international plays not often performed in the US.

FAMOUS DOOR THEATRE COMPANY
☎ 773-404-8283; www.famousdoortheatre.org
This provocative group, which specializes in rarely produced plays, can go from mesmerizingly intense to laugh-out-loud funny at the drop of a hat.

FREE ASSOCIATES
☎ 773-975-7171; www.thefreeassociates.com
This comedy improv group is responsible for works such as *BS*, a much-needed skewering of the TV show *ER*. When not laying waste to pop culture, the group also does a send-up of Shakespeare. It's about time.

GOODMAN THEATRE Map pp282–3
☎ 312-443-3800; www.goodman-theatre.org; 170 N Dearborn St; Blue, Brown, Green, Orange Line to Clark/Lake
The Goodman, named by *Time* magazine as the best regional theater in the US, specializes in new and classic American theater. Its annual production of *A Christmas Carol* has become a local family tradition.

IMPROVOLYMPIC Map pp272–3
☎ 773-880-0199; www.improvolymp.com; 3541 N Clark St; Red Line to Addison
First among the improvs, this comic veteran launched the careers of Mike Myers and MTV's Andy Dick, along with a host of other well-known comics. Shows hinge entirely on audience suggestions, and each turn can run 40 minutes or longer. If you're thoroughly motivated by what you see, ImprovOlympic offers a range of courses to suit every temp's budget (for a personal perspective on these courses, see the boxed text p000). The same stage also hosts various improv groups composed of the talented alums, including the legendary Baby Wants Candy, which has been known to improvise entire musicals. Shows here tend to be a little bawdier than at ComedySportz.

LIVE BAIT THEATER Map pp272–3
☎ 773-871-1212; www.livebaittheater.org; 3914 N Clark St; Red Line to Sheridan
Actors who hoped to lure audiences with the 'bait' of their talent founded this renowned theater in 1987. They've been reeling them in ever since. Mostly the group mounts produc-

Entertainment – Theater & Improv

169

Comedy 101

What do Bill Murray, Fred Willard, Dan Aykroyd, Mike Myers, Rachel Dratch and Tina Fey all have in common?

They – along with a host of other famous names from TV and film – all learned how to be funny in Chicago. Both Second City and ImprovOlympic offer eight-week courses on comedy to all comers, with the cream of each graduating class getting loads of recognition and – just maybe – a shot at the big time.

It has made Chicago's comedy classes a beacon for the city's office cut-ups and wiseacres. We talked to Robyn Nisi, a Chicago office worker and graduate of both Second City and ImprovOlympic, to get the scoop on the classes and find out if people really can *learn* to be funny.

Her first impressions of her fellow comedy school students, it turns out, were less than overwhelming. 'It seemed like a complete disaster,' she says. 'We met in a Catholic elementary school that Second City rented out on weekends for the classes. It was a very weird environment to begin with because we're in this cold, desolate classroom. And so many of the students looked really timid…a lot of quiet looking people. I was thinking "Oh god, this is going to be a total bust."'

As people began talking about their day jobs, Nisi was surprised to discover that a fair number of her mousy colleagues had actually re-arranged their lives just to be there that day. 'A lot of people move to Chicago to do this. You get a lot of kids saying, "Hi, my name is Jim. I just got here from New Mexico."'

Along with the young hopefuls, there were a number of older, solidly established professionals. 'High-level business people do it because they want a break from the monotony of their work week,' says Nisi.

The process of learning to be Jim Belushi, it turns out, isn't as cut and dried as memorizing a roster of punchlines and finding out which funny wigs to wear. 'They don't want you to go out and be the wacky guy with the wacky voice and the wacky hair,' Nisi says. 'They want something that's really pure. Because audiences want to see their realities mirrored. They want to be able to look at you and say "I really relate to that person who's really having the bad day with the jerk who sits next to them."'

It all added up to a thorough introduction to the strange, brainy, hilarious beast that is Chicago comedy. Where learning how to be funny is often just learning how to be yourself. And for a lot of her classmates, that meant coming to terms with the fact that a job at *Saturday Night Live* just wasn't in the cards. But that was OK.

'Some people will never be Tina Fey,' Nisi says. 'Some people will never be Richard Pryor. Their niche is in being a lawyer. Their niche is in being a collections agent. But you definitely see a lot of people reveal new aspects of themselves in the classes.'

---

tions by founders Sharon Evans, Catherine Evans and John Ragir.

LOOKINGGLASS THEATRE COMPANY

Map pp278–9

☎ 312-337-0665; www.lookingglasstheatre.org; 821 Michigan Ave; Red Line to Chicago

This company took a step into the big time with the opening of its new spacious digs on Michigan Ave. The ensemble cast – which includes David Schwimmer of TV's *Friends* – loves to use physical stunts and acrobatics to enhance its thought-provoking plays.

MERCURY THEATRE Map pp272–3

☎ 773-325-1700; 3745 N Southport Ave; Brown, Red Line to Belmont

Michael Cullen, owner of the adjoining bar, Cullen's, has created a fast-rising star among North Side theaters with this classy space.

NEOFUTURISTS Map p274

☎ 773-275-5255; www.neofuturists.org; 5153 N Ashland Ave; Red Line to Berwyn

Best known for their long-running *Too Much Light Makes the Baby Go Blind*, in which the hyper troupe make a manic attempt to perform 30 plays in 60 minutes. Admission cost is based on a dice throw, and they order pizza when the house sells out.

NOBLE FOOL THEATER COMPANY

Map pp282–3

☎ 312-726-1156; www.noblefool.org; 16 W Randolph; Blue Line to Washington

Renowned for its biting and satirical shows, this troupe uses its main stage for bigger productions like *Don't Drink the Water*, and the studio stage for local favorites like *Flanagan's Wake*, a brutal – and of course true – look at an Irish wake that features audience members.

REDMOON THEATER

☎ 773-388-9031; www.redmoon.org

Haunting adaptations of classic works such as *Moby Dick* are the speciality of this innovative troupe, who use masks, complex costumes and puppets to convey universal themes.

ROYAL GEORGE THEATRE Map pp276–7

☎ 312-988-9000; 1641 N Halsted St; Red Line to North/Clybourn

The Royal George is three theaters in one building. The cabaret venue presents long-running mainstream productions such as *Late Nite Catechism*, a nun-centered comedy. The main stage presents works with big-name stars, and the gallery hosts various improv and minor works performed by small troupes.

STEPPENWOLF THEATER Map pp276–7

☎ 312-335-1650; www.steppenwolf.org; 1650 N Halsted St; Red Line to North/Clybourn

This legendary ensemble group helped put Chicago theater on the map when it won a Tony award in 1985 for regional theater excellence. Among the actors who have starred here and then gone on to fame and fortune (and who regularly come back to perform) are John Malkovich, Terry Kinney, Gary Sinise and John Mahoney, the crotchety old coot on *Frasier*.

STRAWDOG THEATRE Map pp272–3

☎ 773-528-9696; www.strawdog.org; 3829 N Broadway; Red Line to Sheridan

Their great sense of humor helps this company perform quirky works in a highly inventive and fun style.

SECOND CITY Map pp276–7

☎ 312-337-3992; www.secondcity.com/theatre /chicago/index.asp; 1616 N Wells St; Brown Line to Sedgwick

A Chicago must-see, this club is best symbolized by John Belushi, who emerged from the suburbs in 1970 and earned a place with the Second City improv troupe with his creative, manic, no-holds-barred style. Belushi soon moved to the main stage, and then to *Saturday Night Live* and fame and fortune. Second City's shows are sharp and biting commentaries on life, politics, love and anything else that falls in the crosshairs of their comedians' rapid-fire, hard-hitting wit. Other famous alums include Bill Murray, Dan Aykroyd, Tina Fey and Elaine May. Try to guess which cast members will be the next to ride the celebrity and success train.

SECOND CITY ETC Map pp276–7

☎ 312-642-8189; www.secondcity.com/theatre /chicago/index.asp; 1608 N Wells St; Brown Line to Sedgwick

Second City's second company often presents more daring work, as actors try to get noticed

and make the main stage. Both theaters offer the city's best comedy value after the last show most nights, when the comics present free improv performances to keep everybody's wit sharp.

THEATRE BUILDING Map pp272–3

☎ 773-327-5252; www.theatrebuildingchicago.org; 1225 W Belmont Ave; Brown, Red Line to Belmont

Lots of small troupes present shows in this flexible space.

TIMELINE THEATRE COMPANY Map pp272–3

☎ 312-409-8463; www.timelinetheatre.com; 615 W Wellington Ave; Brown, Red Line to Belmont

TimeLine has a unique mission of exploring history's place in culture through often-moving theatrical works.

TRAP DOOR THEATRE Map p275

☎ 773-384-0494; www.trapdoortheatre.com; 1655 W Cortland St; bus 9

The latest fundraising goal of this ragtag operation has been to purchase a bathroom for their tiny theater. Despite the limits of the space, the spirited group stages consistently great productions of European avant-garde plays.

WNEP THEATER Map pp272–3

☎ 773-755-1693; www.wneptheater.org; 3209 N Halsted St; Brown, Red Line to Belmont

The name stands for 'what no one else produces,' and that's a perfect summary of this space's mission. Funny, eclectic pop culture–based productions, including many midnight shows for a twentysomething crowd.

VICTORY GARDENS THEATER Map pp276–7

☎ 773-871-3000; www.victorygardens.org; 2257 N Lincoln Ave; Brown, Red Line to Fullerton

Long-established and playwright-friendly, Victory Gardens specializes in world premieres of plays by Chicago authors. The *Wall St Journal* called Victory Gardens 'one of the most important playwright theaters in the US.'

ZANIES Map pp276–7

☎ 312-337-4027; www.chicago.zanies.com; 1548 N Wells St; Brown Line to Sedgwick

The city's main stand-up comedy venue regularly books big-name national acts familiar to anyone with a TV, and also frequently invites comics you're *going to* hear about on TV. The shows last less than two hours and usually include the efforts of a couple of up-and-comers before the main act. The ceiling is low and the seating is cramped, which only adds to the good cheer.

DANCE

The big news in Chicago's small dance community is the opening of the **Joan W and Irving B Harris Theater for Music and Dance** (Map pp282–3; ☎ 312-629-8696; www.madtchi.com; 205 East Randolph Dr), a long-awaited performance space that finally gives Chicago's scattered dance scene a centrally located, high-profile home.

You can find complete listings for the biggies and the handful of smaller companies in the *Reader*'s and the *Tribune*'s arts sections. The **Chicago Dance and Music Alliance** (☎ 312-987-9296; www.chicagomusic.org) has a list of upcoming dance performances on their site.

Festivals

Running for a rhythmic month beginning in November, **Dance Chicago** (☎ 773-989-0698; www.dancechicago.com) brings more than 250 companies to the **Athenaeum Theatre** (Map pp272–3; 2936 N Southport Ave). Styles range from ballet to tap to break dancing. For people interested in getting in on the action themselves, the city sponsors **Chicago SummerDance** (☎ 312-742-4007; Jun-Aug, Thu-Sat evenings, Sun afternoons), where ordinary Chicagoans get a chance to practice their ballroom and Latin dance moves in the Spirit of Music Garden (Map pp282–3) to live orchestral accompaniment. Free lessons are included for folks with two left feet.

BALLET CHICAGO
☎ 312-251-8838; www.balletchicago.org
This pre-professional troupe of younger dancers has received much acclaim for its precision and skill performing classical ballet works.

CHICAGO MOVING CO
☎ 773-880-5402; www.chicagomovingcompany.org
This exciting group was founded by Nana Shineflug, one of the pioneers of modern dance in Chicago. The works and performers are all local.

DANCE CENTER AT COLUMBIA COLLEGE Map pp284–5
☎ 312-344-8300; www.dancecenter.org; 1306 S Michigan Ave
More than an academic institution, the Dance Center has carved out a fine reputation by presenting top local and international talent. The center's new state-of-the-art facility within Columbia College should help it to continue attracting quality dance.

HUBBARD ST DANCE CHICAGO
☎ 312-629-8696; www.hubbardstreetdance.com; Harris Theater for Music and Dance, 205 East Randolph Dr; Brown, Green, Orange Line to Randolph
Hubbard St is the preeminent dance group in the city, with an international reputation to match. The group has become known for energetic and technically virtuoso performances under the direction of the best choreographers in the world, including founder Lou Conte.

JOFFREY BALLET OF CHICAGO
Map pp282–3
☎ 312-739-0120; www.joffreyballet.org; Auditorium Theatre, 50 E Congress Pkwy; Brown, Orange Line to Library
This famous group has flourished since it relocated from New York in 1995. Noted for its energetic work, the company frequently travels the world and boasts an impressive storehouse of pieces it regularly performs.

MUNTU DANCE THEATER OF CHICAGO
☎ 773-602-1135; www.muntu.com
The word 'muntu' means 'the essence of humanity' in Bantu, and this company performs African and American dances that draw on ancient and contemporary movement.

RIVER NORTH DANCE COMPANY
☎ 312-944-2888; www.rivernorthchicago.com
This vibrant young company brings elements of punk, house, hip-hop, mime and more to modern dance.

CINEMA/FILM

In summer, nothing feels better than beating the Chicago heat with a frostbite-inducing bath in one of the city's many air-conditioned movie houses. And in winter, toasty buckets of buttery popcorn will allow you to feel your hands again and give you the

Entertainment – Dance

crucial calories you need to insulate yourself from the snow piling up outside. It's no wonder that the movies are huge in Chicago.

You'll find out everything you need to know about show times in the *Reader*, *New City* or movie sections of either daily paper.

Festivals

Each October, the **Chicago Film Festival** (☎ 312-644-3456; www.chicagofilmfestival.org) brings a score of films from around the world to town for two weeks. Check with the festival for each year's schedule. For less mainstream offerings, check out the **Chicago Underground Film Festival** (www.cuff.org), which runs in late August.

Quirkier still, the **Fast Forward Film Festival** (www.fastforwardfilmfest.com) gives local filmmakers 24 hours to make and edit a three-minute video. The results are then shown to excited, sleep-deprived audiences at a BYOB event in one of the area's converted warehouses. The film fest takes place three times a year, and has included films by up-and-coming local directors such as Julia Cardis; check the website for details. Along the same ambitious lines, the **72 Hour Film Project** (www.72hfp.com) challenges filmmakers from all over the world to shoot and edit a feature-length film in three days. Screenings take place in June at the Gene Siskel Film Center (p173).

Some convenient or worthwhile movie houses are listed here.

600 N MICHIGAN THEATERS

Map pp280–1

☎ 312-255-9340; 600 N Michigan; Red Line to Chicago
Despite the name, the entrance to these theaters is off Rush St. This comfortable complex features six screens of various sizes, plus a café and concessions stand on each of its three floors.

900 N MICHIGAN THEATERS

Map pp278–9

☎ 312-787-1988; 900 N Michigan; Red Line to Chicago
A decent modern theater with two sizable screens hides in the basement of the mall of the same name.

BIOGRAPH THEATER Map pp276–7

☎ 312-444-3456; 2433 N Lincoln; Red, Brown Line to Fullerton
The site of John Dillinger's famous demise in 1934, the Biograph is still showing movies.

BREW & VIEW Map pp272–3

☎ 312-618-8439; www.brewview.com; Vic Theater, 3145 N Sheffield Ave; Brown, Red Line to Belmont
Even the worst film gets better when you've got a pizza in front of you and a pitcher of beer at your side. As you watch second-run Hollywood releases here, you can behave as badly as you would at home – in fact, the staff encourage it. Must be 18 to enter.

FACETS MULTIMEDIA Map pp276–7

☎ 773-281-4114; www.facets.org; 1517 W Fullerton Ave; bus 74
Facets shows interesting obscure movies that would never get booked elsewhere. This is the place to find the denizens of Chicago's film community between Hollywood contracts.

GENE SISKEL FILM CENTER

Map pp282–3

☎ 312-443-3733; www.artic.edu/webspaces /siskelfilmcenter; 164 N State St; Brown, Green, Orange Line to State
The former Film Center of the Art Institute was renamed for the late *Chicago Tribune* film critic Gene Siskel. It shows everything from amateurish stuff by students who should hang onto their day jobs to wonderful but unsung gems by Estonian directors. The monthly schedule includes theme nights of forgotten American classics.

IMAX THEATER Map pp280–1

☎ 312-595-0090; 600 E Grand Ave at Navy Pier; bus 66
The mega-screen theater is out on the pier.

LANDMARK'S CENTURY CENTRE

Map pp272–3

☎ 773-248-7744; 2828 N Clark St; Brown, Red Line to Diversey
This is a useful neighborhood multiplex.

MCCLURG COURT THEATERS

Map pp280–1

☎ 312-642-0723; 330 E Ohio St; bus 66
If your movie is playing in the main theater here, you're in for a treat; it's one of the city's largest screens.

MUSIC BOX THEATRE Map pp272–3

☎ 773-871-6604; www.musicboxtheatre.com; 3733 N Southport Ave; Brown Line to Southport
No matter what's showing, it's worth going to the Music Box just to see the place. This perfectly

restored theater dates from 1929 and looks like a Moorish fantasy. Clouds float across the ceiling, which has twinkling stars. The film programs are always first-rate. A second, small and serviceable theater shows held-over films that have proved more popular than expected.

PIPERS ALLEY Map pp276–7
☎ 312-642-7500; cnr North Ave & Wells St; Brown Line to Sedgwick

Located in the complex of the same name, this is a pretty decent multiplex with good sight lines.

RIVER EAST 21 Map pp280–1
☎ 874-765-7262; 322 E Illinois St; bus 65

The city's newest multiplex is a harbinger of things to come for River East.

THREE PENNY CINEMA Map pp276–7
☎ 773-935-5744; 2424 N Lincoln Ave; Red, Brown Line to Fullerton

The floors creak at this ramshackle, family-run complex of tiny theaters in Lincoln Park. But what the family saves in maintenance expenses, you save in admission. Tickets are cheap for major releases that have passed their prime and for a good selection of the better minor films.

VILLAGE THEATER Map pp278–9
☎ 312-642-2403; 1548 N Clark St; Brown Line to Sedgwick

This is a cool old theater broken up into several smaller ones. It shows quirky new releases and second runs at good prices.

OPERA & CLASSICAL MUSIC

Chicago may have steaks and pizza aplenty, but audiences hungry for classical music will likely go wanting. Not because Chicago doesn't have an orchestra – the Chicago Symphony Orchestra is one of the best in the country. But because tickets to the Symphony are notoriously difficult to get a hold of, scooped up by season-ticket holders.

Opera is similarly loved to exclusivity in Chicago. The Lyric Opera is wonderful, but season-ticket holders hog most of the seats in the ornate opera house. Some good vocal and baroque ensembles make use of the city's theaters and churches, though. And in summer, the classical music moves out-of-doors (see Festivals following), where everyone can enjoy it.

If you're truly dying to see the Chicago Symphony or the Lyric Opera, head on down to the show about 30 minutes before curtain. More often than not, some besuited swell will offer you a pair of tickets at a reasonable (or free) price. Check the *Reader* to see what's being performed when you're in town.

Festivals

During the summer-long Grant Park Music Festival (☎ 312-742-7638), classical music for the masses is performed at the Petrillo Music Shell (Map pp282–3), in Grant Park at Jackson and Columbus Sts between the Art Institute and the lake. Under the auspices of the Chicago Park District, the Grant Park Symphony Orchestra gives free concerts, usually on Wednesday, Friday, Saturday and Sunday evenings, although events such as the jazz festival can alter the schedule. At present Chicago is the only city in the US to boast a free symphony orchestra. The classical orchestra's solid performances span several genres, from opera to Broadway and 'pop.'

In the summer the CSO and other classical, jazz, folk, ethnic and pop groups perform at Ravinia (☎ 847-266-5100; www.ravinia.org; Green Bay and Lake Cook Rds), a vast open-air festival in Highland Park on the North Shore. The main pavilion contains seating for several hundred in a bowl-like setting with a good view of the stage and the performers. But these tickets sell quickly, and most people end up sitting on the acres of lawn. If you do go, avoid the traffic and take the 45-minute Metra/Union Pacific North Line train from Ogilvie Transportation Center (Map pp282–3) to Ravinia Station ($5 round-trip). Trains stop before and after the concerts right in front of the gates.

APOLLO CHORUS OF CHICAGO
☎ 630-960-2251; www.apollochorus.org

A 150-member vocal group founded in 1872, the Apollo usually performs at the Symphony Center (see Chicago Symphony Orchestra p175). Tickets for the chorus' Christmas performance of Handel's *Messiah* sell out every year.

CHICAGO CHAMBER MUSICIANS
☎ 312-225-5226; www.chicagochambermusic.org

This 14-member group has dedicated itself to spreading the sound of chamber music by performing the classics, as well as initiating numerous outreach programs to the community. See local listings for venue information.

CHICAGO OPERA THEATER
Map pp282–3

☎ 312-704-8420; www.chicagooperatheater.org; Harris Theater for Music and Dance, 205 E Randolph St; Brown, Green, Orange Line to Randolph

This innovative group stages contemporary and popular works during the summer. Under general director Brian Dickie, COT has scored some artistic success. It concentrates on little performed 17th- and 18th-century classics as well as contemporary American works.

CHICAGO SINFONIETTA
☎ 312-857-1062; www.chicagosinfonietta.org

This group of notable young musicians, led by the locally well-known Paul Freeman, performs classics as well as adventurous modern works by the likes of Thelonious Monk.

CHICAGO SYMPHONY ORCHESTRA
Map pp282–3

☎ 312-294-3000; www.cso.org; Symphony Center, 220 S Michigan Ave; Brown, Green Orange Line to Adams

The CSO enjoys lavish support locally. The late Sir George Solti was music director from 1969 to '92 and is credited with propelling the CSO to the very front ranks of world symphony orchestras. The current director, Daniel Barenboim, had the classic big pair of shoes to fill and has done so masterfully. He has molded the group with his personality, and the acclaim continues. The CSO season runs from September to May. In the summer, when the orchestra isn't wowing some European capital, it often performs at Ravinia (see Festivals p174). The CSO also oversees the Civic Orchestra of Chicago, the training branch of the symphony. Visiting conductors and musicians often work with the group, which also performs in the Symphony Center. And their tickets are free!

HIS MAJESTIE'S CLERKES
☎ 312-461-0723

This a cappella group, which is named after the 'clerkes' who sang in 16th-century England, produces a clear and haunting sound. Most of their performances take place in the city's grand churches.

LYRIC OPERA OF CHICAGO
Map pp282–3

☎ 312-332-2244; www.lyricopera.com; Civic Opera House, 20 N Wacker Dr; Brown, Orange Line to Washington

One of the top opera companies in the US performs in the grand old Civic Opera House, on the south branch of the river. The Lyric's repertoire is a shrewd mix of old classics and much more modern and daring work. You can catch the *Mikado* one week and some totally new but emotionally stunning piece the next.

The company has had excellent luck luring top international names, such as Placido Domingo. It also has joined the international trend of projecting translations of the lyrics onto a screen above the proscenium. Purists shudder with horror; others, whose Italian or German isn't what it could be, sit back and happily read away. Gregarious Sir Andrew Davis, former music director of the BBC Symphony, took the helm of the Lyric in 2000 to good reviews. The season runs from September to March.

MUSIC OF THE BAROQUE
☎ 312-551-1415; www.baroque.org

One of the largest choral and orchestra groups of its kind in the US, MoB brings the music of the Middle Ages and Renaissance to vibrant life. Its Christmas brass and choral concerts are huge successes.

LIVE MUSIC
There's more music being played any night of the week in Chicago than you could ever listen to, even if you had a year to spare.

Obviously, given the city's blues and jazz roots, you can hear world-class performances in those genres. You can also catch plenty of live rock, by everyone from garage bands to revival groups to cutting-edge names. And with the wealth of ethnic enclaves, you're sure to hear just about anything else you desire. When it comes to finding out what's happening on the live-music scene during your visit, check the *Reader*.

Tickets

Cover charges vary widely depending on the venue, the day of the week, the musicians playing etc. Small places presenting relative unknowns might charge nothing on a Sunday night, while larger venues with top names on the weekend will demand $20 or more. You can get tickets to most of the bigger venues listed through their websites, or by calling **Ticketmaster** (☎ 312-559-1212). We've listed open hours to the clubs like piano bars and the lower-key jazz venues, where performances are likely to continue through the evening. For the start times for concert events, call the venue or check newspaper listings.

Pop, Rock & Country

ABBEY PUB Map pp270–1
☎ 773-478-4408; www.abbeypub.com;
3420 W Grace St; Blue Line to Addison
Along with being a good bet for Irish music some nights, the Abbey Pub in far-out Irving Park has become one of the city's best small rock venues. An adjoining pub is smoky and crowded. This club is located far from the city center, on the northwest side.

CAROL'S PUB Map p274
☎ 773-325-9884; 4659 N Clark; bus 22
The closest thing Chicago has to a honky-tonk, Carol's offers boot-stompin' Bud-drinkin' good times to its patrons, who come out on weekends to dance like crazy to the house band, Diamondback. The live music (and the jukebox that fills in during the week) leans more towards old-school 1950s, '60s and '70s country names like George Jones and Hank Williams rather than more recent acts like Garth Brooks.

DOUBLE DOOR Map p275
☎ 773-489-3160; www.doubledoor.com; 1572 N Milwaukee Ave; Blue Line to Damen
Hard-edged, alternative rock echoes off the walls in this former liquor store, which still has its original sign out front. If you get confused, the bouncer will steer you less than carefully to the proper door.

EMPTY BOTTLE Map p275
☎ 773-276-3600; www.emptybottle.com;
1035 N Western Ave; Blue Line to Damen
As the best-known indie rock venue in Chicago, the Empty Bottle gets their pick of the smaller hot bands to come through town. The impressive programming here doesn't stick to electric guitars and power chords, however – on Tuesday nights free jazz improvisational master Ken Vandermark plays a regular set here.

FIRESIDE BOWL Map pp270–1
☎ 773-486-2700; www.firesidebowl.com;
2648 W Fullerton; Blue Line to California
This energetic, all-ages punk rock, garage rock, and emo venue is in a bowling alley that's seen better days. Sometimes bigger bands like the Jealous Sound or Pansy Division headline, but for the most part it's smaller bands living out of their tour van.

HIDEOUT Map p275
☎ 773-227-4433; www.hideoutchiago.com;
1354 W Wabansia; bus 72
Despite its diminutive size and the middle-of-nowhere location, the Hideout has managed to become a darling of Chicago's discerning bar-goers. In its lodge-like back room, folk, country and rock bands play, and in the dim, cozy front bar, Chicago's local music scene drinks Pabst (or sells it – singers Kelly Hogan and Laurie Stirratt both tend bar here). Come along on Friday nights to enjoy live-band karaoke.

HOUSE OF BLUES Map pp280–1
☎ 312-923-2000; www.hob.com;
Marina City, 329 N Dearborn St; Red Line to Grand
Blues Brother Dan Aykroyd invested in this spot, virtually guaranteeing that the House of Blues would make a big splash in Chicago. On the main floor – a casual eatery in a broken-down bayou setting – video monitors show diners what's happening upstairs in the large and open music venue. Bigger rock and hip-hop acts play here. The Sunday gospel brunch features soul-stirring Chicago groups and Cajun chow. Reserve early – it's usually mobbed. Oh, and try not to notice the gift shop near the door.

Who the hell is Wilco?

Put your ear to the rock-music rails in Chicago and you'll hear one band name coming up over and over again: Wilco. They haven't played the MTV Music Awards and they probably won't be coming to a radio near you any time soon. So who is Wilco? We asked Greg Kot, *Tribune* rock critic and author of the band's biography, *Wilco: Learning to Die*, to give us the lowdown.

Jeff Tweedy and Jay Farrar were the songwriting muscle behind the best band ever to emerge from Belleville, Illinois – Uncle Tupelo. They were a punk band with country influences, and for a bunch of shy blue-collar kids, they had soul. Uncle Tupelo broke up in 1994 after four albums that provided a blueprint for the alternative-country movement. Tweedy then formed Wilco, moved to Chicago and promptly upped the artistic ante.

It took a few years for the erstwhile small-town kid to feel comfortable in his new Rust Belt landscape, but once he did, Tweedy began drawing on the city's rich musical traditions to expand his sound and moved away from the alternative-country roots he's credited with planting. Wilco went about its business with a no-frills modesty and purpose that fit in well with the city's anti–rock star attitude, and graduated from playing to a few hundred people at the legendary (now defunct) Lincoln Ave rock club Lounge Ax, owned by Tweedy's wife, Sue Miller, to 9000 over two nights at the Auditorium Theatre.

Wilco set itself apart by widening its reach with every album: the amiable pop-twang of *A.M.* (1995), the Midwestern response to the Clash's *London Calling* that was *Being There* (1996), the lushly orchestrated song cycle of romantic burnout that became *Summerteeth* (1999), and the avant-garde beauty of *Yankee Hotel Foxtrot* (2002). Sprinkled in between were a pair of acclaimed *Mermaid Avenue* collaborations with Billy Bragg, in which Wilco and the British folksinger wrote new music for previously unheard Woody Guthrie lyrics.

The band might be even better known for its standoff with Reprise Records, which rejected *Yankee Hotel Foxtrot* as too radio-unfriendly for release in 2001. Undaunted, Wilco streamed the new songs on its website and toured to packed houses around the nation while looking for a new label.

The quintet's industry end-around was a risky move that turned into an artistic and commercial coup. When *Yankee Hotel Foxtrot* was finally released nearly a year overdue (ironically, on Nonesuch Records, a subsidiary of the same AOL Time Warner empire to which Reprise belongs), it was already a cause célèbre in international music circles. *Foxtrot* sold 55,000 copies in its first week and debuted at No. 13 on the Billboard 200 Album chart; it has since sold 400,000 copies. Those figures are career bests for Wilco, but they're merely commercial validation for Wilco's most ambitious blend yet of pop melody, lyrical introspection and risk-taking production.

Greg Kot

METRO Map pp272–3

☎ 773-549-3604; www.metrochicago.com; 3730 N Clark St; Red Line to Addison

Indie acts teetering on the verge of stardom play this former classic theater, one of the best venues in Chicago, with sweet sight lines and good sound.

NOTE Map p275

☎ 312-489-0011; 1565 N Milwaukee Ave; Blue Line to Damen

Funk and rock bands play until 2am, and are followed by DJs spinning everything from hip-hop to salsa. It's small, it's full. It's a nice kind of dive.

SCHUBA'S Map pp272–3

☎ 773-525-2508; www.schubas.com; 3159 N Southport Ave; Brown, Red Line to Belmont

Something of an alt-country legend, Schuba's presents a host of twangy, acoustic artists. (Noncountry indie-rock acts too big for the

Empty Bottle also might find themselves playing here.) While the bar area itself is lively and boisterous, the back music room is civilized and music-focused (talkers should expect to be shushed).

Blues & Jazz

ANDY'S Map pp280–1

☎ 312-642-6805; 11 E Hubbard St; Red Line to Grand

This veteran jazz and blues bar/restaurant doesn't charge a cover for its lunchtime shows. Some workers come at lunch and never quite make it back to the office.

BACK ROOM Map pp278–9

☎ 312-751-2433; 1007 N Rush St; Red Line to Clark/Division

In this tiny place you view the jazz musicians via a mirror. If you're on the small main floor, you might find the intimacy reminiscent of a concert held in your own bedroom.

BLUE CHICAGO Map pp280–1

☎ 312-642-6261; www.bluechicago.com; 736 N Clark St; Red Line to Chicago

The talent lives up to the club's name at this mainstream blues club. If you're staying in the neighborhood and don't feel like hitting the road, you won't go wrong here. Admission to Blue Chicago gets you into the branch two blocks down as well, **Blue Chicago on Clark** (Map pp280–1; ☎ 312-661-0100; 536 N Clark). The latter also offers a Saturday early evening alcohol- and smoke-free 'introduce yourself and your kids to the blues' concert. Call for details.

B.L.U.E.S Map pp276–7

☎ 773-528-1012; 2519 N Halsted St; Brown Line to Diversey

Long, narrow and crowded, this veteran club crackles with electric moments where the crowd shares in the music. Look for names like Big James & the Chicago Playboys.

BUDDY GUY'S LEGENDS Map pp284–5

☎ 312-427-0333; www.buddyguys.com; 754 S Wabash Ave; Red Line to Harrison

You're likely to find the namesake here, although instead of playing, Buddy will probably be giving the crowd a circumspect gaze as he adds up a stack of receipts. Look for top national and local blues groups in this no-nonsense, cavernous space.

HOTHOUSE Map pp284–5

☎ 312-362-9707; www.hothouse.net; 31 E Balbo Dr; Red Line to Harrison

Near Grant Park and the Loop, the jazz, world music and hip-hop club HotHouse has been called 'indispensable' by *Tribune* critic Howard Reich. It regularly draws top artists from as far away as South Africa and Japan. Look for the great local saxophonist Ernest Dawkins.

JAZZ SHOWCASE Map pp280–1

☎ 312-670-2473; www.jazzshowcase.com; 59 W Grand Ave; Red Line to Grand

Owner Joe Segal presides over an elegant club that caters to jazz purists. Segal's been promoting be-bop jazz in Chicago since he worked as a student booker at Roosevelt University many, many moons ago.

KOKO TAYLOR'S CELEBRITY

Map pp284–5

☎ 312-566-0555; 1233 S Wabash Ave; Red Line to Roosevelt

Local blues legend Koko Taylor owns this top-notch venue and often performs here herself.

GREEN DOLPHIN STREET Map pp276–7

☎ 773-395-0066; www.jazzitup.com; 2200 N Ashland Ave; bus 6

This classy venue combines excellent and inventive cuisine with good jazz. It's hard to

imagine that this riverside club, which looks like it's been around since the 1940s, used to be a junk-auto dealer before the renovation.

GREEN MILL Map p274
☎ 773-878-5552; 4802 N Broadway;
Brown Line to Lawrence
You can sit in Al Capone's favorite spot at the timeless Green Mill, a true cocktail lounge that comes complete with curved leather booths. Little has changed in 70 years – the club still books top local and national jazz acts. On Sunday night it hosts a nationally known poetry slam where would-be poets try out their best work on the openly skeptical crowd. Would Al have approved?

KINGSTON MINES Map pp276–7
☎ 773-477-4646; www.kingstonmines.com;
2548 N Halsted St; Brown Line to Diversey
It's so hot and sweaty here that the blues neophytes in the audience will feel like they're having a genuine experience – sort of like a gritty theme park. Two stages mean that somebody's always on. The club's popularity means that it attracts big names.

LEE'S UNLEADED BLUES Map pp270–1
☎ 773-493-3477; 7401 S South Chicago Ave;
504 E 75th St; bus 30
Lee's and Rosa's (below) are cut from the same cloth; this is a no-nonsense, nontouristy blues club where the live music runs Thursday to Monday. Dress up.

LILLY'S Map pp276–7
☎ 773-525-2422; 2513 N Lincoln Ave; Brown,
Red Line to Fullerton
Lilly's routinely presents excellent local blues acts inside a club with an odd Mexican air. The largely ignored balcony offers good views on crowded nights.

NEW APARTMENT LOUNGE
Map pp270–1
☎ 773-483-7728; 504 E 75th St; bus 3
The only night to come to this simple storefront venue on the far South Side is Tuesdays, when saxophonist Von Freeman leads his long-running, roof-raising jam session at 10:30pm. Come early.

ROSA'S LOUNGE Map pp270–1
☎ 773-342-0452; www.rosaslounge.com;
3420 W Armitage Ave; bus 73

This is hardcore blues. Top local talents perform at this unadorned West Side club in a neighborhood that's still a few decades away from attracting developers. Take a cab.

VELVET LOUNGE Map pp284–5
☎ 312-791-9050; www.velvetlounge.net; 2128½ S
Indiana Ave; Red Line to Cermak/Chinatown
Tenor saxophonist Fred Anderson owns the Velvet, near the South Side. Visiting jazz musicians often hang out here late at night. The tiny place rocks during frequent impromptu jam sessions.

Reggae, Folk & World
EXEDUS II Map pp272–3
☎ 773-348-3998; www.exeduslounge.com;
3477 N Clark St; closed Tue; Red Line to Addison
This narrow bar fills with smoke and the sounds of good reggae, performed by acts often on their way to or from the Wild Hare.

OLD TOWN SCHOOL OF FOLK MUSIC
Map pp270–1
☎ 773-728-6000; www.oldtownschool.org;
4544 N Lincoln Ave; Brown Line to Western
You can hear the call of the banjos from the street outside this venue, where major national and local acts like John Gorka, Richard Thompson and Joan Baez sometimes play. If you want to join in, you can take classes. The Old Town's original location in **Old Town** (Map pp276–7; ☎ 773-525-7793; 909 W Armitage Ave) offers classes for kids.

WILD HARE Map pp272–3
☎ 773-327-4273; 3530 N Clark St; Red Line to Addison
Dreadlocks meet capitalism at this modern reggae club run by guys from Jamaica but financed by local venture capitalists. It books top touring acts. Beware after Cubs games, when the baseball caps outnumber the dreadlocks by a factor of 10.

Piano Bar & Cabaret
COQ D'OR Map pp278–9
☎ 312-787-2200; The Drake, 140 E Walton St;
⏰ 11am-2am Mon-Sat, 11am-2am Sun;
Red Line to Chicago
Cole Porter, Frank Sinatra and others are part of the repertoire of the highly talented piano players and singers who rotate through this stately lounge. The live music gets going every night at 9:30pm.

DAVENPORT'S PIANO BAR & CABARET Map p275

☎ 773-278-1830; 1383 N Milwaukee Ave; ⏱ 7pm-2am Sun, Mon & Wed-Fri, 7pm-3am Sat, closed Tue; Blue Line to Damen

Old standards get new interpretations and new songs get heard for the first time at this swank place on an up-and-coming stretch of Milwaukee Ave. The front room is a fun, inclusive (read: sing-along) place, with the back reserved for more fancy-pants cabaret events (where singing along will get you thrown out).

ZEBRA LOUNGE Map pp272-3

☎ 312-642-5140; 1220 N State St; ⏱ 2pm-2am Sun-Fri, 2pm-3am Sat; Red Line to Clark/Division

For a funky night dating back to the days before colorization, try this small, smoky joint decorated entirely in black and white. The piano can get as scratchy as the voices of the crowd, which consists mainly of older people who like to sing along. Regular ivory-stroker Tom Oman is a veteran who knows his stuff.

CLUBBING

The dance clubs in Chicago essentially come in two flavors. The first, and most prevalent, are clubs like Le Passage and Circus, where your $20 cover will buy you entry into an over-the-top space where the decor is amazing, the people are good-looking and well-dressed, and a gin and tonic will cost you $8. The house or hip-hop at these places will be handled with aplomb by some competent disc-spinner, but ultimately, dancing is secondary to the experience of being in a fantasy land that transcends the bounds of ordinary life for a night.

The second flavor of club is one where fashion is functional, the cover is lower and people come to dance. Despite a draconian police crackdown on illegal drugs in dance clubs in the late '90s, Chicago still has a fairly strong, very friendly dance-music community. And if when you hear 'dance-music community,' you think of a bunch of E-'d out 19-year-olds with glow sticks, think again: Chicago was one of the hotbeds of house in the early '80s, and the audiences have aged with the music. When you go out to the more music-focused events like Spundae at Vision or weekends at the SmartBar, you'll see plenty of thirtysomethings shaking it out there with the college students.

Top Five Dance Clubs in Chicago

- **Berlin** (p180), where no-attitude, smiling crowds rock hot house mixes.
- **Big Wig** (p180), home to some of the freshest sounds around.
- **Red Dog** (p181), where the big bass tickles just right.
- **Smart Bar** (p182), the basement club where two generations of ravers have come of age.
- **Vision** (p182), where Spundae Saturdays are sweaty fun.

To find out about dance events, the free monthly paper *UR* is far and away the most helpful guide, including detailed listings of all the best one-offs and regular DJ gigs going down around town. *New City* and the *Reader* also have club listings, but they're less helpful. For the more underground events, look for flyers at hip record stores like Gramaphone (p197) or any of the rave-themed clothing stores along Milwaukee in Wicker Park.

BABY DOLL POLKA Map pp270-1

☎ 773-582-9706; 6102 S Central Ave; ⏱ 5pm-2am Mon-Fri, 5pm-3am Sat, 3pm-2am Sun; Orange Line to Midway

This polka bar just west of the Midway Airport is one of the most unique dancing opportunities in town. Middle-aged Polish polka-holics get down seven nights a week to live music starting at 9pm (5:30pm on Sundays). The dancing is fast and furious, the beers are cheap and the views out over the Midway airport runway beautiful.

BERLIN Map pp272-3

☎ 773-348-4975; www.berlinchicago.com; 954 W Belmont Ave; ⏱ 8pm-4am Mon, 5pm-4am Tue-Fri, 5am-5pm Sat, 6pm-4am Sun; Brown, Red Line to Belmont

The excitable crowd at Berlin is very mixed, with straights, gays and in-betweens sharing space on the sweaty dance floor. Video monitors play the latest clips from Bjork and Peaches while DJs take the dance floor in a trancey direction.

BIG WIG Map p275

☎ 773-235-9100; www.bigwignightclub.net; 1551 W Division St; ⏱ 9pm-2am Sun-Fri, 9pm-3am Sat; Blue Line to Division

Garnering a growing reputation as one of Chicago's best underground dance destinations, Big Wig rarely plays the kind of generic booty house you'll hear blaring from other clubs' speakers. Wednesday's drum & bass night is popular.

CLUB EDEN Map pp272–3

☎ 773-327-4646; 3407 N Clark St; 🕑 noon-2am Sun-Fri, noon-3am Sat; Red Line to Addison

This big club features DJs spinning on two levels. Most nights it's hip-hop and soul, with the odd salsa night tossed in.

CIRCUS Map pp276–7

☎ 312-266-1200; www.circusnightclub.com; 901 W Weed St; 🕑 10pm-4am Tue, Fri, Sat; Red Line to North/Clybourn

The name is very appropriate for this huge, crazy club, where fire-blowers, stilt-walkers and other circus entertainment mingle with dancers on the floor. The see-and-be-seen crowd is in their twenties, there more to check out the other twentysomethings than to dance to the house music.

COTTON CLUB Map pp284–5

☎ 312-341-9787; 1710 S Michigan Ave; 🕑 6pm-3am Sun, Mon, Wed, Thu, 5pm-4am Fri, 7pm-5am Sat, closed Tues; bus 1

A dose of R&B is mixed with hip-hop at this swank place near the South Side. The patrons tend to dress sharply to match the elegant surroundings. Some nights you can catch good live jazz at the piano bar out front.

EXCALIBUR Map pp280–1

☎ 312-266-1944; www.excaliburchicago.com; 632 N Dearborn St; 🕑 5pm-4am Sun-Fri, 5pm-5am Sat; Red Line to Grand

Inside its elegant exterior (the building once housed the Chicago Historical Society), Excalibur has three levels of dancing, with mainstream house, hip-hop and 80s booming from various rooms. Other areas in the funhouse include jukeboxes, electronic games, pool and more. Mostly touristy and suburban crowds.

EXIT Map pp276–7

☎ 773-395-2700; www.exitchicago.com; 1315 W North Ave; 🕑 9pm-4am; Blue Line to Damen

A long-running punk/industrial dance club, where the dance floor comes complete with a cage. You'll want to be wearing leather for self-protection if nothing else.

FUNKY BUDDHA LOUNGE

Map pp286–7

☎ 312-666-1695; 728 W Grand; 🕑 9pm-2am Mon-Fri, 9pm-3am Sat, 6pm-2am Sun; Blue Line to Belmont

Though encroachment from suburban types has tarnished the Buddha's cutting-edge rep, this small club is still one of the better dance spots for hip-hop and house in Chicago.

KATACOMB Map pp276–7

☎ 312-337-4040; 1916 N Lincoln Park West; 🕑 8pm-4am Wed-Fri, 8pm-5am Sat, 10pm-4am Sun; Brown Line to Sedgwick

DJs spin soul, house, hip-hop and funk at this weekend favorite with the Lincoln Park crowds.

LE PASSAGE Map pp278–9

☎ 312-255-0022; www.lepassage.tv; 937 N Rush St; 🕑 7pm-4am Wed-Fri, 7pm-5am Sat; Red Line to Chicago

Are you a model? Or just look like one? You've found your niche. If you make it past the doorperson and her clipboard, you'll find a beautiful, vaguely tropical-themed club with French colonial decor and Polynesian drink specials. Music varies with the night; Wednesday's old-school hip-hop night 'Back in the Day' is always fun.

NEO Map pp276–7

☎ 773-528-2622; 2350 N Clark St; 🕑 9pm-4am Tue, Fri, 9pm-5am Sat; bus 22

This veteran industrial and goth venue dates from the time that Lincoln Park was the city's hottest neighborhood. Though the streets have gone quiet and upscale, this gritty dance club holds its own.

PUMP ROOM Map pp278–9

☎ 312-266-0360; Ambassador East hotel, 1301 N State St; 🕑 6pm-midnight; Red Line to Clark/Division

A certain timelessness prevails at this Gold Coast classic, where jazz and dance trios and vocalists provide slow-dance swing Wednesday through Saturday. The black they insist you wear here should be formal, not grunge. For details on the exquisite food, see p000.

RED DOG Map p275

☎ 773-278-1009; 1958 W North Ave; 🕑 10pm-4am Mon, Fri, 10pm-5am Sat; Blue Line to Damen

Some of the hottest DJs in town work weekends and Monday in this kitschy old warehouse, which pulses with funk, hip-hop and house. The lively crowd is as mixed as you can get sexually and ethnically.

REDNOFIVE Map pp286–7
☎ 312-733-6699; www.rednofive.com; 440 N Halsted St; ☽ 10pm-4am Thu & Fri, 10pm-5am Sat; Blue Line to Chicago

Even after its recent face-lift, this somewhat-cramped two-level place is a little rough around the edges, but the twentysomething clientele don't seem to mind. Come down for house music.

SINIBAR Map p275
☎ 773-278-7797; www.soundsofsinibar.com; 1540 N Milwaukee Ave; ☽ 8pm-3am Tue-Sat, closed Sun & Mon; Blue Line to Damen

Though the velvet rope is in effect out in front of this restaurant and club, everyone gets past it after a short wait. The downstairs dance floor bumps with a range of music, from funk to house to salsa.

SLICK'S LOUNGE Map pp276–7
☎ 312-932-0006; www.slickslounge.com; 115 N North Branch St; ☽ 7pm-2am Tue-Thu, 7pm-4am Fri, 7pm-5am Sat & Sun; Blue Line to Chicago

This super-hip dance club and restaurant caters to upscale African Americans. The DJs spin Latin-flavored grooves and soul; all the music reverberates off the nearby waters of the north branch of the Chicago River.

SMART BAR Map pp272–3
☎ 773-549-0203; http://smartbarchicago.com; 3730 N Clark St; ☽ 9pm-4am Sun-Fri, 9pm-5am Sat; Red Line to Addison

This downstairs adjunct to the Metro is a dance-music lover's dream, and the DJs who spin here are often far bigger than the space would have you think. Forward-looking breaks, house and trance.

SPIN Map pp272–3
☎ 773-327-1140; www.spin-nightclub.com; 800 W Belmont Ave; ☽ 4pm-2am Sun-Fri, 4pm-3am Sat; Red Line to Belmont

Though its clientele consists mostly of gay men in their twenties, Spin has also become a popular destination for hetero men and women looking for a fun place to shake it on the weekends. Serious dancers head to the main floor, while those looking to chat and cruise orbit the large bar by the club's entrance. Don't miss the shower contest on Friday nights, where dancing hopefuls of both genders bare (almost) all.

SPY BAR Map pp280–1
☎ 312-587-8779; www.spybarchicago.com; 646 N Franklin St; ☽ 10:30pm-4am Tue, Thu, Fri, 10:30pm-5am Sat; Brown Line to Chicago

The atmosphere at this subterranean spot is cruise-a-rama, as scantily dressed, good-looking twentysomething singles cavort to house music. Enter through the alley and dress nicely (no jeans) to get through the line more quickly.

SUBTERRANEAN Map p275
☎ 773-278-6600; www.subt.net; 2011 W North Ave; ☽ 7pm-2am Mon, 6pm-2am Tue-Fri, 7pm-3am Sat, 8pm-2am Sun; Blue Line to Damen

DJs spin hip-hop and other styles to a stylish crowd at this place, which looks slick inside and out. The cabaret room upstairs draws local bands and popular open-mic events.

VISION Map pp280–1
☎ 312-266-1944; www.visionnightclub.com; 640 N Dearborn St; ☽ 10pm-4am Thu-Fri, Sun, 10pm-5am Sat; Red Line to Grand

Located next to Excalibur, Vision throws some of the best techno parties in Chicago. Big-name DJs like Sasha, Doc Martin and Derrick Carter have all spun here, and the crowds come to dance rather than pose. The newly expanded club plays hip-hop in the smaller of its two spaces. Spundae-hosted events on Saturday are especially good – check the local listings for updates.

ZENTRA Map pp276–7
☎ 312-7870400; 923 W Weed St; ☽ 10pm-4am Wed-Fri, 10pm-5am Sat; Red Line to North/Clybourn

This sumptuous club feels like a cross between a tented harem and the Taj Mahal. Rich colors and textures everywhere combine with loud, thumping house music to create one of the city's most sensual spaces. Swing on the swing, take a hit off the hookah or just sit back and watch the belly dancers work their magic on the dance floor.

Sports, Health & Fitness

Sports, Health & Fitness

When the magazine *Men's Fitness* released its recent list of the 'heaviest cities in America,' Chicago landed with a thud at number two. After a brief period of celebration – Second City title regained! – Chicagoans began shaking their collective heads and asking some questions. How could a city where sports are such an integral part of everyone's lifestyle be one of the most obese cities in the western hemisphere?

The answer came quickly. While Chicagoans love baseball, football, basketball and soccer, they tend to demonstrate that love by sitting in a comfortable chair or stadium seat, eating hot dogs, drinking beer and cheering as their favorite team gets a workout on the field. This, along with the sedentary nature of most office-bound jobs and a meat- and beer-filled diet had caused a crisis of fat in the Midwestern metropolis.

Enter Mayor Daley and the Chicago Park District. Under the auspices of the Chicago Works Out program (www.chicagoworksout.com), the city has begun sponsoring all manner of walking events, biking tours and fitness classes aimed at getting the city out of their La-Z-Boy recliners. Visitors to Chicago will reap the benefits of these programs through improved walking trails, better bike paths, top-notch public tennis courts, skating rinks and easy access to the city's newly beautified parks.

Private health clubs have also been springing up throughout the city to do their part. Most all of them are happy to have you spend a day running around their racquetball courts and scaling their climbing walls. Just ask about a day pass at the most convenient location to where you're staying.

Of course, you *do* owe it to yourself to plant your butt in a stadium seat and take in a game or two while you're here as well. You're on vacation after all – a couple hours of sedentary living won't hurt.

WATCHING SPORTS

For more detailed information on all of Chicago's sports teams, see the sports section (p18) of the City Life chapter. Nearly all sports teams save the Cubs use **Ticketmaster** (☎ 312-559-1212; www.ticketmaster.com) as their ticketing outlet.

Baseball

CHICAGO CUBS Map pp272–3

☎ 773-404-2827; www.cubs.com; Wrigley Field, 1060 W Addison St; Red Line to Addison

Chicago is one of only two US cities that boasts two Major League baseball teams. By far the local favorite, the Cubs play at Wrigley Field on the north side of the city (see the boxed text p185). Tickets are available at the Wrigley Field box office, through the team's website, or by calling 800-843-2827 (within Illinois) or 866-652-2827 (out-of-state).

Both Wrigley Field and US Cellular Field, home of the Chicago White Sox baseball team (see next), are easily reached by public transportation. The baseball season runs from early April to September.

CHICAGO WHITE SOX Map pp270–1

☎ 312-674-1000; www.chisox.com; US Cellular Field, 333 W 35th St; Red Line to Sox-35th

Less loved - but more successful - than the Cubs, the White Sox play at US Cellular Field (aka Comiskey Park) to the south in Bridgeport. Because the stadium is so enormous, White Sox tickets are much easier to come by. You can get them through the team's website, at the US Cellular Field box office, or at any Ticketmaster outlet.

Football

CHICAGO BEARS Map pp284–5

☎ 847-295-6600; www.chicagobears.com; Soldier Field, 425 E McFetridge Dr

The Bears can be found, sleet, snow, or dark of night, at Soldier Field. Since the inauguration of the new stadium, tickets have been hard to come by, and are available only through Ticketmaster.

Soldier Field is a little trickier to get to on public transportation. Metra trains from Randolph St Station stop at nearby 12th St Station, and the Roosevelt Road El stops are a half-mile stroll away. The greatest joy for Bears

A Day At Wrigley Field

by Brad Zibung

Getting into a game oftentimes proves tougher than getting to the game. Tickets for most every weekend and night game sell out far in advance. Ticket vendors around Wrigley abound, but often charge much more than face value. Deciding to go this route is fine, just stick with legitimate vendors who have storefronts rather than sometimes-shady scalpers wandering the area.

If a ticket to the game can't be had, fear not. Much of what makes Wrigley great doesn't require admittance to the park. The Wrigleyville neighborhood is almost always hopping on game days. During batting practice and actual games alike, crowds gather outside Wrigley's outfield walls hoping to snag a frequent monstrous home-run ball. Best places for this are Waveland and Kenmore in left field and approximately 3640 N Sheffield in right field.

If fighting strangers for home-run balls isn't appealing, nearby bars and restaurants overflow with fans on game days. The establishments come and go, but old standbys like **Sports Corner** (956 W. Addison), **Murphy's Bleachers** (3655 W Sheffield), **Cubby Bear** (1059 W Addison), **Bernie's** (3664 N Clark) and **Yak-Zies** (p165) usually offer the most lively crowds. For good, cheap food, be sure to visit **Salt & Pepper Diner** (3537 Clark St).

Before calling it a day, be sure to get a photo snapped by the Harry Caray statue at Sheffield and Addison and the iconic Wrigley Field marquee at Clark and Addison. They'll provide souvenirs for a lifetime. *Brad Zibung is a Cubs fan and editor of the gut-bustingly funny Cubs-centered newspaper the Heckler.*

---

fans of late has been their elaborate tailgate feasts in the parking lots before the games.

The football season runs from August to December, when you can get snowed on while you watch.

Basketball

CHICAGO BULLS Map pp286–7

☎ 312-559-1212; www.nba.com/bulls;
United Center, 1901 W Madison St

Scottie Pippen returning to the Bulls for the 2003–'04 season brought a jolt of energy and excitement to this underachieving team, which holds court at the United Center on the city's West Side. Tickets are available through the United Center box office – located at Gate 4 on the building's east side – and at Ticketmaster outlets.

If you're going to take public transportation to the Bulls game, hop on the Brown, Green or Orange Line to Madison, and take bus 19 or 20 west to the stadium from there.

The basketball season runs from November to April.

Hockey

CHICAGO BLACKHAWKS Map pp286–7

☎ 312-455-7000; www.chiblackhawks.com;
United Center, 1901 W Madison St

The Blackhawks are a strong team who make their home at the United Center.

Hawks tickets are often sold out, but brokers and concierges can usually obtain them for a minimal markup. Transportation and parking information is the same as for the Bulls (above). The hockey season runs October to April.

Soccer

CHICAGO FIRE Map pp284–5

☎ 312-705-7200; www.chicago-fire.com

Soccer is slowly catching on in Chicago, particularly among the European and Latino sports fans in the city.

Tickets are available through Ticketmaster, and are fairly easy to come by. The regular season runs from April to September, with the finals taking place in October.

PLAYING SPORTS
Running & Walking

The lakefront path mentioned under Cycling (p186) also has a runner's side for those looking to get a little bipedal workout. Runners hit the trail around 5am. If you're looking for a good starting point, try the Oak St Beach on the Gold Coast and head north. The path from the beach northward is largely cinder rather than asphalt, which your feet will appreciate.

If you find yourself getting distracted by the great city and park views, you can regain focus on the cinder oval track at Lake Shore Park, at the intersection of Chicago Ave and Lake Shore Dr.

Any questions about running should be directed to the **Chicago Area Runners Association** (☎ 312-666-9836; www.cararuns.org), who offer free downloadable running maps on their website.

For those looking to move at a more leisurely pace, walking through the city's parks is a great way to get exercise. Again, the **Chicago Park District** (www.chicagoparkdistrict.com) has come through in a big way, offering extensive path lists, maps and ratings of their hundreds of city-maintained walking trails on their website. The site even offers a flower and plant finder to help you identify any flora you discovered en route.

Cycling

Curbs are the highest mountains you'll find in Chicago, making the town ideal for biking. The popular, 18½-mile lakefront path from Hollywood Ave in the north to 71st St in the south is an excellent way to see the city from top to bottom, and in hot weather the lake offers cooling breezes.

Lincoln Park is another good spot for biking, with paths snaking around the small lakes and the zoo. Chicago streets themselves, while flat, are not terribly accommodating. Bike lanes don't exist, except in a couple of places, where they have become de facto double-parking zones, and many streets are just wide enough for speeding traffic and parked cars.

The city runs its own biking website (www .cityofchicago.org/transportation/bikes) that has a free downloadable biking map, along with suggestions on routes in the city. Chicago also has a couple of cyclist advocacy groups, which are working to help turn car-centric Chicago into a more bike-friendly place. The **Chicagoland Bicycle Federation** (www.biketraffic.org) is a good place to get an overview of biking issues in Chicago. Their website is a convenient place to order a copy of their useful paper map of Chicagoland bike routes.

A little more chaotic, **Chicago Critical Mass** (www.chicagocriticalmass.org) organizes bike rides through the streets of Chicago the first Friday of the month. The rides, which are intended to celebrate bike use and disrupt the car-dependent status quo, begin at Daley Plaza (cnr Dearborn and Washington Sts) at 5:30pm. The mood among the cyclists is lighthearted and the routes unfold spontaneously.

A few places offer bike rentals.

BIKE CHICAGO Map pp280–1
☎ 312-595-9600; www.bikechicago.com; Navy Pier, 600 E Grand Ave; ☉ 9am-7pm Apr-Oct
Trek mountain bikes, big cruisers with fat tires, bicycles built for two and kids' bikes are available here. The company's main office is at Navy Pier, and when the weather's nice it also operates out of trailers at **North Ave Beach** (☎ 773-327-2706).

Bikes run about $34 per day, and can also be had hourly (about $8). Free guided bike tours are available three times a day for renters, and the company also rents in-line skates.

ON THE ROUTE Map pp272–3
☎ 773-477-5066; www.ontheroute.com; 3146 N Lincoln; ☉ 11am-8pm Mon-Thu, 11am-7pm Fri, 10am-6pm Sat, 11am-5pm Sun
Rents hybrids for around-town riding, or mountain bikes for more serious cycling action. You have to rent by the day, weekend, or week. Rates start at $35. Helmets and locks are $5 extra.

Golf

Chicago golfers stretch the season as far as possible in both directions. The Chicago Park District has six public golf courses and three driving ranges, all overseen by Kemper Sports Management. You can find out more about the courses and find the next available tee times online (www.cpdgolf.com) or by phone on their 24-hour tee time reservation line at ☎ 312-245-0909.

Public courses include those listed.

DIVERSEY DRIVING RANGE Map pp272–3
☎ 312-742-7929; Diversey Pkwy, Lincoln Park ; ☉ 7am-10pm; bus 76
If you just want to knock a bucket of balls around, this driving range in Lincoln Park will let you whack away to your heart's content. Rental clubs are available, and a bucket is about $7. A reconstruction of the building has won kudos for its creative design.

FAMILY GOLF CENTER Map pp282–3
☎ 312-616-1234; 221 N Columbus Dr; Metra to Randolph St Station
In an inspired move, acres of vacant land have been turned into a golf course just east of the Loop. The center features a driving range, nine short holes with a complex green, chipping greens, and a bar and restaurant. You can make reservations to get a round in ($15) before or after a big meeting.

JACKSON PARK GOLF COURSE
Map pp270–1
☎ 312-747-2763; E 63rd St at S Stoney Island Ave
The district's only 18-hole course is considered moderately challenging. Fees range from $10 to $23. Reservations are recommended.

SYDNEY R MAROVITZ COURSE

Map pp272–3

☎ 773-742-7930; Irving Park Rd in Lincoln Park

The nine-hole course enjoys sweeping views of the lake and skyline. The course is very popular, and in order to secure a tee time, golfers cheerfully arrive at 5:30am. You can avoid that sort of lunacy by spending a few dollars extra to get a reservation. Fees vary widely through the year, from $7 to $17, with extra charges for nonresidents and reservations. You can also rent clubs here.

Tennis

Some of Chicago's public tennis courts require reservations and charge fees, while others are free and players queue for their turns on the court. Place your racket by the net and you're next in line. The season runs from mid-April to mid-October.

At Grant Park's **Daley Bicentennial Plaza** (Map pp282–3; ☎ 312-742-7650; south side of the 300 block of Randolph St), you can pay a fee to use 12 lighted courts. **Waveland Tennis Courts** (Map pp272–3; ☎ 312-868-4132; east side of N Lake Shore Dr where Waveland Ave meets Lincoln Park) charges fees for its 20 lighted courts. **Lake Shore Park** (Map pp278–9; ☎ 312-742-7891; 808 N Lake Shore Dr), near the lake, features two very popular (and free) lighted courts. In **Grant Park** (Map pp272–3; 900 S Columbus Dr near E Balbo Dr) you'll find several courts. No reservations are taken, but fees are charged at peak times.

Ice-skating & In-line Skating

The ice-skating season is depressingly long for sunbathers and even skaters. The Chicago Park District operates a first-class winter rink at **Daley Bicentennial Plaza** (☎ 312-742-7650; on the south side of the 300 block of E Randolph St) and at the **McCormick-Tribune Ice Rink** (55 N Michigan Ave) in Millennium Park. Both offer skate rental and free admission.

In summer months, you can strap on a pair of in-line skates and explore the city in fine wheeled fashion. Sources of rental skates include **Windward Sports** (p201) and **Bike Chicago** (☎ 312-944-2337; Navy Pier, 600 E Grand Ave). Be prepared to pay a large deposit and rates of about $20 a day.

Swimming & Watersports

Between Lake Michigan and Chicago's public pools, there are limitless ways to make a splash in the city.

Lakefront beaches (see the boxed text p84) have lifeguards from late in May through early September. However, you can swim at your own risk whenever you want, depending on what you think of the temperature. The water in August is usually in the 70°s F (21 to 26°C).

Chicago's Lucky Strikes

Bowling is a distinctly Midwestern activity. People of all shapes, sizes and ages gather in boisterous groups to send balls crashing into pins. Talent is not a prerequisite, but the willingness to consume copious pitchers of cheap beer is. The lanes draw the most crowds during the cold months, when bowling is a great indoor sport (although the preponderance of beer bellies should tell you everything you need to know about how athletic this so-called sport is).

To try your luck on the lanes, visit one of the following.

- **Diversey-River Bowl** (Map pp270–1; ☎ 773-227-5800; 2211 W Diversey Pkwy)
- **Marigold Arcade** (Map pp272–3; ☎ 773-935-8183; 828 W Grace St)
- **Waveland Bowl** (Map pp270–1; ☎ 773-472-5900; 3700 N Western Ave).

For bowling with charm, try Wrigleyville's **Southport Lanes** (p164). This 80-year-old bar has four lanes with hand-set pins in the basement.

HOLSTEIN PARK Map p275

☎ 312-742-7554; 2200 N Oakley Ave; admission free;
☀ daylight hours

Try this large and refreshing pool in the heart of Bucktown. You can rent a suit and leave your sweaty duds in a locker. Best of all, the pool has frequent adult-only hours, when squealing kids are sent packing.

CHICAGOLAND CANOE BASE

Map pp270–1

☎ 773-777-1489; 4019 N Narragansett Ave

Canoeists and kayakers can retrace the route of French trapper Louis Jolliet by paddling up the Chicago river in a boat from Chicagoland Canoe Base. The outfitter will rent you a canoe for about $40 plus deposit, (kayaks are $10 more) and owner Vic Hurtowy will give you tips on where to paddle. Note: the company isn't located on a body of water, so having a car is key to picking up and returning the boats.

HEALTH & FITNESS
Health Clubs, Yoga & Pilates

Hotels almost always have either their own facilities or agreements with nearby clubs. Otherwise, here are some other options.

BIKRAM YOGA Map p275

☎ 773-315-9150; 1344 N Milwaukee Ave;
Blue Line to Damen

If you're looking for a yoga-only experience, try this place in Wicker Park, where classes run seven days a week and cost $15 per session.

GORILLA SPORTS Map pp280–1

☎ 312-828-9777; 38 E Grand Ave; Red Line to Grand

Located in Near North, Gorilla offers more extreme workout opportunities, with martial arts classes and a heated yoga room.

HALSTED STREET MULTIPLEX

Map pp272–3

☎ 773-755-3232; www.multiplexclubs.com; 3228 N Halsted St; Brown, Purple, Red Line to Belmont

A more recent addition to the Chicago gym scene, Multiplex welcomes guests to its half-dozen Chicago locations. Along with the usual workout machines, swimming pools, and basketball courts, the clubs also offer yoga and pilates classes. Other branches include the Gold Coast Multiplex (Map pp278–9; ☎ 312-944-1030; 1030 N Clark St) in the, you guessed it, Gold Coast. The chain's Fitplex (Map pp278–9;

☎ 312-640-1235; 1235 N. La Salle) also offers a rock-climbing wall. Day-use fees are about $20, and you'll need to bring proof that you don't live in Chicago.

LAKESHORE ATHLETIC CLUB

Map pp280–1

☎ 312-644-4880; 441 N Wabash Ave

Offers pools, full equipment, jogging tracks and more, with another convenient location in Lincoln Park (Map pp276–9; ☎ 773-477-9888; 1320 W Fullerton Ave). Day-use rates average $20 and don't include tennis.

Massage & Day Spas

Tennis, golf, canoeing… Being on vacation can become dreadfully exhausting. After all your activity head to one of Chicago's day spas to unwind.

FOUR SEASONS SPA Map pp278–9

☎ 312-280-8800; Four Seasons Hotel, 120 East Delaware Pl; Red Line to Chicago

If you really want to do it in style, head to the Four Seasons Spa, where pleasures such as the elixir paraffin wrap and the green tea and ginger mud body mask will 'revitalize your energy meridians.' They also feel pretty great. You can do quick 30-minute sessions or have a luxurious all-day affair. Prices start sky high and go up from there.

SPA SPACE Map pp282–3

☎ 312-466-9585; www.spaspace.com; 161 N Canal St; Green Line to Clinton

Men and women face a dizzying array of massages and body treatments in this sleek, relaxing space. Along with the usual seaweed body wraps, Swedish massages, sports massages, and other familiar rubbings, you can get an aromatherapy workout or a 'Heaven and Earth Stone Therapy' massage, where heated river stones are used to melt away tension. Treatments run about $100.

URBAN OASIS Map pp278–9

☎ 312-587-3500; www.urban-oasis.com; 3rd fl, 12 W Maple St; Red Line to Clark/Division

Exactly what the name implies. This calm, friendly place focuses exclusively on massage therapy, offering Shiatsu, Reiki and deep tissue massages along with a host of other options. Guests are treated to fresh fruit juices and an array of specialized showers before their massages. Try the invigorating salt glow massage. Hour sessions cost around $85.

Shopping

Shopping

From the grand department stores of the Loop to the freak boutiques of Lake View and Wicker Park, Chicago is a city that lives to shop. Every bizarre hobby, niche passion, and underground fashion trend has a retailer or three somewhere in the city, and Chicagoans have elevated shopping to a pastime almost as revered as baseball or New Yorker-baiting.

Though you'll find Gaps and Banana Republics throughout the city, Chicago has also managed to maintain a thriving culture of independent and family-run stores. The friendly atmosphere of a small-town pervades the shopping scene here, even among the stores along the Magnificent Mile, where low-key kindness prevails despite high-end prices.

If you're in the market for antiques, you're especially in luck. Chicago is a magnet for the best antiques and collectibles between the two coasts. Serious shoppers can easily make a week of it. Casual collectors or browsers will enjoy the many antique malls that bring scores of dealers together under one roof. You will find clusters of them in the blocks around the Merchandise Mart and Kinzie St in River North, along the stretch of Lincoln Ave north from Diversey Pkwy to Irving Park Rd and along Belmont Ave west from Ashland Ave to Western Ave. Cruising that last strip is like driving along a country road laced with antique stores without ever leaving the city.

If you're looking for souvenirs of a more recent vintage, grab a bag of Tootsie Rolls. They're cheap, they're made in Chicago and you can get them everywhere. Feeling more generous? Try the one-pound 'Chicago Assortment' of locally made Fanny May chocolates, which feature paintings of the city on the boxes and run about $17. Fanny May's sweet-smelling white outlets blanket the city.

THE LOOP & GRANT PARK

Shopping in the Loop was a legendary experience through the 1970s. Then the rise of suburban shopping malls and the proliferation of stores on N Michigan Ave brought devastation – four of six Loop department stores closed, and scores of smaller stores left. Recently the area has undergone a rebirth, and although it hasn't yet come close to its former glory, numerous national retailers have moved in to serve the huge population of office workers who need to squeeze shopping into their lunch hours.

5 S WABASH AVE Map pp282–3 *Jewelry*
5 S Wabash Ave; Brown, Green, Orange Line to Madison
This old building is the center of Chicago's family jeweler trade. Hundreds of shops in this building sell every kind of watch, ring, ornament and gemstone imaginable. Most are quick to say, 'I can get it for you wholesale!'

AFROCENTRIC BOOKSTORE
Map pp282–3 *Bookstore*
☎ 312-939-1956; DePaul Center, 333 S State St;
☺ 9:30am-6:30pm Mon-Fri, 10am-pm Sat; Brown, Orange Line to Library
'Seeing the world through an Afrikan point of view' is the slogan at this store, where many big-name Black authors give regular readings.

BRENT BOOKS & CARDS
Map pp282–3 *Bookstore*
☎ 312-363-0126; 309 W Washington St;
☺ 8am-7pm Mon-Fri, 10am-4pm Sat; Brown, Orange Line to Washington
This busy, independent bookshop has solid business, art and travel sections.

Chicago's Top Five Shopping Streets
- **The Magnificent Mile** (Near North) Big city shopping at its best.
- **Damen Ave** (Bucktown) The mid-to-high-end boutiques here will have female shopaholics salivating.
- **Milwaukee Ave** (Wicker Park) The funkier cousin to Damen Ave features blocks and blocks of hip stores.
- **Clark St** (Lake View) Everything from human-sized dog collars to humanities tomes on this eclectic street.
- **Oak St** (Gold Coast) The bastion of New York–style chic in one convenient location.

CARSON PIRIE SCOTT & CO

Map pp282–3   *Department Store*
☎ 312-641-7000; 1 S State St; ☼ 9:45am-7pm
Mon-Fri, 9:45am-6pm Sat, noon-5pm Sun; Brown,
Green, Orange Line to Madison

This store has lived in the shadow of Marshall Field's since it opened in 1899. Architecturally, it's a gem. And shopping-wise it's pretty good, too, with moderately priced goods and a varied selection spread over six floors. Carson's has attracted a very loyal following of lunchtime shoppers.

CENTRAL CAMERA Map pp282–3   *Electronics*
☎ 312-427-5580; 232 S Wabash Ave; ☼ 8:30am-
5:30pm Mon-Fri, 8:30am-5pm Sat; Red Line to Jackson

If you're traveling with a shutterbug, be sure to avoid this place until the very end of your trip, lest you risk seeing the sights all by yourself. Once photo-holics step inside this long, narrow store, it will be days before they surface again.

CHICAGO ARCHITECTURE FOUNDATION SHOP

Map pp282–3   *Chicago Souvenirs*
☎ 312-922-3432; Santa Fe Center, 224 S Michigan
Ave; ☼ 9:30am-6:30pm Mon-Sat, 9:30am-6pm Sun;
Brown, Green, Orange Line to Adams

Books, posters, postcards and more celebrate local architecture at this heaven for anyone with an edifice complex. The Frank Lloyd Wright section alone contains enough material to research a doctoral thesis. You'll find another, smaller CAF store in the **John Hancock Center** (Map pp278–9; 875 N Michigan Ave).

ILLINOIS ARTISANS SHOP

Map pp282–3   *Arts & Crafts*
☎ 312-814-5321; 2nd level, James R Thompson
Center, Randolph & Clark Sts; ☼ 9am-5pm Mon-Fri;
Brown, Orange Line to Washington

The best works of artisans throughout the state are sold here, including ceramics, glass, wood, fiber, toys and more, at prices that verge on the cheap. The enthusiastic staff will tell you all about the people who created the pieces. The Illinois Art Gallery, immediately next door, sells paintings and sculptures under the same arrangement.

IWAN RIES Map pp282–3   *Tobacconist*
☎ 312-372-1306; 19 S Wabash Ave; ☼ 9am-5:30pm
Mon-Fri, 9am-5pm Sat; Brown, Green, Orange Line to
Madison

You're witnessing five generations of tobacco know-how at work in this store, which cel-

ebrates its 150th birthday in 2007. The setting is jovial and the selection of pipes, pipe tobacco and cigars (100 kinds at last count) can't be beat.

MARSHALL FIELD & CO

Map pp282–3   *Department Store*
☎ 312-781-1000; 111 N State St; ☼ 9:45am-7pm
Mon-Wed, Fri, 9:45am-8pm Thu, 9:45am-6pm Sat,
11am-6pm Sun; Brown, Green, Orange Line to
Randolph

The grandest old department store in the country, Field's offers 10 floors of designer clothes, furnishings, gifts, housewares, fine china and crystal and more. Dining under the soaring Christmas tree in the 7th-floor Walnut Room is a local family tradition. The basement gourmet food court is a good place for quick snacks. The bottom level also features a wealth of smaller-merchandise areas selling household items, gourmet food, stationery and more. You can buy the popular minty chocolate Frango mints throughout the store.

Clothing Sizes

Measurements approximate only, try before you buy

Women's Clothing

Aust/UK	8	10	12	14	16	18
Europe	36	38	40	42	44	46
Japan	5	7	9	11	13	15
USA	6	8	10	12	14	16

Women's Shoes

Aust/USA	5	6	7	8	9	10
Europe	35	36	37	38	39	40
France only	35	36	38	39	40	42
Japan	22	23	24	25	26	27
UK	3½	4½	5½	6½	7½	8½

Men's Clothing

Aust	92	96	100	104	108	112
Europe	46	48	50	52	54	56
Japan	S		M	M		L
UK/USA	35	36	37	38	39	40

Men's Shirts (Collar Sizes)

Aust/Japan	38	39	40	41	42	43
Europe	38	39	40	41	42	43
UK/USA	15	15½	16	16½	17	17½

Men's Shoes

Aust/ UK	7	8	9	10	11	12
Europe	41	42	43	44½	46	47
Japan	26	27	27½	28	29	30
USA	7½	8½	9½	10½	11½	12½

POSTER PLUS Map pp282–3 *Fine Arts*
☎ 312-461-9277; 200 S Michigan Ave;
🕑 10am-6pm Mon-Sat, 11am-6pm Sun;
Brown, Green, Orange Line to Adams

Located across from the Art Institute, this superlative poster store carries reproductions of many of the museum's best-known works, along with a number of fun, Chicago-specific historical prints dating from the late 19th century. Upstairs in the vintage room, European and American poster originals can go for as much as $30,000.

PRAIRIE AVENUE BOOKSHOP
Map pp282–3 *Bookstore*
☎ 312-922-8311; 418 S Wabash Ave;
🕑 9:30am-5:30pm Mon-Fri, 10am-4pm Sat;
Brown, Orange Line to Library

This is easily the classiest and most lavishly decorated bookstore in the city. The beautiful architectural tomes – including many hard-to-find titles – rest on hardwood shelves, and the thick carpet muffles the noise of customers. Soon you'll want to find a smoking jacket, take up pipe smoking and curl up in a corner leather chair.

ROCK RECORDS
Map pp282–3 *CDs & Records*
☎ 312-346-3489; 175 W Washington St;
🕑 9am-6:30pm Mon-Fri, 10am-6pm Sat;
Brown, Orange Line to Washington

Don't let the surly staff scare you away from this well-stocked independent record store, which has a good number of listening stations and a wide selection of pop, indie rock, hip-hop and country.

SAVVY TRAVELLER
Map pp282–3 *Bookstore*
☎ 312-913-9800; 310 S Michigan Ave;
🕑 10am-6pm Mon-Fri, 10am-7pm Sat;
Brown, Orange Line to Library

The goal here is to carry every travel-related title in print, which means that you'll find plenty of obscure tomes tucked in among the comprehensive selection of Lonely Planet guides. If you can't locate something among the big selection, ask the staffers – who are all travel enthusiasts between vacations – and they'll order it for you. You can also buy gadgets such as electricity converters, luggage and atlases.

SEARS Map pp282–3 *Department Store*
☎ 312-373-6040; 2 N State St; 🕑 10am-8pm Mon-Sat, 11am-6pm Sun; Red Line to Washington

The return of this large department store to State Street was a jubilant moment for the Loop. Offering lower prices and more salt-of-the-earth fashions than its upscale neighbors, Sears is also a great place to pick up a replacement for that power sander you accidentally left at home.

SYMPHONY STORE
Map pp282–3 *CDs & Records*
☎ 312-294-3345; 220 S Michigan Ave; 🕑 10am-5pm Mon-Sat, noon-6pm Sun; Brown, Green, Orange Line to Adams

In this store in Symphony Center the Chicago Symphony Orchestra sells all manner of fun, whimsical classical musical souvenirs (keep an eye out for the Beethoven finger puppets). The shop even carries T-shirts – highly tasteful ones, of course.

Chicago fashion

NEAR NORTH & NAVY PIER

The Greater North Michigan Avenue Association likes to claim that the 'Magnificent Mile,' or 'Mag Mile' as it's widely known, is one of the top five shopping streets in the world. It's hard to argue with that. Even the formerly retail-poor south end of N Michigan Ave, near the river, now boasts a number of shopping options, thanks to the opening of the huge 'Shops at North Bridge' complex.

ABRAHAM LINCOLN BOOK SHOP

Map pp280–1   *Bookstore*
☎ 312-944-3085; 357 W Chicago Ave;
🕙 9am-5pm Mon-Sat; Brown Line to Chicago
In the 'Land of Lincoln' this delightful store is a natural. It carries new, used and antiquarian books about the 16th president, the Civil War and the presidency in general. The knowledgeable staff regularly hold open round-table discussions with Civil War scholars.

ANTIQUARIANS BUILDING

Map pp280–1   *Antiques*
☎ 312-527-0533; 159 W Kinzie St; 🕙 Mon-Sat
10am-6pm; Brown Line to Merchandise Mart
Look for rare items from five continents in 22 shops. The selection of Asian-focused works is especially strong.

ANTIQUES CENTRE AT KINZIE

SQUARE Map pp280–1   *Antiques*
☎ 312-464-1946; 220 W Kinzie St; 🕙 10am-5pm
Mon-Fri, noon-4pm Sat; Brown Line to Merchandise Mart
Twenty dealers peddle high-end pieces from the 18th and 19th centuries here.

BURBERRY

Map pp280–1   *Women's & Men's Clothing*
☎ 312-787-2500; 633 N Michigan Ave; 🕙 9:30am-
7pm Mon-Wed, Fri, Sat, 9:30am-7pm Thu, noon-5pm
Sun; Red Line to Chicago
The Chicago outpost of the British company, known for appealing to both upper-crust Brits and American hip-hop stars.

CARTIER Map pp280–1   *Jewelry*
☎ 312-266-7440; 630 N Michigan Ave;
🕙 10am-5:30pm Mon-Sat; Red Line to Chicago
The celebrated French watchmaker has spent the last 150 years perfecting its simple, beautiful lines. It has also branched out into jewelry, bags and sleek sunglasses.

CHICAGO PLACE MALL

Map pp280–1   *Shopping Mall*
☎ 312-642-4811; 700 N Michigan Ave;
Red Line to Chicago
This eight-story mall is occupied mostly by home furnishings store Room & Board, Saks Fifth Avenue and various outposts of Talbots. Smaller stores filling the gaps between these larger retailers feel a little thrown-together, though **Love From Chicago** (☎ 312-787-0838) is one of the best places to get souvenirs. Chicago Place also boasts one of the most dramatic food courts in the city – the plant- and fountain-filled area has wonderful views.

CHICAGO TRIBUNE STORE

Map pp280–1   *Chicago Souvenirs*
☎ 312-222-3080; Tribune Tower, 435 N Michigan Ave;
🕙 8am-6pm Mon-Fri, 10am-6pm Sat; Red Line to Grand
While this small store doesn't have the selection of other Chicago souvenir places, it does outdo its competitors in the *Tribune*-related merchandise. Cubs jerseys and books by noted Chicago authors also available.

COMPUSA Map pp280–1   *Electronics*
☎ 312-787-6776; 101 E Chicago Ave;
🕙 9am-8pm Mon-Fri, 9am-7pm Sat, 11am-5pm Sun;
Red Line to Chicago
A convenient superstore for those looking to pick up laptop supplies, CompUSA offers unbeatable prices on things like wireless cards and hand-held computing devices. Come with a clear idea of what you want – the teenage 'help' here rarely know more than the customers.

GARRETT POPCORN

Map pp280–1   *Food & Drink*
☎ 312-944-2630; 670 N Michigan Ave;
🕙 10am-10pm; Red Line to Grand
Like lemmings drawn to a cliff, people form long lines outside this kernel-sized store on the Mag Mile. Granted, the caramel corn is heavenly and the cheese popcorn decadent, but is it worth waiting in the rain for a chance to buy some? Actually, yes. But rather than suffering the lines here, try the store in the **Loop** (Map pp282–3; ☎ 312-630-0127; 26 E Randolph St) across from Field's. It's usually line-free.

HAMMACHER SCHLEMMER

Map pp280–1   *Gadgets*
☎ 312-527-9100; 435 N Michigan Ave; 🕙 10am-6pm
Mon-Sat, noon-5pm Sun; Red Line to Grand
Gadget freaks and closet inventors will go nuts at this retail outpost of the catalog company.

JAY ROBERT'S ANTIQUE
WAREHOUSE Map pp280–1 *Antiques*
☎ 312-222-0167; 149 W Kinzie St; ☺ 10am-5pm
Mon-Sat; Brown Line to Merchandise Mart
This vast place boasts more than 60,000 square
feet of antique furniture, clocks and fireplace
mantels.

JAZZ RECORD MART
Map pp280–1 *CDs & Records*
☎ 312-222-1467; 444 N Wabash Ave; ☺ 10am-8pm
Mon-Sat, noon-5pm Sun; Red Line to Grand
Musicians, serious jazz and blues aficionados,
and vintage album collectors flock here. Bob
Koester and his dedicated staff can find just
about anything, no matter how obscure. This
is the place to go to complete your Bix Beiderbecke collection.

MERCHANDISE MART
Map pp280–1 *Shopping Mall*
☎ 312-527-4141; 222 Merchandise Mart Plaza;
☺ 9am-6pm Mon-Fri, 10am-5pm Sat; Brown Line
to Merchandise Mart
Beautifully restored in the early 1990s, the Mart
contains a modest collection of chain stores on
its lower floors. But the real allure lies on the
many floors devoted to distributor showrooms
for home furnishings and other interior fittings.
As you prowl the halls, you can find next year's
hot trends on display today. Technically, only
retailers and buyers can shop on these floors,
but the displays are simply an elevator ride
away for anyone. Don't try to buy anything,
though, because you're not allowed. (But
think of the savings!) Tours (☎ 312-644-4664)
are available. Wrap up your visit here with a
visit to Chicago's version of Easter Island – the
vaguely creepy Merchandise Mart Hall of Fame.
Located on the south side of the building, the
row of oversized sculpted heads is a who's who
of Chicago magnates from eras past.

NIKETOWN Map pp280–1 *Shoes*
☎ 312-642-6363; 669 N Michigan Ave; ☺ 10am-8pm
Mon-Fri, 9:30am-6pm Sat, 10am-6pm Sun; Red Line
to Grand
This Nike temple has all the flash and sparkle
you'd expect from the shoe giant.

NORDSTROM
Map pp280–1 *Department Store*
☎ 312-464-1515; 55 E Grand Ave; ☺ 10am-8pm
Mon-Sat, 11am-6pm Sun; Red Line to Grand
This is one of the biggest branches of the Se-
attle-based department store, which is known

for its lavish customer service. The Chicago
store plans an active schedule of events featuring appearances by designers.

PAPER SOURCE Map pp280–1 *Art Supplies*
☎ 312-337-0798; 232 W Chicago Ave; ☺ 10am-7pm
Mon-Fri, 10am-5pm Sat, noon-5pm Sun;
Brown Line to Chicago
Every kind of paper produced is here, with the
lightweight merchandise ranging from delicate
Japanese handmade creations to iridescent,
neon-hued numbers. Great souvenir shopping
for friends back home with eclectic tastes.

PEARL Map pp280–1 *Art Supplies*
☎ 312-915-0200; 225 W Chicago Ave; ☺ 9am-7pm
Mon-Sat, noon-5pm Sun; Brown Line to Chicago
This huge art-supply store sells discounted art
supplies you can use on the paper you bought
from Paper Source.

RAND MCNALLY
Map pp280–1 *Maps & Guidebooks*
☎ 312-321-1751; 444 N Michigan Ave; ☺ 9am-6pm
Mon-Fri, 10am-6pm Sat, noon-5pm Sun;
Red Line to Grand
Rand McNally, the locally based map publisher, operates this small travel book and
map store. The friendly staff will help you find
what you want on the densely packed shelves.
In addition to books, you can pick up other
travel necessities, like that electrical converter
you forgot.

SHOPS AT NORTH BRIDGE
Map pp280–1 *Shopping Mall*
☎ 312-327-2300; 520 N Michigan Ave; hours vary by
store; Red Line to Grand
The newest of the classy Michigan Ave
malls, the Shops at North Bridge appeals to a
less aggressively froufrou demographic with
stores like Swatch, the Body Shop, Ann Taylor
Loft and the LEGO Store. The multilevel mall
connects anchor Nordstrom to Michigan Ave
via a gracefully curving, shop-lined atrium.

SPORTMART Map pp280–1 *Sporting Goods*
☎ 312-337-6151; 620 N LaSalle St; ☺ 9:30am-9pm
Mon-Sat, 10am-6pm Sun; Red Line to Grand
In a classic rags-to-riches story, Morrie Mages
got his start in his family's store in the old
Maxwell St Jewish ghetto, where some of the
city's leading retailers launched their careers by
selling clothes between WWI and WWII. Mages
built the place into the world's largest sporting

goods store, eventually moving it from Maxwell St into its own renovated eight-story warehouse here. A couple of years ago the Chicago-based national chain Sportmart bought Morrie out for a fortune. Now renamed, the store continues his discounting philosophy, albeit without his inveterate promoter's spirit. Check out Mages' *Chicago Sports Hall of Fame*, on the Ontario St exterior wall.

TIFFANY & CO Map pp280–1 *Jewelry*
☎ 312-944-7500; 730 N Michigan Ave; 10am-6pm Mon-Wed, Fri, Sat, 10am-7pm Thu; Red Line to Chicago
For those of us who can't afford one of their $25,000 rings just now, the legendary jeweler also offers a wide range of china, pens and perfumes.

GOLD COAST
Designer boutiques pop up like mushrooms on the tiny blocks just west of Michigan Ave, particularly in the single block of Oak St between Michigan Ave and Rush St. Lots of little boutiques line Oak St, and the names read like the advertisers' index in *Vogue*.

900 N MICHIGAN
Map pp278–9 *Shopping Mall*
☎ 312-915-3916; 900 N Michigan Ave; hours vary by shop; Red Line to Chicago
This huge mall got off to a rocky start in 1989. But it has found its niche as a home to an upscale collection of boutiques, thanks to the fact that the same people manage both this mall and Water Tower Place, and they simply moved all the expensive stores over here. 900 N Michigan is home to Diesel, Gucci, and J Crew, among many others.

ALTERNATIVES Map pp278–9 *Shoes*
☎ 312-266-1545; 942 N Rush St; 11am-7pm Mon-Fri, 10am-7pm Sat, noon-5pm Sun; Red Line to Clark/Division
The kinds of shoes that delight the eye and appall the feet are the speciality here. Alternatives features one of the most cutting-edge collections of shoes in town, at prices that gladden the hearts of budding Imelda Marcoses everywhere.

ANTHROPOLOGIE
Map pp278–9 *Women's Clothing*
☎ 312-255-1848; 1120 N State St; 10am-8pm Mon-Sat, 11am-6pm Sun; Red Line to Clark/Division
Thirtysomething women flock to this classy, unstuffy store that specializes in simple designs in dresses, suits and shoes.

BALLY
Map pp278–9 *Men's & Women's Accessories*
☎ 312-787-1057; 919 N Michigan Ave; 10am-8pm Mon & Thu, 10am-7pm Tue, Wed & Fri, 10am-6pm Sat, noon-6pm Sun; Red Line to Chicago
From boots to handbags to belts – if it's leather and beautiful, it likely has this Swiss company's logo somewhere on it.

BARNEY'S Map pp278–9 *Men's Clothing*
☎ 312-587-1700; 25 E Oak St; 10am-7pm Mon-Sat, noon-6pm Sun; Red Line to Clark/Division
An anchor at the west end of the street, this branch of the legendary New York men's store went up during an ill-conceived overexpansion in the 1990s (its debt went through the roof, and Barney's barely avoided liquidation). It has never made the splash the original made in New York, but it does carry a nice selection of its own designer wear and lots of trendy shoes.

BORDERS BOOKS & MUSIC
Map pp278–9 *Bookstore*
☎ 312-573-0564; 830 N Michigan Ave; 8am-11pm Mon-Sat, 9am-9pm Sun; Red Line to Chicago
This huge Borders, right across from the Water Tower, is always crowded. Thousands of books, spread over four floors in the bright and airy place, include lots of special-interest titles. You'll find a good selection of magazines and newspapers near the main entrance. Borders has also opened a much-needed branch in the **Loop** (Map pp282–3; ☎ 312-606-0750; 150 N State St) and a less attractive store in **Lake View** (Map pp272–3; ☎ 773-935-3909; 2817 N Clark St).

BULGARI Map pp278–9 *Jewelry*
☎ 312-255-1313; 909 N Michigan Ave;
🕑 10am-5:30pm Mon-Sat; Red Line to Chicago
This stately jeweler offers an expanded line of jewelry, watches, perfumes and accessories.

CAMPER Map pp278–9 *Shoes*
☎ 312-787-0158; 61 E Oak St; 🕑 10am-7pm Mon-Sat, noon-6pm Sun; Red Line to Clark/Division
Thanks to an inexplicable dearth of customers, the young employees at the only Midwestern outpost of the hip European shoemaker have plenty of time to talk to you about the fun designs they sell.

CHANEL
Map pp278–9 *Women's Clothing & Accessories*
☎ 312-787-5500; 935 N Michigan Ave; 🕑 10am-6pm Mon-Sat, noon-5pm Sun; Red Line to Chicago
Yep, you read the price tag right: $2500 for a sweater is par for the course at this sumptuous Chanel store.

CITY OF CHICAGO STORE
Map pp278–9 *Chicago Souvenirs*
☎ 312-742-8811; Chicago Visitor Information Center, 163 E Pearson St; 🕑 7:30am-7pm; Red Line to Chicago
This city-run store is a mecca for those wise enough not to try to steal their own 'official' souvenirs. Cheerful city workers will sell you anything from a decommissioned city parking meter ($200) to street signs for famous local streets ($50). The usual array of Chicago books, shot glasses etc is also available.

EUROPA BOOKS Map pp278–9 *Bookstore*
☎ 312-335-9677; 832 N State St; 🕑 8:30am-8pm Mon-Fri, 9am-8pm Sat & Sun; Red Line to Chicago
As the name promises, this store carries newspapers, magazines and books, primarily in European languages.

HERMES
Map pp278–9 *Men's & Women's Accessories*
☎ 312-787-8175; 110 E Oak St; 🕑 10am-6pm Mon-Sat; Red Line to Clark/Division
The Parisian retailer operates a Chicago fashion base here.

JIL SANDER Map pp278–9 *Women's Clothing*
☎ 312-335-0006; 48 E Oak St; 🕑 9:30am-6pm Mon-Sat; Red Line to Clark/Division
Jil Sander's minimalist colors and simple designs somehow manage to remain fashionable long after other trendsetters have disappeared from the scene.

KATE SPADE
Map pp278–9 *Women's Clothing & Accessories*
☎ 312-604-0808; 101 E Oak St; 🕑 10am-6pm Mon-Sat, noon-5pm Sun; Red Line to Clark/Division
Beloved by the women of Lincoln Park, Kate Spade specializes in clean-lined bags. This store also offers jewelry, shoes and sunglasses by a host of designers.

NORTH FACE Map pp278–9 *Outdoor Gear*
☎ 312-337-7200; John Hancock Center, 875 N Michigan Ave; 🕑 10am-7pm Mon-Sat, noon-6pm Sun; Red Line to Chicago
This well-known brand operates a large store that peddles the company's first-rate line of backpacks, sleeping bags and other outdoor gear at full retail prices. You can also buy maps, books and doodads.

PRADA
Map pp278–9 *Men's & Women's Clothing*
☎ 312-951-1113; 30 E Oak St; 🕑 10am-6pm Mon-Sat, noon-6pm Sun; Red Line to Clark/Division
This large store carries the designer's full line.

SUGAR MAGNOLIA
Map pp278–9 *Women's Clothing*
☎ 312-944-0885; 34 E Oak St; 🕑 10am-6pm Mon-Sat, noon-5pm Sun; Red Line to Clark/Division
One of the youngest-feeling of the Oak St boutiques, Sugar Magnolia specializes in women's clothes by European designers.

URBAN OUTFITTERS
Map pp278–9 *Clothing & Accessories*
☎ 312-640-1919; 935 N Rush St 🕑 10am-9pm Mon-Fri, 10am-9pm Sat, 11am-7pm Sun; Red Line to Chicago
Male and female twentysomethings looking for the perfect ironic/retro T-shirt or sloppily cool sweatshirt should make a beeline to this two-story UO outpost. Along with clothes, the store also carries a huge range of fun knickknacks and cheap, style-heavy home furnishings.

WATER TOWER PLACE
Map pp278–9 *Shopping Mall*
☎ 312-440-3166; 835 N Michigan Ave; Red Line to Chicago
Featuring the coolest fountain in all of Chicago mall-land (you'll see it on your ride up the main escalator), Water Tower Place brought the concept of vertical shopping malls to Chicago, driving a stake through the heart of State St

retail and forever changing the character of N Michigan Ave. The mall features 100 stores on seven levels, including Abercrombie & Fitch, Sharper Image, the Limited, Express and Marshall Field & Co.

LINCOLN PARK & OLD TOWN

Clark St, the main thoroughfare for shopping in Lincoln Park, contains shops of every description, but record-store hounds are especially well-served.

2ND HAND TUNES

Map pp276–7   *CDs & Records*
☎ 773-929-6325; 2602 N Clark St; ☽ 11am-8pm
Mon-Sat, noon-7pm Sun; Brown, Red Line to Diversey
This used store focuses on out-of-print, harder to find CDs, along with esoteric newer indie and punk titles.

ACT 1 Map pp276–7   *Bookstore*
☎ 773-348-6757; 2221 N Lincoln; ☽ 10am-8pm
Mon-Wed, 10am-6pm Thu-Sun; Brown,
Red Line to Fullerton
What would a great theater town be without a great theater bookstore? Act 1 takes its bow in this category with plays, anthologies, works by local authors and a large area devoted to production and the often-ignored business end of theater.

ACTIVE ENDEAVORS

Map pp276–7   *Outdoor Gear*
☎ 773-281-8100; 935 W Armitage Ave; ☽ 10am-8pm
Mon-Thu, 10am-6pm Fri & Sat, noon-6pm Sun;
Brown, Red Line to Armitage
Prices are high here, but so is the quality. If you need lots of personal help choosing top-end outdoor gear, come here.

BARBARA'S BOOKSTORE

Map pp276–7   *Bookstore*
☎ 312-642-5044; 1350 N Wells St; ☽ 9am-10pm
Mon-Sat, 10am-9pm Sun; Red Line to Clark/Division
For serious fiction, you can't touch this locally owned store. The staff have read what they sell, and touring authors regularly give readings. There's another location near the entrance to Navy Pier (Map pp280–1; ☎ 312-222-0890).

BARNES & NOBLE Map pp276–7   *Bookstore*
☎ 773-871-9004; 659 W Diversey Pkwy; ☽ 9am-11pm;
Brown, Red Line to Diversey
This bustling location draws crowds every day of the week and has become a prime meeting

place for Lincoln Park yuppies. There's also a branch in the **Gold Coast** (Map pp278–9; ☎ 312-280-8155; 1130 N State St).

CHICAGO HISTORICAL SOCIETY STORE Map pp276–7   *Chicago Souvenirs*
☎ 312-642-4600; 1601 N Clark St; ☽ 9:30am-4:30pm
Mon-Sat, noon-5pm Sun; Brown Line to Sedgwick
The shop in the museum (p74) boasts an excellent selection of books devoted to local history, many of which are hard to find elsewhere.

CRATE & BARREL OUTLET

Map pp276–7   *Home Furnishings*
☎ 312-787-4775; 800 W North Ave; ☽ 10am-8pm
Mon-Fri, 10am-7pm Sat, 11am-6pm Sun;
Red Line to North/Clybourn
The 'outlet' in the name means you can score plates, glasses and other discontinued home items at very cheap prices.

DAVE'S RECORDS

Map pp276–7   *CDs & Records*
☎ 773-929-6325; 2604 N Clark St; ☽ 11am-8pm
Mon-Sat, noon-7pm Sun; Brown, Red Line to Diversey
Right next to 2nd Hand Tunes, Dave's is an all-vinyl shop that feels a little like the setting of Nick Hornby's music-nerd classic, *High Fidelity*. Whether that's a good thing or not probably depends on your level of music nerddom. You'll find everything from vocal jazz to techno.

GRAMAPHONE RECORDS

Map pp276–7   *CDs & Records*
☎ 773-472-3683; 2663 N Clark St; ☽ 11am-9pm
Mon-Fri, 10:30am-8:30pm Sat, noon-6pm Sun;
Brown, Red Line to Diversey
Gramaphone is the hippest record store in Chicago – you'd have to either be a DJ or be dating one to have heard of most of the hip-hop and electronic music sold here. Along with their collection of trendsetting sounds, Gramaphone offers record needles and DJ supplies, and a host of info on upcoming parties.

GUITAR CENTER

Map pp276–7   *Musical Instruments*
☎ 773-327-5687; 2633 N Halsted St; ☽ 10am-9pm
Mon-Fri, 10am-7pm Sat, 11am-6pm Sun;
Brown, Red Line to Diversey
This large store caters to the instrument needs of bands from all over Chicagoland, and has also recently branched out into DJ equipment like mixers and turntables.

HIFI RECORDS

Map pp276–7   *CDs & Records*

☎ 773-880-1002; 2570 N Clark St; ⊙ 11am-8pm
Mon-Sat, noon-7pm Sun; Brown, Red Line to Diversey

Check out the selection of dirt-cheap old soul and jazz LPs and new indie CDs at this friendly store. The Technics record bags ($45) will make you look cool, no matter what you have in them. HiFi is also a good bet for local music magazines like *Venus* and *Stop Smiling*.

LORI'S, THE SOLE OF CHICAGO

Map pp276–7   *Shoes*

☎ 773-281-5655; 824 W Armitage; ⊙ 11am-7pm
Mon-Thu, 11am-6pm Fri, 10am-6pm Sat, noon-5pm
Sun; Brown, Red Line to Armitage

Chicago women swear by this place, where designer shoes can be bought for a song. Even if you're not in the market for shoes, drop by on a weekend just to take in the orgy of boxes, tissue paper, and frenzied shoppers.

SATURDAY'S CHILD

Map pp276–7   *Toys & Games*

☎ 773-525-8697; 2146 N Halsted St; ⊙ 10am-6pm
Mon-Sat, 11am-5pm Sun; Red, Brown Line to Fullerton

Remember the episode of the *Brady Bunch* wherein Peter constructed a working volcano that covered the whole clan in poop? Your own kid can get the makings of his or her own mess here. However, the vast majority of the toys and games for sale are a blast creatively and intellectually, rather than literally.

TOWER RECORDS

Map pp276–7   *CDs & Records*

☎ 773-477-5994; 2301 N Clark St; ⊙ 9am-midnight;
Brown, Red Line to Fullerton

Besides all types of mainstream music, this large store sells books and concert tickets, plus an excellent selection of 'zines and products from the alternative press. There's another Tower location in the **Loop** (Map pp282–3; ☎ 312-663-0660; 214 S Wabash Ave).

UNCLE DAN'S

Map pp276–7   *Outdoor Gear*

☎ 773-477-1918; 2440 N Lincoln Ave; ⊙ 10am-8pm
Mon-Thu, 10am-7pm Fri & Sat, 11am-5pm Sun;
Brown, Red Line to Fullerton

The smell of leather hits you in the face as you walk into this outdoor gear store, which offers a big selection of hiking boots and equipment, plus camping supplies and many brands of backpacks. It's a very relaxed place to buy out-

door gear without the derisive looks of lurking sales dudes who consider anything less than a frontal assault on K2 to be for wimps.

VIDEO BEAT

Map pp276–7   *CDs & Records*

☎ 773-871-6667; 2616 N Clark St; ⊙ 11am-8:30pm
Mon-Sat, noon-8pm Sun; Brown, Red Line to Diversey

Choose among a large selection of music videos on tape as well as funky recordings. We were fascinated and horrified by *Ronald Reagan's Favorite Ballads*.

LAKE VIEW

Stuff that's never worn – let alone sold – on Michigan Ave is de rigueur on Halsted and Clark Sts in Lake View. Even if you're not buying, the browsing is entertainment in itself. Near Belmont Ave several stores serve the rebellious needs of full-on punks and teens. On weekend days the sidewalks attract a throng of characters – rich teens from the North Shore, black-clad punks with blond roots, the rest of Lake View's diverse tribes and people selling socialist newspapers. A true Chicago people-watching treat.

99TH FLOOR   Map pp272–3   *Costumes*

☎ 773-348-7781; 3406 N Halsted St; ⊙ noon-9pm;
Red Line to Addison

You can still buy 'Dead Elvis Masks' ($36) here. For more formal occasions, the store carries black pumps with 8-inch heels in men's sizes.

AIR WAIR   Map pp272–3   *Shoes*

☎ 773-244-0099; 3240 N Clark St; ⊙ noon-9pm
Mon-Fri, noon-6pm Sat & Sun; Red Line to Belmont

This shop features perennial sales on huge, heavy boots of minimal practical value outside of a steel mill (read: Doc Martens). Celebrate your third piercing with a pair.

ALLEY

Map pp272–3   *Men's & Women's Clothing*

☎ 773-525-3180; 3218 N Clark St; ⊙ 11am-10pm
Mon-Thu, 11am-midnight Fri & Sat, noon-9pm Sun;
Red Line to Belmont

A vast emporium based on counterculture and pop trends, the Alley offers everything from head-shop gear to band posters to human-size dog collars. Loud, obnoxious punk-rock tees ('I've got the biggest dick in the band' etc) are a speciality of the house. The labyrinth of rooms includes one devoted to the Alley's 'Architectural Revolution' store, which sells plaster reproductions of gargoyles,

Oak St shopping (p190)

Ionic pillars and other items that have found a mainstream market with non-dog-collar-wearing interior designers. The Alley's adjoining store, **Taboo-Tabou** (☎ 773-548-2266; 858 W Belmont Ave), sells condoms in more flavors than Baskin-Robbins sells ice cream.

ARMY NAVY SURPLUS USA
Map pp272–3   *Outdoor Gear*
☎ 773-348-8930; 3100 N Lincoln Ave; 🕑 8am-5pm Mon-Fri, 10am-5pm Sat; Brown Line to Southport
The merchandise area here would send a drill sergeant into a conniption. The place is a huge mess. But among the torn boxes and shambles of merchandise are actual military surplus items of the highest quality the taxpayer can afford.

BATTERIES NOT INCLUDED
Map pp272–3   *Erotic Toys*
☎ 773-935-9900; 3420 N Halsted St;
🕑 11am-midnight; Red Line to Addison
You think kids cry when the batteries in their toys run out? You oughta see the frustrated looks on the faces of the adult customers of this place when *their* toys run out of juice. Some of the vibrating items for sale might have been nuclear missiles in a former life.

BOOKWORKS Map pp272–3   *Bookstore*
☎ 773-871-5318; 3444 N Clark St; 🕑 noon-10pm Mon-Thu, noon-11pm Fri & Sat, noon-6pm Sun; Red Line to Belmont
This small bookstore selling used titles has an excellent Chicago-specific section, and also sells used jazz and blues records. Contemporary fiction is a speciality.

BROWN ELEPHANT
Map pp272–3   *Secondhand*
☎ 773-549-5943; 3651 N Halsted St; 🕑 noon-6pm; Red Line to Addison
Everything from furs to studs lines the simple pipe coatracks at this resale shop, which helps to raise funds for the Howard Brown Health Center, an acclaimed clinic serving the gay, lesbian and bisexual community. Among last year's satin dresses you can find some gems, price- and style-wise. The used CD selection is especially good.

CHICAGO COMICS Map pp272–3   *Bookstore*
☎ 773-528-1983; 3244 N Clark St; 🕑 noon-8pm Mon-Thu, noon-10pm Fri, 11am-10pm Sat, noon-6pm Sun; Red Line to Belmont
This comic emporium has won 'best comic book store in the US' honor from all sorts of people

who should know. Old Marvel *Superman* back issues share shelf space with hand-drawn works by cutting-edge local artists. Chicago Comics also has enough arcane *Simpsons* toys to keep Matt Groening's children in high-tuition private schools for decades.

CHICAGO MUSIC EXCHANGE

Map pp272–3   *Musical Instruments*
☎ 773-477-0830; 3264 N Clark St; ⏱ 11am-7pm Mon-Fri, 11am-6pm Sat, noon-5pm Sun; Brown, Red Line to Belmont

This is the place for vintage and classic guitars and other instruments. Watch out for the drool left by garage-band hopefuls.

CUPID'S TREASURE

Map pp272–3   *Erotic Toys*
☎ 773-348-3884; 3519 N Halsted St; ⏱ 11am-midnight Mon-Thu, 11am-1am Fri & Sat, 11am-midnight Sun; Red Line to Addison

Here's the place to buy all those things you wondered if your neighbors owned. Spread through three large rooms, the adult toys on display leave adult browsers giggling like children. The goods – frilly, aromatic, battery-powered, leathery and more – should satisfy even the most imaginative of consenting adults. If you're having trouble deciding, ask the friendly staff, who are always eager to help and earnest in their advice. Consider the following guidance given to one couple: 'The whip requires more skill. With the paddle, it's easy – you just spank.'

DISGRACELAND

Map pp272–3   *Men's & Women's Clothing*
☎ 773-281-5875; 3338 N Clark St; ⏱ 11am-7pm Mon-Sat; noon-6pm Sun; Red Line to Belmont

You won't find loud '70s polyester shirts at this used clothing store, which specializes in secondhand (but up-to-date) fashions. The men's stuff is downstairs.

EVIL CLOWN Map pp272–3   *CDs & Records*
☎ 773-472-4761; 3418 N Halsted St; ⏱ noon-10pm Mon-Fri, 11am-9pm Sat, noon-7pm Sun; Red Line to Addison

This small store is covered with posters from Radiohead, Weezer, the Flaming Lips and other alternative favorites. Evil Clown sells used CDs acquired from people liquidating their collections ahead of the creditors. The staff know where to find the good stuff. If you want to check out some local bands live, take a look at all the fliers advertising performances.

FLASHY TRASH

Map pp272–3   *Men's Clothing*
☎ 773-327-6900; 3524 N Halsted St; ⏱ 11am-8pm Mon-Sat, noon-6pm Sun; Red Line to Addison

This trendy, stylish store offers all the accoutrements for a gay ol' time, including cool Puma gear and the popular 'switch hitter' T-shirt.

GAY MART Map pp272–3   *Toys & Novelties*
☎ 773-929-3459; 3457 N Halsted St; ⏱ 11am-7pm Sun-Thu, 11am-9pm Fri & Sat; Red Line to Addison

The Woolworth of the strip sells toys, novelties, calendars, souvenirs, you name it. One of the top sellers is Billy, the heroically endowed 'world's first out and proud gay doll.' Ken would just wilt in Billy's presence – that is, if Ken had anything to wilt.

MEDUSA'S CIRCLE

Map pp272–3   *Men's & Women's Clothing*
☎ 773-935-5950; 3268 N Clark St; ⏱ noon-8pm Mon-Sat, 1am-6pm Sun; Brown, Red Line to Belmont

Not sweating enough? Medusa's carries everything for raven-haired folks who like to wear dark velvet clothes on hot days.

MIDWEST STEREO

Map pp272–3   *Electronics*
☎ 773-929-5523; 2806 N Clark St; ⏱ 10:30am-8pm Mon-Fri, 10am-7pm Sat, 10am-6pm Sun; Brown, Red Line to Belmont

A hub for DJ gear, both used and new. If you're looking for a basic mixer or a Technics turntable (or a PA system that will quickly make you the talk of your neighborhood), this is your store.

POSH Map pp272–3   *Home Furnishings*
☎ 773-529-7674; 3729 N Southport Ave; ⏱ noon-7pm Tue-Fri, 11am-7pm Sat, noon-5pm Sun; Brown Line to Southport

This gem of a store carries vintage china, old posters, and furnishings from (or stylized to look like) the 20s and 30s.

SILVER MOON

Map pp272–3   *Vintage Clothing*
☎ 773-883-0222; 3337 N Halsted St; ⏱ noon-6pm Tues-Sun; Brown, Red Line to Belmont

This prim vintage store offers 1920s cloche hats, 1900s top hats and other museum-quality clothes priced high enough to make you nervous about handling them.

SPORTS WORLD

Map pp272–3   *Chicago Souvenirs*
☎ 312-472-7701; 3555 N Clark St; ☻ 9am-6pm;
Red Line to Addison
This store across from Wrigley Field is crammed with authentic Chicago sports duds. All-wool Cubs and White Sox caps just like those worn by the players are $25. All-synthetic baseball caps just like those worn by nerds are $10.

STRANGE CARGO

Map pp272–3   *Men's & Women's Clothing*
☎ 773-327-8090; 3448 N Clark St; ☻ 11:30am-6:45pm
Mon-Sat, noon-5:30pm Sun; Red Line to Belmont
One of the coolest stores in Chicago for retro T-shirts and thrift-store-esque hipster wear, Strange Cargo also sells wigs, clunky shoes and leather jackets. Have something you want to get off your chest? You can use their iron-on machine to enliven vintage-style tees (or, ahem, panties) with the message of your choice.

UNCLE FUN Map pp272–3   *Toys & Novelties*
☎ 773-477-8223; 1338 W Belmont Ave; ☻ noon-7pm
Wed-Sat, noon-6pm Sun; Brown, Red Line to Belmont
This weird toy and novelty shop is one of the best spots in Chicago for goofy gifts, kitschy postcards and vintage games. The shelves are overflowing with strange finds such as fake moustache kits, 3-D Jesus postcards and Chinese-made tapestries of the US lunar landing (just $5, baby).

WINDWARD SPORTS

Map pp272–3   *Sporting Goods*
☎ 773-472-6868; 3317 N Clark St; ☻ 11am-8pm
Tue-Fri, 11am-5pm Sat & Sun; Red Line to Belmont
One-stop shopping for sporty gear, whether you're into windsurfing, snowboarding, in-line skates, or the see-it-to-believe-it 'flowboard' (kind of like a cross between a skateboard and a snowboard). Ask at the store about various beach rentals of windsurfing equipment during the summer.

WISTERIA Map pp272–3   *Vintage Clothing*
☎ 773-880-5868; 3715 N Southport Ave; ☻ 4pm-9pm
Thu-Fri, noon-9pm Sat, noon-5pm Sun;
Brown Line to Southport
Here you can find classic, vintage Hawaiian shirts ($38) and other bits of clothing from the Swing and '70s eras.

YESTERDAY

Map pp272–3   *Toys & Novelties*
☎ 773-248-8087; 1143 W Addison St; ☻ 1pm-7pm
Mon-Sat; 2pm-6pm Sun; Red Line to Addison
If you've ever actually lived through the classic tale about discovering that your mom has thrown out all of your baseball cards, you can come here to find out what a fortune you've lost. Old sports memorabilia is the speciality of this shop, which is older than some of the goods on sale.

ANDERSONVILLE & UPTOWN

ALAMO SHOES Map p274   *Shoes*
☎ 773-784-8936; 5321 N Clark St; ☻ 9am-8pm Mon-Fri,
9am-6pm Sat, 10am-6pm Sun; Red Line to Berwyn
This throwback to the 1960s focuses on comfortable Swedish shoes and Birkenstocks for both men and women, all at really good prices. The enthusiastic staffers hop off to the backroom and emerge with stacks of boxes until you find what you want or you're entirely walled in by the possibilities.

PAPER TRAIL

Map p274   *Greeting Cards & Gifts*
☎ 773-275-2191; 5307 N Clark St; ☻ 10am-6:30pm
Tue-Fri, 10am-6pm Sat, 11am-4pm Sun;
Red Line to Berwyn
Here's where you find the cards the designers at Hallmark probably want to create, if only such creativity wouldn't cost them their jobs. The store's Chihuahua card collection is matched in scope only by the 'boxing rabbi' puppets.

STUDIO 90 Map p274   *Women's Clothing*
☎ 773-878-0097; 5239 N Clark St; ☻ 11am-7pm
Mon-Fri, 10am-6pm Sat, 11am-5pm Sun;
Red Line to Berwyn
Everything here is designed by the owners, who have built a growing reputation on their loose-fitting, sophisticated women's clothes.

SURRENDER

Map p274   *Greeting Cards & Gifts*
☎ 773-784-4455; 5225 N Clark St; ☻ 11am-7pm
Mon-Wed, 11am-8pm Thu-Fri, 10am-6pm Sat,
11pm-5pm Sun; Red Line to Berwyn
If all your shopping has you stressed out, drop by this serene boutique for some aromatherapy candles and other sensual bath products.

2nd Hand Tunes (p197)

Shopping – Wicker Park/Bucktown & Ukrainian Village

WIKSTROM'S GOURMET FOODS
Map p274   *Food & Drink*
☎ 773-275-6100; 5243 N Clark St; 🕑 9am-6pm
Mon-Sat; Red Line to Berwyn
Scandinavians from all over Illinois flock here for homemade *limpa* bread, herring and lutefisk. They sell over 4000lb of Swedish meatballs around Christmas time.

WOMEN & CHILDREN FIRST
Map p274   *Bookstore*
☎ 773-769-9299; 5233 N Clark St; 🕑 11am-7pm Mon & Tue, 11am-9pm Wed-Fri, 10am-7pm Sat, 11am-6pm Sun; Red Line to Berwyn
Hillary Clinton caused a mob scene when she came to this Andersonville feminist mainstay for her 2003 reading. High-profile book-signings and author events happen every week at the welcoming shop, which features fiction and non-fiction by and about women, along with an expanding children's book selection.

WICKER PARK/BUCKTOWN & UKRAINIAN VILLAGE
Damen and Milwaukee Aves in Wicker Park are two of the city's best shopping drags. You'll find the more oddball and youth-oriented shops residing on Milwaukee, while Damen holds a wealth of women's clothing boutiques.

APARTMENT NO. 9
Map p275   *Men's Clothing*
☎ 773-395-2999; 1804 N Damen; 🕑 11am-7pm Mon-Wed, Fri & Sat, 11am-8pm Thu, noon-5pm Sun; Blue Line to Damen
One of Chicago's only shops catering to metrosexuals (straight guys with a strong style sense and desire to pamper their bodies), Apartment No. 9 has a slim array of stylish shirts, pants and shoes, along with fancy shaving accessories.

(Continued on page 211)

1 Fun mirror, Navy Pier (p68)
2 Street musician, the Loop 3
Vendor on 18th St, Pilsen 4 In
the Loop

1 Mr Beef (p134), Near North 2
Earwax Cafe (p163), Wicker Park
3 Frontera Grill (p131), Near North
4 Eatery neon

1 Berghoff (p128), the Loop **2** Pizzeria Uno (p135), Near North **3** Nuevo Leon (p154), Pilsen **4** Cyrano's Bistrot (p131), Near North

1 Chicago Theater (p169), the Loop 2 Billy Goat Tavern (p131), Near North 3 Chinatown scene (p156) 4 Crowds at the annual Chicago Blues Festival (p10), Grant Park

1 *City Sole/Niche (p211), Wicker Park* 2 *Hermes (p196), Gold Coast* 3 *Merchandise Mart (p194), Near North* 4 *Mannequin wearing Belmont Ave fashion, Lake View*

1 Oak St Beach (p84), Gold Coast 2 Fun with the kids at Navy Pier (p68) 3 Rosehill Cemetery (p81), Andersonville 4 Statues, Grant Park (p63)

1 *In the Loop* **2** *Wrigley Field (p77)*
3 *Oak St Beach (p84), Gold Coast*
4 *Chicago Marathon official*

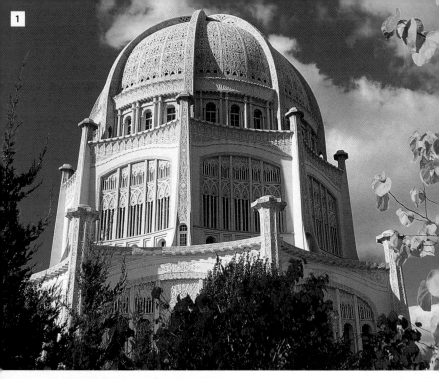

1 Baha'i House of Worship (p232), Wilmette 2 Frank Lloyd Wright Home & Studio (p234), Oak Park 3 Indiana Dunes State Park (p240) 4 Starved Rock State Park, Utica (p238)

(Continued from page 202)

BOTANICA Map p275 *Religious Paraphernalia*
☎ 773-486-5894; 1524 N Milwaukee Ave; ☼ 9am-5pm
Mon-Fri, 10am-5pm Sat; Blue Line to Damen
This old storefront sells devotional art and paraphernalia without an ounce of irony. What you do with your sacred candle once out of the store is your business.

CITY SOLE/NICHE Map p275 *Shoes*
☎ 773-489-2001; 2001 W North Ave; ☼ 11am-8pm;
Blue Line to Damen
One of the hippest shoe stores in Chicago is divided into two sections. Niche is where high-priced designs frolic and City Sole is the more down-to-Earth cousin. Regardless of which side you pick, you can count on discovering gorgeous men's and women's shoes and a somewhat absurdly haughty staff.

CLIMATE Map p275 *Greeting Cards & Gifts*
☎ 773-862-7075; 1702 N Damen Ave; ☼ 11am-8pm
Mon-Fri, 10am-9pm Sat, 11am-6pm Sun;
Blue Line to Damen
'Eclectic' doesn't do justice to the array of cute little items packed into this small store. Cocktail party kits, cheeky dating guides, and other tongue-in-cheek essentials for urban living.

CLOTHES MINDED
Map p275 *Women's Clothing*
☎ 773-227-3402; 1649 N Damen; ☼ 11am-7pm
Mon-Wed, Fri, 11am-8pm Thu, 11am-6:30pm Sat;
Blue Line to Damen
A regular winner in Chicago 'best of' lists, Clothes Minded offers everyday women's fashions in a fun, inviting shop.

DUSTY GROOVE Map p275 *CDs & Records*
☎ 773-342-5800; 1120 N Ashland; ☼ noon-7pm
Sat-Wed, noon-8pm Thu-Fri; Blue Line to Division
Be sure to check out the battery powered record players ($100) at this mecca for soul, jazz and electronica.

JOHN FLUEVOG SHOES Map p275 *Shoes*
☎ 773-772-1983; 1539-41 N Milwaukee Ave;
☼ 11am-7pm Mon-Sat, noon-5pm Sun;
Blue Line to Damen
Bold and colorful shoes by the eccentric designer are the order of the day at this close-out haven.

LILLY VALLENTE Map p275 *Secondhand*
☎ 773-645-1537; 1746 W Division St; ☼ noon-8pm
Mon-Fri, noon-6pm Sun; Blue Line to Damen
You'll need an adventuresome spirit and a cleared afternoon to tackle this resale shop, which features deliriously wonderful amount of clothes, art and useful junk.

MEBLE Map p275 *Home Furnishings*
☎ 773-772-8200; 1462 N Milwaukee Ave;
☼ 11am-6pm Tue-Sun; Blue Line to Damen
It's worth just browsing here to see the weird and wonderful mix of pricey props, antiques and conceptual art pieces. If you're thinking of buying, beware – much of the stuff is made of metal and probably won't work as carry-on baggage.

Comic Books for Grown-Ups
by Archer Prewitt

Chris Ware's 380-page Pantheon graphic novel, *Jimmy Corrigan, The Smartest Kid On Earth*, won the prestigious British Guardian First Book Award, an American Book Award, France's L'Alph Art award, and unanimous praise from the likes of the *Village Voice* and *Time* magazine. Ware has redefined the comics medium by developing intricate visual constructs which unravel like storytelling maps or challenging musical compositions. His entire output is elegantly designed, masterfully paced, intelligent, melancholic and brutally funny. He is currently working on two (or more) lengthy stories that appear in the *Chicago Reader* as full-page, full-color weekly installments, designing books and CDs, and exhibiting (he was in the 2002 Whitney Biennial).

For savage and shocking humor, look no further than the nihilistic work of Ivan Brunetti. The two issues of *Schizo* published by Fantagraphics are existential nightmares that erupt as damaged philosophical rants on everything from suicidal self-loathing to perverse fantasies of mutilations meted out on former bullies. Brilliant, obsessive, claustrophobic and hilarious, Ivan's work has garnered several Harvey and Ignatz nominations.

Jeffrey Brown's work is prolific and confessional. His loose drawing style and writing is intimate and affecting, and his self-published debut, *Clumsy*, reads like a cathartic diary of the pleasures and pains of a relationship. It was nominated for the Ignatz award for Best New Talent in 2002. His second book, *Unlikely*, is available through Top Shelf Books.

Archer Prewitt draws the comic Sof' Boy *when not playing music solo or with his band, The Sea and Cake.*

MYOPIC BOOKS Map p275 *Bookstore*
☎ 773-862-4882; 1564 N Milwaukee; ⏰ 11am-1am
Mon-Sat, 11am-10pm Sun; Blue Line to Damen
An eclectic used-book store with an enormous
fiction collection, Myopic contains large sections for special interests such as lesbian, gay,
geek and more.

NOIR FOR MEN Map p275 *Men's Clothing*
☎ 773-862-9960; 1740 W Division; ⏰ 11am-8pm;
Blue Line to Damen
A cool men's store with refreshingly friendly
staff and simple, affordable fashions, Noir is
a must for those put off by the showy clothes
and snooty attitudes of most boutiques. Pants,
shirts and shoes here are unpretentious and
classic cuts from the '50s predominate. Women
can visit the parent store two shops east on
Division St for similarly hip, laid-back fashions.

P45 Map p275 *Women's Clothing*
☎ 773-862-4523; 1643 N Damen; ⏰ 11am-7pm
Mon-Wed, Fri & Sat, 11am-8pm Thu, noon-5pm Sun;
Blue Line to Damen
The international buyers at this ultra-hip
boutique ensure that the latest styles arrive
in Chicago roughly the same time they hit
the coasts. Whether it's a black mesh vest by
Tree or a bright orange leather blazer from Ulla
Johnson, the clothes here deliberately push the
fashion envelope.

PENELOPE'S
Map p275 *Clothing & Accessories*
☎ 773 395-2351; 1913 W Division St; ⏰ 11am-7pm
Mon-Sat, noon-5pm Sun; Blue Line to Damen
Named after the owners' ridiculously cute pug,
Penelope's is a warm boutique for twenty- and
thirtysomethings. Offering both women's and
men's fashions along with really cool gifty
things (check out the flask/cigarette holder
combo), Penelope's further ups the ante by
providing an arcade-style stand-up Ms Pac-
Man game to keep significant others occupied
while loved ones try on clothes.

QUIMBY'S Map p275 *Bookstore*
☎ 773-342-0910; 1854 W North Ave; ⏰ 11am-8pm
Mon-Fri, noon-8pm Sat & Sun; Blue Line to Damen
The epicenter of Chicago's comic and 'zine
worlds, Quimby's is one of the linchpins of
underground culture in Chicago. You can
find everything here from crayon-powered
punk-rock manifestos to slickly produced
graphic novels. See the boxed text on p211
for some of the names in Chicago's words-
with-pictures scene.

RECKLESS RECORDS
Map p275 *CDs & Records*
☎ 773-235-3727; 1532 N Milwaukee Ave; ⏰ 10am-
10pm Mon-Sat, 10am-8pm Sun; Blue Line to Damen
Chicago's best indie-rock record and CD
emporium allows you to listen to everything
before you buy. If you're looking for CDs by
local bands like Tortoise or Gastro del Sol,
come here first.

RED BALLOON CO Map p275 *Children*
☎ 773-489-9800; 2060 N Damen Ave; ⏰ 11am-6:30pm
Mon-Wed, 11am-7pm Thu, 11am-6pm Fri & Sat, noon-
5pm Sun; Blue Line to Damen
When hipsters get good jobs and start having
kids, this is where they outfit the li'l pups. Ador-
able clothes, classic children's books, and '50s-
ish toys predominate in this cozy store.

SAFFRON Map p275 *Women's Clothing*
☎ 773-486-7753; 2064 N Damen Ave; ⏰ 11am-6pm
Tue-Wed, Fri & Sat, noon-8pm Thu, noon-5pm Sun;
Blue Line to Damen
This women's clothing store specializes in
classic-cut evening wear and accessories,
along with jewelry, shawls, and bath and
beauty products.

TANGERINE Map p275 *Women's Clothing*
☎ 773-772-0505; 1719 N Damen; ⏰ 11am-7pm
Mon-Wed, Sat, 11am-8pm Thu, noon-5pm Sun;
Blue Line to Damen
The designers featured at this perky boutique
are mostly American with some Europeans
thrown in too. The service-oriented staff will
help you find what you need.

UNA MAE'S FREAK BOUTIQUE
Map p275 *Men's & Women's Clothing*
☎ 773-276-7002; 1422 N Milwaukee Ave;
⏰ noon-8pm Mon-Fri, 11am-8pm Sat, 11am-7pm Sun;
Blue Line to Damen
It's unlikely that the solid suburban women
who once wore the pillbox hats and fine Republican cloth coats on sale here would ever
have thought of themselves as freaks. Along
with the vintage wear, Una Mae's has a growing collection of new accessories like scarves,
hats and cosmetics.

US #1 Map p275 *Men's Clothing*
☎ 773-489-9428; 1509 N Milwaukee Ave;
⏰ 11am-7pm; Blue Line to Damen
This place looks like a dump from the outside.
Inside, however, you'll find rack after rack of
excellent, affordable vintage '70s and western
wear shirts, as well as towers of old Levi's jeans.

VAGABOND Map p275 *Bookstore*
☎ 773-227-6140; 2010 N Damen 🕙 10am-8pm;
Blue Line to Damen
This store offers weary travelers guidance in
the form of guidebooks, maps, backpacks and
more. If you can think of it, Vagabond can help
you get there.

VIVE LA FEMME
Map p275 *Women's Clothing*
☎ 773-772-7429; 2115 N Damen; 🕙 noon-8pm
Mon-Wed, noon-9pm Thu, noon-5pm Sat & Sun;
Blue Line to Damen
Plus-size shops for women are often woefully
lacking in style. Not so at Vive La Femme,
where larger women can find cute and cutting-edge designs in a variety of sizes.

SOUTH LOOP & NEAR SOUTH SIDE

HOYPOLOI Map pp284–5 *Home Furnishings*
☎ 312-225-6477; 2235 S Wentworth Ave;
🕙 11am-8pm Mon-Thu, Sun, 11am-9pm Fri & Sat;
Red Line to Cermak-Chinatown
This neat store is filled with Asian artwork and
other funky interior items.

New Maxwell St Market

Much changed from the original, the **New Maxwell
St Market** (Map pp286–7; Canal St; Sun 7am-3pm)
has moved from Maxwell St to a stretch of S
Canal St between Taylor St and the equivalent of
15th St, near the river. This relocation was supposedly
sparked by the University of Illinois' insatiable need
to expand southward (which is partly true), but
mostly it was caused by the city's desire to reclaim
the original market's area, which had become
Chicago's own wild bazaar, with drug dealers and
vendors of stolen hubcaps openly competing for
customers. One whole block had even seceded from
the US and declared itself an anarchist state. In a
postscript, years after the market was snuffed out at
its old Maxwell St location, the battered VW buses
of the anarchist state remain.

The city bureaucracy closely monitors the new
location, but the rough edges remain. Nonetheless,
every Sunday morning hundreds of vendors set up
stalls that sell everything from Cubs jerseys in the
wrong colors to tacos for $1. You can still buy hub-
caps, but the odds that they're fresh from your own
car are somewhat diminished.

SANDMEYER'S BOOKSTORE
Map pp284–5 *Bookstore*
☎ 312-922-2104; 714 S Dearborn St; 🕙 11am-6:30pm
Mon-Wed, Fri, 11am-8pm Thu, 11am-5pm Sat, noon-5pm
Sun; Red Line to Harrison
Suitably located in the heart of Printer's Row,
Sandmeyer's holds a good selection on travel.
The family-run store also emphasizes fiction
and architecture.

SUN SUN TONG Map pp284–5 *Food & Drink*
☎ 312-842-6398; 2260 S Wentworth Ave;
🕙 10am-7pm; Red Line to Cermak-Chinatown
Hundreds of varieties of tea and herbs make
for great aromas here.

WOKS N THINGS Map pp284–5 *Kitchen*
☎ 312-842-0701; 2234 S Wentworth Ave; 🕙 9am-7pm;
Red Line to Cermak-Chinatown
This busy store carries every kind of utensil and
cookware you could want.

SOUTH CHICAGO
Bibliophiles should hop on the next Metra
train to Hyde Park to check out the great
selection of bookstores around the University of Chicago campus.

57TH STREET BOOKS
Map pp288–9 *Bookstore*
☎ 773-684-1300; 1301 E 57th St; 🕙 10am-10pm
Mon-Sat, 10am-8pm Sun; Metra to 57th
A vast selection of general-interest titles here
fills the basements of two buildings. The travel
section features a commendable choice of
Lonely Planet guides, a table and chairs for
careful choosing and a chilled-water dispenser
to cool the sweaty tourist.

O'GARA & WILSON LTD
Map pp288–9 *Bookstore*
☎ 773-363-0993; 1448 E 57th St; 🕙 9am-10pm
Mon-Sat, noon-10pm Sun; Metra to 57th
The tone here is set by the leaded glass in the
oaken door. The titles range from humanities
tomes to old *Life* magazines and $1 paper-
backs.

POWELL'S Map pp288–9 *Bookstore*
☎ 773-955-7780; 1501 E 57th St; 🕙 9am-11pm;
Metra to 57th
The leading local used bookstore can get you
just about any book ever published – for a
price. Another store is located in **Lake View** (Map
pp272–3; ☎ 773-248-1444, 2850 N Lincoln
Ave). Both stores are all very well arranged.

SEMINARY COOPERATIVE
BOOKSTORE Map pp288–9 *Bookstore*

☎ 773-752-1959; 5757 S University Ave;
🕑 8:30am-9pm Mon-Fri, 10am-6pm Sat, noon-6pm Sun;
Metra to 57th

This is the bookstore of choice for several University of Chicago Nobel Prize winners, including Robert Fogel, who says, 'For a scholar, it's one of the great bookstores of the world.' The store carries more than 100,000 academic and general titles.

UNIVERSITY OF CHICAGO
BOOKSTORE Map pp288–9 *Bookstore*

☎ 773-702-7712; 970 E 58th St; 🕑 8am-6pm Mon-Fri,
9am-4pm Sat; Metra to 57th

Gussied up under Barnes & Noble management, the campus store still stocks textbooks on everything you can imagine (color titles in the medical section will put you off smoking, drinking, meat and perhaps even life itself), plus titles by faculty and students. On the 2nd floor is a souvenir and U of C gift section.

Sleeping

Sleeping

As the most popular convention city in the US, Chicago abounds with hotels. In the Loop and North Side, more than a hundred hotels of all types offer more than 25,000 rooms. That's the good news. The bad news is that the conventions can attract tens of thousands of visitors, who fill up even the most remote locations and pay top dollar for the chance to do so. During one of the major shows it might be better to skip Chicago entirely: the best hotels and restaurants will be packed.

To find out if your intended visit coincides with a major show, you can try calling the Chicago Convention and Tourism Bureau (☎ 312-567-8500; www.choosechicago.com), but these folks – the ones who market McCormick Place – may not give you complete information on upcoming shows because of contractual agreements. The best sources are probably the major convention hotels, such as the Hyatt, the Sheraton and the Hiltons. If they have room for the dates of your visit, then most other places will as well.

Not so long ago, you could usually count on great lodging deals when conventions weren't in town and hotels were scrambling to fill their rooms at almost any cost. Sadly, though, Chicago's popularity means that this is no longer the case. The average downtown room rate runs about $150. During non-holiday weekends in the dead of winter, the best hotels sometimes offer rooms for $125 a night, or even less. Package deals may include in-room treats such as champagne, as well as free theater tickets and parking. The latter can shave $20 a night off your bill.

When we list room rates in this chapter, we are listing average prices for a standard double occupancy room. The range noted takes into account seasonal fluctuations and the vagaries of weekend versus weekday lodging. Use the prices quoted for comparison purposes only, since a large convention in town can make them laughably off-base.

> ## Top Five Unique Hotels
> - **W Chicago-Lakeshore** (p222) For its tantalizing 'goodie boxes.'
> - **House of Blues Hotel** (p220) For the original artwork hand-painted by kids from the Chicago Housing Authority.
> - **Hotel Sofitel** (p223) For the Euro panache.
> - **Peninsula** (p221) For the bathtub views.
> - **Drake** (p223) For the non-stop pampering.

The Internet is your best bet in finding special deals in Chicago (see the boxed text p247). Almost every hotel in Chicago has a website offering special 'Internet only' deals. If your laptop is broken, try calling the chain-affiliated hotels directly rather than calling their national toll-free numbers – sometimes the local desk staff will know of deals not listed in the national computer banks. Families should note that suite hotels can be a good deal; the kids can be exiled to the sofa bed while the adults take refuge in the real bed behind a closed door.

Beware of a nasty surprise you will find on your bill – the hotel tax is a gnarly 14.9%. Also, the more a hotel charges per night, the more likely it is to levy some sort of ridiculous fee on local calls. These can run $1.25 or more per call, so if you have a lot of business to conduct and you're paying your own bill, ask about these charges when making reservations.

Finally, if you do arrive in town and everything seems to be full, try the hotels by the O'Hare and Midway Airports. Because these are a trek from the city center, they often have a few beds available when no one else does.

B&Bs

Chicago is slowly catching on to the bed-and-breakfast concept. **Bed & Breakfast Chicago** (☎ 773-549-0962; www.chicago-bed-breakfast.com; 607 W Deming Place 60614), a booking service, handles rooms at more than 60 places throughout the city, most of them in the Gold Coast, Old Town and Lincoln Park areas. The units run the gamut from bedrooms in upscale old graystones to whole apartments where you're left to your own devices. This is an excellent way to experience life in the more interesting neighborhoods. The service provides you with a list of places based on your desires for price, location and proximity of the owners. Rates for singles and doubles range anywhere from about $95 to over $300. The minimum stay at most of the places is two or three nights.

Long Stays

Lucky enough to have to extend your time in Chicago? Hotels often offer very attractive rates for stays of a week or longer, so you can start your hunt for a long-term stay with them. You can also look in the Yellow Pages under 'Apartments': several of the large management companies run advertisements of their furnished apartments, geared toward corporate clients.

Another good resource is the **Habitat Corporate Suites Network** (☎ 312-902-2090, 800-833-0331; www.habitatcsn.com), which manages many of the city's upscale high-rises in the Near North. The fully equipped rental units come with cable TV and voice mail, and they enjoy good locations, in buildings with door attendants. Rates tend to run $70 to $120 per day.

If you don't want to work through a middleman, try the **Residence Inn by Marriott** (Map pp278–9; ☎ 312-943-9800, 800-331-3131; www.residenceinn.com; 201 E Walton St). It offers apartment-sized units, each with a full kitchen. The Gold Coast hotel also provides breakfast every day, as well as a free buffet (with beer and wine) in the lobby on Monday to Thursday evenings. Rooms are bigger than typical hotel rooms and make good homes for the person stuck on the road. There's even a laundry room where you can wash your dirty duds.

THE LOOP & GRANT PARK

Loop hotels are convenient to Grant Park, the museums and the central business and financial districts. They are usually no more than a 15-minute walk away from River North and N Michigan Ave (and for those near the river, much less). But despite several promising signs, such as the development of the theater district, the area is still a few years away from having its own hopping nightlife.

FAIRMONT Map pp282–3 _Hotel_
☎ 312-565-8000, 800-527-4727; www.fairmont.com; 200 N Columbus Dr; r $169-389; Brown, Green, Orange Line to Randolph
Overall, the Fairmont would rank among the elite of Chicago hotels if it weren't lost in the depths of the otherwise odious Illinois Center. Tall people will be thrilled with the extra-long beds, and less lofty-heighted souls will enjoy the spacious rooms, well-equipped work areas, opulent bathrooms and other luxuries provided by this San Francisco-based company. Rooms near the top of the hotel's 45 stories can enjoy excellent views if they face the park or lake. The public spaces are equally grand, and the hotel is convenient to the museums and Grant Park.

HOTEL ALLEGRO Map pp282–3 _Hotel_
☎ 312-236-0123, 800-643-1500; www.allegrochicago.com; 171 W Randolph St; r $119–295; Brown, Orange Line to Randolph
Located in what was once the Bismarck Hotel, the Allegro has a notorious past to live down. For years it was home to various Chicago political organizations, and its hallways and rooms were the scene of all manner of dubious dealings. Now, however, its hip makeover has chased out the pinky-ring-clad political fat cats. Bright primary colors dominate the public spaces and the rooms, which vary widely in size. Try not to get one overlooking another building.

HOTEL BURNHAM Map pp282–3 _Hotel_
☎ 312-782-1111, 877-294-9712; www.burnhamhotel.com; 1 W Washington St; r $169-399; Red Line to Washington
Architecture buffs might have a hard time going to sleep in one of the most historic buildings in Chicago. Built as the Reliance Building in the early 1890s, this one languished in recent decades as tenants shunned its small floors. However, small floors proved perfect for a hotel, and it's been lavishly restored and reopened as the Hotel Burnham, in honor of one of its architects. The rooms all feature period-inspired decor to lavish and elegant effect. The hotel's Atwood Café is tops among hotel restaurants.

HYATT REGENCY CHICAGO

Map pp282–3 *Hotel*

☎ 312-565-1234, 800-233-1234;
www.chicago.hyatt.com; 151 E Wacker Dr; r $170-368;
Brown, Green, Orange Line to State

A vast convention hotel with 2019 rooms, the Hyatt Regency was best known for being big. And kind of blah. A $60 million renovation completed in 2002, however, has given the rooms a more modern look, and added free DSL Internet access for all guests. Drinkers will rejoice at the fact that the Hyatt boasts the longest free-standing bar in North America. The big downside: no swimming pool. Lots of specials keep all those rooms filled in off-peak times.

PALMER HOUSE HILTON

Map pp282–3 *Hotel*

☎ 312-726-7500 ☎ 800-445-8667; www.hilton.com;
17 E Monroe St; r $94-219; Brown, Green, Orange Line
to Adams

Built in 1927, the Palmer House hotel has gone through three incarnations in its long lifetime. As in many hotels of its era, the Hilton's 1640 rooms vary greatly in size, so ask for a big one when you check in. Up one flight on an escalator, the lobby is the stunning feature of the place, with enough gilding to cover several lesser establishments. Even if you're staying in a nearby hotel, the lobby here is worth a visit.

RENAISSANCE CHICAGO HOTEL

Map pp282–3 *Hotel*

☎ 312-372-7200, 888-236-2427;
www.renaissancehotels.com; 1 W Wacker Dr;
r $168-400; Brown, Green, Orange Line to State

This luxury hotel, next to the offices of advertising giant Leo Burnett, is lavish in its decor and amenities, but feels a touch dated. The public spaces are actually much nicer than the somewhat bland exterior would suggest, with ornate tapestries and other elegant touches. The rooms are large and include sitting areas, which will be appreciated by those who don't want to spend all their time in their room in bed. Bay windows offer good views of the skyline and the river. All rooms contain modem ports, and the business traveler rooms come with fax machines and printers. In addition, a 24-hour Kinko's business-service facility is on the premises. The hotel offers packages that include tickets to shows in Loop theaters.

SILVERSMITH Map pp282–3 *Hotel*

☎ 312-372-7696, 800-227-6963;
www.ichotelsgroup.com; 10 S Wabash Ave; r $109-319;
Brown, Green, Orange Line to Madison

Another Loop architectural gem that has been converted into a hotel, the Silversmith was built in 1894. Although the exterior was designed by Daniel Burnham's firm, the hotel's interior recalls Frank Lloyd Wright. The rooms are big, and the furniture has a distinct Prairie-style charm. Try to get one of the rooms that doesn't look right into another building.

SWISSÔTEL CHICAGO

Map pp282–3 *Hotel*

☎ 312-565-0565, 800-654-7263; www.swissotel.com;
323 E Wacker Dr; r $169-595; Brown, Green, Orange
Line to Randolph

On the eastern frontier of Illinois Center, the Swissôtel – in a striking triangular mirrored-glass high-rise – is easy to spot. The 632 large rooms offer the expected good views from their individual sitting areas. Separate showers and bathtubs mean that one can douse while the other dunks. The casual Cafe Suisse bakes its own bread and pastries, and the Palm is a notable steak house. Anyone wandering through can lay waste to the huge bowl of mini Swiss chocolates on the concierge counter. This place fills up for weekday stays *months* in advance, so reserve early.

W CHICAGO CITY CENTER

Map pp282–3 *Hotel*

☎ 312-332-1200, 877-946-8357; www.whotels.com;
172 W Adams St; r $199-319; Brown, Orange Line to Quincy

The employees all wear black at this hip hotel, where the soaring, beautiful lobby feels a little like a European cloister remade into a sleek dance club. The smallish rooms are simple to the point of starkness, using lots of grays and dark-wood trim to maintain the Euro feel. Rooms come with wireless web TV and high-speed Internet access. Look for good deals on weekends, when the moneyed neighborhood folks working in the surrounding financial district have gone home and you can expect to find a tumbleweed or two rolling up the street.

NEAR NORTH & NAVY PIER

North of the river you can't go a block in any direction without finding a hotel. If you want to be near the center of Chicago's tourist action, stay here and enjoy all the eating, drinking, shopping and entertainment you could possibly desire.

BEST WESTERN CHICAGO RIVER

NORTH Map pp280–1 *Hotel*

☎ 312-467-0800, 800-727-8088;
www.bestwestern.com/rivernorthhotel; 125 W Ohio St;
r $89-225; Red Line to Grand

A renovation in 2002 made this one of the better value options in River North. Large rooms have a vaguely Asian flair, and the pool and sundeck overlook the Loop. In-room coffeemakers and free parking(!) sweeten the deal.

BEST WESTERN INN OF CHICAGO

Map pp280–1 *Hotel*

☎ 312-787-3100, 800-557-2378;
www.bestwestern.com; 162 E Ohio St; r $89-169;
Red Line to Grand

One of the neighborhood's best values, the Best Western Inn of Chicago offers less-than-fancy rooms in an older building, but you can't beat the location. The hotel has been going through a slow renovation that's brought a fresh look to 90% of its rooms. If you're looking for rooms that are basic without being depressing, this is a good choice. It's a favorite with tour groups, so hold your breath as you pass all the buses idling outside.

CHICAGO MARRIOTT HOTEL

Map pp280–1 *Hotel*

☎ 312-836-0100, 800-228-9290; www.marriott.com;
540 N Michigan Ave; r $185-369; Red Line to Grand

Barring a good deal, there's little reason to stay here. Several nicer places lie within a two-block radius. Long one of Chicago's ugliest hotels, the Marriott now sports new exterior cladding that does nothing more than cover up the old cladding. The inside isn't much better, with gloomy public spaces and so-so restaurants. The cracker-box rooms on the high floors of this 46-story behemoth enjoy good views. The car entrance is off Rush St.

COURTYARD BY MARRIOTT CHICAGO DOWNTOWN

Map pp280–1 *Hotel*

☎ 312-329-2500, 800-321-2211;
www.courtyard.com; 30 E Hubbard St; r $149-269;
Red Line to Grand

Billing itself as 'the hotel designed by business travelers,' this outpost charges rates that fall at the high end of the moderate range. However, unlike at its hulking corporate brother a few blocks away on Michigan Ave, here you get what you pay for. Rooms on the high floors in the fairly new building enjoy excellent views,

Hotel Sofitel (p223)

and all contain good work areas for travelers needing to pound away at the laptop. There's also a sundeck, a whirlpool and an indoor lap pool. The management has cut deals with several nearby restaurants, so you can charge your meals at those places to your room account.

EMBASSY SUITES CHICAGO-

DOWNTOWN Map pp280–1 *Hotel*

☎ 312-943-3800, 800-362-2779;
www.embassysuites.com; 600 N State St; r $179-249;
Red Line to Grand

A good deal for families, this chain hotel offers all the expected suite features, including the two-room layout with beds in one room and a sofa bed in the other. The kitchenette has a microwave, which means you can nuke up some sort of popcorn and pizza delight for the kids and then head out into River North for some real food. Speaking of food, you can feast on a free full – not continental – breakfast served in the atrium each morning, and the indoor pool is a great way to wake up.

EMBASSY SUITES CHICAGO-RIVER
EAST Map pp280–1 *Hotel*
☎ 312-836-5900, 866-866-8095;
www.chicagoembassy.com; 511 N Columbus Dr;
r $209-245; Red Line to Grand

It's the usual Embassy Suites deal here – an all-suite layout with complimentary happy hour and breakfast. True to Embassy Suites form, the rooms all overlook a central atrium. This version, though, is more stunning than most, with a chic airplane-hangar feel and a small forest of trees growing in the lobby. The place opened in 2002, and the rooms still feel fresh and new.

HAMPTON INN & SUITES-CHICAGO
RIVER NORTH Map pp280–1 *Hotel*
☎ 312-832-0330, 800-426-7866; www.hamptoninn.com;
33 W Illinois St; r $159-239; Red Line to Grand

The relatively new Hampton features 230 rooms (including 100 suites, some with full kitchen), an indoor pool, a hot tub, a sauna, an exercise room, a free continental breakfast buffet, a guest coin laundry and a 24-hour business center. It's fairly generic, but the location is good.

HILTON GARDEN INN
Map pp280–1 *Motel*
☎ 312-595-0000, 800-774-1500; www.hilton.com;
10 E Grand Ave; r $149-224; Red Line to Grand

This 23-story hotel opened in 2000 as part of the vast North Bridge development. Rather bland, it does feature bright, good-sized rooms that boast microwaves. There's a small pool and the usual – for this price range – business and fitness centers. Grill-o-philes will be happy to note that the adjoining restaurant is run by the Weber Grill company.

HOLIDAY INN-CHICAGO CITY
CENTRE Map pp280–1 *Hotel*
☎ 312-787-6100, 800-465-4329; www.basshotels.com;
300 E Ohio St; r $136-230; bus 66

Though nearly generic, this hotel is better than many of its namesake brethren, but it's still unremarkable in most respects. Views aren't bad, and you do get access to a health club with an indoor pool in the same complex.

HOTEL INTER-CONTINENTAL
CHICAGO Map pp280–1 *Hotel*
☎ 312-944-4100, 800-327-0200; www.interconti.com;
505 N Michigan Ave; r $179-429; Red Line to Grand

The Inter-Continental has a split personality. The older portion, on the south side, dates from 1929 and underwent a careful restoration in the 1990s. Once a health club for rich men, it holds such classic details as a beautifully mosaicked indoor swimming pool in a setting worthy of William Randolph Hearst. The rooms got the same treatment and have become both elegant and convenient, with all the facilities business travelers expect. Just north is the cheesy aluminum addition that used to house the Inter-Con's budget chain, now dead. When reserving and checking in, be sure to go for the classic side. Swimmers should note that the pool is the largest inside any hotel in the city.

HOUSE OF BLUES HOTEL
Map pp280–1 *Hotel*
☎ 312-245-0333, 800-235-6397; www.loewshotels.com;
333 N Dearborn St; r $150-299; Red Line to Grand

Once upon a time, this concrete building was the grim office component of the noted Marina City complex. However, it's been reborn in a big way as the hotel component of the adjacent House of Blues club (p176). You need look no further than the huge gold Buddha near the door to get a sense of the over-the-top decor. If you get a room with a view (many have none), you might just be distracted from the many goofy and colorful details. Expect to luxuriate in the huge bathrooms, and keep an eye out for the musicians playing at the House of Blues club who often stay here.

LENOX SUITES Map pp280–1 *Hotel*
☎ 312-337-1000, 800-445-3669; www.lenoxsuites.com;
616 N Rush St; r $119-239; Red Line to Grand

While none of the rooms are striking (sometimes the beds fold down from the wall), the location and prices of the Lenox are hard to beat. Some of the suites are barely bigger than one room (when we were there last, a confused guest stood at the counter asking how the room she had reserved could be considered a suite, but others are fairly sizable. Be sure to make a point of asking for one of the remodeled rooms, which are a few notches above their un-remade counterparts. A free continental breakfast (aka muffin basket) is delivered to your room daily.

LE MERIDIEN Map pp280–1 *Hotel*
☎ 312-645-1500; www.lemeridien.com;
520 N Michigan Ave (entrance at 520 N Rush St);
r $209-465; Red Line to Grand

If you're looking for a little urban pampering, this chic hotel connected to the upscale North Bridge Shops is for you. The Euro-sleek, blonde-wood rooms – each with a CD player, voice mail, a thick bathrobe, and free high-speed Internet – are discreetly luxurious. During the day you can visit the spa to massage and whirlpool the urban din away.

OMNI CHICAGO HOTEL

Map pp280–1 *Hotel*
☎ 312-944-6664, 800-843-6664;
www.omnihotels.com; 676 N Michigan Ave; r $188-379;
Red Line to Chicago

One of the nicest properties on Michigan Ave (the entrance is just west on Huron St), the modern all-suite Omni rises high above a retail and office building. The rooms are decked out in rich colors and cherry wood. The living room of each of the 347 units features an excellent work area with a two-line phone – perfect for leaving the boss on hold while you talk nice-nice to a loved one on the other line. Other amenities include free DSL Internet access, an indoor pool, whirlpools and an exercise room.

PENINSULA Map pp280–1 *Hotel*
☎ 312-337-2888, 866-288-8889;
www.peninsula.com; 108 E Superior St; r $395-475;
Red Line to Chicago

Hailed as the best place to stay in Chicago by everyone from *Zagats* to *Condé Nast Traveler*, the Peninsula is truly an experience. Each of the large, luxurious rooms comes equipped with no fewer than five(!) phones, three of which are located in the bathroom. Lighting and electronics are all tied into impressively complicated high-tech systems, and DVD players come standard in the rooms. Some of the rooms have bathtub views, and the rooftop glass-enclosed pool is enough to weep over. How's the service? The staff here are all required to take personal grooming classes to ensure there's never a hair out of place.

RADISSON HOTEL & SUITES

Map pp280–1 *Hotel*
☎ 312-787-2900, 800-333-3333; www.radisson.com/chicagoil; 160 E Huron St; r $159-309; Red Line to Chicago

Newly renovated, this Radisson is excellent value. Many of the rooms come with microwaves and refrigerators, and the hotel contains a small heated rooftop pool and sundeck. The miniscule exercise room feels a little like a garage sale waiting to happen, but at these rates, you won't sweat it. The furniture has a funky, fun feel. Weekend Internet deals here can border on the amazing, dropping the room rates down to as little as $89 for two people.

Chicago Hostels

Arlington House (Map pp276–7; ☎ 773-929-5380; www.arlingtonhouse.com; 616 W Arlington Place; dm $17, private r $24-68 per person; Blue Line to Washington) This occupies an excellent location in the heart of Lincoln Park, one block west of Clark St. The rooms in the classic brick building look pretty beat-up and the staff borders on indifferent. Choose a renovated room if you have a choice, and steer clear of the dark basement rooms. Open year-round, 24 hours a day.

Chicago International Hostel (Map pp270–1; ☎ 773-262-1011; www.chicagointernationalhostel.com; 6318 N Winthrop Ave; dm $17; Red Line to Loyola) Near Loyola University, this major year-round hostel housed in a 1960s building lies three blocks south of the Loyola El stop on Sheridan, then two blocks east. Though the location is safe enough, you're far from the action. The El takes at least 35 minutes to get you to Chicago Ave.

Hostelling International-Chicago (Map pp282–3; ☎ 312-360-0300; www.hichicago.org; 24 E Congress Pkwy; dm $34-44; Blue, Red Line to Jackson) OK, so the prices are a little outrageous for a hostel. But oh, what a hostel. Just three years old, this bright and cheery place is the best hostelling option in Chicago by far, with a super-convenient location and clean, cared-for sleeping areas. It does double duty as Columbia College dorms during the academic year, so the number of available beds is lower September to May. If you can get a room here, you'll enjoy 24-hour access (hello, nightclubs!) and a kitchen. Check-in starts after 2pm.

SHERATON CHICAGO HOTEL AND TOWERS Map pp280–1 *Hotel*
☎ 312-464-1000, 877-242-2558 or ☎ 800-325-3535;
www.sheratonchicago.com; 301 E North Water St;
r $199-219; bus 56

The best of the monster convention hotels contains 1204 rooms, all with excellent views, especially those on the river. The vast public spaces feature huge plate-glass walls and fountains made with black granite, while the room decorations are typical of corporate hotels – nice but nothing special. The lower level lies on the River Esplanade, which runs east from Michigan Ave. The hotel's bizarre address means it is just behind the NBC Tower, one block east of Michigan Ave along Columbus Dr.

WESTIN RIVER NORTH

Map pp280–1 *Hotel*

☎ 312-744-1900, 800-228-3000 or ☎ 800-937-8461; www.westinrivernorth.com; 320 N Dearborn St; r $199-359; Brown, Green, Orange Line to State

On the north bank of the river, the former Hotel Nikko continues to reflect its Asian roots; the rock garden, for example, is still carefully tended. But fans of the Westin chain can now rest easily in a hotel that's much better than its older sibling further north. Rooms are large, views are good and the service is splendid. The lobby bar, with its minimalist decor and open feel, makes an excellent place for a casual meeting.

W CHICAGO-LAKESHORE

Map pp280–1 *Hotel*

☎ 312-943-9200, 877-946-8357; www.whotels.com; 644 N Lake Shore Dr; r $209-279; bus 66

This Near North outpost of the clubby hotel is located within walking distance of Navy Pier and the Oak St beach, making it a good choice for families. The hotel's location on the inner access road away from other high-rises means that the rooms are sunny and the views of either the lake or the city are good. Rooms are less gray-feeling than its Loop counterpart. Low rooms on the Lake Shore Dr side suffer from traffic noise.

Cheap Sleeps

CASS HOTEL Map pp280–1 *Motel*

☎ 312-787-4030, 800-227-7850; 640 N Wabash Ave; r $74-89; Red Line to Grand

Not much to look at inside or outside, the Cass won't give you much to look at in the bill department either. Rooms are very simple and rather small; in some the TV sits on a shelf at an angle hard to see from the beds. The location, however, is excellent.

HOTEL WACKER

Map pp280–1 *Motel*

☎ 312-787-1386; 111 W Huron St; r $55-60; Red Line to Chicago

This beat-up place is kept clean, but it's far from romantic and teeters dangerously close to the edge of flophouse-dom. If you're really hard up for cash, and are traveling with a friend, this place will do fine for a night or two. Everyone else is advised to keep looking. Rooms include TVs and air-conditioning, but you need to leave a $5 deposit for linen and your key.

HOWARD JOHNSON INN

Map pp280–1 *Motel*

☎ 312-664-8100, 800-446-4656; www.hojo.com; 720 N LaSalle St; r $85-125; Brown Line to Chicago

Straight out of your old family vacation in the minivan (or station wagon, if you have gray hair), the HoJo offers free parking in a lot surrounded by a classic American motel. The 1995-era rooms include free cable.

OHIO HOUSE MOTEL Map pp280–1 *Motel*

☎ 312-943-6000; 600 N LaSalle Dr; r $85-115; Red Line to Grand

Make your reservations quick at the Ohio House, before developers turn it into a trendy restaurant. This throwback auto-court motel, with its cement-block detailing, has remained resolutely unchanged since JFK was president. A few of the rooms have been remodeled in the past couple years – ask for one of them when checking in. Free parking.

RED ROOF INN Map pp280–1 *Motel*

☎ 312-787-3580, 800-466-8356; www.redroof.com; 162 E Ontario St; r $80-109; Red Line to Grand

The couches in the lobby here are stained, and the staff seem perpetually confused as to how they got their jobs and what they're supposed to do with them. But this Red Roof Inn is ideally located and very affordable. Rooms are the definition of utilitarian, bordering on cell-like.

GOLD COAST

Home to many of the city's best hotels, the Gold Coast also has a few moderately priced gems.

AMBASSADOR EAST Map pp278–9 *Hotel*

☎ 312-787-7200, 800-843-6664; www.omnihotels.com; 1301 N State St; r $149-179; Red Line to Clark/Division

In Hitchcock's *North by Northwest*, Cary Grant gets to hang out at the Ambassador East with Eva Marie Saint before he meets that crop-duster in the Indiana cornfield. Your stay may lack the same glamour or danger, but you will still be in swank surroundings that include the famous Pump Room off the lobby (p181). Grand touches abound, from the marble floors to the heavy woodwork. Rooms vary widely in size and style, with some seemingly untouched since Grant and Saint made eye contact. Aim for one of the large, bright ones. To reflect its chain affiliation, the hotel has added 'Omni' in front of its name.

CLARIDGE HOTEL Map pp278–9 *Hotel*
☎ 312-787-4980, 800-245-1258;
www.claridgehotel.com; 1244 N Dearborn St; r $165-255;
Red Line to Clark/Division

A nicely renovated neighborhood hotel in the heart of the Gold Coast, the Claridge features rooms that range from tiny to spacious, so inquire carefully when you make your reservation and again at check-in. Parks, the lake and nightlife are all short strolls away. Amenities include complimentary continental breakfast and newspaper, as well as complimentary morning limo shuttles around the immediate neighborhood.

DOUBLETREE GUEST SUITES HOTEL
Map pp278–9 *Hotel*
☎ 312-664-1100, 800-222-8733;
www.doubletree.com; 198 E Delaware Place;
r $179-279; Red Line to Chicago

Dysfunctional couples love it here: each room includes two TVs, two phones and other amenities in pairs, including the freshly baked cookies. There's only one indoor pool, however. The striking modern lobby rises a few notches above the usual hotel entry.

DRAKE Map pp278–9 *Hotel*
☎ 312-787-2200, 800-553-7253;
www.thedrakehotel.com; 140 E Walton St;
r $239-259; Red Line to Chicago

The ageless Drake is Chicago's grandest hotel. Listed on the National Register of Historic Places, the hotel has hosted the likes of Queen Elizabeth and other glitterati since opening in 1920. It enjoys a commanding location at the head of Michigan Ave and offers convenient access to Oak St Beach, a short stroll through the pedestrian tunnel under Lake Shore Dr. The quiet rooms are built like bank vaults, with heavy old doors and marble baths. The suitably grand public places include restaurants and bars many notches above the norm. The Cape Cod Room serves excellent seafood. The Coq d'Or (p179) is one of the classiest bars in town.

FOUR SEASONS HOTEL
Map pp278–9 *Hotel*
☎ 312-280-8800, 800-332-3442;
www.fourseasons.com/chicagofs; 120 E Delaware Pl;
r $305-975; Red Line to Chicago

Rising high above the 900 N Michigan Ave mall, the Four Seasons is often considered the best in Chicago. It pampers its guests and firmly believes in the old maxim 'your wish is our command.' For instance, room service will endeavor to rustle up whatever you desire, whether it's on the menu or not, 24 hours a day. Each of the 343 rooms is unique, thanks to the handmade rugs and other decor. Needless to say, the amenities include an indoor pool, a health club, a whirlpool, a sauna and just about anything else spa-related short of a mud bath. (On the other hand, if you wanted one...) Seasons restaurant serves superb American cuisine in a plush setting. The casual café is good as well, and the commodious bar overlooking Michigan Ave makes an excellent meeting place.

GOLD COAST GUEST HOUSE
Map pp278–9 *B&B*
☎ 312-337-0361; www.bbchicago.com; 113 W Elm St;
r $119-189; Red Line to Clark/Division

Visitors from abroad will be especially welcomed by innkeeper Sally Baker at the Gold Coast Guest House. Baker has been steadily refining her 1873 classic three-flat for 15 years. Her experience as a travel guide based in London helps her understand the needs of travelers new to the US or to Chicago. Each of the four guest rooms includes a private bath and individual air-conditioning controls. Guests receive a bounteous breakfast and can help themselves to sodas and snacks in the refrigerator at other times. The walled-in garden out back makes a pleasant escape from the city.

HOTEL SOFITEL Map pp278–9 *Hotel*
☎ 312-324 4000; www.sofitel.com; 20 E Chestnut St;
r $159-369; Red Line to Chicago

The Sofitel looks a little like some state-of-the-art Mac computing device from the outside, its triangular glass tower leaning gracefully forward into space. Inside, stylish staff tend to stylish thirty- and fortysomething guests, who come here for the luxuriously minimalist vibe. Rooms feel a little like they were decorated from a high-end Ikea, all blonde wood and rectangular lines. All rooms come with high-speed Internet access and a cute bottle of European water.

PARK HYATT Map pp278–9 *Hotel*
☎ 312-335-1234, 800-233-1234; www.parkchicago
.hyatt.com; 800 N Michigan Ave; r $285-445;
Red Line to Chicago

This flagship of the locally based Hyatt chain spares no expense, from the flat-screen TVs to the DVD players to the oodles of phones in every one of the 203 rooms. For once, the word 'stunning' adequately describes the NoMi restaurant and bar (p132), with its views over Michigan Ave and the Water Tower, plus a nice outdoor area looking west. The hotel's amenities include a pool and concierges ready and willing to jump at your request. Suites come with balconies and cost the moon.

RAPHAEL HOTEL Map pp278–9 *Hotel*
☎ 312-943-5000, 800-983-7870;
www.raphaelchicago.com; 201 E Delaware Pl;
r $99-149; Red Line to Chicago

The Raphael is one of several boutique hotels in older buildings in this neighborhood near Water Tower Place. You won't find many amenities in the building itself, but the rooms are spacious, and many also have sitting rooms. The hotel serves a continental breakfast in the morning, and at night you can unwind in the quaint little bar downstairs or with the in-room honor bars. The Raphael has a very loyal following.

RITZ-CARLTON Map pp278–9 *Hotel*
☎ 312-266-1000, 800-621-6906;
www.fourseasons.com/chicagorc; 160 E Pearson St;
r $300-910; Red Line to Chicago

One of the city's finest hotels, it occupies 32 stories above Water Tower Place. The lobby, mostly understated, bursts with stunning floral arrangements. The large rooms embody refinement, with antique armoires and floral prints. The concierges have earned a reputation for being able to conjure up the answer to any guest's demand. The well-equipped health club includes an indoor pool. The Dining Room is an excellent French restaurant serving prix-fixe and degustation menus, including vegetarian options.

SENECA Map pp278–9 *Hotel*
☎ 312-787-8900, 800-800-6261;
www.senecahotel.com; 200 E Chestnut St; r $145-209;
Red Line to Chicago

Another boutique hotel, the Seneca is popular with people who want a nice room but don't need all the accoutrements of a major hotel. The place has the feel of a well-maintained older apartment complex from the 1920s. Accommodations include voice mail, coffeemakers and refrigerators, and range in size from one room to large suites.

SUTTON PLACE HOTEL
Map pp278–9 *Hotel*
☎ 312-266-2100, 800-606-8188;
www.suttonplace.com; 21 E Bellevue Pl; r $199-305;
Red Line to Clark/Division

This hotel works hard at staying true to its European roots. Built as a German-owned Kempinski Hotel in the mid-1980s, it was bought by the French chain Le Meridian in the early 1990s before adopting its rather anonymous

The Drake hotel (p223)

name now. Electronics freaks will enjoy the rooms, which all come with CD players, VCRs and stereo TVs. When not exercising your finger on the remotes, you can work out at the nearby health club or check in to the 'Aerobics Suite' and feel the burn. The contemporary decor is accented by Robert Mapplethorpe's lush floral photos (the controversial stuff is over at the Museum of Contemporary Art). Gaunt models haunt the Whisky Bar, off the lobby.

TREMONT Map pp278–9 *Hotel*
☎ 312-751-1900, 800-621-8133;
www.tremontchicago.com; 100 E Chestnut St;
r $139-199; Red Line to Chicago
The priciest of the neighborhood boutique hotels, the Tremont boasts fully wired rooms with fax machines, VCRs, CD players and more. The decor – sort of whimsical European – is fairly bright for an older, somewhat staid building like this one. The clientele leans toward the tasseled-loafer lawyer set, who enjoy the speaker phones in the rooms.

WESTIN HOTEL, CHICAGO
Map pp278–9 *Hotel*
☎ 312-943-7200, 800-228-3000;
www.westinmichiganave.com; 909 N Michigan Ave;
r $215-399; Red Line to Chicago
This 751-room hotel is a shopper's dream, located within pouncing distance of all the Michigan Ave malls. The hotel got a facelift recently, and the work has transformed what was a dark, homely hotel into a cheerier place to stay. Rooms come with high-speed Internet plus all the basics like coffeemakers, CD players and in-room safes. Note that the hotel entrance is well east of Michigan Ave, on Delaware Pl.

LINCOLN PARK, OLD TOWN & WICKER PARK
These hotels and inns, often cheaper than the big ones downtown, place you near a lot of the city's best nightlife. Daytime pleasures at the museums and in the Loop and Near North are a short El or bus ride away.

COMFORT INN OF LINCOLN PARK
Map pp276–7 *Motel*
☎ 773-348-2810; www.choicehotels.com; 601 W
Diversey Pkwy; r $99-169; Brown, Red Line to Diversey
The Comfort Inn sits right on enjoyable Diversey Pkwy, east of Clark St, and about five

minutes' walk from Lincoln Park and the lake. Built in 1918, the building was modernized in the 1980s, bringing it up to true anonymous Comfort Inn standards. Amenities include free continental breakfast and free parking. Some rooms come with king beds, and a couple feature whirlpool tubs. If you pay one of the lower rates here, you'll get a good deal.

DAYS INN GOLD COAST
Map pp276–7 *Motel*
☎ 312-664-3040, 800-325-2525 or ☎ 800-544-8313;
www.daysinn.com; 1816 N Clark St; r $89-119;
Brown Line to Sedgwick
Once a flophouse called the Hotel Lincoln, this place has been upgraded to the low standards of Days Inn. However, it's clean, and the furniture is much younger than you are. The best feature, besides the rate, is the excellent location across from the zoo and in the midst of Old Town. You can easily walk to many of the top destinations on the North Side from here.

DAYS INN LINCOLN PARK NORTH
Map pp276–7 *Motel*
☎ 773-525-7010, 800-325-2525 or ☎ 800-544-8313;
www.daysinn.com; 644 W Diversey Pkwy; r $99-141;
Brown, Red Line to Diversey
With 122 rooms near the busy intersection of Clark St, Diversey and Broadway, this good-sized hotel occupies a prime location. Otherwise, it's not the most charming place, situated in an old retail building above one of the North Side's four gazillion coffee bars. The free breakfast includes bagels.

HOUSE OF TWO URNS BED & BREAKFAST Map 275 *B&B*
☎ 773-235-1408; www.twourns.com; 1239 N
Greenview Ave; r $80-160; Blue Line to Division
Not a long walk from the diverse charms of Wicker Park, this B&B sits on a classic Chicago residential street. Inside the typical former two-flat brownstone, you'll find a long list of amenities like VCRs, free local calls, a laundry and a great roof deck. Owner Kapra Fleming can chat you up in German, Spanish and French (and Anglaise, *oui*).

LAKE VIEW
These places all lie near great nightlife spots and away from the tourist bustle of N Michigan Ave.

BEST WESTERN HAWTHORNE
TERRACE Map pp272–3 *Motel*
☎ 773-244-3434, 888-675-2378; www.hawthorneterrace.com; 3434 N Broadway; r $140-165; bus 152
A very good northern option, this hotel in a 1920s residential building features in-room fridges, microwaves and speakerphones (so you can sound like an annoying big shot).

CITY SUITES HOTEL Map pp272–3 *Hotel*
☎ 773-404-3400, 800-248-9108; www.cityinns.com; 933 W Belmont Ave; r $99-189;
Brown, Red Line to Belmont
Location, location, location. The City Suites Hotel, between Clark St and the El, definitely has it. You won't go hungry or thirsty or get bored in this stylish little place, full of brightly redone rooms (not all of which are suites). This is one of the best-kept lodging secrets in Chicago, and it will remind European visitors pleasantly of home. The same company, Neighborhood Inns of Chicago, also operates the Majestic and Willows. All three serve complimentary continental breakfasts.

MAJESTIC HOTEL Map pp272–3 *Hotel*
☎ 773-404-3499, 800-727-5108; www.cityinns.com; 528 W Brompton Ave; r $99-199; bus 145
The Majestic, one block south of Addison St, lies close to Wrigley Field and the Halsted St gay scene. The inside has a bit of a Laura Ashley feel.

WILLOWS HOTEL Map pp272–3 *Hotel*
☎ 773-528-8400, 800-787-3108; www.cityinns.com; 555 W Surf St; r $79-169; bus 22
The architectural pick of the Neighborhood Inns of Chicago trio, the Willows puts up an ornate terra-cotta facade on a very narrow strip of property. Built in 1925 and renovated in 2001, the hotel contains a small lobby but big rooms with traditional decor.

WEST SIDE
Unless you have a compelling reason to stay on the West Side, your Chicago stay will be much more enjoyable at one of the places that's more central.

HOLIDAY INN-CHICAGO DOWNTOWN
Map pp286–7 *Hotel*
☎ 312-957-9100, 800-465-4329; www.basshotels.com/holiday-inn; 506 W Harrison St; r $136-204; Blue Line to Clinton
On the west side of the river, this Holiday Inn offers convenient access to such exciting attractions as Union Station, the bus station and the post office. Its location is a bit bleak, but okay if you don't plan to hang around. Amenities include a small rooftop pool with a good view of the Sears Tower, a guest laundry and a business center. All rooms come with high-speed wireless Internet access.

HYATT AT UNIVERSITY VILLAGE
Map pp286–7 *Hotel*
☎ 312-491-1234, 800-233-1234; www.hyatt.com; 625 S Ashland Ave; r $149-239; Blue Line to Polk
This Hyatt is in the middle of the vast medical center complex and the University of Illinois at Chicago campus. Rooms are large and rather posh, and if you're visiting friends or family at the University of Illinois, you're set. Otherwise, try for a closer-in option.

SOUTH LOOP & NEAR SOUTH SIDE
Places in this area offer convenient access to the Museum Campus and McCormick Place but are far from the North Side action.

BEST WESTERN GRANT PARK INN
Map pp284–5 *Motel*
☎ 312-922-2900, 800-472-6875; www.bestwesterm.com; 1100 S Michigan Ave; r $119-139; Green, Orange Line to Roosevelt
This hotel is not much to look at inside or out, though it does feature a great view. The neighborhood is still in transition – it's not bad, just dead – but the hotel lies close to the Museum Campus, only about a mile from McCormick Place and three blocks from the Roosevelt El stop. At night there's not much going on except at the Chicago police headquarters, a half-block away. If you plan on getting in trouble, you'll have a short walk home from the pokey.

CHICAGO HILTON & TOWERS
Map pp284–5 *Hotel*
☎ 312-922-4400, 800-445-8667; www.hilton.com; 720 S Michigan Ave; r $184-279; Red Line to Harrison
When it was built in 1927, this was the largest hotel in the world, with close to 2000 rooms. A $225-million renovation in the mid-1980s brought that total down to a still huge 1543. Some of the resulting rooms now have two bathrooms, perfect if one member of a party locks him- or herself away for hours of ablutions.

Catching Some Sleep (and a Plane in the Morning)

Hotels near the airport don't offer any price advantage over those downtown, and you're stuck in the suburbs around O'Hare – places that might be nice for raising a family but are hardly of interest to visitors. The airport hotels may come in handy if you have a very early flight, or if all other accommodations in the city have been sucked up by visiting conventioneers.

Most of the hotels in Rosemont are linked to an enclosed pedestrian walkway that leads to the Rosemont Convention Center, a growing collection of buildings hosting trade shows and fairs for collectors of limited-edition plates and the like. If you're stuck at one of these places, you're probably within walking distance of the Rosemont CTA station for the 30-minute ride to downtown.

All the following places offer free shuttle service to and from O'Hare. But remember, the same traffic that plagues the expressways around O'Hare will swallow up your hotel shuttle bus; many people instead use the CTA for its five-minute ride to O'Hare from Rosemont.

Chicago O'Hare Rosemont Travelodge (Map pp270–1; ☎ 847-296-5541, 800-578-7878; www.travelodge.com; 3003 Mannheim Rd, Des Plaines; r $66-86; Blue Line to O'Hare) The sleepy bear comes alive at this Travelodge – the aggressive management provides free incoming fax service, cable TV, newspapers, coffee and more. The place looks like a throwback, but the staff really do aim to please. It's also the closest cheap hotel to the airport.

Clarion Hotel Barcelo (Map pp270–1; ☎ 773-693-5800, 800-252-7466; www.choicehotels.com; 5615 N Cumberland Ave; r $119-195; Blue Line to Cumberland) Pop-culture buffs will be keen to stay at the Clarion, where OJ Simpson checked in after his flight from California on the night of his ex-wife's murder. The broken glass and other memorabilia are long gone, as is the name of the place; in 1994 it was the O'Hare Plaza. Now this rather undistinguished hotel only begs the question – why did OJ opt to stay here in the first place?

Excel Inn of O'Hare (Map pp270–1; ☎ 847-803-9400, 800-367-3935; 2881 Touhy Ave, Elk Grove Village; r $60-85; Blue Line to O'Hare) A favorite dumping ground for airline passengers whom the airlines don't like (eg, non-frequent fliers with dirt-cheap tickets) but who still have to be put up for the night, the Excel is a simple motel in a town that claims to be America's largest industrial park. All rooms include coffeemakers, ironing boards and other useful touches.

Holiday Inn O'Hare International (Map pp270–1; ☎ 847-671-6350, 888-642-7344 or 800-465-4329; www.basshotels.com; 5440 N River Rd, Rosemont; r $99-123; Blue Line to O'Hare) The Holiday Inn O'Hare International features a Holidome and a whole bunch of other delights: an indoor pool, whirlpools, arcade games and more. Its ambience has remained unchanged since Richard Nixon was president.

Hotel Sofitel (Map pp270–1; ☎ 847-678-4488, 800-763-4835; www.sofitel.com; 5550 N River Rd, Rosemont; r $99-179; Blue Line to O'Hare) The pick of the O'Hare litter is the Sofitel, member of the friendly French chain of the same name; the hotel even makes especially flaky croissants in its own bakery. The large rooms include a number of amenities.

Hyatt Regency O'Hare (Map pp270–1; ☎ 847-696-1234, 800-233-1234; www.hyatt.com; 9300 W Bryn Mawr Ave, Rosemont; r $119-225; Blue Line to O'Hare) This ever-expanding property contains 1099 rooms, many with views of the expressway or the enclosed parking garage. It's across from the convention center and a short walk away from the El.

Marriott Suites Chicago O'Hare (Map pp270–1; ☎ 847-696-4400, 800-228-9290; www.marriott.com; 6155 N River, Rosemont; r $159-189; Blue Line to O'Hare) Compared with the O'Hare Marriott this one offers much bigger rooms in a much newer building.

O'Hare Hilton (Map pp270–1; ☎ 773-686-8000, 800-445-8667; www.hilton.com; r $134-254; Blue Line to O'Hare) If you want a real airport hotel, you can't get closer than the Hilton – it's right in the middle of the airport, across from Terminals 1, 2 and 3. Underground tunnels link the hotel with the terminals, the shuttle tram and the CTA. The rooms are large and soundproof. Amenities include an indoor pool, a sauna, whirlpool and exercise center. The restaurants aren't bad, either – definitely better than what you'll find in the terminals.

O'Hare Marriott (Map pp270–1; ☎ 773-693-4444, 800-228-9290; www.marriott.com; 8535 W Higgins Rd, Chicago; r $99-179; Blue Line to O'Hare) This Marriott often becomes a temporary home for bumped passengers. It's big and has a big parking lot, but it's otherwise unremarkable.

The public spaces are exquisitely grand, reaching a crescendo in the gilded ballroom, which is modeled after one at Versailles. Even if you're not staying here, it's worth a peek. The lobby bar that overlooks Michigan Ave at the north end of the block-size building has also played a minor role in history: Chicago police tossed protesters through the plate-glass windows here at the height of the riots during the 1968 Democratic National Convention.

ESSEX INN Map pp284–5 *Motel*

☎ 312-939-2800, 800-621-6909; www.essexinn.com; 800 S Michigan Ave; r $99-149; Green, Orange Line to Roosevelt

Once down at heel, the Essex has been spruced up a bit, although its 1964-vintage motel roots are very apparent. Still, it's a fine enough place to rest your head and even good value if you can manage to get a room under $100. Try for a park view.

HYATT ON PRINTER'S ROW

Map pp284–5 *Hotel*

☎ 312-986-1234, 800-233-1234; www.printersrow .hyatt.com; 500 S Dearborn St; r $155-240; Red Line to Harrison

With nice-sized rooms and good amenities, this is the pick of the South Loop litter. On weekends, when the streets are tranquil (read: dead), it's an even better deal. The resident restaurant, Prairie, is a worthy destination in itself (p155). The rates vary widely depending on what's going on in town. On weekends you might get a double here in the $100–200 range, but when occupancy is high, rates can climb to $300 or more.

HYATT REGENCY MCCORMICK PLACE

Map pp284–5 *Hotel*

☎ 312-567-1234, 800-233-1234; www.mccormickplace.hyatt.com; 2233 S Martin Luther King Jr Dr; r $274-314; Metra to McCormick Place

If you're manning a booth at McCormick Place during a show, this is the most convenient arrangement imaginable; after a short walk you can pass out in bed with memories of a day spent glad-handing dolts – er, potential clients – dancing in your head. The 800 rooms come with all the usual conveniences and boast good views of the Loop, more than 2 miles north. Of course, if you're not doing anything at McCormick Place, then there's no reason to stay down here, so far from most of the city's action.

Excursions

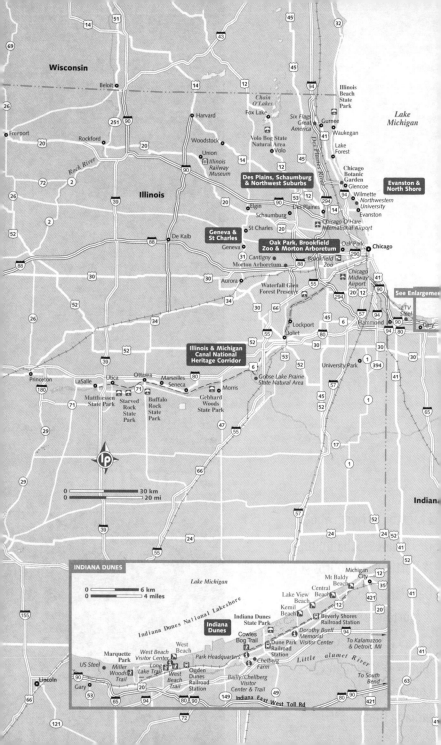

Excursions

Surrounded by farmlands and small towns, Chicago doesn't offer a whole lot in the way of ravishingly beautiful nature getaways or one-of-a-kind day trips. If you find yourself with an extra day on your hands and some extra gas in your rental car though, you'll find plenty to do outside city limits.

SUBURBAN TREASURES

You've come all this way to see one of America's great cities, and the last thing you want to do is get stuck in the suburbs, right? Wrong. **Evanston** (p231) and **Oak Park** (p234) both have some fascinating sights and attractions. You want crazy temples? Scandalous architects? Ernest Hemingway? Sure you do. And you'll find them in and around Evanston and Oak Park, both of which are just a 15-minute drive or short El ride from the Loop.

BEACHES

Surf's up (sort of) on the edge of Lake Michigan southeast of Chicago. Either ride the South Shore train line out from the Loop, or hop on I-90 and take it past Gary to the split with I-12. From there, you can explore the **Indiana Dunes National Lakeshore** (p239) at your leisure, staking your claim on any of the dozen or so pleasant beaches in the area, or hiking through **Indiana Dunes State Park** (p239).

FREAKS OF CAPITALISM

The area around Chicago offers some freakishly oversized shopping opportunities. Love them or hate them, the gigantic malls in **Gurnee** (p232) and **Des Plaines** (p233) are inarguably prime places to see American culture writ large (and pick up a nice sweater while you're at it). Gurnee also offers the decidedly American experience of paying a not-inconsiderable amount of money to be wrenched, torqued, spun and looped by roller coasters and other machines of torture and delight. Yep, there's a Six Flags Great America amusement park in Gurnee, and if your kids are reading this right now, you're already done for. After Six Flags, you can round out your ethnographic tour of American consumerist shrines with a visit to the most sacred sight of all: the First McDonald's Store Museum (p233) in Des Plaines.

SMALL-TOWN GETAWAYS & REGIONAL HISTORY

Geneva and **St Charles** (p236), about an hour outside Chicago along Hwy 31, are both popular weekend getaways from Chicago, offering charming small-town atmosphere for city slickers, good antique stores and the former stomping grounds of the area's most notoriously eccentric millionaire. The Illinois & Michigan Corridor, to the south of Chicago, brought the city much of its wealth in the first half of the 19th century, allowing goods to travel from Chicago factories all the way down the Mississippi river. Now a historic corridor, the area boasts plenty of quaint towns to explore.

EVANSTON & NORTH SHORE

A pleasant town 14 miles north of the Loop, Evanston combines stately old houses with a compact and walkable downtown shopping district. Bibliophiles will find one of Chicago's best bookstores in Evanston, **Bookman's Alley**, which feels like a cross between a garage sale and the eccentric English country estate you had always hoped to inherit. Old musical instruments, art and curios are everywhere, and the rooms are a warren of first-editions, new books and used fiction. The bookishness is right in keeping with the city's tone – Evanston is home to **Northwestern University**, one of the Midwest's most prestigious private schools.

Founded in 1851, the university has grown to more than 10,000 students, and is known especially for its top-notch graduate programs in journalism, law and medicine. Northwestern's campus doesn't have quite the fairy-tale feel of its rival, the University of Chicago. Still, wandering through campus can make for a pleasant afternoon. The main campus is just north of Evanston's center (NU's medical, legal and business graduate programs are located in Near North). Once you've exhausted yourself traipsing through campus, go get a mocha at Evanston's best coffeehouse, **Cafe Express**, and continue your explorations with a visit to the **Mitchell Museum of the American Indian**. The museum documents the lives of Native Americans in the Midwest, both past and present. The artwork on display – including pottery, textiles, clothing, baskets and quilts – illustrates aspects of the Indians' daily existence. Special exhibits let visitors handle traditional everyday objects, such as the stone tools used to make cornmeal. You'll never eat a corn tortilla so nonchalantly again – making one is wrist-killing work. Many Native Americans who live in the area take an active role in the displays, temporary exhibitions and lectures that the museum hosts.

Continue north from Evanston and you'll discover some pleasant and gracious neighborhoods that are worth every dollar the residents pay in property taxes. Quiet yet urbane, the North Shore became popular in the late 19th century, when the carriage set had experienced enough of Chicago's fires, riots, tainted water and other big city excitement and beat an eager retreat to the bucolic shores of Lake Michigan. One of the highlights of a visit to the area is the oft-photographed **Baha'i House of Worship** in Wilmette. The glistening white temple is surrounded by lovely gardens and enjoys a dramatic location near the lake. You might have seen the huge white-domed edifice as you flew over Wilmette on the way into Chicago. Completed in 1953 by members of the Baha'i faith, a Persian sect, the temple is one of seven major Baha'i houses of worship worldwide. In summer the abundance of blooming flowers provides a colorful contrast to the white cement.

The flowers of the Baha'i House of Worship, though, look like a discount florist's shop compared to the blooms at the **Chicago Botanic Garden** in tony Glencoe, five miles north of Wilmette. The Chicago Horticultural Society runs the facility, which features thousands of plants in 20 distinctive settings on 385 acres. There is a tram tour of the site, but come on, it's not that big and what better way to explore gardens than on foot? Among the leafy sights you'll see are a prairie garden, an herb garden, a Japanese garden and a rose garden. Frequent demonstrations show you how to try to replicate the gardens at home. Although admission is free, the garden still collects plenty of dough by charging $8.75 for parking. Public transportation is not an easy option.

Hopefully you have your credit card handy for the next town on your northward trek. Gurnee is home to **Six Flags Great America**, a 300-acre amusement park where you can feel your stomach drop and heart palpitate on any number of screamingly fun rides. Don't leave without subjecting yourself to the Superman ride, where patrons 'fly' headfirst through the loops and hairpin turns at 60mph. If your children are reading this right now, you're probably already on the way out the door. But note that anyone less than 54in tall is kept away from the wilder rides. If you have any energy left over, hurl yourself towards the North

Transport

Distance from Chicago Evanston 15 miles; Wilmette 20 miles; Glencoe 25 miles; Gurnee 40 miles.
Direction North.
Travel time 15 min to Evanston; 25 min to Wilmette; 30 min to Glencoe; 45 min to Gurnee.
Car Head north from Chicago on Lake Shore Dr. When it ends, turn right on Sheridan Rd, drive northward, and you're on your way to both Evanston and Wilmette. Glencoe is five miles north of Wilmette. Getting to Gurnee requires a jaunt on Highway 90/94; Six Flags Great America and the Gurnee Mills Mall are both off the Grand Ave exit.
El During rush hour you can ride the CTA Purple Line Evanston Express to Evanston from the Loop. At other times, ride the Red Line to Howard and transfer to a Purple Line local. The Davis Station is in the heart of Evanston. For Wilmette, take the Purple Line to Linden, the final stop. The temple is a short walk east.
Metra Take the Union Pacific North Line from the Richard B Ogilvie Transportation Center in the West Loop to the Davis St stop (for Evanston), the Wilmette stop, or the Glencoe stop.
Bus For Evanston, take bus 147 north from the Loop to the end of the line, and transfer to bus 201.

Shore's final adventure: the **Gurnee Mills Mall**. This over-the-top creation contains nearly 200 'outlet stores,' clearinghouse versions of big-name retailers like the Gap, Abercrombie & Fitch and Sears. There's also a Bass Pro Shops Outdoor World, where you practice your aim on the store's indoor shooting range. Chartered buses disgorge shoppers at the mall from all over the state, and the scene is a little overwhelming, even for the most hard-core shopper. As a field trip into the heart of Middle America, though, it ranks right up there with the Woodfield Mall (below), and provides some amazing insights on our shopping-obsessed culture.

Sights & Information

Bookman's Alley (☎ 847-869-6999; 1712 Sherman Ave; ⊙ noon-7pm Mon, noon-8pm Tue-Wed, noon-6pm, Fri-Sun)

Northwestern University (Map p230; ☎ 847-491-7271; www.northwestern.edu)

Mitchell Museum of the American Indian (☎ 847-475-1030; www.mitchellmuseum.org; Kendall College, 2600 Central Park Ave, Evanston; adult/student/child, $5/2.50/2.50; ⊙ 10am-5pm Tue-Sat, Thu to 8pm, noon-4pm Sun)

Baha'i House of Worship (☎ 847-853-2300; 100 Linden Ave, Wilmette; admission free; ⊙ 10am-10pm, shorter hours in winter)

Chicago Botanic Garden (Map p230; ☎ 847-835-5440; www.chicago-botanic.org; 1000 Lake-Cook Rd, Glencoe; admission free, parking $8.75; ⊙ dawn-dusk)

Six Flags Great America (Map p230; ☎ 847-249-1776; www.sixflags.com; off I-94 at Grand Ave, Gurnee; adult/senior/child/under 3yrs $40/30/30/free; ⊙ call ahead for hours)

Gurnee Mills Mall (☎ 847-263-7500; west of I-94 at the Grand Ave exit, Gurnee; ⊙ 9am-9pm)

Eating

Cafe Express (☎ 847-328-7940; 500 Main St, Evanston) Strong coffee, wrap-around windows and sidewalk seating make this café a good stopover.

DES PLAINES, SCHAUMBURG & NORTHWEST SUBURBS

Your journey into the northwestern reaches of the Chicago suburbs starts, fittingly, at a first – the **First McDonald's Store Museum**, in Des Plaines. This oddball recreation of the first outlet fast-food magnate Ray Kroc built on the spot back in 1955 features male mannequins dressed up in the dark-blue outfits that were apparently de rigueur for the still-embryonic fast-food industry at the time. You'll see a video presentation and lots of mementos and original equipment. As the book *Fast Food Nation* proved, McDonald's has a huge effect on the global economy. From the effort they put into this dusty museum, though, you'd think the store had never made it out of the Chicago suburbs. Still, it's fun in a kitschy sort of way.

In nearby chain-filled Schaumburg is the **Woodfield Mall**, where the cheery motto is 'Shop happily ever after.' Boasting that it contains the largest amount of retail space in the world (the Mall of America, in suburban Minneapolis, is bigger but much of its space is devoted to an amusement park), Woodfield features a municipality's-worth of stores, scores of restaurants, big department stores and an ocean of a parking lot. It's a teenagers' vision of heaven, and it's also one of the biggest tourist draws in the state of Illinois.

Further out along Highway 90, the **Illinois Railway Museum** is one of the best of its kind in the US. The grounds of the museum boast more than 200 acres full of historic trains that

Transport

Distance from Chicago Des Plaines 20 miles, Schaumburg 32 miles, Volo Bog 33 miles.
Direction Northwest.
Travel time 25 min to Des Plaines, 36 min to Schaumburg, 35 min to Volo Bog.
Car Des Plaines lies 17 miles northwest of the Loop off I-294, Schaumburg and the Woodfield Mall are located at the junction of the Northwest Tollway (I-90) and I-290. To get to the railway museum, the exit for US Hwy 20 and Marengo off the Northwest Tollway (I-90), then drive north for 4½ miles to Union and follow signs.
Metra For Des Plaines, take the Union Pacific Northwest Line from the Ogilvie Transportation Center in the Loop to the Des Plaines station; for Schaumburg, take the Milwaukee District West Line from Union Station to Schaumburg.

date from the mid-1800s to the present. Models on display include steam, diesel and electric locomotives, plus passenger and freight cars, many of which are protected by large sheds. This is ground zero for the state's train nerds, and part of the fun is just watching the older patrons and museum volunteers giddily discussing the intricacies of each engine, coupler and car.

Sights & Information

First McDonald's Store Museum (☎ 847-297-5022; 400 N Lee St, Des Plaines; ☺ call for hours)

Woodfield Mall (☎ 847-330-1537; www.shopwoodfield.com; Golf Rd, at Route 53, Schaumburg; ☺ 10am-9pm Mon-Fri, 10am-9pm Sat, 11am-6pm, Sun)

Illinois Railway Museum (Map p230; ☎ 815-923-4000; www.irm.org; 1712 Sherman Ave; admission varies by season; ☺ call for hours and steam train schedule)

Detour: Volo Bog State Natural Area

'Malls...fast food....greasy trains,' you say. 'Where's the nature?' The answer is found just off Highway 12 at the **Volo Bog State Natural Area**. The bog, left over from glacial melt-off about 12,000 years ago, has an open-water center and no true bottom (the bog turns to mushy peat about 50ft down). Among the plants and animals that make their home in this anomalous environment are minks, great blue and green-backed herons, sandhill cranes, orchids, sphagnum moss and the coolest-sounding plant ever – the bog buckbean. A short nature trail winds through the area, and on weekends experts are on hand to get to the bottom of your boggy questions.

To get here, take I-94 north from Chicago to Route 120. Turn west on 120 and drive until you turn north onto Hwy 12. Two miles later, turn left on Brandenburg Rd. The park is 1.25 miles ahead.

OAK PARK, BROOKFIELD ZOO & MORTON ARBORETUM

Oak Park is the place to go if you admire the designs of Frank Lloyd Wright. For 10 years – from 1889 until 1908, when he took a surprise trip to Europe (see the boxed text p235) – Wright worked and lived in a studio in Oak Park. Strolling the streets of this pleasant old town is like stepping back into one of those 1950s TV sitcoms, with all its bland charm. Native son Ernest Hemingway was unmoved, though – he called Oak Park a 'village of wide lawns and narrow minds.'

Transport

Distance from Chicago Oak Park 8 miles; Brookfield Zoo 14 miles; Morton Arboretum 25 miles.
Direction West.
Travel time 15 min to Oak Park; 25 min to Brookfield Zoo; 30 min to Morton Arboretum.
Car Take I-290 west, exiting north on Harlem Ave; take Harlem north to Lake St and turn right. For the zoo, go west on the Eisenhower Expressway (I-290) to the 1st Ave exit, then south to 31st and follow the signs. The arboretum is 25 miles west of Chicago on Route 53, just north of I-88.
El To get to Oak Park, take the Green Line to Oak Park.
Metra Union Pacific West Line has an Oak Park stop; the Brookfield zoo is reachable via the Burlington Northern Line from the loop (exit at the Hollywood stop).
Bus 72 skirts the northern border of Oak Park.

To see some examples of Wright's work, which dots the town, ask for the architectural walking-tour map at the **Oak Park Visitors Center**. The helpful, plain-talking volunteers provide a wide variety of information.

Staff at the **Frank Lloyd Wright Home & Studio** offer tours of the complex, the neighborhood and some other Wright-designed homes. Self-guided walking tours, including audio tours, are also available.

The studio is a fascinating place, filled with the details that made Wright's style distinctive. Note how he molded plaster to look like bronze and stained cheap pine to look like rare hardwood. Always in financial trouble, spendthrift Wright was adept at making the ordinary seem extraordinary. The studio's bookstore sells mountains of Wright-related paraphernalia. Unfortunately, all the books seem to have been written by supplicants, sycophants and adoring relatives.

One block away, the **Moore House** is Wright's bizarre interpretation of an English manor house that was first built in 1895. In later years of his life, Wright called the house 'repugnant' and said he had only taken the commission originally because he needed the money. He claimed that he walked out of his way to avoid passing it.

Oak Park honors another famous local – despite the crack about the lawns – at the **Ernest Hemingway Museum**. The exhibits begin with his middle-class Oak Park background and his innocent years before he went off to find adventure. Other displays follow the rest of his life, focusing on his writings in Spain and during WWII. Admission includes admittance to **Hemingway's Birthplace**, where you can see his first room. 'Papa' was born here in 1899 in the home of his maternal grandparents.

To see the wide variety of animals Hemingway likely shot and killed on some of his famed hunting expeditions, head from Oak Park southwest to the **Brookfield Zoo**. With 2700 animals and 215 acres, Brookfield Zoo can easily sustain a day's wanderings. More extensive than the free Lincoln Park Zoo in Chicago, the zoo features dolphin shows, African- and Australian-themed exhibits, several primate areas, a kids' zoo and a ton more.

Because most visitors use the north gate and tend to stop at the nearby attractions first, you can avoid some of the crowds by starting in the southern part of the zoo and working back north.

Tree-lovers traumatized by the arboreal grazing going on at the zoo can view their favorite specimens unmolested at the **Morton Arboretum**, 15 miles west. A private nature preserve on more than 1700 acres, the Morton Arboretum combines a wide variety of terrain and trees. The sights range from manicured shrubs to special plantings of trees not native to the area, to long stretches of local forest and prairie. Many trees are marked with small informational signs. Twenty-five miles of trails wind through the arboretum, but a realistic circular path covering most of the preserve runs for 6 to 7 miles. Plan your course using the map you receive at the entrance. Parts of the arboretum are quite hilly, with paths that feel pleasantly rural. However, large sections of the park seem to have been designed with drivers, rather than walkers, in mind. Many people tour the entire location without once leaving their car, a situation befitting the park's suburban location. If you find your way to the middle of the arboretum, you'll enjoy the relative quiet there.

'He Was Not Morally Up to Snuff'

Oak Park might boast a good portion of Frank Lloyd Wright's legacy, but you can't accuse locals of glossing over his checkered reputation. That Wright was 'not morally up to snuff' was an observation made by a woman who worked in Oak Park's official visitor information center. She made a variety of cutting comments about the acerbic and philandering Wright, who once ran off to Europe with Mamah Borthwick Cheney, the wife of a client, instead of going home to his own wife and six kids at his Oak Park studio.

Born in Wisconsin in 1867 and always a prodigy, Wright went to Chicago in 1887 to work for Louis Sullivan as a drafter. But in 1893 that relationship ended when Sullivan found out that Wright was moonlighting and not cutting the firm in on his profits.

After his European escapade in 1908, Wright worked from studios on a Wisconsin farm, where he lived with Cheney although he was still married to his first wife. Public condemnation was harsh. On Christmas Day in 1911, Wright held a press conference to explain his infidelity, proclaiming that he, as a 'thinking man,' did not have to follow the rules of 'the ordinary man.'

In 1914, a deranged servant murdered Cheney. Wright found consolation with Miriam Noel, who had sent him a letter of sympathy. They married in 1923 and divorced in 1927. In 1928 Wright married his third and final wife, Olga Hinzenberg, with whom he had had a child in 1925.

Wright spent most of his later years working at his home in the Arizona desert, where he died in 1959 at the age of 90. His personal life notwithstanding, Wright was already rightfully recognized as the most original of all American architects when he died.

On the same day that the visitor center staffer passed moral judgment, a touring architect outside the Moore House offered the following anecdote about his own run-in with the tart-tongued Wright: 'I was 19 and going to a small architecture school back east. Wright came and spoke. Afterwards I tried to speak to him because I admired him. He looked at me and said, "You'll never be an architect, because you go to school in a shoe factory." Then he hit me with his cane and drove away.'

Sights & Information

Oak Park Visitors Center (☎ 708-848-1500; 158 N Forest Ave, Oak Park; 🕙 10am-5pm)

Frank Lloyd Wright Home & Studio (☎ 708-848-1976; www.wrightplus.org; 951 Chicago Ave, Oak Park; adult/child $9/7; 🕙 tours Mon-Fri 11am, 1pm, 3pm, more frequently Sat & Sun)

Moore House (333 N Forest Ave, Oak Park)

Ernest Hemingway Museum (☎ 708-848-2222; www.ehfop.org; 200 N Oak Park Ave, Oak Park; adult/senior/child $7/5.50/5.50; 🕙 Sun-Fri 1pm-5pm, Sat 10am-5pm)

Hemingway's Birthplace (339 N Oak Park Ave, Oak Park)

Brookfield Zoo (Map p230; ☎ 708-485-0263; www.brookfieldzoo.org; 8400 W 31st St, Brookfield; adult/senior/child $8/4/4; 🕙 9:30am-6pm, shorter hours Sep-May)

Morton Arboretum (Map p230; ☎ 630-719-2400; www.mortonarb.org; $7 per car, $3 on Wed; 🕙 7am-5pm, until 7pm Apr-Oct)

Brookfield Zoo aquarium

GENEVA & ST CHARLES

The two towns of Geneva and St Charles on the Fox River are major weekend destinations. Both Geneva and St Charles feature nicely restored downtowns with a plethora of antique shops. The **Geneva Chamber of Commerce** and the **St Charles Convention & Visitors Bureau** can provide lists of the ever-growing number of restaurants and B&Bs.

Geneva, despite its hour-out location, has become a commuter city for Chicago-bound workers, thanks to the Metra train line. One hundred years ago, those rails were new in town, laid by hardy Swedes who ended up settling in Geneva. In 1895, half of Geneva's population spoke Swedish as their first language.

The most famous of all Genevans, though, was Colonel George Fabyan, an eccentric millionaire who bought a farm outside Geneva in 1905 with his wife, and built a kind of wacky empire there. The grounds came to be known as Riverbank, and over time the sprawling farmland grew to include a zoo, a Dutch windmill, 18,000 chickens (yep, 18,000), a lighthouse (for disoriented mariners on their way to Atlantic ports, apparently), formal gardens and a Frank Lloyd Wright–redesigned farmhouse.

The grounds were a curiosity, but Riverbank soon became better known as a testing ground for the Colonel's myriad theories and ideas on everything from trench warfare to levitation to cryptology. Fabyan was particularly interested in the latter, and would hire researchers to come live at Riverbank and work on his pet projects. In one of Riverbank's finer episodes, Fabyan got a Cook County judge to rule in 1916 that all of Shakespeare's works had been written by Francis Bacon (based on encrypted messages deciphered by Fabyan's research team).

Not everything going on at Riverbank was quite so fantastical, though, and the cryptology teams there were essential in cracking enemy codes during WWI. The acoustical studies begun by Fabyan also ended up blossoming into one of the foremost research institutions dedicated to sound in the country.

Transport

Distance from Chicago Geneva 45 miles; St Charles 43 miles.
Direction West.
Travel time 1 hr to Geneva; 55 min to St Charles
Car Take I-90 W to Hwy 31 S.
Metra Geneva is accessible via the Union Pacific West Line from the Ogilvie Transportation Center in the Loop.

The area now is the **Fabyan Forest Preserve**, and the sculpture-decorated grounds are open to the public. The Frank Lloyd Wright–redesigned home houses the **Fabyan Villa Museum**, where you can see some mementos and papers from the Colonel's life.

Over in St Charles, the **Kane County Flea Market** draws hundreds of dealers selling everything from junk to books to rare curios.

Sights & Information

Geneva Chamber of Commerce (☎ 630-232-6060; www.genevachamber.com; 8 S Third St; ☼ 9am-4:30pm Mon-Fri)

St Charles Convention & Visitors Bureau (☎ 630-377-6161; www.visitstcharles.com; 311 N Second St)

Fabyan Forest Preserve (☎ 630-232-2631; off Route 31 south of Geneva; ☼ dawn-dusk)

Fabyan Villa Museum (☎ 630-232-4811; in Fabyan Forest Preserve; ☼ call ahead for hours)

Kane County Flea Market (☎ 630-377-2252; www.kane countyfleamarket.com; 525 S Randall Rd; ☼ noon-5pm Sat, 7am-5pm Sun 1st weekend every month)

ILLINOIS & MICHIGAN CANAL CORRIDOR

Dubbed a National Heritage Corridor, the Illinois & Michigan Canal Corridor is a linear park run by the National Park Service which encompasses 41 towns, 11 state parks and scores of historic sites. The I&M Canal resulted from merchants' desire for a waterway that linked the Mississippi River basin with the Great Lakes and made it possible to ship goods by boat from the eastern US to New Orleans and on to the Caribbean. In 1836 the first shovelful of dirt was turned, and during the next 12 years, thousands of immigrants, primarily Irish, were lured to Chicago to work on the 96-mile course.

After the canal opened in 1848, the constant flow of goods through Chicago propelled the city's economic development. In 1900 the I&M Canal was supplemented by the much deeper Chicago Sanitary & Ship Canal, a much more navigable waterway that, sadly, became Chicago's de facto drainpipe.

Competition from railroads and other waterways caused the I&M Canal to molder for most of the 20th century. The establishment of the park in 1984 has spurred restoration and development of the I&M Canal's remaining sites and of some of the historic towns along the route.

The Heritage Corridor driving route can be hard to follow, and the sites are greatly dispersed. It's a good idea to get some of the available free maps in advance so you can plan your itinerary – the trip can easily fill a day. One bonus – most sites are free.

The **Heritage Corridor Visitors Bureau** in Joliet offers information on the parks as well as food and lodging details for the region.

The **Illinois & Michigan Canal Heritage Corridor Commission** in Lockport is the source for all the excellent National Park Service brochures and maps of the corridor. The one devoted to archaeology is especially good. The staff here also know when various information centers along the canal are open, and can tell you about the I&M Canal State Trail. The

Transport

Distance from Chicago Lockport is 34 miles from Chicago, and the corridor stretches 65 miles southwest from there.

Direction Southwest.

Travel time 45 min to Lockport, 90 min from Lockport (start point) to LaSalle (end point).

Car To reach Lockport, take I-55 S to Hwy 53 S, eventually turning left onto Hwy 7. The towns and sites along the I&M Corridor roughly follow Hwy 57, but there are exceptions. Pick up a map at one of the visitor centers.

Metra Lockport is located on the Metra Heritage Corridor Line.

61-mile path follows the canal and makes an ideal route for biking, hiking and snowmobiling. You can also wilderness camp along the length of the canal. For many activities, such as snowmobiling and camping, advance registration is required at one of three information centers: **Gebhard Woods State Park**, **Channahon Access** and **Buffalo Rock State Park**. The centers also have information about the portions of the canal suitable for canoeing. Call for details.

A good place to start the tour of the canal corridor is the town of Lockport, 33 miles southwest of Chicago on Hwy 171, a historic place that's been bypassed by most of the development that has afflicted much-larger Joliet, to its south. The center of Lockport, which is on the National Register of Historic Places, includes the **I&M Canal Museum**, which is housed in the original 1837 home of the canal commissioners. It contains all the maps and brochures you didn't get in advance, as well as displays about life along the waterway when more flowed by than just the odd fallen leaf. The surviving Lock No 1 is the highlight of the 2½-mile Gaylord Donnelley Canal Trail, which follows the canal through town and passes several exhibits along the way.

Further down the canal, the Kankakee and Des Plaines Rivers join near Morris, home to the **Goose Lake Prairie State Natural Area**, which contains the largest surviving portion of tall-grass prairie in Illinois. The plants, which early pioneers likened to an ocean of color, grew up to 10 or more feet in height and blossomed in waves through the growing season; what little survives is still worth seeing. A visitor center explains the unique ecology of the prairie, and on weekends a naturalist is usually around to answer questions.

Viewing platform in Starved Rock State Park

Seneca, the next town on the route, is home to the Seneca Grain Elevator, a fascinating affair that towers over the canal, which is little more than a muddy ditch here. Completed in 1862, the 65ft building is one of the oldest survivors from the early grain industry. Check with the Heritage Corridor Commission for hours, and be sure to get a copy of the heavily illustrated Park Service brochure that explains the workings of the place. Seneca is 65 miles from Chicago, on Route 6 off I-80.

Located off Hwy 178, the charming small town of Utica has found itself a profitable place near the end of the I&M Canal zone and across the river from Starved Rock State Park. It's a good place to stroll or to stay if you're planning a visit to either Starved Rock or Matthiessen State Park. In Utica, the **LaSalle County Museum** features displays of items used by the people who lived and worked near the I&M Canal.

One of the most popular parks in Illinois, **Starved Rock State Park** features more than 2600 acres of wooded bluffs, with 18 canyons that were carved through the limestone during the last ice age. After heavy rains a waterfall cascades down the head of each canyon.

According to legend, a band of Illinois Native Americans got trapped atop the park's 130-foot sandstone butte during a battle with the Ottawa and starved to death – hence the park name. Today the highest bluff here offers spectacular views. Some 15 miles of hiking trails wander through the park, and the Illinois River and canyon waterways provide opportunities for paddled canoe jaunts. You can also take guided nature tours.

The park **visitor center** offers full information on the many rental opportunities – including canoes, horses, bikes and skis – as well as the hiking trails and other park features. Although the park gets very crowded on summer weekends, you can always leave the throngs behind by hiking beyond Wildcat Canyon, which is less than a mile east of the main parking area. Less than a mile from this point is La Salle Canyon, where a waterfall turns into a glistening ice fall in the winter.

The park has become a popular spot for camping, with 133 electrified sites. The **Starved Rock Lodge**, right in the park, manages to be rustic and modern at the same time. If you'd like to stay in Utica, try the **Starved Rock Inn**.

And if the crowds at Starved Rock are too much, try **Matthiessen State Park**, just across Hwy 178. It features dramatic limestone cliffs and chasms formed by water runoff to the river. Hiking, skiing and equestrian trails meander through the park.

Sights & Information

Heritage Corridor Visitors Bureau (☎ 815-727-2323, 800-926-2262; www.heritagecorridorcvb.com; 81 N Chicago St, Joliet; ⏰ 9am-5pm Mon-Fri)

Illinois & Michigan Canal Heritage Corridor Commission (☎ 815-588-1100; www.canalcor.org; 200 W Eighth St, Lockport; ⏰ 9am-5pm Mon-Fri)

Gebhard Woods State Park (Map p230; ☎ 815-942-0796; 401 Ottawa St, Morris)

Channahon Access (Map p230; ☎ 815-467-4271; PO Box 54, Channahon)

Buffalo Rock State Park (Map p230; ☎ 815-433-2224; PO Box 2034, Ottawa)

I&M Canal Museum (☎ 815-838-5080; 803 S State St; admission free; ⏰ 1pm-4:30pm)

Goose Lake Prairie State Natural Area (Map p230; ☎ 815-942-2899; 5010 N Jugtown Rd; ⏰ dawn-dusk)

LaSalle County Museum Map p230; ☎ 815-667-4861; www.lasallecountymuseum.org; Mill St at Canal St;

adult/child $1/0.50; ⏰ 10am-4pm Wed-Fri, noon-4pm Sat & Sun, shorter hours Sep-May)

Starved Rock State Park & Visitor Center (Map p230; ☎ 815-667-4906, PO Box 509; admission free; ⏰ visitor center 8am-8pm, shorter hours Sep-May)

Matthiessen State Park (Map p230; ☎ 815-667-4868; PO Box 509, Utica)

Sleeping

Starved Rock Inn (☎ 815-667-4238; at Routes 6 and 178; r $60) The eight rooms at this old-fashioned place are decorated with handmade wood furnishings.

Starved Rock State Park Campgrounds (☎ 815-667-4906; sites $11) The 133 sites here come with electrical hook-ups.

Starved Rock Lodge (☎ 815-667-4211, 800-868-7625; Routes 178 and 71; r & cabins from $90) This rustic place has an indoor pool.

INDIANA DUNES

The Indiana Dunes are easily the most scenic part of the state. The prevailing winds of Lake Michigan have created more than 20 miles of sandy beaches and dunes here. On a windy day you can place an obstacle on the beach and watch a dune form behind it. Behind the sands, large areas of woods and wetlands have become major wildlife habitats.

Preserving the dunes, which today stretch about 21 miles east from Gary to Michigan City, has always been a struggle. The occasional vast and stinky steel mill amid the bucolic beauty shows which way the struggle has frequently gone. Initial

Transport

Distance from Chicago 50 miles.
Direction Southeast.
Travel time 75 min.
Car Take I-90 through Gary to Hwy 12, most sites are located off Hwy 12.
Metra South Shore Line trains depart frequently from Randolph St Station in the Loop, offering access to Ogden Dunes, Dune Park, Beverly Shores and the state park.

attempts to designate the area as a national park in 1913 flopped under pressure from industry. The state of Indiana did manage to wrest some territory away from hungry industrialists in 1923, with the creation of **Indiana Dunes State Park** near Chesterton. In the 1950s Bethlehem Steel's construction of what was then the world's largest steel mill, on prime dunes at Burns Harbor, solidified public pressure to save the remaining stretches. Activist Dorothy Buell and Illinois Senator Paul Douglas led the fight, which resulted in the creation of the Indiana Dunes National Lakeshore in 1966. In the decades since, the designation has also effectively saved the dunes from full-scale real estate development. The areas where such development occurred in the 1950s and early '60s give some idea of the horrors that could have spread.

Today the entire area attracts huge crowds in summer months, when people from Chicago to South Bend flock to the shores for good swimming and general frivolity. Most don't take the time to explore the area's diverse natural wonders, but hikes offer escape from the crowds. Swimming is allowed anywhere along the national lakeshore. On busy days, a short hike away from the folks clogging up a developed beach will yield an almost deserted strand. Other times of year, the lake winds and pervasive desolation make the dunes a moody and memorable experience. You may well hear the low hum of the 'singing sands,' an unusual sound caused by the zillions of grains of sand hitting each other in the wind.

A good place to start your trip is the **Dorothy Buell Memorial Visitor Center**. The helpful center features a section on the park's flora and fauna. The free, official map is up to the usual excellent park-service standards. From the visitors center, it's time to hit the beaches. Of the developed beaches, Central Beach is a good place to escape the crowds. Mt Baldy Beach boasts the highest dunes, with namesake Mt Baldy offering the best views all the way to Chicago from its 120ft peak. Don't look east or you'll see the environmental travesty of downtown Michigan City's coal-powered electric plant and huge cooling tower. The closest beach to Michigan City, this is by far the busiest of the lot. West Beach is one of the best beaches because it draws fewer crowds than the others and features a number of nature hikes and trails. It's also the only beach with an on-duty lifeguard.

If you'd rather be on your feet than flat on your back on the sand, the park service has done a good job of developing hiking trails through a range of terrain and environments. One good trail begins at the **Bailly/Chellberg Visitor Center**, a major site that's some distance from the beaches. The trail winds through the forest, whose diversity continues to astound botanists. Among the plants growing here are dogwood, Arctic berries and even cactus. The 1¾-mile trail passes restored log cabins from the 1820s and a farm built by Swedes in the 1870s.

The nicely varied 4-mile walk at Cowles Bog Trail combines marsh and dunes. The Miller Woods Trail passes dunes, woods and ponds, plus the **Paul H Douglas Center for Environmental Education**, which offers day programs. At West Beach the Long Lake Trail is a classic wetlands walk around an inland lake.

Much of the national park area is good for cycling, although the traffic and the narrow shoulders on Hwy 12 can make that road dangerous. However, the Calumet Bike Trail runs west from near Michigan City almost to the Chellberg Farm, in the middle of the national lakeshore. Cross-country skiing is popular in the inland areas, especially along the trails described above.

In the heart of the dunes, **Indiana Dunes State Park** has more amenities, but is also more regulated (and crowded). Away from its mobbed beaches, the park features many secluded natural areas. In winter cross-country skiing is very popular; a ski rental facility operates near Wilson shelter. In summer, the hiking can be excellent. Some highlights among the numbered trails include Trail 2, which is good for spring flowers and ferns and popular with cross-country skiers, Trail 4, which passes through dunes that are in the process of being colonized by black oak trees, and Trail 8, which surmounts three of the highest dunes and offers great views as a reward

Sights & Information

Dorothy Buell Memorial Visitor Center (Map p230; ☎ 219-926-7561 ext 225; www.nps.gov/indu; Kemil Rd, just off Hwy 12, near the Beverly Shores rail station; ☘ 8am-5pm)

Paul H Douglas Center for Environmental Education (☎ 219-926-7561 ext 245; ☘ 10am-4pm Mon-Fri)

Bailly/Chellberg Visitor Center (Map p230; ☎ 219-926-7561 ext 218; Mineral Springs Rd, south of Hwy 12 ☘ 11am-4:30pm, Sat & Sun only Sep-May)

Indiana Dunes State Park (Map p230; ☎ 219-926-1952, 1600 North 25 E in Chesterton; $5 per car; ☘ beaches open 9am-sunset , park open 7am-11pm, shorter hours Sep-May)

Directory

Directory

TRANSPORT
AIRLINES

Between O'Hare and Midway (below), you'll likely find a way to get anywhere in the US and abroad. Airlines flying into and out of Chicago include the following:

Aer Lingus (☎ 800-474-7424; www.aerlingus.ie)

Aeromexico (☎ 800-237-6639; www.aeromexico.com)

Air Canada (☎ 888-247-2262; www.aircanada.ca)

Air France (☎ 800-237-2747; www.airfrance.com)

Air-India (☎ 800-221-6000; www.airindia.com)

Air Jamaica (☎ 800-523-5585; www.airjamaica.com)

Air New Zealand (☎ 800-262-2468; www.airnz.co.nz)

AirTran Airways (☎ 800-247-8726; www.airtran.com)

Alaska Airlines (☎ 800-252-7522; www.alaskair.com)

Alitalia (☎ 800-223-5730; www.alitaliausa.com)

America West Airlines (☎ 800-247-5692; www.americawest.com)

American Airlines (☎ 800-433-7300; www.aa.com)

ATA (American Trans Air; ☎ 800-883-5228; www.ata.com)

Austrian Airlines (☎ 800-843-0002; www.austrianair.com)

Bangkok Airways (☎ 312-222-9833; www.bangkokair.com)

BMI (British Midland Airways; ☎ 800-788-0555; www.flybmi.com)

British Airways (☎ 800-247-9297; www.britishairways.com)

Cathay Pacific Airways (☎ 733-686-0808; www.cathaypacific.com)

China Southern Airlines (☎ 773-601-8868; www.cs-air.com/en)

Continental Airlines (☎ 800-523-3273; www.continental.com)

Delta Airlines (☎ 800-325-1999; www.delta-air.com)

El Al Israel Airlines (☎ 800-223-6700; www.elal.co.il)

Finnair (☎ 800-950-5000; www.finnair.com)

Frontier Airlines (☎ 800-432-1359; www.frontierairlines.com)

Iberia Airlines (☎ 800-772-4642; www.iberia.com)

Japan Airlines (☎ 800-525-3663; www.jal.com)

KLM Royal Dutch Airlines (☎ 773-462-9428; www.klm.com)

Korean Air (☎ 800-438-5000; www.koreanair.com)

Kuwait Air (☎ 800-458-9248; www.kuwait-airways.com)

Lufthansa (☎ 800-645-3880; www.lufthansa.com)

Mexicana Airlines (☎ 800-531-7921; www.mexicana.com)

Northwest Airlines (☎ 800-447-4747; www.nwa.com)

Pan Am (☎ 800-359-7262; www.flypanam.com)

Qantas Airways (☎ 800-227-4500; www.qantas.com)

Singapore Airlines (☎ 800-742-3333; www.singaporeair.com)

South African Airways (☎ 800-722-9675; www.flysaa.com)

Southwest Airlines (☎ 800-435-9792; www.iflyswa.com)

Spirit Airlines (☎ 800-772-7117; www.spiritair.com)

Sun Country Airlines (☎ 800-359-6786; www.suncountry.com)

Swiss International Air Lines (☎ 877-359-7947; www.swiss.com)

United Airlines (☎ 800-822-2746; www.ual.com)

US Airways (☎ 800-943-5436; www.usair.com)

Virgin Atlantic (☎ 800-862-8621; www.virgin-atlantic.com)

Flights

In addition to the airline companies' own sites, which often offer Internet-only deals, a number of third-party websites can be helpful in finding you discounts on flights.

- www.cheaptickets.com
- www.expedia.com
- www.go-today.com
- www.hotwire.com
- www.orbitz.com
- www.priceline.com
- www.site59.com
- www.smarterliving.com
- www.travelocity.com
- www.travelzoo.com

If you're trying to work out a complex itinerary or would like someone to handle the bookings for you, try **STA Travel** (Map pp282–3; ☎ 312-786-9050; www.statravel.com; 429 S Dearborn St), which has another branch in the **Gold Coast** (Map pp278–9; ☎ 312-951-0585; 1160 N State).

AIRPORTS

Chicago is served by two main airports. O'Hare International (ORD) is the world's busiest hub and located 17 miles northwest of the city. Midway (MID) is smaller and located 10 miles to the south of the city center.

O'Hare

O'Hare's four terminals bustle day and night. Terminal 1, designed by architect Helmut Jahn is home to United and Lufthansa. Terminal 5 is the international terminal. Terminal 4 is no longer used.

For general airport info call ☎ 773-686-2200. You'll find ATMs and phones (including TTY phones) available in every terminal. Airport information and customer-service counters are in Terminals 1, 3 and 5. The Children's Museum on Navy Pier (p68) runs an exhibit space for children 12 and under in Terminal 2. **Currency exchanges** (☎ 773-462-9973; ☽ 8am-8pm Mon-Fri) are located in Terminals 3 and 5. Police kiosks/lost-and-found counters can be found on the upper levels of all terminals. The **Travelers and Immigrants Aid Office** (☎ 773-894-2427; ☽ 8:30am-9pm Mon-Fri, 10am-9pm Sat & Sun) is on the lower level of Terminal 2. It provides information, directions and special assistance to travelers.

For medical help, the University of Illinois at Chicago's Medical Center runs a **clinic** (☎ 773-894-5100) on the upper level of Terminal 2. There's also a **post office** (☎ 773-686-0119; ☽ 7am-7pm Mon-Fri) on the upper level of Terminal 2. If you're looking to hook into email or other business services, **Laptop Lane** (☎ 773-894-3100) in Terminal 1 offers faxing, printing and Internet access.

Each terminal has one taxi stand outside the baggage claim area; you may have to line up. The fare to the Near North and Loop runs $35 to $40, depending on tip (usually about 10% to 15%) and traffic (taxi meters keep running even when the car is at a standstill). If there are other travelers heading downtown, it may make sense to share a cab. Inform the driver you want to share the cab before you start off.

The CTA offers 24-hour train service on the Blue Line to and from the Loop. Unfortunately, the O'Hare station is buried under the world's largest parking garage. Finding it can be akin to navigating a maze – directional signs are variously marked as 'CTA,' 'Rapid Transit' and 'Trains to City.' Unless you are staying right in the Loop, you will have to transfer to

another El or bus to complete your journey. For recommendations on which one to take, ask your hotel when you reserve your room. A good alternative is to ride the El as close as you can get to your hotel and then take a taxi for the final few blocks. Again, ask your hotel or consult the neighborhood map in this book to see which El stop is closest to your hotel.

As for shuttle vans, **Airport Express** (☎ 312-454-7800, 800-654-7871; www.airportexpress.com) has a monopoly on services between the airport and hotels in the Loop and Near North. The fare is $17.50 per person, plus the usual 10% to 15% tip. Once downtown, you may ride around while others are dropped off before you. You also may have to wait until the van is full before you leave the airport. If there are two or more of you, take a cab – it's immediate, direct and cheaper per person. If you're heading directly to the Midway airport, you can take the **Omega Shuttle** (☎ 773-483-6634) for $17 per person.

For trips further afield, regional bus companies serve southern Wisconsin, suburban Illinois and northwest Indiana from the bus/shuttle center, installed in the ground level of the central parking garage. Use the tunnels under the Hilton Hotel to get there from Terminals 1, 2 and 3. Terminal 5, the international terminal, has its own pickup area.

If you're renting a car, take I-190 east from the airport to I-90 east into the Loop.

Midway

A recent renovation has turned formerly dowdy Midway into a modern, attractive airport with three concourses. You'll enter and exit through the magnificent New Terminal, home to almost all of the airport's services and amenities. Midway is mostly known as a home to cut-rate carriers such as Southwest and ATA.

Airport Information/Customer Service (☎ 773-838-0600), airport police, ATMs and Travelers Aid are located in the New Terminal building. Additionally, there is a helpful City Information Center in the baggage claim area of the new terminal building offering transportation and accommodations information.

Follow the signs to ground transportations to catch a taxi. The taxis are available on a first-come, first-served basis, and you can split the costs by sharing a ride. Tell the driver you'd like to ride-share before heading off. Costs are based on the meter (there are no flat rate rides), and will likely run about $20 plus tip into the Loop.

You can take the CTA Orange Line from Midway to the Loop. A one-way ride will cost you $1.50; if you need to transfer to another El line during your ride (which is likely), it will cost an extra $0.30. To reach the CTA station, follow the signs from the New Terminal.

The same shuttle-van operators that service O'Hare (above), also work out of Midway. A ride with Continental Airport Express from Midway to the Loop costs $12.50 per person. For shuttle rides between Midway and O'Hare airports use the Omega Shuttle (☎ 773-483-6634; $17 per person).

If you're renting a car at the airport, take S Cicero Ave north to I-55N. You can tune in to the airport radio station – 800 AM – for traffic and airport parking updates.

Airport Security

Since the September 11, 2001 terrorist attacks, airport security in the US has adopted a zero-tolerance policy for even the slightest infractions of airport rules. These rules mean confiscations of tiny pocketknives and other entirely innocuous-seeming (but potentially malicious) instruments are routine at the X-ray detectors: plan on checking any belongings that might be construed as threatening. Also, know that if the Transportation Safety Administration (www.tsa.gov) decides to screen your checked luggage and you have a lock on it, they will simply break off the lock. Visit their website for more information.

Expect to have to take off your shoes and belt as you go through the metal detectors, and know that the people clumsily waving those wands over you are now federal employees; however inept they may seem at times, they do carry the weight of the government and can cause you no end of delays if angered.

BICYCLE

Bikes can be rented for about $35 per day. Try the following:

Bike Chicago (Map pp280–1; ☎ 312-595-9600; www.bikechicago.com; Navy Pier; bus 66)

On The Route (Map pp272–3; ☎ 773-477-5066; www.ontheroute.com; 3146 N Lincoln Ave; Red, Brown Line to Belmont)

Bicycles on the El & Buses

Bikes are allowed on all CTA trains, save for during high-use commuter hours (7-9am and 4-6pm Mon-Fri). When entering the station, tell the customer service assistant you are there with your bike, and look for the handicapped-accessible swing gate. Go through it, depositing your bike on the other side, and then return through the same gate, running your transit card through the scanner-turnstile. If there is no swing gate, the customer service person will open a gate for you. To get to the platform, use elevators when possible. Only two bikes are allowed per train car.

Many CTA buses are equipped with bike racks on the front. These racks accommodate two bikes at a time, and there is no extra cost associated with using them. Tell the driver you have your bike with you, and he or she will lower the rack (if it isn't already accessible). Before boarding the bus, swing the rack's support arm down over your bike to secure it.

BUS

Along with local buses run by the CTA (see El & Buses earlier, long-distance bus carrier **Greyhound** (Map pp286–7; ☎ 312-408-5800 ☎ 800-231-2222; www.greyhound.com; 630 W Harrison St) sends dozens of buses in every direction every day. Trips are slower than they would be by car, with the bus making many stops along the way to pick up people traveling from small towns. Sample one-way fares and times include Minneapolis ($54, 10 hours), Memphis ($63, 10 hours) and New York City ($93, 18 hours) The station's ticketing windows are open 24 hours. The Clinton El stop on the Blue Line is two blocks away.

CAR & MOTORCYCLE

Driving

Driving in Chicago is a challenge. The pace is speedy and reckless, and Chicago drivers have little patience for slow-driving tourists. And during rush hour, the highways and surface roads become a crawling mess. With public transportation being what it is, there is little reason to have a car, unless you're heading out of town.

Rental

Both O'Hare and Midway have a plethora of car rental options, supplementing the in-town branches. Online bookings have become common for all major rental agencies; reserving your car through the Web is also a good way to take advantage of frequent

Internet-only rates. You'll need a credit card to rent a car, and many agencies rent to those 25 and older only. Of the agencies listed here, Enterprise sets itself apart by picking up customers.

Expect to pay $30 to $45 per day for a compact car, with rates going down somewhat if you rent for an entire week. Rates are also lower on weekends, sometimes dramatically so. Most agencies offer unlimited mileage on their cars; if they don't, ask about it – the per mile costs can add up quickly. Also be aware of redundant insurance coverage – liability and medical insurance provided by the car rental companies is optional and can often add 50% on to the cost of your rental. Many credit cards have built-in liability coverage on car rentals – check with yours before renting so you know exactly how much supplemental insurance you need to get from your rental car company. For motorcycle rental, contact **Illinois Harley-Davidson** (Map pp270–1; ☎ 708-749-1500, 888-966-1500; www.eaglerider.com; 1301 S Harlem Ave, Berwyn). Their range of rental motorcycles includes several Harley-Davidson touring models and Buell sports bikes. Rentals start at $75 per day.

Some of the larger car rental agencies in Chicago include the following:

Alamo (☎ 800-462-5266; www.alamo.com)

Avis (☎ 800-230-4898; www.avis.com)

Budget (☎ 800-527-0700; www.budget.com)

Dollar (☎ 800-800-4000; www.dollar.com)

Enterprise (☎ 800-7368-2227; www.enterprise.com)

Hertz (☎ 800-654-3131; www.hertz.com)

National (☎ 800-227-7368; www.nationalcar.com)

Thrifty (☎ 800-847-4389; www.thrifty.com)

Parking

Parking in Chicago can range from effortless to excruciating. Meter spots and on-street parking are plentiful in outlying areas, but the Loop, Near North, Lincoln Park, and Lake View neighborhoods can require up to an hour of circling before you find a spot. Valet parking, even at $11, can be worth it in these congested neighborhoods.

Parking meter rates vary from neighborhood to neighborhood, but in many, 25¢ will buy you 30 minutes or more of time, up to the posted limit. Watch out for streets where parking meters are only posted at every other parking spot. These are 'double' meters, and you'll need to examine them closely to figure out which meter applies to your spot.

Some common curb colors and their meanings include:

Red – no parking or even stopping

Yellow – loading zone from 7am-6pm

Green – 10-minute parking zone from 9am-6pm

White – For picking up or dropping off passengers

Blue – Disabled parking only; identification required

The biggest rule of parking in Chicago is to never park in a spot or parking area marked 'Tow-Away.' Your car will be towed. Period. Tow-truck drivers are like vultures in Chicago, circling the streets on the lookout for illegally parked cars. Towing fees run $125, plus the cost of the cab ride to retrieve your car from the lot. Almost every Chicago driver has had their car towed at some point. It's not pretty.

Parking in a garage can be expensive, but will save you time and traffic tickets. Try the downtown garages off Michigan Ave at Washington St and at Van Buren St.

EL & BUS

The **Chicago Transit Authority** (☎ 312-836-7000; www.transitchicago.com) consists of the El and buses. Between the two systems, you'll be able to get most everywhere you want to go in the city. Pace buses handle outlying suburbs. For help on routes, call the number listed above, or visit the CTA's helpful trip planning website http://tripsweb.rtachicago.com. Fares for single adult riders on both bus and the El are $1.50, with transfers costing an additional $0.30. The plastic tickets have a magnetized strip that allows you to add as much fare as you'd like (up to $100), and a 'free' dollar is added to the ticket for every $10 you put on it. Fares (and transfers) are deducted automatically when you enter the El system or board the bus.

Single- and multiday passes are available for one day ($5), two days ($9), three days ($12), five days ($18), seven days ($20) and 30 days ($75). Inexplicably, these passes are not available at all CTA stations. You can buy them at the O'Hare and Midway airport El stops, and in local retail outlets such as Jewel and at tourist attractions such as the Sears Tower, the Shedd Aquarium and the Field Museum. You can also buy them through the CTA's website, listed above.

You can get useful free system maps at all CTA stations.

The El

The El is an efficient, air-conditioned way to get around Chicago. Though most lines run occasional trains through the wee hours of the night, only the Blue Line from O'Hare to the Loop and the Red Line from Howard to 95/Dan Ryan run trains 24 hours.

Bus

Local CTA buses go almost everywhere, but they do so on erratic schedules. The bus stops are clearly marked, with signs showing which buses stop there but little else. Buses make frequent stops and don't go very fast. At rush hour you'll have to stand, and during the summer many buses lack air-conditioning.

Pace buses (www.pacebus.com) handle Chicago's outlying suburban areas.

TAXI

Taxis are easy to find in many of the northern parts of the city, from the Loop through Wrigleyville. Stand on the curb and raise your arm to hail one. In other parts of the city, you can either call a cab or face what may be a long wait for one to happen along. Fares are $1.90 when you enter the cab and $1.60 for each additional mile; extra passengers cost 50¢ apiece. Drivers expect a 10% to 15% tip. All major companies accept credit cards. Of the three reliable companies listed below, Flash is very popular with locals because it has a reputation for hiring older, more experienced drivers. To report a taxi, call the taxi complaint hotline ☎ 312-744-9400.

Checker Taxi (☎ 312-243-2537)

Flash Cab (☎ 773-561-4444)

Yellow Cab (☎ 312-829-4222)

TRAIN
Amtrak

Chicago's **Union Station** (Map pp282–3; 210 S Canal St between Adams St and Jackson Blvd) is the hub for **Amtrak** (☎ 800-872-7245; www.amtrak.com), and it has more connections than any other city. Trains leave regularly for Midwestern cities like Milwaukee ($20, two hours) and Indianapolis ($31, five hours), as well as long-haul destinations like Boston ($106, 23 hours). During much of the year it's crucial to reserve your Amtrak tickets well in advance. Amtrak is usually faster than Greyhound, and much, much more comfortable.

Metra

A web of commuter trains running under the **Metra** (☎ 312-836-7000; www.metrarail.com); banner serves the 245 stations in the suburbs surrounding Chicago. The primary riders are people who work in the city and live elsewhere. The clean, timely trains have two levels, with the second offering tight seating but better views. Some of the Metra lines run frequent schedules seven days a week; others operate only during weekday rush hours. The four main Metra stations in Chicago have schedules available for all the lines and other information.

Short trips start at $1.85; buy tickets from agents and machines at major stations. At small stations where nobody is on duty, you can buy the ticket without penalty from the conductor on the train; normally there is a $2 surcharge for doing this.

PRACTICALITIES
ACCOMMODATIONS

Because of the near-constant stream of business travelers coming to Chicago, the city has no off-season rates when it comes to lodging. That said, more rooms tend to be available on the weekend, and you can sometimes find special weekend deals that will knock up to 50% off the normal rates. See the Sleeping chapter for more information.

Along with the hotels' own websites, some helpful websites for finding discounted rooms include those listed under Flights earlier in this chapter (p241), and sites that allow you to 'bid' for rooms (see the boxed text p247).

BABY-SITTING

Check with the concierge at your hotel for a list of recommended sitters. **North Shore Nannies** (☎ 847-864-2424; www.northshore nannies.com; 520-B Lee St, Evanston) offer rigorously screened sitters who will do in-hotel sitting. Rates start at $10, plus parking and a placement fee. Booking a couple days ahead is recommended, especially on weekends.

BUSINESS

The pace of business in Chicago is bounding, though it's much less manic than New York. You'll find that the larger stores keep late hours, but few – save Walgreens and a handful of other chain retailers – are open all night. If you're burning the midnight oil and are looking for some place to make some quick photocopies or send a fax, head to the Near North **Kinko's** (Map pp280–1; ☎ 312-670-4460; 444 N Wells) or the branch in **Wrigleyville** (Map pp272–3; ☎ 312-975-5031; 3524 N Southport); both stay open 24 hours.

Business Hours

Normal business hours:

Shops 10am-7pm Mon-Sat, noon-6pm Sun

Restaurants 11am-10pm

Banks 8am-5pm Mon-Fri

Bars & pubs Until 2am Sun-Fri, until 3am Sat

CHILDREN

Chicago is a welcoming place for children. From the dinosaurs at the Field Museum to the carousel on Navy Pier, the city will probably come across as endlessly thrilling for kids. For more on specific child-friendly attractions, see the boxed text on p60. And for a comprehensive overview on traveling with kids, check out Lonely Planet's book *Travel With Children*.

CLIMATE

The nickname 'Windy City' actually has nonmeteorological origins. It was coined by newspaper reporters in the late 1800s in reaction to the oft-blustery boastfulness of Chicago's politicians. Nevertheless, Chicago is windy, with everything from cool, God-sent lake breezes at the height of summer to skirt-raising gusts in the spring to spine-chilling, nose-chiseling blasts of icy air in the winter. You'll experience all four seasons here, with late spring and early fall being generally warm, clear and dry times. Winter and summer behave as expected (see climate chart), but early spring and late fall can freely mix nice days with wretched ones. Chicago has no true rainy season; its 34 inches of average annual precipitation are spread throughout the year. For a blow-by-blow on Chicago's annual weather, see the City Calendar section of the City Life chapter.

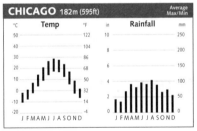

Directory – Practicalities

CUSTOMS

International travelers will be familiar with the red-and-green line system at O'Hare. Those with nothing to declare can opt for the green line, which is still subject to spot checks. Those with something to declare should definitely do so, because if you try to smuggle something in and are caught, your day will immediately go downhill. Penalties for drug smuggling are especially severe. Remember, until you clear all the formalities, you have no rights. Non–United States citizens over the age of 21 are allowed to import 1 liter of liquor and 200 cigarettes (or 100 non-Cuban cigars) duty free. Gifts may amount to no more than $100 in value. You may bring any amount of money less than $10,000 into or out of the US without declaration. Amounts greater than $10,000 must be declared.

Certain goods such as ivory and tortoiseshell anything are a no-no, as are drug paraphernalia, absinthe, and, oddly, dog and cat fur. For more information, visit the website www.customs.gov.

DISABLED TRAVELERS

Chicago can be a challenge for people with reduced mobility. The preponderance of older buildings means that doorways are narrow and stairs prevalent. Much of the El is inaccessible. If you do find a station with an elevator, make sure that there's also one at your destination. The CTA has, however, made progress on making its buses wheelchair-friendly, installing lifts in over 80% of the routes. To see a list of wheelchair-accessible routes and El stations, head to www.transitchicago.com/maps/accessible.html or call ☎ 312-836-7000.

For hotels, you are best off with the newer properties. But call the hotel itself – not the 800 number – and confirm that the room you want to reserve has the features you need. The phrase 'roll-in showers' is interpreted very loosely by some properties.

The **Mayor's Office for People with Disabilities** (Map pp282–3; ☎ 312-744-6673 ☎ TTY 312-744-7833; Room 1104, 121 N LaSalle St, 60602) is a good spot to start asking questions about the availability of services.

DISCOUNT CARDS

Chicago CityPass (www.citypass.net) costs $49 for adults and $38 for children (ages three to 11) and gets the bearer into the Hancock Observatory, the Art Institute of Chicago, the Field Museum, the Shedd Aquarium, the Adler Planetarium and the Museum of Science and Industry. You can buy the passes at the attractions themselves, or at any of Chicago's Visitor Information bureaus (see Tourist Information, p253).

ELECTRICITY

Electric current in the US is 110-120 volts, 60Hz AC. Outlets accept North American standard plugs, which have two flat prongs and an occasional third round one. If your appliance is made for another system, you will need a converter or adapter. These are best bought in your home country. Otherwise, try a travel bookstore (see the Shopping chapter).

CONSULATES

Australia (Map pp282–3; ☎ 312-419-1480; Suite 1330, 123 N Wacker Dr)

Austria (Map pp280–1; ☎ 312-222-1515; 400 N Michigan Ave)

Brazil (Map pp280–1; ☎ 312-464-0244; 410 N Michigan Ave)

Canada (Map pp282–3; ☎ 312-616-1860; Suite 2400, 180 N Stetson Ave)

France (Map pp278–9; ☎ 312-327-5229; Suite 3760, 205 N Michigan Ave)

Germany (Map pp280–1; ☎ 312-580-1199; Suite 3200, 676 N Michigan Ave)

Ireland (Map pp280–1; ☎ 312-337-1868; Suite 911, 400 N Michigan Ave)

Italy (Map pp280–1; ☎ 312-467-1550; 500 N Michigan Ave)

Japan (Map pp280–1; ☎ 312-280-0400; Suite 1100, 737 N Michigan Ave)

Mexico (Map pp282–3; ☎ 312-332-7352; 300 N Michigan Ave, Suite 200)

New Zealand (Map pp270–1; ☎ 773-714-9461; 8600 W Bryn Mawr)

South Africa (Map pp282–3; ☎ 312-939-7929; Suite 600, 200 S Michigan Ave)

Sweden (Map pp282–3; ☎ 312-781-6262; Suite 1250, 150 N Michigan Ave)

Switzerland (Map pp280–1; ☎ 312-915-0061; 737 N Michigan Ave)

UK (Map pp280–1; ☎ 312-970-3800; 400 N Michigan Ave)

EMERGENCIES

For all emergencies (police, ambulance, fire), call 911. For non-emergency police matters call 311.

GAY & LESBIAN TRAVELERS

The heart of Chicago's large and vibrant gay and lesbian community lies on N Halsted St between Belmont Ave and Addison St, but Andersonville, Lincoln Park, Bucktown and other neighborhoods are also gay- and lesbian-friendly. Outside the Halsted neighborhood, however, open affection between same-sex partners often draws confused or disapproving stares. Some good local gay weeklies include the Chicago Free Press (www.chicagofreepress.com) and the Windy City Times (www.windycitytimes.com). For a list of gay-owned and gay-friendly businesses found in Chicago, contact the **Chicago Area Gay & Lesbian Chamber of Commerce** (Map pp270–1; ☎ 773-303-0167; www.glchamber.org; 1210 W Rosedale Ave).

HOLIDAYS

Chicago's governmental offices and services shut down on public holidays, as do many of the city's shops. To find out how you can join in on Chicago holiday celebrations, see the City Calendar section of the City Life chapter. Major public holidays include:

New Year's Day Jan 1

Martin Luther King, Jr Day Third Mon in Jan

President's Day Third Mon in Jan

St Patrick's Day Mar 17 (government offices remain open)

Memorial Day Last Mon in May

Independence Day July 4

Labor Day First Mon in Sept

Columbus Day Second Mon in Oct

Veteran's Day Nov 11

Thanksgiving Day Fourth Thu in Nov

Christmas Day Dec 25

INSURANCE

A travel insurance policy to cover theft, loss and medical problems is a good idea, especially when traveling in the US, where dismal medical coverage means routine trips to the doctor can cost the uninsured hundreds of dollars. Some policies specifically exclude dangerous activities, which can include motorcycling.

You may prefer a policy that pays doctors or hospitals directly rather than you having to pay on the spot and claim later. If you have to claim later ensure you keep all documentation.

Check that the policy covers ambulances or an emergency flight home.

INTERNET ACCESS

Free high-speed Internet access has become a regular enticement at many of Chicago's higher-end hotels. To take advantage of it, you'll need a laptop equipped with an Ethernet card and plug-in. It's also a good idea to bring 5ft or so of Ethernet cable with you. As wireless Internet becomes more popular, hotels and cafés are offering it as well, either for free or at a per-hour charge. To access it, you'll need a laptop with a Wi-Fi card. If you need to buy any of these things, try CompUSA (p193).

For those traveling without laptop, you can access the Internet for free at any public library (try the Harold Washington Library in the Loop), or visit Internet cafés, where you can get on a machine right away, and costs range from $6 to $9 per hour.

Cybercafe 1020 (Map pp272–3; ☎ 773-832-1020; www.cybercafe1020.com; 3330 N Clark St; $6 per hr; ☾ noon-4am; Red Line to Addison)

Screenz (Map pp276–7; ☎ 773-348-9300; www.screenz.com; 2717 N Clark St; $8.50 per hr; ☾ 8:30am-1am Mon-Fri, 9am-1am Sat & Sun; Brown, Red Line to Diversey)

LEGAL MATTERS

The basics of Chicago's legal system are identical to other US cities. If stopped and questioned by the police, you should cooperate, though you are not required to give them permission to search either your person or your car (though they can do both if they determine they have 'probable cause'). If arrested, you have the right to remain silent – which you should do – and the right to make one phone call from jail. If you don't have a lawyer or friend or family member to help you, call your consulate. The police will give you the number upon request.

It's generally against the law to have an open container of alcoholic beverage in public, whether in a car, on the street, in a park or at the beach. But during festivals and other mass events, this rule is waived. The drinking age of 21 is pretty strictly enforced. If you're younger than 35 (or just look like it), carry an ID to fend off overzealous barkeeps and the like. The legal driving age is 16, age of consent is 17 and the voting age is 18. There is zero tolerance at all times for any kind of drug use.

MAPS

Maps are widely sold at hotels, drug stores and newsstands. Try Lonely Planet's Chicago city map, a laminated map that folds into a compact size. The Rand McNally store (p194) sells it, along with their house-brand Chicagoland map, which is good, though it doesn't show El lines or stations and is better for driving than walking or touring. You can pick up free maps of the Chicago transit system at any CTA station, or download one from www.transitchicago.com.

MEASUREMENT

Chicago uses the imperial measurement system.

MEDICAL SERVICES

If you are ill or injured and suspect that the situation is in any way life-threatening, call ☎ 911 immediately. This is a free call from any phone. If you have a less serious malady, such as the flu or a sprained ankle, and want to see a doctor, ask your hotel for a recommendation. Though Chicago is filled with clinics and doctors, none of their services come cheap, so make sure you have insurance, or try the free Cook County Hospital (below).

Clinics & Emergency Rooms

The following hospitals offer medical services through their emergency rooms. If your condition is not acute, call first, because many also operate clinics that can see you in a more timely and convenient manner. If you are broke and have no insurance, head to **Cook County Hospital** (Map pp286–7; ☎ 312-864-6000; 1969 W Ogden; Blue Line to Medical Center), one block south of the El stop. If your problem is not life-threatening, you will be seated in a waiting room where you will do just that for perhaps 12 hours while you're surrounded by people sicker than yourself.

Children's Memorial Hospital (Map pp276–7; ☎ 773-880-4000; 2300 N Lincoln Ave; Brown, Red Line to Fullerton)

Illinois Masonic Hospital (Map pp272–3; ☎ 773-975-1600; 836 W Wellington Ave; Brown, Red Line to Wellington)

Northwestern Memorial Hospital (Map pp280–1; ☎ 312-926-2000; 251 E Huron St; Red Line to Chicago)

University of Chicago Hospital (Map pp288–9; ☎ 773-702-1000; 5841 S Maryland Ave; Metra to 57th)

MONEY

The US currency is the dollar ($), divided into 100 cents (¢). Coins come in denominations of 1¢ (penny), 5¢ (nickel), 10¢ (dime), 25¢ (quarter), 50¢ (half dollar – rare) and $1 (silver dollar – rare). A gold-colored $1 coin, introduced in 2000, features the face of Native American Sacagawea. Notes ('bills') come in denominations of $1, $2 (rare), $5, $10, $20, $50 and $100.

See Economy & Costs (p22) for where the money goes in Chicago.

ATMs

ATMs are everywhere in Chicago, with many convenience stores such as White Hen getting in on the action as well. All machines are connected to Cirrus and Plus, the world's two largest banking networks. Unless you find an ATM belonging to your bank, you will be charged a fee of around $2 to withdraw money from one of the machines. The exchange rate you get by taking money out of the ATM is usually the very best available (though the fees may nullify that advantage).

Changing Cash & Traveler's Checks

You'll find that exchanging foreign cash and non-US dollar traveler's checks in Chicago is a hassle, although it can be done. One cautionary note: shortly after arriving in Chicago, you will begin noticing 'currency exchanges' on many street corners. These primarily serve people without bank accounts who want to cash checks, and will not exchange foreign currencies. Head instead to the banks and exchange places listed below.

Traveler's checks are usually just as good as cash in the US, provided they are in US dollars. Most places will accept them as long as you sign them in front of the cashier, waiter etc. To exchange international monies or traveler's checks for dollars, you can visit the arrivals area of O'Hare's Terminal 5, which has a foreign exchange service. Otherwise, try one of the following:

Bank One (Map pp282–3; ☎ 312-661-5000; 120 S LaSalle St; ⏰ 8am-5pm Mon-Fri; Brown, Orange Line to Washington)

Northern Trust Bank (Map pp282–3; ☎ 312-630-6000; 50 S LaSalle St; ⏰ 8am-5pm Mon-Fri; Brown, Orange Line to Washington)

Travelex (Map pp282–3; ☎ 312-807-4941; 19 S LaSalle St; 🕙 9am-5pm Mon-Fri; Brown, Orange Line to Washington)

World's Money Exchange (Map pp282–3; ☎ 312-641-2151; Suite M-11, 203 N LaSalle St; 🕙 9am-5pm Mon-Fri; Blue, Brown, Green, Orange Line to Clark)

Credit Cards

Major credit cards are widely accepted by car rental firms, hotels, restaurants, gas stations, shops, large grocery stores, movie theaters, ticket vendors, taxi cabs and other places. In fact, you'll find certain transactions impossible to perform without a credit card: you can't reserve theater or other event tickets by phone without one, nor can you guarantee room reservations by phone or rent a car. The most commonly accepted cards are Visa and MasterCard. American Express is widely accepted but not as universally as the first two. Discover and Diners Club cards are usually good for travel tickets, hotels and rental cars, but they're less commonly accepted in other situations.

If your credit card is lost or stolen, call the card issuer.

American Express (☎ 800-628-4800)

Diners Club (☎ 800-234-6377)

Discover (☎ 800-347-2683)

MasterCard (☎ 800-307-7309)

Visa (☎ 800-336-8472)

NEWSPAPERS & MAGAZINES

For specifics on Chicago's newspapers and magazines, see Media (p20). Daily papers include the following:

Chicago Sun-Times (www.suntimes.com)

Chicago Tribune (www.chicagotribune.com)

Weekly arts and entertainment papers include:

Chicago Reader (www.chireader.com)

New City (www.newcitychicago.com)

UR (www.urchicago.com)

Worthwhile local magazines include:

Chicago Magazine (www.chicagomag.com)

Crain's Chicago Business (www.chicagobusiness.com)

Found Magazine (www.foundmagazine.com)

Roctober (www.roctober.com)

The Baffler (www.thebaffler.com)

Venus Magazine (www.venuszine.com)

PHARMACIES

Both Walgreens and Osco pharmacies are convenient places to get your prescriptions filled. The following branches are open 24 hours:

Osco (Map pp272–3; ☎ 773-871-8242; 2940 N Ashland Ave; Brown, Red Line to Diversey)

Walgreens (Map pp280–1; ☎ 312-664-8686; 757 N Michigan Ave; Red Line to Chicago)

Walgreens (Map pp280–1; ☎ 312-587-1416; 641 N Clark St; Red Line to Grand)

POST

At press time, it cost 37¢ to mail a 1oz 1st-class letter within the US. Each additional oz cost 23¢. Domestic postcards cost 23¢ to mail. It costs 60¢ to mail a 1oz letter to Canada or Mexico, 80¢ for other international destinations. Attach 50¢ of postage for postcards to Canada and Mexico, 70¢ for those going overseas. All aerogrammes cost 70¢.

Parcels mailed to foreign destinations from the US are subject to a variety of rates. First class can be very expensive. If you're not in a hurry, consider mailing your items fourth class, which goes by boat. Those rates can be very low, but delivery to Europe, for instance, takes six to eight weeks. If all you are sending is printed matter such as books, you qualify for an extra-cheap rate.

If you'd like to get mail while traveling but don't have an address, have it sent to you in Chicago via 'general delivery'. This is the same as poste restante. Letters should be addressed:

Your Name
c/o General Delivery (Station Name)
Chicago, IL Zip Code
USA

General delivery mail is held for at least 10 days (sometimes as long as 30) before being returned to sender. Bring some photo ID when you come to pick up your mail. Full-service post offices that also accept general delivery include the following:

Fort Dearborn Station (Map pp280–1; ☎ 312-644-3919; 540 N Dearborn St, Chicago, IL 60610; 🕙 7:30am-5pm Mon-Fri, 7:30am-1pm Sat, 9am-2pm Sun)

Loop Station (Map pp282–3; ☎ 312-427-4225; 211 S Clark St, Chicago, IL 60604; 🕙 7am-6pm Mon-Fri)

Main Post Office (Map pp286–7; ☎ 312-983-8182; 433 W Harrison St, Chicago, IL 60607; 🕙 24hr)

Shipping Services

Shipping companies such as **UPS** (domestic ☎ 800-742-5877, international ☎ 800-782-7892; www.ups.com) and **FedEx** (domestic ☎ 800-463-3339, international ☎ 800-247-4747; www.fedex.com) specialize in getting packages across the country and around the world in the blink of an eye. Call them to find the closest Chicago location to you.

RADIO

Of the options listed below, WBEZ can be heard on the Internet, at www.wbez.com.

Q101 101.1 FM (modern rock)

WHPK 88.5 FM (eclectic)

WBEZ 91.5 FM (national public radio)

WXRT 93.1 FM (rock)

SAFETY

The areas written about in this book are all reasonably safe during the day. At night, the lakefront, major parks and certain neighborhoods (especially south and west of the Loop) can become bleak and forbidding places. The Loop, Near North, Gold Coast, Old Town, Lincoln Park and Lake View, on the other hand, are tolerably safe (and bustling) night and day.

TAXES

The basic sales tax is 8.75%. Some grocery items are taxed at only 2%. Newspapers and magazines, but not books, are tax free. The hotel tax is 14.9%; the car rental tax is 18%. And for meals in most parts of town you are likely to visit, there's an extra 9.75% added to the bill.

TELEPHONE
Area Codes

The city has two area codes, with more soon to come as the proliferation of pagers, faxes and Internet connections sops up the available supply of numbers. The area code 312 serves the Loop and an area bounded roughly by 1600 North (ie 1600 block, north of Madison St in the Loop), 1600 West and 1600 South. The rest of the city falls in area code 773. The northern suburbs use area code 847, those close to the west and the south 708, and the far west suburbs 630.

Dialing

All phone numbers within the US and Canada consist of the three-digit area code followed by a seven-digit local number. If you are calling locally, just dial the seven-digit number. If you are calling from within the US to another area code, dial 1 + the three-digit area code + the seven-digit local number. In the city, if you don't use the area code when you should or you do use it when you shouldn't – both of which are common mistakes – you'll get an ear-shattering screech, followed by advice on what to dial.

The country code for the US is 1. The international access code is 011 for calls you dial directly; dial it first, before you dial the country code. To find out the country code of the place you're trying to call, look in the front of the local phone directory.

Toll-free phone numbers start with the area codes 800, 877 or 888. Numbers that begin with 900 will cost you a small fortune (up to several dollars per minute). You'll most often see such numbers advertised late at night on TV in ads asking, 'Lonely? Want to have some hot talk?'

Local directory assistance can be reached by calling ☎ 1411. If you are looking for a number outside of your local area code but know what area code it falls under, dial ☎ 1 + the area code + 555-1212. These calls are no longer free, even from pay phones. To obtain a toll-free phone number, dial ☎ 800-555-1212.

Pay Phones & Hotel Phones

Unfortunately, pay phones do not use the same high-tech card systems in the US that they do in Europe. This is fine for local calls, which cost 35¢ for about 10 minutes of talk time. But trying to make a long-distance call at a pay phone if you don't have a credit card calling card or a pre-paid calling card (see below) requires an outrageous amount of change. When using hotel phones, know that some places will charge up to $2 per local call. Ask in advance to avoid a shock later.

Collect Calls

You can call collect (reverse the charges) from any phone. The main service providers are **AT&T** (☎ 800-225-5288) and **MCI** (☎ 800-365-5328). These generally charge rates that will be less stressful to the lucky recipient of your call than the fees levied by local phone companies or the dreaded third-party firms. Just dial 0 to begin the call.

Prepaid Calling Cards

Convenience stores and other places sell telephone cards good for a prepaid amount of long-distance phone time; these are typically available in amounts of $5, $10, $20 and $50. To use one, you dial an 800 number and then enter the code number on your card. At a prompt from an automated operator, you simply enter the number you are calling. The company's computer keeps track of how much value you have left on the card. These cards are often a good deal and a good way to circumnavigate the swamp of phone-call-making minutiae.

Mobile Phones

The US uses a mess of incompatible formats for mobile (or 'cell') phones. Many still use an old analog format, while the newer digital models primarily use the competing TDMA or CDMA formats. Few use the GSM format that is popular in the rest of the world. If you really can't be separated from your mobile phone, it is a good idea to check with your service provider to see if there's any hope it will work in the US.

TIME

Chicago falls in the US Central Standard Time (CST) zone. 'Standard time' runs from the last Sunday in October to the first Sunday in April. 'Daylight saving time,' when clocks move ahead one hour, runs from the first Sunday in April to the last Sunday in October, when clocks go back to standard time.

Chicago is one hour behind Eastern Standard Time, which encompasses nearby Michigan and Indiana, apart from the northwestern corner of Indiana, which follows Chicago time. The border between the two zones is just east of the city. Note that Indiana doesn't take a cotton to notions like daylight saving time. In the summer Indiana keeps the same time as Chicago; in winter, with the exception of its northwestern corner, it is one hour ahead.

The city is one hour ahead of Mountain Standard Time, a zone which includes much of the Rocky Mountains, and two hours ahead of Pacific Standard Time, the zone which includes California. Chicago is six hours behind Greenwich Mean Time (but remember daylight saving time).

TIPPING

Restaurant wait staff, hotel maids, valet car parkers, bartenders, bellhops and others are paid a mere pittance in wages and expect to make up the shortfall through tips. But whom to tip? And how much?

Bartenders – 50¢ to $1 per drink

Bellhops – from $2 total to $1 per bag or more, depending on the distance covered

Cocktail servers – at least 10% to 15%, when you pay for the drinks

Concierges – nothing for answering a simple question, $5 or more for securing tickets to a sold-out show

Doormen – $1 to $2 for summoning you a cab, depending on the weather

Hotel cleaning staff – $1 to $2 per day, left on the pillow each morning

Restaurant wait staff – 15% is standard, but leave 20% if you're really pleased with the service; an easy rule is to pay the same amount as the tax (which is 18.5% in Chicago restaurants)

Skycaps – at least $1 per bag

Taxi drivers – 10% to 15% of bill

Valet car parkers – $2 to $5, when the keys to the car are handed to you

For more on tipping in restaurant situations, see the Tipping section of the Eating chapter (p127).

TOURIST INFORMATION

For sheer tonnage of leaflets, maps and coupon books, you can't beat the Visitor Information Center in the Chicago Cultural Center. (The friendly staff don't hurt either.) The second location, in the Water Tower Pumping Station, is close to both Near North and Gold Coast sights and shops. The Chicago Office of Tourism also has set up a 24-hour hotline to answer questions about sights, events and lodging, call ☎ 877-244-2246.

Illinois Marketplace Visitor Information Center (Map pp280–1; ☎ 312-744-2400; 700 E Grand Ave; ☺ 10am-8pm Mon-Thu, 10am-10pm Fri & Sat, 10am-8pm Sun; bus 66)

Visitor Information Center in the Chicago Cultural Center (Map pp282–3; ☎ 312-744-2400; 77 E Randolph St; ☺ Mon-Fri 10am-6pm, Sat 10am-5pm, Sun 11am-5pm; Brown, Green, Orange Line to Randolph)

Visitor Information Center in the Water Tower Pumping Station (Map pp278–9; ☎ 312-744-2400; 163 E Pearson St; ☺ 7:30am-7pm; Red Line to Chicago)

Internet Resources

The best resource on the city's restaurant and nightlife scene is the review-heavy www.metromix.com website, which is run by the *Chicago Tribune*. The *Chicago Reader* website – www.chireader.com – also has top-notch dining reviews. Citysearch Chicago – http://chicago.citysearch.com – offers up broad coverage of venues, and their 'best of' lists in dozens of genre are a good way to get a handle on the city's latest places.

Various wings of the city's tourism powers that be have set up several websites to help spread the word about Chicago.

www.877chicago.com

www.ci.chi.il.us/Tourism

www.chicago.il.org

VISAS

A reciprocal visa-waiver program applies to citizens of certain countries, who may enter the US for stays of 90 days or fewer without having to obtain a visa. Currently these countries are Andorra, Australia, Austria, Belgium, Brunei, Denmark, Finland, France, Germany, Iceland, Ireland, Italy, Japan, Liechtenstein, Luxembourg, Monaco, the Netherlands, New Zealand, Norway, Portugal, San Marino, Singapore, Slovenia, Spain, Sweden, Switzerland, the Netherlands and the UK.

In order to travel to the US visa-free, visitors from the above countries must have a machine-readable passport. If your passport cannot be scanned by a computer, you'll need to get a visa regardless. Consult with your airline or the closest US consulate or embassy for more information.

With heightened security concerns showing no sign of abating, travelers should be aware that US Visa rules are subject to change with little warning. Check the government website http://travel.state.gov/visa_services.html for the latest developments.

Visa Extensions

Tourists using visas are usually granted a six-month stay on first arrival. If you try to extend that time, the first assumption will be that you are working illegally, so come prepared with concrete evidence that you've been behaving like a model tourist: receipts to demonstrate you've been spending lots of your money from home in the US or ticket stubs that show you've been traveling extensively. Requests for visa extensions in Chicago are entertained at the **US Citizenship and Immigration Services office** (Map pp282–3; ☎ 800-375-5283; www.uscis.gov; Suite 600, Kluczynski Building, Federal Center, 10 W Jackson Blvd).

WOMEN TRAVELERS

Women will be safe alone in most parts of Chicago, though they should exercise a degree of caution and awareness of their surroundings. The El is safe, even at night, though you might want to seek out more-populated cars or the first car, to be closest to the driver. Or you can take one of the buses that parallel many train lines.

In the commonly visited areas of Chicago, you should not encounter troubling attitudes from men. In bars some men will see a woman alone as a bid for companionship. A polite 'no thank you' should suffice to send them away. Chicagoans are very friendly, so don't be afraid to protest loudly if someone is hassling you. It will probably send the offending party away and bring helpful Samaritans to your side.

WORK

It is very difficult for foreigners to get legal work in the US. Securing your own work visa without a sponsor – meaning an employer – is nearly impossible. If you do have a sponsor, the sponsor should normally assist or do all the work to secure your visa. Contact your embassy or consulate for more information.

Behind the Scenes

THE LONELY PLANET STORY

The story begins with a classic travel adventure: Tony and Maureen Wheeler's 1972 journey across Europe and Asia to Australia. There was no useful information about the overland trail then, so Tony and Maureen published the first Lonely Planet guidebook to meet a growing need.

From a kitchen table, Lonely Planet has grown to become the largest independent travel publisher in the world, with offices in Melbourne (Australia), Oakland (USA), London (UK) and Paris (France).

Today Lonely Planet guidebooks cover the globe. There is an ever-growing list of books and information in a variety of media. Some things haven't changed. The main aim is still to make it possible for adventurous travelers to get out there – to explore and better understand the world.

At Lonely Planet we believe travelers can make a positive contribution to the countries they visit – if they respect their host communities and spend their money wisely. Since 1986 a percentage of the income from each book has been donated to aid projects and human rights campaigns, and, more recently, to wildlife conservation.

THIS BOOK

This third edition of *Chicago* was researched and written by Chris Baty. Some of it was based on the second edition researched and written by Ryan Ver Berkmoes. The guide was commissioned in Lonely Planet's Oakland office, and produced by:

Commissioning Editors Michele Posner, Valerie Sinzdak, Jay Cooke
Coordinating Editor Dan Caleo
Coordinating Cartographer Sarah Sloane
Coordinating Layout Designer Adam Bextream
Cartographer Natasha Velleley
Proofreaders Simon Williamson, Susannah Farfor
Cover Designer Ruth Askevold
Series Designer Nic Lehman
Series Design Concept Nic Lehman, Andrew Weatherill
Managing Cartographer Alison Lyall
Managing Editor Darren O'Connell
Layout Manager Adriana Mammarella
Mapping Development Paul Piaia
Project Manager Andrew Weatherill
Regional Publishing Manager Maria Donohoe
Series Publishing Manager Gabrielle Green
Series Development Team Jenny Blake, Anna Bolger, Fiona Christie, Kate Cody, Erin Corrigan, Janine Eberle, Simone Egger, James Ellis, Nadine Fogale, Roz Hopkins, Dave McClymont, Leonie Mugavin, Rachel Peart, Ed Pickard, Michele Posner, Howard Ralley, Dani Valent
Thanks to Kate McDonald, Chris Love, Katrina Webb, Laura Jane, Dianne Zammit

Cover photographs by Raymond Hillstrom/Lonely Planet Images

Internal photographs by Ray Laskowitz/Lonely Planet Images except for the following: p210 (#4), p238 Charles Cook/Lonely Planet Images; p210 (#1), p236 Richard Cummins/Lonely Planet Images; p128 Rick Gerharter/Lonely Planet Images; p210 (#3) Mark & Audrey Gibson/Lonely Planet Images; p105 (#2), p204 (#2) Tom Given/Lonely Planet Images; p1, p100 (#2), p164, p206 (#4), p210 (#2) Raymond Hillstrom/Lonely Planet Images; p2 (#2), p207 (#3) Peter Ptschelinzew/Lonely Planet Images. All images are the copyright of the photographers unless otherwise indicated. Many of the images in this guide are available for licensing from Lonely Planet Images: www.lonelyplanetimages.com.

ACKNOWLEDGMENTS

Many thanks to the following for the use of their content:

Ryan Ver Berkmoes for his contribution to the History chapter and boxed text on Charlie Trotter's. Kathleen Munnelly, Brad Zibung, Archer Prewitt, Mara Vorhees and Greg Kot for their contributions to boxed texts.

Transit map © Chicago Transit Authority, 2004.

THANKS
CHRIS BATY

First and foremost, I would like to thank Amy and Julia at Kitty City for all their kind-hearted assistance. The barbecue grill is only a fraction of what I owe you, ladies.

SEND US YOUR FEEDBACK

We love to hear from travelers – your comments keep us on our toes and help make our books better. Our well-traveled team reads every word on what you loved or loathed about this book. Although we cannot reply individually to postal submissions, we always guarantee that your feedback goes straight to the appropriate authors, in time for the next edition. Each person who sends us information is thanked in the next edition – and the most useful submissions are rewarded with a free book.

To send us your updates – and find out about LP events, newsletters and travel news – visit our award-winning website: www.lonelyplanet.com.

Note: We may edit, reproduce and incorporate your comments in Lonely Planet products such as guidebooks, websites and digital products, so let us know if you don't want your comments reproduced or your name acknowledged. For a copy of our privacy policy visit www.lonelyplanet.com/privacy.

Also a tremendous thank you to my friends and informants on the ground: Regan Kappe and the Kappe family, Marie Marasovich, Michael Hansel, Dana Dubriwny, Marjory Clements Rudiak, Katie and Tim Tuten, Laurie Stirratt, Sheila McCoy, Megan Kellie, Karla Zimmer, Scott Mathews, Jeff Ruby, Sam Hallgren, Robyn Nisi, Derek Hull, John Hindman, Kathleen Judge, Kate Clark, Jason Ankeny, Scott Sikkema, Keith Greenwalt, Matt Kobylar, Javier Ayala, Jessica Linker, Howard Greynolds, Mike Bulington and Amy Schroeder.

At Lonely Planet, a big hat-tip is due to Ryan, Valerie, and Kathleen for all the legwork, Michele for the invitation, Wendy for the good advice, Jay for seeing it through, and Dan for his sense of humor and editorial acumen.

And a final thanks to Elly. For the drive to and from, and all the love in-between.

OUR READERS

Many thanks to the following travellers who used the last edition and wrote to us with helpful hints, useful advice and interesting anecdotes. Your names follow:

Pichya Anavil, Sola Bankole, Carl Banner, Nazim Bharmal, David Bossiere, Jack Breisacher, Joost Brugman, Neil & Sandra Burditt, Dennis Cox, Roberta Dal Cero, Matteo Del Grosso, Jennifer Duggan, Gerard Evans, Thommy Frantzen, Sandra Friede, Bob Froehlig, Andrea Gould, Ronalie Green, Marco Heusdens, Laura Jeffrey, Robert L Johnson, Dirk Kasulke, Tim Langan Jr, Abraham A Leib, Shin Lim, Stuart Lipnick, Ann Lippmann, Kate Mahon, Cynthia O'Keefe, Shannon O'Loughlin, Jan Onno Reiners, Matt Roberts, Amartya Saha, J Stefan, Diego Tonelli, Brian Turbyfill, Christina Urban, Debbie Weijers, Jodi Whitlock, Andrew Young

Notes

Notes

Index

See also separate indexes for Eating (pp 266-7), Drinking (p267), Shopping (p267) and Sleeping (pp 267-8).

Index

000 map pages
000 photographs

Index

Index

Index

000 map pages
000 photographs

MAP LEGEND

ROUTES

	Tollway		Track
	Freeway		Unsealed Road
	Primary Road		Mall/Steps
	Secondary Road		Tunnel
	Tertiary Road		Walking Tour
	Lane		Walking Trail
	Under Construction		Walking Path

TRANSPORT

	Ferry		Rail
	Metro		Rail (Underground)
	Monorail		Tram
	Bus Route		Cable Car, Funicular

HYDROGRAPHY

	River, Creek		Water
	Intermittent River		Swamp

BOUNDARIES

	International		Regional, Suburb
	State, Provincial		Ancient Wall
	Disputed		

AREA FEATURES

	Airport	+ + +	Cemetery, Christian
	Area of Interest	× × ×	Cemetery, Other
	Beach, Desert		Forest
	Building, Featured		Land
	Building, Information		Park
	Building, Other		Sports
	Building, Transport		Urban
	Campus		

POPULATION

◎	**CAPITAL (NATIONAL)**	◉	CAPITAL (STATE)
●	**Large City**	●	Medium City
●	Small City	●	Town, Village

SYMBOLS

Sights/Activities

	Beach
	Buddhist
	Canoeing, Kayaking
	Castle, Fortress
	Christian
	Islamic
	Jewish
	Monument
	Museum, Gallery
	Picnic Area
•	Point of Interest
	Ruin
	Surfing, Surf Beach
	Taoist
	Wheelchair Access
	Winery, Vineyard
	Zoo, Bird Sanctuary

Eating

🍴	Eating

Drinking

	Drinking
	Café

Entertainment

	Entertainment

Shopping

	Shopping

Sleeping

	Sleeping
	Camping

Transport

	Airport, Airfield
	Border Crossing
	Bus Station
	General Transport
	Taxi Rank

Information

	Bank, ATM
	Embassy/Consulate
	Hospital, Medical
	Information
@	Internet Facilities
Ⓟ	Parking Area
	Petrol Station
	Police Station
	Post Office, GPO
	Telephone
	Toilets

Geographic

	Lookout
▲	Mountain, Volcano
	National Park
)(	Pass, Canyon
→	River Flow
	Shelter, Hut
	Waterfall

Map Section

Lake Michigan

See Andersonville & Uptown Map (p274)

See Lake View Map (pp272–3)

See Lincoln Park & Old Town Map (pp276–7)

See Gold Coast Map (pp278–9)

See Near North & Navy Pier Map (pp280–1)

See The Loop & Grant Park Map (pp282–3)

See Wicker Park/Bucktown & Ukrainian Village Map (p275)

Northwestern University

Calvary Cemetery

Loyola Beach
Loyola Park
Loyola

Granville
Thorndale

Lincoln Park Montrose Beach

Andersonville

Wrigleyville

Old Town

Wicker Park

Bucktown

Greektown

Little Italy

Ukrainian Village

Humboldt Park

Garfield Park
Laramie
Garfield Park Conservatory

Evanston

Central
N Sheridan Rd
Ridge Ave
Davis
Dempster
Main
Howard
South Blvd
Jarvis
Morse
Warren Park

Western Ave
Rosehill Cemetery

Rockwell
Horner Park
Kimball
Montrose Ave

North Branch Chicago River
East River Park

Skokie

W Dempster St
W Touhy Ave
N Lincoln Ave
W Devon Ave
W Peterson Ave
W Foster Ave

North Shore Channel

Lake Ave

Jefferson Park
Montrose
W Irving Park Rd
W Addison St
W Belmont Ave
W Fullerton Ave

Nagle Ave
N Harlem Ave

Oak Park
Ridgeland
Harlem/Lake
W Lake St
W Washington St
Oak Park
Columbus Park
Austin
Central
N Central Ave

Hanson Park

N Milwaukee Ave

John F Kennedy Expwy

Metra Milwaukee District North Line

Metra North Central Line

Metra Milwaukee District West Line

Metra Union Pacific West Line

Metra/ Union Pacific North Line

Metra Union Pacific Northwest Line

Green Bay Rd
Clinden
Glenn

Des Plaines
Rand Rd

O'Hare
Chicago O'Hare International Airport

Park Ridge
Higgins Rd
Cumberland Ave
Rosemont
N Cumberland Ave

W Golf Rd
Waukegan Rd
Milwaukee Ave
Northwest Hwy

W North Ave
Mannheim Rd
W Grand Ave

Maywood
Butterfield Rd
Eisenhower Expwy
Oak Park Ave
W Washington St

Greektown

SIGHTS & ACTIVITIES 🎟 (pp125–58)
Chicago White Sox	1 E5
Diversey-River Bowl	2 D3
Ida B Wells House	3 E5
Pilgrim Baptist Church	4 E5
Robert W Roloson Houses	5 E5
Supreme Life Building	6 E5
Union Stockyards Gate	7 D5
Victory Monument	8 E5
Waveland Bowl	9 D3

EATING 🍴 (pp125–58)
Army & Lou's	10 E6
Gladys' Luncheonette	11 E5
Hot Doug's	12 D3
Indian Garden	13 D2
Leon's Bar-B-Q	14 E7
Sabri Nehari	15 E7
Udupi Palace	16 D2

DRINKING 🍸 (pp159–66)
Puffers	17 D5

ENTERTAINMENT 🎭 (pp167–82)
Abbey Pub	18 C3
Baby Doll Polka	19 C6
Lee's Unleaded Blues	20 E6
New Apartment Lounge	21 E6
Old Town School of Folk Music	22 D3
Rosa's Lounge	23 C4

SLEEPING 🛏 (pp215–28)
Chicago International Hostel	24 D2
Chicago O'Hare Rosemont Travelodge	25 A2
Clarion Hotel Barcelo	26 B2
Excel Inn of O'Hare	27 A2
Holiday Inn O'Hare International	28 B3
Hotel Sofitel	29 B3
Hyatt Regency O'Hare	30 B2
Marriott Suites Chicago O'Hare	31 B2
O'Hare Hilton	32 A3
O'Hare Marriott	33 B2

INFORMATION
Chicagoland Canoe Base	34 C3
Gay and Lesbian Chamber of Commerce	35 D2
Illinois Harley Davidson	36 B5
New Zealand Consulate	37 B3

LAKE VIEW

See Andersonville &
Uptown Map (p274)

Montrose

Gracelan
Cemetery

W Irving Park Rd

Hebrew
Cemetery

Wunders
Cemetery

W Byron St

Wrigleyvill

W Grace St

Metra/Union Pacific North Line

N Hermitage Ave
N Paulina St
N Marshfield Ave
N Magnolia Ave

W Waveland Ave

W Eddy

N Lakewood Ave
N Racine Ave

W Cornelia Ave

N Jansen Ave
N Southport Ave

Paulina

W Roscoe St   Southport

W Henderson St

N Clifton Ave

W School St

W Melrose St

N Ravenswood Ave
N Ashland Ave

W Belmont Ave

W Fletcher St

W Barry Ave

W Nelson St

W Wellington Ave

W Oakdale Ave

See Lincoln Park & Old Town Map (pp276–7)

N Southport Ave
N Lakewood Ave

W Wolfram St

N Paulina St

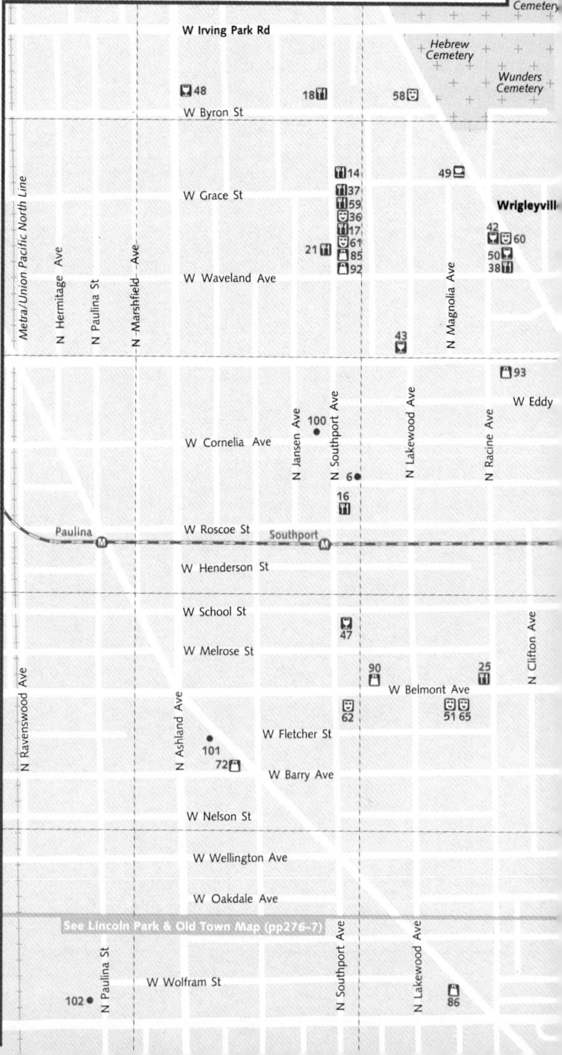

0 ——————— 500 m
0 ——————— 0.3 miles

See Lake View Map (pp272–3)

WICKER PARK/BUCKTOWN & UKRAINIAN VILLAGE

0 — 500 m
0 — 0.3 miles

SIGHTS & ACTIVITIES
2135 W Pierce Ave................................ 1 A4
2138-2156 W Caton St.......................... 2 A3
Bikram Yoga... 3 B4
Flat Iron Building................................. 4 B3
Nelson Algren House............................ 5 B4
Polish Museum of America................... 6 C5
Saints Volodymyr & Olha Church........ 7 A6
St Mary of the Angels Church.............. 8 B3
St Nicholas Ukrainian Catholic
  Cathedral.. 9 A5
Ukrainian Institute of Modern Art....... 10 A5

EATING 🍴 (pp125–58)
Alliance Bakery.................................... 11 B4
Bari Foods... 12 D6

Clothes Minded................................... 13 B3
Flo... 14 C5
Fortunato.. 15 B4
Irazu.. 16 A3
Le Bouchon... 17 B2
Leo's Lunchroom................................. 18 B4
Margie's.. 19 A2
Meritage Cafe & Wine Bar.................. 20 B3
Miko's... 21 B3
Milk and Honey................................... 22 B4
Mirai Sushi.. 23 B4
MOD.. 24 B4
Northside.. 25 B3
Pontiac Cafe....................................... 26 B4
Silver Cloud.. 27 B3
Smoke Daddy Rhythm & Bar-B-Que... 28 B4
Soul Kitchen.. 29 B3
Spring.. 30 A3
Tecalitlan.. 31 B5
West Town Tavern............................... 32 D6

DRINKING 🍷 (pp159–66)
Atomic Café.. 33 B6
Charleston... 34 A2
Club Foot.. 35 B5
Danny's... 36 B2
Earwax.. 37 B3
Gold Bar... 38 B4

Lemmings.. 39 B3
Map Room... 40 A2
Nick's.. 41 B4
Quenchers... 42 A1
Rainbo Club... 43 A4
Sonotheque... 44 C6

ENTERTAINMENT 😀 (pp167–82)
Big Wig... 45 C4
Chicago Dramatists............................. 46 D6
Davenport's Piano Bar & Cabaret....... 47 B4
Double Door.. 48 B3
Empty Bottle....................................... 49 A5
Note.. 50 B3
Red Dog.. 51 B3
Sinibar... 52 B4
Slick's Lounge..................................... 53 D5
Subterranean....................................... 54 B3
Trap Door Theatre............................... 55 B3

SHOPPING 🛍 (pp189–214)
Apartment No 9................................... 56 B3
Botanica.. 57 B4
City Sole/Niche................................... 58 B4
Climate.. 59 B3
Dusty Groove...................................... 60 C5
Jambalaya... 61 B3
John Fluevog Shoes............................. 62 B4
Lilly Vallente....................................... 63 B4
Meble.. 64 B4
Myopic Books...................................... 65 B4
Noir for Men.. 66 B4
p45.. 67 B3
Penelope's... 68 B4
Quimby's... 69 B3
Reckless Records................................. 70 B4
Red Balloon Co.................................... 71 B4
Saffron.. 72 B2
Tangerine.. 73 B3
Una Mae's Freak Boutique.................. 74 B4
US #1.. 75 B4
Vagabond.. 76 B2
Vive la Femme..................................... 77 B2

SLEEPING 🛏 (pp215–28)
House of Two Urns Bed & Breakfast.. 78 C4

N Medill Ave
V Belden Ave
N Lyndale St
Holstein Park

W Shakespeare Ave
W Charleston St
W Dickens Ave
W McLean Ave
W Armitage Ave
Bucktown
W Homer St

N Winchester Ave
N Wolcott Ave

W Cortland St
W Moffat St
W Churchill St

Churchill Field Park

N Wilmot Ave
N Milwaukee Ave

N Western Ave
N Bell Ave
N Claremont Ave

W St Paul Ave
W Wabansia Ave
Caton St
W North Ave
W Pierce Ave
W Le Moyne St
Wicker Park
Wicker Park Ave
W Schiller St
W Hirsch St

N Honore St
N Wood St
N Hermitage Ave
N Paulina St
N Marshfield Ave

W Wabansia Ave

Wicker Park

W Le Moyne St
W Julian St

John F Kennedy Expwy
To Hideout

W Blackhawk St

Goose Island

N Hickory Ave
N Cherry Ave

Pulaski Park
N Ashland Ave
N Bosworth Ave
N Greenview Ave
N Cleaver St

W Oakley Blvd
N Leavitt St
W Evergreen Ave
W Potomac Ave
W Crystal St
W Division St

Clemente Park
N Damen Ave
N Winchester Ave
N Wolcott Ave
N Wood St
N Hermitage Ave
N Paulina St
N Marshfield Ave

Division
W Division St

See Lincoln Park & Old Town Map (pp276–7)

N Milwaukee Ave

W Haddon Ave
W Thomas St
W Cortez St
W Augusta Blvd
W Watton St

W Thomas St
W Cortez St

W Walton St
W Chestnut St

N Noble St

See Gold Coast Map (pp278–9)

N North Branch St

N May St
N Ogden Ave

Ukrainian Village
W Iowa St
W Rice St
W Chicago Ave

W Rice St

Elkhart Park

Chicago

N Racine Ave
N Elston Ave

W Superior St
W Huron St

See West Side & Pilsen Map (pp286–7)

W Erie St
W Ohio St
W Race Ave
W Ferdinand St

N Wood St
N Armour St
N Bishop St
N Noble St

W Grand Ave

LP

275

LINCOLN PARK & OLD TOWN

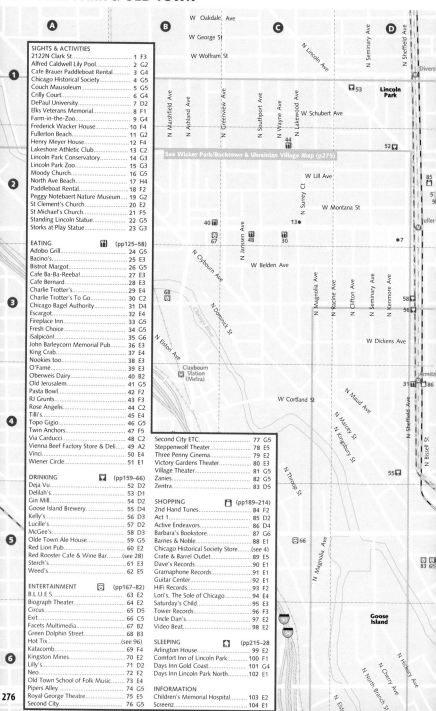

GOLD COAST

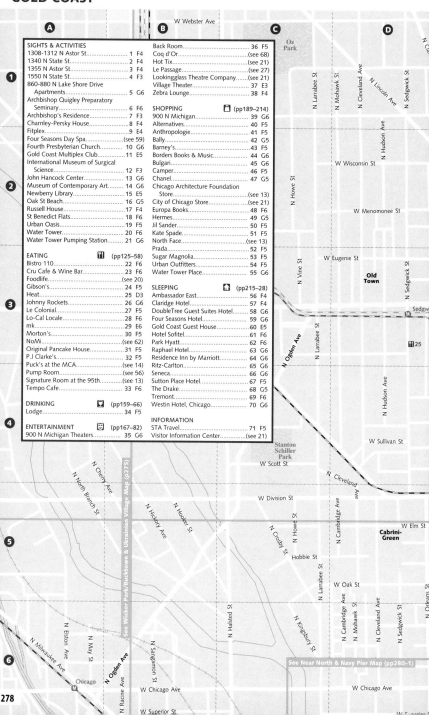

SIGHTS & ACTIVITIES
1308-1312 N Astor St.................... 1 F4
1340 N State St............................ 2 F4
1355 N Astor St............................ 3 F4
1550 N State St............................ 4 F3
860-880 N Lake Shore Drive
   Apartments............................. 5 G6
Archbishop Quigley Preparatory
   Seminary................................. 6 F6
Archbishop's Residence................ 7 F3
Charnley-Persky House................. 8 F4
Fitplex... 9 E4
Four Seasons Day Spa................(see 59)
Fourth Presbyterian Church......... 10 G6
Gold Coast Multiplex Club............ 11 E5
International Museum of Surgical
   Science.................................... 12 F3
John Hancock Center.................... 13 G6
Museum of Contemporary Art...... 14 G6
Newberry Library......................... 15 E5
Oak St Beach............................... 16 G5
Russell House............................... 17 F4
St Benedict Flats.......................... 18 F6
Urban Oasis.................................. 19 F5
Water Tower................................. 20 F6
Water Tower Pumping Station....... 21 G6

EATING 🍴 (pp125–58)
Bistro 110.................................... 22 F6
Cru Cafe & Wine Bar.................... 23 F5
Foodlife.....................................(see 20)
Gibson's....................................... 24 F5
Heat... 25 D3
Johnny Rockets........................... 26 G6
Le Colonial.................................. 27 F5
Lo-Cal Locale............................... 28 F6
mk... 29 E6
Morton's...................................... 30 F5
NoMi..(see 62)
Original Pancake House................ 31 F5
P.J Clarke's................................... 32 F5
Puck's at the MCA.....................(see 14)
Pump Room...............................(see 56)
Signature Room at the 95th......(see 13)
Tempo Cafe.................................. 33 F6

DRINKING 🍸 (pp159–66)
Lodge... 34 F5

ENTERTAINMENT 😊 (pp167–82)
900 N Michigan Theaters.............. 35 G6

Back Room.................................... 36 F5
Coq d'Or...................................(see 68)
Hot Tix.....................................(see 21)
Le Passage................................(see 27)
Lookingglass Theatre Company...(see 21)
Village Theater............................. 37 E3
Zebra Lounge............................... 38 F4

SHOPPING 🛍 (pp189–214)
900 N Michigan............................ 39 G6
Alternatives.................................. 40 F5
Anthropologie............................... 41 F5
Bally... 42 G5
Barney's.. 43 F5
Borders Books & Music................. 44 G6
Bulgari.. 45 G6
Camper... 46 F5
Chanel.. 47 G5
Chicago Architecture Foundation
   Store.......................................(see 13)
City of Chicago Store.................(see 21)
Europa Books............................... 48 F6
Hermes... 49 G5
Jil Sander...................................... 50 F5
Kate Spade................................... 51 F5
North Face.................................(see 13)
Prada.. 52 F5
Sugar Magnolia............................. 53 F5
Urban Outfitters........................... 54 F5
Water Tower Place......................... 55 G6

SLEEPING 🛏 (pp215–28)
Ambassador East........................... 56 F4
Claridge Hotel.............................. 57 F4
DoubleTree Guest Suites Hotel...... 58 G6
Four Seasons Hotel........................ 59 G6
Gold Coast Guest House............... 60 E5
Hotel Sofitel................................. 61 F6
Park Hyatt.................................... 62 F6
Raphael Hotel............................... 63 G6
Residence Inn by Marriott............. 64 G6
Ritz-Carlton.................................. 65 G6
Seneca.. 66 G6
Sutton Place Hotel........................ 67 F5
The Drake..................................... 68 G5
Tremont.. 69 F6
Westin Hotel, Chicago................... 70 G6

INFORMATION
STA Travel.................................... 71 F5
Visitor Information Center...........(see 21)

Oz
Park

N Larrabee St
N Mohawk St
N Cleveland Ave
N Lincoln Ave
N Sedgwick St
N Clar...

N Hudson St

W Wisconsin St

N Howe St

W Menomonee St

W Eugenie St

N Vine St

Old
Town

N Sedgwick St

Sedgw...

N Larrabee St

N Ogden Ave

N Hudson Ave

W Sullivan St

Stanton
Schiller
Park
W Scott St

W Division St

N Howe St
N Crosby St
N Cambridge Ave

Cabrini-
Green
W Elm St

See Wicker Park/Bucktown & Ukrainian Village Map (p275)

N Cherry Ave
N North Branch St
N Hickory Ave
N Hooker St

Hobbie St

N Larrabee St

W Oak St

N Cambridge Ave
N Mohawk St
N Cleveland Ave
N Sedgwick St
N Orleans St

N Elston Ave
N May N
N Milwaukee Ave

N Halsted St
N Sangamon St
N Kingsbury St

See Near North & Navy Pier Map (pp280–1)

N Ogden Ave
N Racine Ave

Chicago

W Chicago Ave

W Chicago Ave

W Superior St

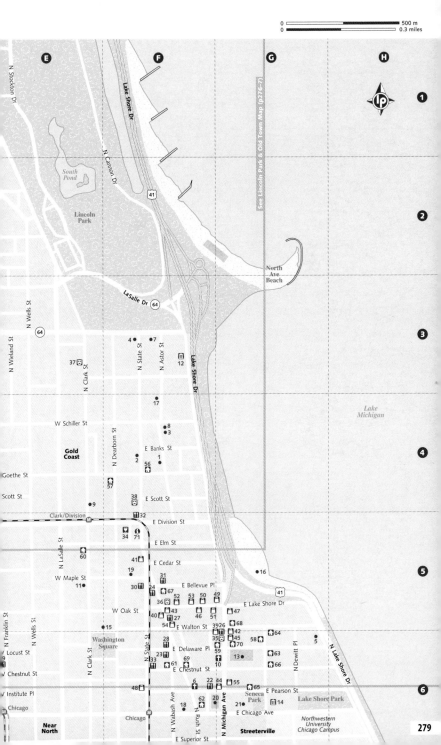

0 — 500 m
0 — 0.3 miles

E

F

G

H

1

N Stockton Dr

Lake Shore Dr

N Cannon Dr

South Pond

Lincoln Park

41

2

North Ave Beach

Lake Michigan

La Salle Dr 64

N Wells St

64

N Wieland St

3

4 7

N State St

N Astor St

37

N Clark St

12

Lake Shore Dr

17

W Schiller St

N Dearborn St

8
3

Gold Coast

E Banks St

2 1

56

4

Goethe St

57

Scott St

9

38

E Scott St

Clark/Division

32

E Division St

34 71

N LaSalle St

E Elm St

60

41

E Cedar St

19

16

5

W Maple St

11

30

31

E Bellevue Pl

24

52 67

36

53 50

49

41

N Franklin St

N Wells St

W Oak St

40

43

51

46

47

E Lake Shore Dr

15

54 E Walton St

3926 68

Washington Square

28

42
45
70

58

5

N Clark St

N State St

E Delaware Pl

35
59

13

63

N Dewitt Pl

N Lake Shore Dr

Locust St

23

61

69

33

10

66

Chestnut St

E Chestnut St

48

6
22 44

55

Institute Pl

Chicago

18

62

20

65

21

E Pearson St

14

Seneca Park

Lake Shore Park

6

Chicago

N Wabash Ave

N Rush St

N Michigan Ave

E Chicago Ave

Near North

Chicago

Streeterville

Northwestern University Chicago Campus

E Superior St

A　B　C　D

1

Seneca Par

W Chicago Ave　　Chicago

N Sedgwick St　N Orleans St　Chicago

89

W Superior St　　70　　Near North

4

W Huron St　　23　13　　77　46　　11　　51　130　98　143　139

River North Gallery District　52　34　125　55　74　68　　61　96　131

56　　123　47　65　　129　99　67　104

W Erie St　87　69　　58　80　88　　114　95　37　132　94

54　50　　　　　　　　127　29　　　

W Ontario St　43　110　118　93　38　75　113　　

128　　　59　73　115　35　40

44　78　112　W Ohio St　120　53　144　　

W Grand Ave　Grand　109　126　122

49　　83　63　105　138

64　57　36　119　　116　102　108　100

N Wells St　48　66　W Illinois St　　15　39　31

W Illinois St　41　W Hubbard St　76　62　33　142　97

W Hubbard St　140

91　W Kinzie St　E Kinzie St

90　124　7

101　W Carroll Ave　12

103　Merchandise Mart　135　81　16

Chicago River

W Wacker Dr　E Wacker Pl

E Wacker Dr

Illinois Center

Clark　State　E Lake St

W Lake St　Lake　N Stetson Ave

Clinton　Randolph　Randolph St Station

W Randolph St

Wrigley Square

W Washington St　Washington

The Loop

W Madison St　Madison

Bank One Promenade

W Monroe St

Monroe

W Marble Pl

Union Station　Sears Tower　Quincy　W Adams St

W Adams St　W Quincy St

W Jackson Blvd　Jackson

See South Loop & Near South Side Map (pp284–5)

LaSalle　Library

LaSalle St Station (Metra)　Van Buren St Station (Metra)

W Van Buren St

Clinton　W Congress Pkwy　E Congress Pkwy

290　LaSalle

W Harrison St　Harrison

280

W Polk St

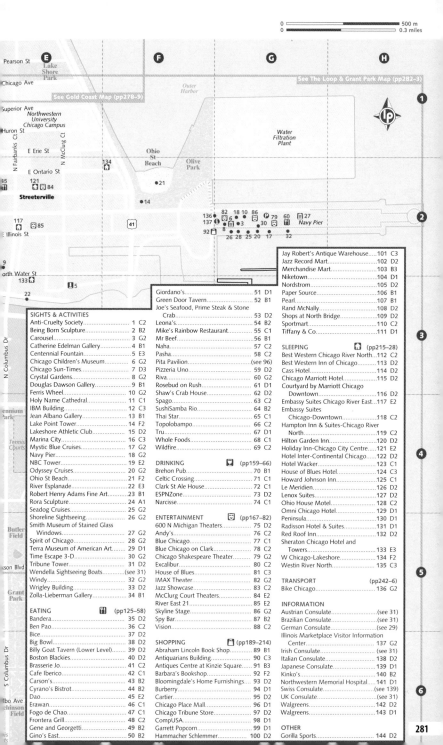

0	500 m
0	0.3 miles

See The Loop & Grant Park Map (pp282–3)

See Gold Coast Map (pp278–9)

SIGHTS & ACTIVITIES

Anti-Cruelty Society	1 C2
Being Born Sculpture	2 B2
Carousel	3 G2
Catherine Edelman Gallery	4 B1
Centennial Fountain	5 E3
Chicago Children's Museum	6 G2
Chicago Sun-Times	7 D3
Crystal Gardens	8 G2
Douglas Dawson Gallery	9 B1
Ferris Wheel	10 G2
Holy Name Cathedral	11 C2
IBM Building	12 C3
Jean Albano Gallery	13 B1
Lake Point Tower	14 F2
Lakeshore Athletic Club	15 D2
Marina City	16 C3
Mystic Blue Cruises	17 G2
Navy Pier	18 G2
NBC Tower	19 E2
Odyssey Cruises	20 G2
Ohio St Beach	21 F2
River Esplanade	22 E3
Robert Henry Adams Fine Art	23 B1
Rora Sculpture	24 A1
Seadog Cruises	25 G2
Shoreline Sightseeing	26 G2
Smith Museum of Stained Glass Windows	27 G2
Spirit of Chicago	28 G2
Terra Museum of American Art	29 D1
Time Escape 3-D	30 D2
Tribune Tower	31 D2
Wendella Sightseeing Boats	(see 31)
Windy	32 G2
Wrigley Building	33 D2
Zolla-Lieberman Gallery	34 B1

EATING 🍴 (pp125–58)

Bandera	35 D2
Ben Pao	36 C2
Bice	37 D2
Big Bowl	38 D2
Billy Goat Tavern (Lower Level)	39 D2
Boston Blackies	40 C2
Brasserie Jo	41 C2
Cafe Iberico	42 C1
Carson's	43 B2
Cyrano's Bistrot	44 B2
Dao	45 C2
Erawan	46 C1
Fogo de Chao	47 C1
Frontera Grill	48 C2
Gene and Georgetti	49 B2
Gino's East	50 B2
Giordano's	51 D1
Green Door Tavern	52 B1
Joe's Seafood, Prime Steak & Stone Crab	53 D2
Leona's	54 B2
Mike's Rainbow Restaurant	55 C1
Mr Beef	56 B1
Naha	57 C2
Pasha	58 C2
Pita Pavilion	(see 96)
Pizzeria Uno	59 D2
Riva	60 G2
Rosebud on Rush	61 D1
Shaw's Crab House	62 D2
Spago	63 C2
SushiSamba Rio	64 B2
Thai Star	65 C1
Topolobampo	66 C2
Tru	67 D1
Whole Foods	68 C1
Wildfire	69 C2

DRINKING 🍷 (pp159–66)

Brehon Pub	70 B1
Celtic Crossing	71 C1
Clark St Ale House	72 C1
ESPNZone	73 D2
Narcisse	74 C1

ENTERTAINMENT 🎭 (pp167–82)

600 N Michigan Theaters	75 D2
Andy's	76 C2
Blue Chicago	77 C1
Blue Chicago on Clark	78 C2
Chicago Shakespeare Theater	79 G2
Excalibur	80 C2
House of Blues	81 C3
IMAX Theater	82 G2
Jazz Showcase	83 C2
McClurg Court Theaters	84 E2
River East 21	85 E2
Skyline Stage	86 G2
Spy Bar	87 B2
Vision	88 C2

SHOPPING 🛍 (pp189–214)

Abraham Lincoln Book Shop	89 B1
Antiquarians Building	90 C3
Antiques Centre at Kinzie Square	91 B3
Barbara's Bookshop	92 F2
Bloomingdale's Home Furnishings	93 D2
Burberry	94 D1
Cartier	95 D2
Chicago Place Mall	96 D1
Chicago Tribune Store	97 D2
CompUSA	98 D1
Garrett Popcorn	99 D1
Hammacher Schlemmer	100 D2
Jay Robert's Antique Warehouse	101 C3
Jazz Record Mart	102 D2
Merchandise Mart	103 B3
Niketown	104 D1
Nordstrom	105 D2
Paper Source	106 B1
Pearl	107 B1
Rand McNally	108 D2
Shops at North Bridge	109 D2
Sportmart	110 C2
Tiffany & Co	111 D1

SLEEPING 🛏 (pp215–28)

Best Western Chicago River North	112 C2
Best Western Inn of Chicago	113 D2
Cass Hotel	114 D2
Chicago Marriott Hotel	115 D2
Courtyard by Marriott Chicago Downtown	116 D2
Embassy Suites Chicago River East	117 E2
Embassy Suites Chicago-Downtown	118 C2
Hampton Inn & Suites-Chicago River North	119 C2
Hilton Garden Inn	120 D2
Holiday Inn-Chicago City Centre	121 E2
Hotel Inter-Continental Chicago	122 D2
Hotel Wacker	123 C1
House of Blues Hotel	124 C3
Howard Johnson Inn	125 C1
Le Meridien	126 D1
Lenox Suites	127 D2
Ohio House Motel	128 C2
Omni Chicago Hotel	129 D1
Peninsula	130 D1
Radisson Hotel & Suites	131 D1
Red Roof Inn	132 D2
Sheraton Chicago Hotel and Towers	133 E3
W Chicago-Lakeshore	134 F2
Westin River North	135 C3

TRANSPORT (pp242–6)

Bike Chicago	136 G2

INFORMATION

Austrian Consulate	(see 31)
Brazilian Consulate	(see 31)
German Consulate	(see 29)
Illinois Marketplace Visitor Information Center	137 G2
Irish Consulate	(see 31)
Italian Consulate	138 D2
Japanese Consulate	139 D1
Kinko's	140 B2
Northwestern Memorial Hospital	141 D1
Swiss Consulate	(see 139)
UK Consulate	(see 31)
Walgreens	142 D2
Walgreens	143 D1

OTHER

Gorilla Sports	144 D2

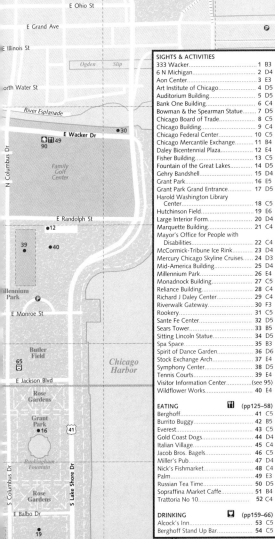

See Gold Coast Map (pp278-9)

Northwestern University Chicago Campus

Streeterville

N Fairbanks Ct
N McClurg Ct
N Lake Shore Dr
E Erie St
E Ontario St
E Ohio St
E Grand Ave
E Illinois St

Ogden Slip

orth Water St

River Esplanade

E Wacker Dr

N Columbus Dr

Family Golf Center

E Randolph St

E Monroe St

Butler Field

E Jackson Blvd

Rose Gardens

Grant Park

Rose Gardens

E Balbo Dr

Lake Shore Park

Outer Harbour

Water Filtration Plant

Ohio St Beach
Olive Park

Navy Pier

Chicago Harbor

Millennium Park

Buckingham Fountain

S Columbus Dr
S Lake Shore Dr

Hutchinson Field

0 — 500 m
0 — 0.3 miles

SIGHTS & ACTIVITIES

333 Wacker	1	B3
6 N Michigan	2	D4
Aon Center	3	E3
Art Institute of Chicago	4	D5
Auditorium Building	5	D5
Bank One Building	6	C4
Bowman & the Spearman Statue	7	D5
Chicago Board of Trade	8	C5
Chicago Building	9	C4
Chicago Federal Center	10	C5
Chicago Mercantile Exchange	11	B4
Daley Bicentennial Plaza	12	E4
Fisher Building	13	C5
Fountain of the Great Lakes	14	D5
Gehry Bandshell	15	D4
Grant Park	16	E5
Grant Park Grand Entrance	17	D5
Harold Washington Library Center	18	C5
Hutchinson Field	19	E6
Large Interior Form	20	D4
Marquette Building	21	C4
Mayor's Office for People with Disabilities	22	C4
McCormick-Tribune Ice Rink	23	D4
Mercury Chicago Skyline Cruises	24	D3
Mid-America Building	25	D4
Millennium Park	26	E4
Monadnock Building	27	C5
Reliance Building	28	C4
Richard J Daley Center	29	C4
Riverwalk Gateway	30	F3
Rookery	31	C5
Sante Fe Center	32	D5
Sears Tower	33	B5
Sitting Lincoln Statue	34	D5
Spa Space	35	B3
Spirit of Dance Garden	36	D6
Stock Exchange Arch	37	E4
Symphony Center	38	D5
Tennis Courts	39	E4
Visitor Information Center	(see 95)	
Wildflower Works	40	E4

EATING 🍴 (pp125-58)

Berghoff	41	C5
Burrito Buggy	42	B5
Everest	43	C5
Gold Coast Dogs	44	D4
Italian Village	45	C4
Jacob Bros. Bagels	46	C5
Miller's Pub	47	D4
Nick's Fishmarket	48	C4
Palm	49	E3
Russian Tea Time	50	D5
Sopraffina Market Caffe	51	B4
Trattoria No 10	52	C4

DRINKING 🍷 (pp159-66)

Alcock's Inn	53	C5
Berghoff Stand Up Bar	54	C5

ENTERTAINMENT (pp167-82)

Auditorium Theater	55	D5
Cadillac Palace Theater	56	C3
Chicago Symphony Orchestra	(see 38)	
Chicago Theater	57	C3
Civic Opera House	58	B4
Ford Center/Oriental Theater	59	C3
Gene Siskel Film Center	60	C3
Goodman Theatre	61	C3
Hot Tix	62	C3
Joan W and Irving B Harris Theater for Music and Dance	63	D3
Joffrey Ballet of Chicago	(see 55)	
Noble Fool Theatre Company	64	C3
Petrillo Music Shell	65	E5
Shubert Theater	66	C4
Skate on State	67	C4

SHOPPING 🛍 (pp189-214)

5 S Wabash Ave	68	D4
Afrocentric Bookstore	69	D5
Borders Books & Music	70	C3
Brent Books & Cards	71	B4
Carson Pirie Scott & Co	72	C4
Central Camera	73	D5
Garrett Popcorn	74	D3
Illinois Artisans Shop	75	C3
Iwan Ries	76	D4
Marshall Field & Co	77	D4
Poster Plus	78	D5
Prairie Avenue Bookshop	79	D5
Rock Records	80	C4
Santa Fe Center	(see 32)	
Savvy Traveller	81	D5
Sears	82	C4
Symphony Store	(see 38)	
Tower Records	83	D5

SLEEPING 🛏 (pp215-28)

Fairmont	84	E3
Hotel Allegro	85	C3
Hotel Burnham	(see 28)	
Hyatt Regency Chicago	86	D3
Palmer House Hilton	87	D4
Renaissance Chicago Hotel	88	C3
Silversmith	89	D4
Swissôtel Chicago	90	E3
W Chicago City Center	91	B5

INFORMATION

Australian Consulate	92	B4
Bank One	93	C4
Canadian Consulate	94	D3
Chicago Cultural Center	95	D4
French Consulate	96	D3
Mexican Consulate	97	C3
Northern Trust Bank	98	C4
South African Consulate	(see 78)	
STA Travel	99	C5
Swedish Consulate	100	D3
TravelEx	101	C4
World's Money Exchange	102	C3

283

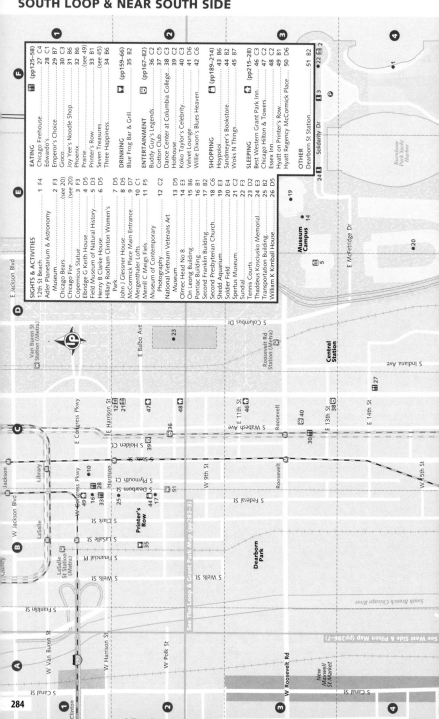

SIGHTS & ACTIVITIES
12th St Beach	1 F4
Adler Planetarium & Astronomy Museum	2 F3
Chicago Bears	(see 20)
Chicago Fire	(see 20)
Copernicus Statue	3 F3
Elbridge G Keith House	4 D5
Field Museum of Natural History	5 D3
Henry B Clarke House	6 D5
Hillary Rodham Clinton Women's Park	7 D5
John J Glessner House	8 D5
McCormick Place Main Entrance	9 D7
Mergenthaler Lofts	10 C1
Merrill C Meigs Field	11 F5
Museum of Contemporary Photography	12 C2
National Vietnam Veterans Art Museum	13 D5
Olmec Head No 8	14 E3
On Leong Building	15 B6
Pontiac Building	16 B1
Second Franklin Building	17 B2
Second Presbyterian Church	18 C6
Shedd Aquarium	19 E3
Soldier Field	20 E4
Spertus Museum	21 C2
Sundial	22 F3
Tennis Courts	23 D2
Thaddeus Kosciusko Memorial	24 B6
Transportation Building	25 B2
William K Kimball House	26 D5

EATING 🍴 (pp125–58)
Chicago Firehouse	27 C4
Edward's	28 C1
Emperor's Choice	29 B7
Gioco	30 C3
Joy Yee's Noodle Shop	31 B6
Phoenix	32 B6
Prairie	(see 49)
Printer's Row	33 B1
Seven Treasures	(see 45)
Three Happiness	34 B6

DRINKING 🍷 (pp159–66)
Blue Frog Bar & Grill	35 B2

ENTERTAINMENT 🎭 (pp167–82)
Buddy Guy's Legends	36 C2
Cotton Club	37 C5
Dance Center at Columbia College	38 C3
Hothouse	39 C3
Koko Taylor's Celebrity	40 C3
Velvet Lounge	41 D6
Willie Dixon's Blues Heaven	42 C6

SHOPPING 🛍 (pp189–214)
Hoypoloi	43 B6
Sandmeyer's Bookstore	44 B2
Woks N Things	45 B7

SLEEPING 🛏 (pp215–28)
Best Western Grant Park Inn	46 C3
Chicago Hilton & Towers	47 C2
Essex Inn	48 C2
Hyatt on Printer's Row	49 B1
Hyatt Regency McCormick Place	50 D6

OTHER
Dearborn St Station	51 B2

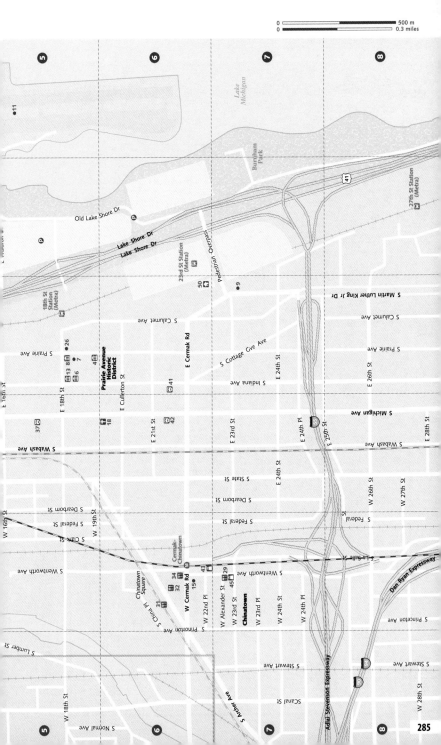

0   500 m
0   0.3 miles

⑤
⑥
⑦
⑧

●11

Lake Michigan

Burnham Park

41

27th St Station (Metra) 🚉

Old Lake Shore Dr

Ⓟ

Lake Shore Dr
Lake Shore Dr

Pedestrian Overpass

23rd St Station (Metra) 🚉

50

●9

S Martin Luther King Jr Dr

18th St Station (Metra) 🚉

S Calumet Ave

E Cermak Rd

S Calumet Ave

S Cottage Gve Ave

E Prairie Ave

S Prairie Ave

E 26th St

E 16th St

●26

13 8🏛
6● 7
4🏛

Prairie Avenue Historic District

E 18th St

E Cullerton St

S Indiana Ave

E 24th St

S Prairie Ave

37🏛

18

E 21st St

41🏛

42🏛

E 23rd St

S Michigan Ave

E 25th St

E 28th St

S Wabash Ave

E 24th Pl

S Wabash Ave

S State St

S Dearborn St

E 24th St

W 26th St

W 27th St

S Clark St

W 19th St

S Federal St

S Federal St

W 16th St

S Dearborn St

Cermak-Chinatown

S Federal St

Dan Ryan Expressway

S Princeton Ave

W 18th St

S Normal Ave

Chinatown Square

S China Pl

31

Princeton Ave

34
32

W Cermak Rd
15●

Chinatown

43🏛

29

45🏛

W Alexander St

W 23rd St

W 23rd Pl

W 24th St

W 24th Pl

S La Salle St

S Wentworth Ave

S Wentworth Ave

S Stewart Ave

S Stewart Ave

S Canal St

S Lumber St

S Archer Ave

Adlai Stevenson Expressway

W 28th St

Ⓑ
Ⓑ

285

Greektown

See Near North & Navy Pier Map (pp280-1)

To United Center,
Chicago Blackhawks &
Chicago Bulls

SIGHTS & ACTIVITIES

Bat Column	1	E3
Bodybuilder & Sportsman	2	E3
Bucket Rider Gallery	3	F7
Chicago Fire Department Academy	4	F5
Cooper Dual Language Academy	5	B7
Dogmatic Gallery	6	E7
Donald Young Gallery	7	D3
Gallery 1R	(see 2)	
Gallery 312	8	D2
Haymarket Riot Monument	9	D3
Holy Family Church	10	C4
Italian-American Sports Hall of Fame	11	D6
Jane Addams Hull House	12	C5
Mexican Fine Arts Center Museum	13	E5
moniquemeloche Gallery	14	A8
Old St Patrick's Church	15	D2
Piazza DiMaggio	16	E4
SixFourFive Gallery	17	C5
St Adalbert Church	18	D7
St Pius Church	19	E7
Thalia Hall	20	B8
Unit B Gallery	21	D7
Vedanta	22	E7
University Center Housing & Commons	23	E4
University Center Housing &	24	E3

EATING (pp125–58)

Artopolis Bakery & Cafe	25	E4
Cafe Jumping Bean	26	C7
Conte di Savoia	27	C5
Jim's Original	28	E6
Lou Mitchell's	29	F4
Marché	30	E3
Mario's	31	D5
Mr Greek Gyros	32	E4
Nuevo Leon	33	B7
Nuevo Leon Panderia	34	B7
onesixtyblue	35	C2
Red Light	36	E2
Rosebud	37	C5
Santorini	38	E3
Taqueria El Milagro	39	C8
Thyme	40	E1
Tufano's Vernon Park Tap	41	D5
Wishbone	42	D3

DRINKING (pp159–66)

Hawkeye's	43	C5

ENTERTAINMENT (pp167–82)

Funky Buddha Lounge	44	E1
rednofive	45	E1

SLEEPING (pp215–28)

Holiday Inn-Chicago Downtown	46	F4
Hyatt at University Village	47	B4

TRANSPORT (pp242–6)

Main Bus Station	48	E4

INFORMATION

Cook County Hospital	49	A5
Old Cook County Hospital	50	B4

HYDE PARK & KENWOOD

SIGHTS & ACTIVITIES

4944 S Woodlawn Ave	**1**	E1
David & Alfred Smart Museum	**2**	D4
DuSable Museum of African American History	**3**	C4
Elijah Muhammed House	**4**	E1
Isidore Heller House	**5**	E2
Kehilath Anshe Ma'ariu-Isaiah Israel Temple	**6**	D2
Madison Park	**7**	E1
Museum of Science and Industry	**8**	G4
Nuclear Energy Sculpture	**9**	D4
Oriental Institute Museum	**10**	E5
Robie House	**11**	E4

EATING 🍴 (pp125–58)

Caffé Florian	**12**	F4
Medici	**13**	E4
Valois	**14**	F2

DRINKING 🍷 (pp159–66)

Jimmy's Woodlawn Tap	**15**	E3

ENTERTAINMENT 🎭 (pp167–82)

Court Theatre	**16**	D3

SHOPPING 🛍 (pp189–214)

57th Street Books	**17**	E4
O'Gara & Wilson Ltd	**18**	F4
Powell's	**19**	F4
Seminary Cooperative Bookstore	**20**	E4
University of Chicago Bookstore	**21**	D4

INFORMATION

University of Chicago Hospital	**22**	D5

E 49th St

S Drexel Blvd

S Ellis Ave

S Vincennes Ave

S Forrestville Ave

S St Lawrence Ave

S Champlain Ave

S Langley Ave

S Cottage Gve Ave

Drexel Square

E Drexel Sq

Bowen Dr

S Drexel Ave

S Ingleside Ave

S Ellis Ave

S Greenwood Ave

Washington Park

E 55th St

Garfield Ⓜ E Garfield Blvd

E 55th Pl

Ratner Athletic Club

☐16

🏛2

E 56th St

Rainey Dr

Morgan Dr

🛢9

E 57th St

Russell Dr

🏛3

Payne Dr

University of Chicago

Ht Co

21 ☐

E 58th St

S Cottage Grove Ave

Maryland Ave

E 57th St

Main Quadrans

Bond Chapel

⚕22

E 59th St

William Rainey Ha Memorial Libra

E Best Dr

S Midway Plaisance

E 60th St

E 61st St

S Indiana Ave

S Prairie Ave

S Calumet Ave

S Martin Luther King Dr

S Vernon Ave

S Eberhart Ave

S Rhodes Ave

S Lawrence Ave St

S Champlain Ave

S Langley Ave

S Evans Ave

S Drexel Ave

S Ingleside Ave

S Ellis Ave

S Greenwood Ave

E 62nd St

CHICAGO TRANSIT AUTHORITY TRAIN SYSTEM MAP

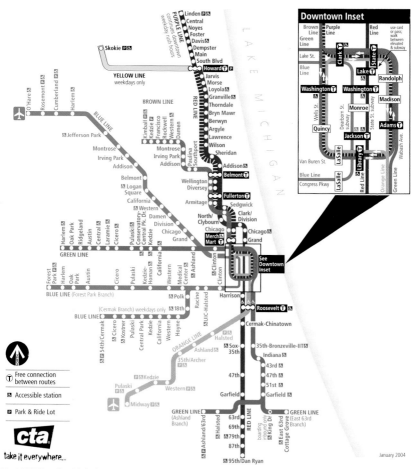